International Labour Office
Geneva

An Introductory Course in Teaching and Training Methods for Management Development

Management Development Branch

Training Department

Man Dev Manual

36

ISBN 92-2-101006-6

First published 1972
Seventh impression 1981

Printed in Switzerland

Table of Contents

⑳ In-Basket Exercises

㉑ Evaluation of Training

㉒ Designing Training Programmes II (Preparation)

㉓ Field Training

㉔ Open (reserved for special methods)

㉕ Designing Training Programmes III

㉖ Designing Training Programmes IV

㉗ Course Administration

㉘ Follow-Up of Training

㉙ Conclusion

Foreword

This manual on Teaching and Training Methods for Management Development has been prepared for the use of ILO technical co-operation experts assigned to developing countries. It is presented in the form of a five-day introductory course for the training of management trainers, but the instructor who wishes to treat a single theme only, or to design a shorter or longer course, will find the resource material equally valuable for his purpose.

Many of the articles in the manual were first prepared for use in a briefing course for management development experts organised by the Management Development Branch of the ILO. Some papers and exercises were developed by ILO experts working in developing countries, and some material was collected by Man.Dev. staff in the course of research into training methods and training courses.

The present manual is the direct result of work by H.E. Frank, M. Kubr and the late J.D. Hounsell. Special acknowledgement must be made to C. Gilbert and B. Crowther for editing the vast amount of material, and to P. Allen for the graphic art. Grateful acknowledgement is also due to the several publishers who have given us permission to reprint articles.

In practice, the manual will, no doubt, be changed by those who use it. Most instructors will want to add their own material and adjust the course design so that it is appropriate to the local situation. We hope that users will let us know of their experiences and make recommendations for revision, so that we may gradually improve the present text.

The manual is by no means the last word on training methods. Nevertheless, it does aim to encourage both international experts and national trainers to enlarge their repertoire of training techniques. Its usefulness will depend largely upon the ingenuity and imagination of those who seek to apply its principles.

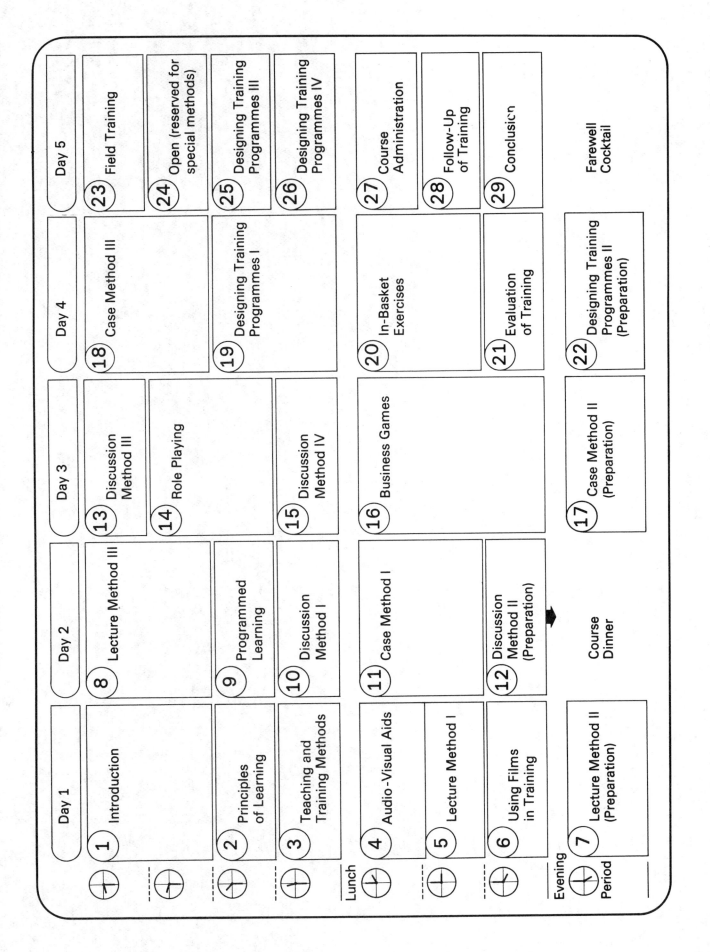

General Notes

Objectives of the Course

A five-day programme of the type presented in this manual should familiarise course participants with the broad concepts of learning theory and a variety of teaching and training methods, and promote a stimulating exchange of ideas and experiences. If a participant leaves the course anxious to try out some of the teaching methods; if he has acquired a rough understanding of learning theory to guide his use of them; and if he realises the importance of using them in a creative manner, then the seminar can be said to have achieved its broad objective.

Each session has a stated objective and it is wise to keep this in mind throughout the session. It is often difficult, in a course of such short duration, to be sure of accomplishing the objective of a particular session without a clear idea of time allottment beforehand. The timing indicated on the session guides should help to solve this problem.

The co-ordination between sessions will depend largely on the instructor's own preparation and emphasis. In general, he will need to be thoroughly acquainted with all sessions in order to make appropriate links between them and ensure that he is accomplishing his over-all objective.

It goes without saying that the course itself should set the example for the principles of good teaching which it advocates. This applies to lectures, visual aids, discussion leadership, adaptation to individual needs, and over-all course design and administration. A good model will make a greater impact on participants than any single session on teaching technique.

Organisation of the Material

Each session is covered in a separate section and bound in loose-leaf form to permit insertion of additional material or the revision of a particular section without re-editing the manual as a whole.

For each of the twenty-nine sessions, the manual contains a session guide, background reading material, handouts and, occasionally, visual aid displays. Among the readings, there is some intentional duplication to show various points of view on the same subject. Certain session guides recommend additional readings which are fully referenced in the general List of Literature. The wealth of material there - not exhaustive, but a sound basis for study - will be helpful not only for broadening the instructor's background, should he wish to refresh or update his thinking on training techniques, but also for supplementing the case studies, role plays and business games, or for making other modifications in the programme.

Some readers may regret that the session guides are not more detailed. The abbreviated format is intentional, however, in view of the many different ways in which the manual is likely to be used. No two instructors will conduct the course in the same way, just as no two groups of participants will have the same needs. We have preferred to leave the material in easily adjustable, outline form, to be filled in by the instructor with the help of background reading, rather than to present it in a pre-synthesized manner which might limit its application.

Course Design

Total Duration

It will be obvious from the master programme that the schedule is extremely condensed and most sessions operate under the absolute minimum time limit. It is therefore recommended that where at all possible, the programme be extended in order to have more time available for participant preparation and practice, and to add training in other methods or general subjects which would be appropriate to participants' interests and needs.

Adaptation

The needs of participants on the course and the local conditions under which training is carried out by them should be taken into account in a creative way, especially in selecting and scheduling subjects. Session 24 has been left open for this purpose, but the entire schedule is potentially subject to change and adaptation as required. It is also expected that instructors will insert their best training material into the manual - cases, discussion topics, handouts, visual aids, films - so that it becomes more suited to their own needs.

Balance

A careful look at the programme will show that slightly less than half of the sessions are devoted to instruction and somewhat more than half to the preparation and carrying out of practical work. A course leader may find it necessary or desirable to make adjustments in the sequencing of the Master Programme, but he should try to maintain this balance between practice and theory; in general, participants attending a "training of trainers" course should spend the greater part of their time _practicing_ methods of training.

Organising the Programme

Most of what needs to be said about course organisation is covered in the background reading and handouts for Session 27 on Course Administration. The checklists there are especially recommended for the constant checking and re-checking of arrangements which are essential to a well-run programme. Instructions relevant to this particular course are given below.

Briefing Letter to Participants

If it is possible to issue invitations to participants several weeks in advance, and to confirm the enrolments soon thereafter, each participant should receive a briefing letter which contains the following:

(a) the seminar programme (even if tentative);

(b) information about the training centre (maps, accommodation, etc.);

(c) a list of background literature, indicating whether it will be distributed or whether participants should try to get hold of it;

(d) key handouts for advance study;

(e) advance instructions as to practical assignments. For example, they can be advised to prepare a lecture topic and a discussion topic which they will present during the course; in this case they should bring appropriate visual aids with them or other supplementary material;

(f) a suggestion that they bring their own case studies, management exercises or other training materials, including visual aids, which might be used for discussion or demonstration during the course;

(g) a short questionnaire or personal history form to be returned by mail to the course director, the purpose being to inform him about the participant's experience and interests, in particular, his present or anticipated training functions. Such advance information would help in adjusting the programme to the group's needs. The course leader should make a summary review of these forms during the opening introductions, indicating how he has taken account of participants' backgrounds in designing the course.

Timing

The course has been programmed in 45-minute modules which are sometimes combined into periods of 90 minutes or longer. Although a 15-minute break is scheduled during a double period, the instructor should feel free to eliminate it if the session is particularly lively or if he needs more time. In fact, the 15-minute pause scheduled between modules will probably not be necessary every hour, and many of the sessions can easily be extended into the extra 15 minutes. This would be especially desirable for the lecture and discussion practice sessions.

Of course, where these timings do not suit local conditions or the aims of instruction, they should be adjusted accordingly. For this reason, no time limits have been set for the evening preparation sessions.

Number of Participants

The programme has been designed for a group of approximately twenty members. Appropriate adjustments will have to be made according to the number in attendance. For more than twenty, the leader will probably require an assistant.

Staffing

The course assumes that a single staff member will be able to conduct the programme, but it would clearly be preferable to have the collaboration of other instructors so that participants become acquainted with other training centre staff and profit from their varied views and personalities. This would leave the course leader somewhat freer to attend to arrangements and to get to know the participants personally, and would also be helpful when the group is divided into sub-sections.

Another possible source of staff would be the more experienced members of the group who could be invited (in advance) to lead certain sessions.

Involvement of Participants

As stressed earlier under "Balance", one of the most important features of the course is the opportunity for participants to practice training skills. Because of the limited time available for this, however, assignments should be very carefully planned to: (a) give each participant an opportunity to practice as many different skills as possible; and (b) to make sure that no one person has too heavy a load. (For example, see the schedule of assignments for Session 17. Here, to balance out the study load, the two people named as observers for the case study discussion could be asked to prepare for the role play). To increase participation in the lecturing and discussion leading sessions, a large group should be split in two, especially if another instructor is available to advise the second group.

Social Events

Apart from their collaboration in course work, participants should have an opportunity to get to know each other on a personal basis, since a relaxed interchange of ideas will be one of the greatest benefits to be obtained from the programme. To promote this, a friendly and welcoming atmosphere should prevail at the training centre, and the course leader should schedule appropriate occasions which will encourage informal exchange. The regular coffee breaks, a course dinner and a farewell cocktail serve this purpose in the present programme.

Handouts

A complete List of Handouts appears in this introductory section. In general, the papers identified as handouts are working papers essential to the session: e.g. exercises or evaluation forms, study assignments (cases), or reference forms and checklists. It is important to ensure that sufficient copies of all handouts are ready in advance.

The articles which provide theoretical background on training methods are treated as background reading and not as handouts. The instructor wishing to use this material as handouts will have to put it into a suitable form for duplication and distribution to participants. Due acknowledgement should, of course, be made of the source (and where applicable, the author) of the material from which such handouts are compiled.

Some of the inexpensive booklets mentioned in the List of Literature could also serve as reference handouts.

Visual Aids and Films

The number and variety of visual aids used on the course is somewhat limited, and instructors are encouraged to design supplementary displays appropriate to the aids they are accustomed to using. Several diagrams in the background readings have been drawn so that they may be directly photocopied onto transparencies for the overhead projector. Before photocopying, be sure to block out the page number and other irrelevant information typed on the manual page.

Films, for which full descriptions appear in the List of Films, are suggested for various sessions but the choice is optional and the instructor will have to adapt the session guide if he decides to use a film. Date, length and availability will influence his choice.

Meeting Room

A meeting room should have the following features and equipment:

- good ventilation
- power outlets
- curtains or shades so that the room can be darkened
- a table or tables which will accommodate participants comfortably
- ash trays
- notice board
- spare table for books or displays
- tray with drinking water and glasses
- lectern
- chalkboard with different coloured chalks and an eraser; and/or
- flip chart with crayons or felt pens
- flannel board (optional)
- overhead projector with acetate sheets, writing pens
- cinema screen
- storage boxes
- folders, pens and writing tablets for participants.

Additional small meeting rooms, equipped with chalkboard or flip chart, will be needed when the group splits up for discussion sessions.

Evaluation by the Participants

There is some difference of opinion as to whether evaluation by participants should be undertaken as a continuous process throughout the duration of a seminar or at the conclusion only. It can be contended that participants are not in a position to judge until they have acquired some background knowledge and that asking participants to evaluate makes them excessively critical, especially in the initial sessions. The contrary view is that the evaluation forms help the seminar leader to have a frequent assessment of how the instruction is being received, so that if necessary, he can make appropriate adjustments in the later stages of the programme. In some cases, filling in the forms may also help participants to clarify their own ideas about training. Later on, the forms will be useful for guidance in the planning of a future seminar.

In this course, the use of the evaluation form is part of the training and the manual indicates which sessions should be concluded by the completion of an evaluation form to be handed over to the seminar leader. Each participant will require ten to twelve of these forms which can all be issued with an appropriate explanation at the end of the introductory session. The benefits of this exercise will be discussed during Session 21. If all of the participants complete the forms regularly throughout the week, Session 21 on Evaluation of Training should produce a stimulating exchange of ideas.

List of Literature

Items frequently referenced during the course and containing essential background reading, are marked with an (*). Copies should be available or be purchased for the course.

Books

Andrews, Kenneth R. <u>The Effectiveness of University Management Development Programs</u>. Boston: Harvard University, Graduate School of Business Administration, 1966.

<u>BACIE Case Studies</u>. London: British Association for Commercial and Industrial Education, 1970.

Bass, Bernard, and Vaughan, J.A. <u>Training in Industry: The Management of Learning</u>. London: Tavistock Publications, 1966.

Bigge, Morris L. <u>Learning Theories for Teachers</u>. New York: Harper and Row Publishers, Inc., 1964.

*Craig, Robert L., and Bittel, Lester R. <u>Training and Development Handbook</u>. New York: McGraw-Hill, 1967.

Desatnick, Robert L. <u>A Concise Guide to Management Development</u>. American Management Association, Inc., 1970.

Drucker, Peter F. <u>Preparing Tomorrow's Business Leaders Today</u>. Englewood Cliffs, New Jersey: Prentice-Hall, 1969.

Gould-Marks, Langton. <u>Management Communication through Audio-Visual Aids</u>. London: Leonard Hill, 1966.

Graham, R.G. and Grey, C.F. <u>Business Games Handbook</u>. New York: American Management Association, Inc., 1969.

Hesseling, P. <u>Strategy of Evaluation Research in the Field of Supervisory and Management Training</u>. Assen: van Gorcum, 1966.

Kelly, Joe. <u>Organizational Behavior</u>. Homewood, Illinois: Richard D.Irwin,Inc.,1969.

King, David. <u>Training within the Organisation</u>. London: Tavistock Publications,1964.

Lynton, Rolf P. and Pareek, Udai. <u>Training for Development</u>. Homewood, Illinois: Richard D. Irwin, Inc., 1967.

Markwell, D.S. and Roberts, T.J. <u>Organisation of Management Development Programmes</u>. London: Gower Press Ltd., 1969.

Odiorne, George S. <u>Training by Objectives: An Economic Approach to Management Training</u>. New York: The Macmillan Company, 1970.

Pigors, Paul, and Pigors, Faith. <u>Case Method in Human Relations - The Incident Process</u>. New York: McGraw-Hill, 1961.

Powell, L.S. <u>Communications and Learning</u>. London: Pitman, 1969.

Revans, R.W. <u>Developing Effective Managers</u>. London: Longman Group Ltd., 1971.

Rigg, R.P. <u>Audiovisual Aids and Techniques</u>. London: Hamish Hamilton, 1969.

Skertchly, A.R.B. <u>Tomorrow's Managers</u>. London: Staples Press, 1968.

Taylor, B. and Lippitt, G.L. <u>Management Development and Training Handbook</u>. London: McGraw-Hill, 1975.

Towl, Andrew R. <u>To Study Administration by Cases</u>. Boston: Harvard University, Graduate School of Business Administration, 1969.

Tracey, William R. <u>Designing Training and Development Systems</u>. USA: American Management Association, Inc., 1971.

Warr, Peter. Bird, Michael and Rackham, Neil. <u>Evaluation of Management Training</u>. London: Gower Press Ltd., 1970.

Whyte, William Foote. <u>Organisational Behavior - Theory and Application</u>. Homewood, Illinois: Richard D. Irwin, Inc. and The Dorsey Press, 1961 and 1969.

Zoll, A.A. <u>Dynamic Management Education</u>. 2nd edition. Reading, Mass.: Addison-Wesley Publishing Co., 1969.

Booklets

Inexpensive; can be ordered for distribution to course participants.

*Debenham, A.I.S. A Training Officer's Guide to Discussion Leading. BACIE Training Manual No. 5. London: British Association for Commercial and Industrial Education, 1968. (BACIE, 16 Park Crescent, Regent's Park, London W.1).

Powell, L.S. A Guide to the Overhead Projector. London: BACIE, 1964.

-----------. A Guide to the Use of Visual Aids. 2nd edition. London: BACIE, 1968.

-----------. Lecturing to Large Groups. London: BACIE, 1966.

Tips on Talking. London: BACIE, 1959.

Using Sound Filmstrips. 3rd edition revised. London: Industrial Welfare Society, 1962. (now the Industrial Society), Robert Hyde House, 48 Bryanston Square, London W. 1.

ILO Publications

The following is a selection of papers and manuals prepared by the Management Development Branch which deal especially with management training methods.

Man.Dev. 6 (1968) "The Effectiveness of Management Development Programmes", by C.R. Wynne-Roberts. A summary and commentary on the book by Kenneth R. Andrews, The Effectiveness of University Management Development Programs.

Man.Dev. 12: Career Planning and Development

Man.Dev. 13: Management and Productivity. An International Directory of Institutions and Information Sources

Management Consulting: A Guide to the Profession

Promoting Sales (programmed book, available only in English)

*How to Read a Balance Sheet, Geneva, 1966.

*Creating a Market, Geneva, 1968.

* These programmed books are available in English, French and Spanish.

Management Development Manuals:

No. 4   Human Relations - Case Studies and Role Playing
No. 15   Films - Management Development (Eng-Fr)
No. 16   Plays for Management Training - "The XYZ Company"
No. 21   Case Studies for Management Decisions (Eng-Fr-Sp)
No. 21(a)   Instructor's Guide to Case Studies for Management Decisions
No. 25   Introduction to Programmed Learning (Eng-Fr-Sp)
No. 27   An Introduction to Business Games
No. 28   In-Basket Exercises for Management Development
No. 30   Case Studies for Management Development (Eng-Fr-Sp)
No. 31   Radio Plays for Management Training, "Double Your Money"
No. 35   Planning Training Courses by Network Analysis (Eng-Fr-Sp)

```
 _____
/                                                  \
|                   List of Films                   |
_____/
```

Films are not always easy to obtain, so a large number of titles have been included
here to facilitate the search in film libraries and private commercial collections.
Instructors should add to the list films which are locally available. For sources
of films, see the article "Using Films in Training" in Session 6.

With a few exceptions, no evaluation is implied in the film summaries. Instructors
are advised to verify, through preview, that the film is up-to-date, suitable for
adult training (many of those listed under Audio-Visual Aids and Programmed
Learning were originally prepared for school teacher training), and that it is
appropriate to their instruction.

Numbers refer to the ILO library of management development films. ILO projects
may borrow these films from Geneva Headquarters. For further information, consult
the film catalogue, ILO Man.Dev. Manual 15, Films - Management Development.

Audio-Visual Aids

See Rigg's book, Audiovisual Aids and Techniques,pp. 73-75 and 191-195, for
additional films related to this subject. Suppliers of photographic equipment
may provide demonstrations, such as Kodak's "Effective Visual Presentations"
(a multi-media package) and their film entitled "Movies Move People".

Better Bulletin Boards, 13 min., colour
Indiana University, USA , 1956
Presents various types of bulletin boards and how they can be used with a variety
of materials.

Bulletin Boards: An Effective Teaching Device, 11 min., colour
Bailey Films, USA , 1956
Suggestions for the planning and layout of creatively designed bulletin boards.
Materials needed for background, writing, mounting, achievement of third
dimensional effects.

Design, 10 min., colour
Bailey Films, 1955
Shows how to make a flat surface interesting and offers a non-technical formula
for basic design, using animated drawings to provide examples.

Film Tactics, 22 min., black and white
United States Department of the Navy, 1945
Demonstrates through dramatised episodes how training films should and should not
be used by instructors, and shows the results of good and poor teaching. Five
different persons use the same film describing a manoeuvre known as the
"Countermarch".

Flannel Boards and How to Use Them, 15 min., colour   (ILO No. 60)
Bailey Films, USA., 1958
The display possibilities of the flannel board are demonstrated, as well as how
to construct the board and the materials used on it.

Handmade Materials for Projection, 20 min., colour
Indiana University, 1955
Shows how to make a variety of materials suitable for projection by non-
photographic techniques and suggests numerous instructional uses.

Lettering Instructional Materials, 22 min., colour
Indiana University, 1955
Demonstration of various lettering methods to prepare charts, posters, bulletin
boards, etc.

The Unique Contribution, 35 min., colour
Encyclopaedia Britannica Films, USA , 1960
A comprehensive review of the role that audio-visual aids, and particularly film, can play in teaching.

Using Visual Aids in Training, 10 min., black and white
United States Office of Education, 1944
An instructor teaching the use of the micrometer, follows a carefully planned procedure, involving the use of a training motion picture, a co-ordinated film-strip and an instructor's manual.

Using Visuals in Your Speech, 10 min., black and white   (ILO No. 70)
McGraw-Hill Book Company, USA , 1959
An introductory demonstration of a variety of visual aids: chalkboard, flannel board, charts, graphs, working models, slides, overhead projector, filmstrips, motion pictures. The film stresses the idea that while aids increase the degree of communication, they will not make a bad speech good, or make the job of the lecturer any easier.

Visual Aids, 27 min., colour   (ILO No. 346)
Ministry of Defence, UK , 1966   Also in French
Suitable, well-planned visual aids which are simple, bold and clear, can greatly increase the effectiveness of instruction. This film demonstrates the use of the chalkboard, flannel and magnetic boards, diagrams, models, movies, slides, episcope and an overhead projector. Strengths and weaknesses of each media are emphasised. Some nice touches of humor and imaginative direction make this an outstanding training film for instructors. Part of the "Instructional Techniques" series.

Case Method

The Case Method of Instruction - Department of the Army, USA ,1959
Part I, 19 min., black and white   (ILO No. 431)
The case method encourages people to think and reason for themselves; its purpose is to teach the analytical process that is a prerequisite to decision-making.
A training officer at the US Army logistics school explains, in conversation with an interviewer, the use of the case method: its history, rationale, advantages and disadvantages. The case discussion process is outlined and the role of the instructor - as discussion leader and summariser - is stressed. The film is a suitable introduction for anyone quite unfamiliar with the method.

Part II, 23 min., black and white   (ILO No. 432)
A complete case is dramatised and discussed in this film. The Peter Robbins Case concerns a complex of personnel problems at top management level in an Army supply depot. The class discussion illustrates, in particular, the techniques of discussion leadership.

Part III, 19 min., black and white   (ILO No. 433)
A class case discussion and case-leading demonstration based on the Throw-Away Wrist Watch. The case deals with a problem of decision on three alternative pro-grammes for the supply and maintenance of watches. The case material is basically a set of figures on each programme, but the discussion brings out hidden factors which bear on the decision.

The Personal Problem, 6 min., black and white   (ILO No. 154)
McGraw-Hill Book Company, USA , 1959
This film is a dramatised case of a worker whose concern about his wife's poor health is affecting his efficiency on the job and the quality of production. Ending without a solution, the film raises the question as to the nature and extent of help that a supervisor should give to the solution of personal problems of workers. Clear, brief, and an excellent discussion opener.

The Trouble with Archie, 12 min., colour   (ILO No. 350)
Bureau of National Affairs, USA
The subject of constructive discipline is illustrated through a dramatised case, dealing with a plant foreman, the manager he reports to, and a plant worker. The film emphasises the importance of fairness in disciplinary action, and out-lines the constructive rather than punitive approach, to promote the improvement of employee attitudes and habits. There is an accompanying instructor's guide.

Discussion Method/Conference Leadership

All I Need is a Conference, 28 min., black and white   (ILO No. 308)
Henry Strauss and Company, USA , 1954   Also in French
Depicts an impromptu business meeting to solve a problem. The conference leader
demonstrates various techniques for encouraging participation and directing the
discussion, and emphasises the human relations skills needed to bring diverse
personalities together to work on a problem.

How to Conduct a Discussion, 24 min., black and white
Encyclopaedia Britannica Films, USA , 1953
Explains some of the basic principles of a method which discussion leaders can use
in order to ensure effective and satisfying group discussion. Each of eleven
principles is dramatised, and all are tied together by the narrative of a seasoned
administrator of discussion programmes.

How to Lead an Effective Sales Conference, 20 min., black and white
Porter Henry and Co., New York, USA
The method of setting the stage for the conference is shown together with
suggestions as to how the meeting should be managed, discussions stimulated and
attention maintained. The importance of organising the subject matter is stressed.

Let's Discuss It, 32 min., black and white
National Film Board of Canada, 1956
A presentation of group discussion methods, demonstrating the principles by which
a healthy and active discussion group can be maintained. The camera moves around
among several groups meeting in a hall to illustrate right and wrong ways of
eliciting participation. The film describes steps in organising a group and rules
for a discussion leader to follow in bringing about effective and satisfying
discussion.

Meeting in Progress, 43 min., black and white/colour
Roundtable Films, USA
The film presents examples of twelve typical meeting problems encountered by a
conference leader, such as what to do when people do not participate, when there
is an awkward silence, or when the meeting seems to be getting nowhere. At each
of these moments, the film asks the audience to decide, among three alternatives,
which course of action the leader should take.

Running a Meeting, 30 min., black and white
BBC-TV Productions, UK , 1969
How can a manager use the social skills which enable people to participate
effectively in meetings? A meeting in a headmaster's study is followed by an
example of training in these skills from Esso. Professor Singleton of Aston
analyses a working framework for chairmen. Part of a series of films entitled
"Skills for Managers".

A Shift of Opinion, 30 min., black and white
SB Modules, UK , 1970
Designed to help supervisors improve their skills in leading group discussions.
A plant foreman is seen involving the whole of his production team in formulating
suggestions for possible improvements to a plant modification scheme. Part of a
training package entitled "Preparing for Change".

Instruction (General)

A Class of Your Own (see under "Lecture Method")   (ILO No. 434)

Management Training, 23 min., colour
EMI Special Films Unit, UK, 1971
Based on a situation in an imaginary company, the film suggests how to satisfy
management training needs within an organisation. Senior management decides on a
four-stage process: identify the needs (present job, future job, new techniques,
etc.); plan the training that will satisfy those needs: do the training (internal,
external, on-the-job, etc.); and evaluate, to make sure the training objectives
are achieved and that the company is getting good value for money. Part of the
"Management by Objectives" series prepared in consultation with John Humble.

The New Instructor, 18 min., colour   (ILO No. 435)
Ministry of Defence, UK , 1963
Having learned how to teach, a young Navy instructor is faced with preparing his
first class. The film reviews the various points he must consider: the time
schedule and the scope of the syllabus, teaching policy of the institution, use
of texts and visual aids, suggestions of experienced staff members, teaching notes
for the class, preparation of the classroom environment. A review of basic
teaching preparation for technical classes to Navy apprentices. A film from the
"Instructional Techniques" series.

Pattern for Instruction, 21 min., black and white   (ILO No. 437)
Roundtable Films, USA , 1960
This film presents and demonstrates the steps in job instruction training and
relates them to the essential elements in the learning process. The training
officer conducting the discussion demonstrates his points on film, by showing
how a football coach trains his team using the same four steps.

Steps in Learning Process	Steps in Instruction
	Get ready to instruct: prepare training schedule; job breakdown; arrange the work place.
Motivation	Prepare: put him at ease; find out what he knows; arouse his interest; place him correctly.
Understanding	Present: tell; show; explain; demonstrate.
Participation	Try-out performance: have him perform the operation; have him explain key points; correct his errors; re-instruct.
Application	Follow-up: put him on his own; encourage questions; check frequently; taper off.

Successful Instruction, 38 min., black and white   (ILO No. 153)
The Army Kinema Corporation, UK , 1956
The film is an illustrated lecture by a competent speaker. The theme is that
successful instruction is made possible through the application of three basic
principles: prepare and plan; promote and maintain the desire to learn; confirm
that instruction has been assimilated. These principles are described in detail
with the aid of some humorous examples and an outline of the main points,as follows:

1.   Prepare and plan

     (a)   Time to prepare
     (b)   Consider the aim: 1. Length   2. Prior knowledge
     (c)   Instructor's knowledge
     (d)   Subject matter: 1. Size of class   2. Logical order
                                                    (Beginning/Middle/End)
     (e)   Aids: 1. Availability 2. Suitability 3. Improvisation
     (f)   Conditions of work
     (g)   Lesson plan

2.   Promote and maintain the desire to learn

     (a)   Enthusiasm
     (b)   Interest: 1. Incentive 2. Realism 3. Curiosity 4. Variety 5. Competition
     (c)   Lack of distraction
     (d)   Use of the right senses
     (e)   Maximum activity
     (f)   Simplicity
     (g)   Human factor: 1. Be firm 2. Be honest 3. Be fair 4. Be approachable

3.   Confirm that instruction has been assimilated

     (a)   Confirm by stages
     (b)   Check by questions......etc.

The film was made to train Army instructors and the dramatic examples are drawn
from Army classroom and field training situations; this does not detract from
the primary message of the film, nor from the presentation.

xix

Lecture Method

Anatomy of a Presentation, 35 min., black and white
Roundtable Films, USA
Taking the case example of an assistant manager who must prepare a presentation for a staff committee, the film is designed to show how such presentations can be made more informative and convincing. It discusses how to handle the fear of speaking before groups, how to establish objectives, analyse the audience, "talk their language", gather material, anticipate objections, appeal to the audience's point of view, prepare and organise the content, capture attention, support key points, and make an effective closing that prompts action. After a pause in the film, the actual 5-minute presentation is shown.

A Class of Your Own, 25 min., colour   (ILO No. 434)
Ministry of Defence, UK, 1966
There are two parts to this film: the Classroom Lesson and the Practical Lesson. In both, good teaching technique is demonstrated in a Navy instructor's lesson on the micrometer. The film stresses the value of a motivating introduction, logical sequence, continuity between lesson stages, the use of questions and answers, a judicious use of visual aids, careful timing, class activity, periodic review and chalkboard notes or summary. Despite the technical nature of the lesson, the teaching points are convincingly demonstrated. Part of the "Instructional Techniques" series.

How to Make an Effective Sales Presentation, 30 min.,black and white (ILO No. 62)
Dartnell Corporation, USA , 1963
Richard Borden and Alvin Busse demonstrate four key steps essential to an effective sales presentation, techniques which are used by successful speakers and salesmen to capture and hold the attention of their audiences. These techniques are:

- 	overcoming initial disinterest ("Ho hum");

- 	using the prospect's self-interest as a logical bridge ("Why bring that up?") toward getting a favourable and interested hearing;

- 	using case histories ("For instance") and other documentary proof;

- 	clinching buying benefits into a signed order ("So what?").

This lively and entertaining presentation of how to improve sales interview technique can be adapted for training in public speaking.

The Lecture Method, 15 min., colour
IBM Poughkeepsie, USA, 1964
Describes the lecture method of teaching.

The Lecturer and the Student, 13 min., black and white   (ILO No. 124)
Poland
The do's and don'ts of lecture delivery are illustrated through narrated pantomime. Humorous exaggeration in the acting demonstrates how physical poise and manner can increase or decrease the effectiveness of a talk. Good and bad facial expressions, posture, tone of voice, gestures, and choice of words are illustrated.

Planning Your Talk, 13 min, black and white   (ILO No. 98)
McGraw-Hill Book Company, USA, 1951
A professor of speech offers advice to a student on how to overcome the pitfalls of lecturing. He shows how a bad speech can be improved by thorough organisation, development of a central theme, and firm conclusions. Speeches should be divided into five main parts:

Opening:	- attention getter
	- why speech is important
Body:	- main idea
	- actual cases
Conclusion:	- what to do about it.

Successful Instruction (see under "Instruction")   (ILO No. 153)

Unaccustomed as They Are, 30 min., colour
BNA Films, USA
The film begins by demonstrating the contrast in effectiveness between two speakers facing an audience of top executives. Joe Powell then outlines 11 pointers for improved speaking technique and gives a short demonstration presentation.

Programmed Learning

Programmed Learning, 31 min., colour
Stewart Films for Ministry of Defence, UK , 1971
An introductory film in two parts. The first part introduces technical terms,
discusses target population and objectives and the need for pre- and post-pro-
grammed tests. After a break for class discussion, the second part takes up
programming styles, validation and presentation techniques.

Teaching Machines and Programmed Learning, 29 min., black and white (ILO No. 69)
Norwood Studios, USA , 1961
The film aims through lecture and demonstration to introduce school personnel to
the principles of programmed learning and the use of teaching machines. The four
speakers are men who have pioneered in the study and use of programmed learning
in America.

Teaching Machines and Programmed Learning, 17 min., black and white
Educational Systems/Sound Services, UK
Made to introduce teachers and educators to the principles and techniques of
programmed learning. Shows American and British teaching machine programmes and
research work. Most of the film was made at Cambridge University Department of
Education; other sequences were filmed at Sheffield University and Brighton College
of Technology.

List of Handouts

The following material should be reproduced for distribution to course participants. The instructor may wish to supplement the list with additional background readings on the various teaching methods, by selecting other articles from the manual or from his own files.

All handouts will be found with the session in which they are used. They are listed below in their order of distribution. Items with an asterisk (*) are optional, or require preparation by the instructor.

S e s s i o n		Title
Distr.	Used	
Whole Course		Master Programme
1	3, 6, 9, 11,14,15, 16,20,21	Session Evaluation Form (several copies per participant)
3	3	A Brief Guide to Teaching and Training Methods
4	4	Equipment Checklist for Visual Aid Presentations
4	4	* Selections from background reading on Audio-Visual Aids
5	5, 8	Lecture Rating Form
5	5	Lecture Presentation by Course Participants
6	6	Specimen Evaluation Sheet for Films
6	6	* List of local sources for hiring or borrowing films, compiled by the instructor
8	8	Lecture Rating Form (as for Session 5; several copies per participant)
9	9	How to Read a Balance Sheet (excerpts)
9	9	* Programmed Learning (background reading)
10	10	Discussion Leading
10	10	Discussion Planning Sheet
10	10, 13	Discussion Leading - Evaluation Sheet
11	11	Case Study: Union President and Works Manager
11	11	Writing a Case
11	11,17,18	Questions for Case Study Analysis
11	17, 18	Case Study: The Plywood Factory
11	17, 18	Case Study: The Northern Cement Factory
12	14	Role Play Exercise/Role Briefs (to two or more participants playing roles)
14	14	Role Playing as Teaching Aid
16	16	Business Games: Ilo Control, Instructions for Participants
16	16	Ilo Control: Decision Sheet
19	19,22,25	A Systems Concept of Training
19	19	Designing Training Programmes
19	19	Tips for Lesson Preparation and Presentation
19	19,22,26	* Instructions for Designing a Course Programme (prepared by the instructor)
20	20	The In-Basket
20	20	In-Basket Exercise - The Confidential File: Instructions to the Players, Contents of the Confidential File
21	21	Stages in Evolving an Evaluation Instrument (a diagram)
21	21	Individual Session Evaluation Sheet
21	27, 29	Course Review Form
27	27	The Organisation of Courses and Conferences
27	27	Organising Conferences, Study Groups and Courses - Checklist

Objective

To introduce course participants, course leaders and training centre officials to each other and to put everyone at ease

To explain the course programme, its design and purpose; how it has been adapted to specific needs of the participants

To discuss some of the general issues relating to management training

Handout Material

Master Programme (if not distributed on arrival), p. vii

I - Session Evaluation Form (10 copies per participant), p. 17

Background Reading

Introduction to a Course on Management Training, pp. 1-3

Some Basic Thoughts on Training for Industry and Commerce, pp. 5-9

The Training and Consultancy Cycle in ILO Management Development Projects, pp. 11-13

Note on Terms, p. 15

Session 19, The Determination of Training Needs within an Enterprise

Recommended Reading

ILO, <u>Management and Productivity No. 35, 1970/4</u>, "Management Education in the Second Development Decade", pp. 3-19

Special Equipment and Aids

Check to be sure that the meeting room is equipped with the items mentioned on page xii of the General Notes.

90 min.	**Session Guide** 1
	Before beginning the session, be sure that each participant has a master programme.
8:30	Welcome the participants. Introduce yourself and your co-leaders. Ask each member to introduce himself briefly to the group by saying something about his work and the way in which he is involved in management training.
8:45	Go over the master programme and explain the purpose and design of the course, indicating in particular how it has been adapted to meet the needs of the group. Stress that instruction is balanced with practice; every participant will be asked to practice a number of training techniques. Preparation periods for the practice sessions are scheduled for the evenings.
9:00	Discuss formalities such as the handouts to be issued, the amount of note-taking required, last minute changes in the programme, arrangements for the course dinner and the periods of evening study.
9:10	HAND OUT and explain the session evaluation form: how it is to be completed, when you want it handed in (certain sessions only). Mention that its use as a training instrument will be discussed in Session 21 on Evaluation of Training.
9:15	BREAK
9:30	In the seminar, management training programmes and techniques will be shown as instruments used to improve managerial competence. The rest of this introductory session should therefore be devoted to a discussion of problems such as:
	- how managers acquire their competence
	- what is management education, development and training
	- how and under what circumstances can training help the manager in his growth
	- what are the more recent trends in management education and training
	- what should enterprises and other organisations do to make full use of the advantages of well-designed management development programmes.
	All this should relate to the environment for training in which participants are involved.
10:10	Summarise points made in the discussion.
10:15	Close the session.

INTRODUCTION TO A COURSE ON MANAGEMENT TRAINING

by A.N. Giles,
Management Development Branch
International Labour Office

Whilst teaching methods can be applied to nearly any subject matter with regard to the circumstances in which they are used, this manual is concerned primarily with providing an introduction to their use for developing and training managers.

The unprecedented growth in management training activities in the industrialised world since the Second World War tends to obscure the fact that the concept of management as a body of knowledge with its own specialist skills only began to gain general acceptance between 1918 and 1939.

The Second World War saw the successful application of "scientific management" techniques to industry in support of military operations. Following the cessation of hostilities, techniques devised for military purposes were applied to the solution of industrial problems.

The very considerable mass of techniques, empirical data, skills and concepts built up during this period resembled, it must be admitted, a rag-bag of recipes rather than a body of knowledge. It was not until the late fifties that management education was based squarely on the study of economics, quantitative analysis and sociology.

Whilst business school curricula are now capable of turning out a university graduate adequately trained to fill a managerial post in the modern world, the problem of developing the manager who has some years of experience and who may, indeed, have never studied management at all, becomes even more acute.

The post-war technological explosion means for example that an electronic engineer's basic training has a half life of ten years. That is to say, in his early thirties, he is already out of date. This is equally true of management knowledge. Consequently, it is currently recognised that managers must receive continuous training throughout their working life to keep them abreast of new developments. The fact that facilities for training are available does indeed help to dispel some of the insecurity and frustration inherent in this situation.

The manager, then, may require retraining in his technology or in managerial skills several times during his working life. He will also require guidance in his present job to make him a more effective manager. It has been found that the climate created by his organisation's policy and practice is the most important factor in developing him, i.e. preparing him for successively increasing responsibilities. In this process, the attitude of his immediate superior is decisive since it must be the latter who provides him with the necessary guidance.

Only quite sophisticated companies have well-planned training programmes which may include job rotation, planned reading, special projects, membership committees, etc. in addition to running internal training courses and sending managers on external courses, having ascertained the individual's training needs.

In a developing country, the enterprise or organisation will probably not have a training department, and the superior may not have the knowledge to be able to guide his subordinates effectively. Consequently, in the absence of on-the-job training by the superior, "classroom" training will become of outstanding significance for the developing country.

The preparation of training programmes will, therefore, involve special problems in a developing country. Those in authority will not be automatically abreast of the latest accepted developments in more industrialised countries. The expert may even have to sell the idea that training is necessary at all. The opinion that managers are "born not made" is only just dying out in industrialised countries. In a country where engineers and chemists are in short supply, quite a lot of persuasion may be necessary to induce those in authority to spare scarce resources for management training.

Special care will also have to be taken to ensure that what a manager learns on a course can be applied in his own environment or else he will lose interest and his last state will be worse than his first.

A manager's training needs may be divided into three categories:

- Intellectual knowledge.
- Problem-solving skills.
- Skills of social interaction[1] (changing attitudes).

The transfer of knowledge is a fairly straightforward process provided the individual feels that he wants the new knowledge. However, if he does not want the knowledge, it will be extremely difficult to induce him to learn it. Consequently the individual must be motivated to learn, either preferably through his own recognition of a need for knowledge in a given field or by means of incentives such as the possibility of promotion, higher salary, and so on. Motivation can also be lost if, for example, the manager feels the need to take a course in statistics, and finds he has to attend a course in production planning. Whoever is responsible for planning the over-all programme must analyse existing training needs to ensure that not only the individual courses are useful and practical, but also that they meet "felt" needs.

The executive development programmes which are undertaken by many universities provide a more general educational experience. They have the objective of "broadening" the manager, i.e. making him aware of the social, political and economic trends in his environment. They do not usually have an immediate result but in the long run they have profound effects on his behaviour and preconceptions and provide him with a more realistic understanding of the causes and effects with which he must deal. Such programmes usually have a prestige value of their own and the problem in this case is not to motivate the manager but to decide which manager ought to go on the course.

Since much of a manager's work is solving problems, the skills involved in diagnosing problems, acquiring and interpreting data, and testing alternative solutions are of immediate use. As with any skill, practice and feedback are essential for learning. Consequently, the case method is widely used for improving problem-solving skills. There is, however, some evidence that the case study can improve diagnostic skills without materially changing the quality of the solutions. Underlying theoretical assumptions are likely to determine the answers given by the participant and they should therefore be critically examined before the case is studied. The balance between providing background knowledge and sharpening skills must be carefully gauged. Discussion groups and role playing also have value in developing these skills. But the most important source of feedback comes from the critical examination of mistakes that have been committed by the manager in solving a problem on the job. Depending on the way a manager deals with his subordinate's mistakes, the latter will learn and develop. In fact, without being permitted to make mistakes, he will never learn. For this reason all courses in developing countries other than seminars and appreciation courses should include a project in the participant's own organisation which will give him the opportunity of making mistakes. Only in this way can he develop confidence and sharpen his powers of analysis and synthesis.

The skills of social interaction are much more difficult to instill. In a difficult situation, we react unconsciously to internal hopes and fears rather than reacting with regard to the situation itself. What we need, therefore, is feedback concerning the impact of our behaviour on others. T-groups and sensitivity training are the most outstanding means of providing meaningful feedback. Nevertheless, teaching methods such as discussion groups, role playing and even informal conversations within the training group can, under the guidance of an imaginative training officer, provide new insights and lasting value.

Other factors which may affect the motivation of the manager and his ability to learn are:

- Managers tend to be product-oriented. For example, the selling of electric power plants is a different problem from selling cornflakes. If a manager from an electric power plant company was attending the average marketing course, he would feel that the course did not really concern him.

---

[1] The terminology of the late Douglas McGregor is used here.

- There are problems of scale. The small entrepreneur cannot afford the specialisation of the large enterprise. Consequently, detailed descriptions of techniques requiring a specialist team for their operation would not interest him.

- There are problems of status. A manager who is status-conscious, may resent participating in courses with lower-grade managers. This resentment would be expressed in criticism of the course and resistance to learning.

- There are problems of age and education. The bright young boys from the universities tend to have a depressing effect on the older members of the group.

These and other factors are brought out in the various sessions of the manual. The techniques and methods described are not a means of transferring knowledge in a vacuum to automatically receptive participants. They are a means of overcoming the mental blockages which are the reaction of the participant to the personal, political, social and economic environment in which he lives.

The trainer, therefore, whilst he cannot be held responsible for the motivation of participants before they attend a course, must be quite clear in his mind what he thinks management is and why he thinks management training is necessary at all. He must also try to understand the reasons why he thinks training is important in the particular environment in which he is operating. Finally, he should have his answer ready as to the results expected from training.

In practice, the justification for training in general is usually expressed in terms of results: higher productivity, better use of resources, better labour relations, greater job interest and so on. For a particular course the results are more detailed in accordance with the level of the participant.

Bearing all these factors in mind, participants in a course on training methods should, in the introductory session, exchange views and ideas in order to reach a consensus of agreement as to why training is necessary, what they expect to achieve in the light of the difficulties of their own environment and what they hope to get out of the course.

SOME BASIC THOUGHTS ON TRAINING
FOR INDUSTRY AND COMMERCE

by Rex Strayton,
Associate Professor of
Personnel Administration,
International Centre for Advanced
Technical and Vocational Training, Turin

1. WHAT IS IT ALL ABOUT?

Training for industry and commerce is concerned with the acquisition or development of those knowledges, skills, techniques, attitudes and experiences which enable an individual to make his most effective contribution to the combined effort of the team of which he is a member. Its objective may be to prepare the individual to carry out his present job satisfactorily, or to prepare him for greater responsibility.

As we progress from the shop floor to the board room, the importance of intellectual capacity and personality characteristics increases, until eventually the object of training becomes, essentially, the development of sound judgment.

Much ink has been spilt in an attempt to define non-existent boundaries between education and training, between activities which are vocational and those which are not. One cannot be interested and involved in training without at the same time being interested and involved in education. The results which can be achieved in industry and commerce by training will be limited in a very real sense by the quality of the basic education which the trainees have received and which it may sometimes be necessary to supplement.

2. WHOSE RESPONSIBILITY IS IT?

Training in industry or commerce is, primarily, the responsibility of the line manager.

A. What the trainee does tomorrow in the factory or the office depends much more on the impression he has of what his own supervisor wants and expects him to do than on all that may have been said by all the instructors in all the training courses he ever attended.

B. In any case, training consists of something more than formal training courses carried out in a lecture room. Every line manager has many opportunities and techniques for training and developing his team in the workshop or office including, above all, his own personal example, regular departmental meetings, job rotation, projects, etc.

C. The majority of the experiments which have been carried out to evaluate training activities show that these activities are always more successful when two basic conditions are satisfied:

(i) when there is not only an interest but also an active participation in these activities by line managers;

(ii) when there is a very close relation between what is taught in the training course and the demands of the day-to-day work situation of the trainees.

3. WHAT IS THE FUNCTION OF THE TRAINING OFFICER?

The function of the training officer, basically, is to help the line manager to carry out his training responsibility.

The training officer cannot be an expert in all the specialisms which we find within a company - in engineering, in accountancy, in administration, in selling. His indispensable expertise is in education and training for industry and commerce.

The function of the training officer is to help the line manager to analyse his problems, to identify those which are training problems, and to provide all possible advice, information, help, services, etc. to help him to resolve them.

Thus the specialist knowledges and skills which figure in an "internal" training programme are contributed largely by the line manager. The training officer contributes his specialist knowledge and experience in the whole area of instructional techniques, the psychology of learning, audio-visual aids, manpower planning and development, evaluation, performance appraisal, follow-up, and so on.

It may be that sometimes the training officer's task will be to stimulate line managers to accept their training responsibility and carry it out but an enlightened board of directors will usually do this job for him.

4.   WHERE DOES THE TRAINING FUNCTION "BELONG" ORGANISATIONALLY?

Training is an integral part of the personnel function, i.e., of the process which begins with the writing of the job description and ends with superannuation.

At board level, the senior executive who carries the total responsibility for the personnel function should have reporting to him the senior training officer. He may report direct or through the chief personnel officer. At lower levels the training department, like the personnel department, could be centralised or decentralised according to the needs of the enterprise.

5.   WHAT IS THE BASIC OBJECTIVE IN TRAINING?

To be quite frank it is doubtful whether any line manager or training officer can ever "develop" any employee.

In fact, they can only help those employees to develop themselves who have already decided that this is what they are going to do. Hence the fundamental importance of motivation in all training activities. The true training function of any line manager or training officer is to stimulate, to motivate people so that they want to improve themselves, and then to help them to do it.

6.   WHAT ARE THE MAIN AREAS IN WHICH TRAINING CAN OPERATE?

There are really only five:

Knowledge. We can teach knowledge. Here we are helping the trainee to learn, to understand and to remember facts, information, principles.

Skills. A skill is a physical act or action. Examples are shorthand writing, operating an adding machine, playing a trumpet.

Techniques. A technique usually involves the application in a dynamic situation of both knowledge and skill. It is a way of behaviour or thinking. Driving a car, commanding troops in battle, salesmanship, are examples of techniques.

Attitudes. This is a very wide subject on which much has been written and a very broad range of different opinions are held. In brief, it may be said that not all attitudes can be changed, that not all "attitude changers" know what they are trying to do or why, that some of the methods used by the "attitude changers" are highly questionable to say the least of them, and often without any validation whatever. We have to define what an attitude is in the first place. Then we have to decide whether it is an attitude based upon superstition, fear, prejudice, ignorance, etc., etc., or whether it is the product of the social group to which the individual belongs. If we are trying to change "undesirable" attitudes based upon ignorance, then there is a reasonable hope of achieving this in an industrial training situation. In the case of attitudes based upon the other elements outlined above, the situation is much more complex. There are very few training officers who have the ability to properly diagnose the bases of attitudes or the knowledge and skill with which to seek to change them - or indeed, the time to devote to either.

Experience. Clearly this differs from the four previous items in that it cannot be taught in a classroom. It is the result of practising the use of knowledges, skills and techniques over a period of time and often in a number of different situations. One of the training officer's many tasks is to "arrange" the experience of trainees on an organised basis. Frequently this is achieved by means of job rotation and sometimes by exchanges between companies.

Is there a sixth?

In addition to the five main areas listed above, we might perhaps mention a sixth, which is particularly applicable in the field of executive development. Here we may well be focusing on knowledge, skills, techniques, experience and attitudes, but we are usually aiming at something else besides which, to put it simply, is the development of sound judgment.

Application of the foregoing principles to a specific situation.

Example   driving a motor car.

Knowledge   would include such things as the position of the various controls, how to operate them and what happens when you do.

Skills   would include such things as how to start up the car, how to move off, how to steer it around obstacles, how to change gears, how to reverse, etc. All of these things could be practised at the beginning in a field where there is no danger or inconvenience to other people.

Techniques   would include the ability to apply all this knowledge and these skills to real life conditions on the open road and in the busy city.

Attitudes   the training course would clearly need to try to develop in the trainees the proper attitudes towards such things as road safety, vehicle maintenance, etc.

Experience   according to the objectives of our training course it may be necessary for our trainee driver to have experience of driving under special conditions, for example, on very rough mountain roads or even in another country where they drive on the other side of the road. The training officer must arrange the training accordingly.

7.   WHAT TECHNIQUES ARE AVAILABLE TO HELP US WITH OUR TRAINING TASK?

The list is a very long one as any textbook on training for industry and commerce will show. The basic instructional techniques such as the lecture, the lesson, the discussion and job instruction would figure high on the list but the post-war years have seen the development of scores of others. The case study, the business game, the in-basket exercise, the incident process, the syndicate method, role-playing, to quote but a few, are in regular use in management training courses throughout the world.

New ones and variations of old ones are constantly appearing on the scene. Some of them are highly controversial and some are as yet "unproven". Like tools in a toolbag, each one is more suitable for certain tasks than for others, and again, like tools, skill in their use is only achieved by practice and still more practice.

8.   WHAT MAKES A SUCCESSFUL INSTRUCTOR?

Within any organisation, in addition to the training officer who has over-all company responsibility, there will usually be a number of instructors. Some of these will report direct to the training officer and some to line managers. One of the training officer's tasks is to see that the right people are selected for this work and then to train them in instructional techniques.

The following paragraphs simply set out what are considered the basic minimum requirements for a successful instructor. Some instructors can meet all these requirements and many more besides. On the other hand, it is doubtful whether a man can perform successfully as an instructor unless and until he can meet the minimum specification set out below.

He must:

A.   Want to instruct. Above all, the instructor must really want to instruct and enjoy doing it. Enthusiasm is infectious and readily transmits itself from instructor to students. So does the lack of it!

B. Know what to instruct. Do we need to stress that the instructor must know what he is talking about - and know it "inside out"? Not only must he know his subject well, he must know more than he will be expected to teach. Remember the iceberg. Only about one-fifth of its mass is visible above the water. The rest of it is there all right - below the water, invisible, but supporting the part which is visible. Much of your knowledge and skill may never "rise above the water" in the lecture room, but it has to be there to support the rest.

C. Know how to instruct. He must be trained in instructional techniques - being the best operator or the best technician in the department is not enough. As we said in paragraph 7, there are many instructional techniques which are used in the industrial training situation. Each one has its advantages and disadvantages and may be more effective in one situation than another. So the instructor must know how to choose the right one and, having chosen it, how to use it.

D. Know how people learn. A great deal of research has been done over the years into the way people learn and more particularly in recent years into the way in which they acquire industrial skills. There are a number of obstacles which act as barriers to learning and there are ways of overcoming them and making the learning process easier, quicker, more effective. The instructor must know about these including the use of audio-visual aids.

E. Have the right personality. Much could be written under this heading but we are going to assume that most readers of this handout really know already what we are talking about. A very well-known booklet on instructional techniques says that a good instructor is "firm, fair and friendly". We could write pages on personality and not improve on this.

F. Be able to communicate. This is self-evident but it needs to be said. We have all met people who simply cannot communicate. Some of their faults may be "curable" by training, others not. Possibly they fail to communicate because they have not learned to put themselves in our shoes and see the problem through our eyes, and thus to understand our difficulties. This is what the instructor must do vis-à-vis the learner.

G. Be flexible. He must be flexible enough to make changes, very often at the last minute, in his programme or his approach. With the best will in the world and the best management, there will always be crises and unforeseen circumstances. The instructor will naturally want to avoid too many changes and interruptions in his training programme, but if he remembers that fundamentally his task is to offer a service to management, his reaction in any emergency will usually be the wise one.

9. WHAT IS THE REAL JUSTIFICATION FOR TRAINING AND DEVELOPMENT ACTIVITIES?

In the opinion of the writer, there is only one justification for the investment of time, money or any other resources in training and development activities, and that is, that it can contribute to the profitability of the enterprise. Training activities often lead to many other highly desirable side effects especially in the area of employee morale and industrial relations, for example. But these, however desirable, are not the fundamental reasons why an enterprise should take training seriously.

Over fifty years ago, the board of a well-known life insurance company was surprised by the results of a survey which revealed that 10 per cent of their salesmen were handling 90 per cent of their business. There were a number of factors which contributed to this situation, but prominent among them were two - poor selection and poor training. The company introduced a systematic plan for the selection and training of its salesmen. Twelve years later, although the company's business had increased from US$20,500,000 to US$52,000,000 per year, the number of salesmen employed had, in fact, gone down from 1,700 to 375.

In the following fifty years, countless similar surveys in all types of enterprises have revealed similar situations. In the badly selected and badly trained working group the best operator is often turning out twice as many units per hour or per shift as the worst. In this situation the unit cost is high, the overhead recovery is low, the training periods are excessively long, the labour turnover is high and costly. Put the other way around, for a little investment in the improvement of selection and training techniques the potential return is extremely high.

It is relatively easy to assess the performance of salesmen or to count units per hour or per shift at operative level. Management performance is not so easy to assess quantitively but there is ample evidence that the same situation exists not only at shop floor level, but also at all levels in industrial and commercial organisations. Some managers are outstanding, some are average, and some we would rather not talk about.

Training activities, properly planned, conducted and evaluated, help to raise the productivity of the enterprise through the more effective use of human resources.

And if, as sometimes happens, the employee whom we have carefully trained leaves us to join another company, this is not always the "dead loss" we sometimes pretend it is. Presumably we have benefitted from having a better employee in our service whilst he was still with us. Presumably we realise that if we had not helped him to improve, he might well have left us in any case to work for someone who would. Presumably we would admit that what we lose on the swings we sometimes gain on the roundabouts. And wherever our "lost" employee is now working, is he not still contributing to the economic development of the nation as a whole? And is not the prosperity of our enterprise inseparably tied up with the prosperity of the nation?

THE TRAINING AND CONSULTANCY CYCLE
IN ILO MANAGEMENT DEVELOPMENT PROJECTS

The main lesson drawn from ILO experience in the field has been that there is a marked difference between the knowledge of a management technique and the ability to use it properly in a practical management situation. This ability can be defined as a management skill. In most cases, knowledge of the technique can be acquired through theoretical study and through simulation exercises in the classroom or laboratory. But the essential skills in practical use and application of the technique cannot be acquired in the same way as the theory. Acquisition of these skills involves identification of practical situations to which the technique can be applied; the adaptation of the technique to the requirements of these situations; co-ordination of the efforts of those people concerned with introduction of the technique, and the overcoming of diverse obstacles. Such skills are only developed and refined through practice and first-hand experience. The aptitudes and efforts of the individuals concerned as well as opportunities provided by the environment, greatly influence the process of acquiring management skills.

In technical assistance in the management development field, the upgrading of the theoretical knowledge of management techniques, including the most advanced and difficult ones, does not represent a major problem. Today in many developing countries there are a number of capable young university graduates who have studied management techniques and other aspects of management theory in their home countries or abroad. Normally, they are able to quickly understand the theoretical aspects of any new technique. As a rule, national management development institutes and centres and, to some extent, public administration in developing countries have such people.

On the other hand, the skills of effective practical application of management techniques to live situations are a major problem. Coupled with motivation, this is, in fact, the major problem of technical co-operation in management. To be really useful, however, to the countries who have requested assistance in building up their national management development services, the transfer of management skills and the whole range of personal, organisational, cultural and other problems of application of management techniques and theories to the practice of developing countries must be considered collectively. Properly designed and executed training programmes can reduce the period of learning the practical skills which would otherwise be needed, and thus help developing countries to acquire the necessary managerial and administrative competence in a shorter time than that required for industrialised countries. A shorter development period is essential if we are to contribute to closing the much publicised gaps between the developing and the industrialised countries.

This approach to technical co-operation is reflected in the cycle of operations followed in a typical UNDP/ILO management development project (see Figure 1).

Most commonly, the first activity in which the managers, or young people trained for future management jobs participate, are training courses. To the extent that is necessary, these courses deal with management techniques and concepts in a theoretical way. This is only the initial step, however, because as soon as possible, and normally right from the very beginning of the course, many practical exercises and case studies are used to bring the theory closer to practice and present it in a form which appeals to the practitioner/trainee.

The next activity in the development cycle is guided practical application of the new techniques and concepts. In some cases, this is done during the training programme concerned, which consists thus of two major phases: the first, as a rule shorter, phase of classroom or laboratory training is followed by a phase during which the participants work as individuals or in groups on practical projects. In other cases, the formal training programme does not include this second phase. But it is almost invariably followed by a follow-up period which is very similar in objectives and scope. Before the end of the course, each participant is assisted in selecting a practical problem-solving task in which he will apply, in the conditions of his own enterprise, what he has learned in the course. The professional training staff keep in touch with the participants and work with them in their enterprise enough to ensure that each participant does, in fact, produce practical results. It is considered that this approach is the only way to ensure that participants receive adequate training in, and exposure to, practical management skills. Further, top management is unlikely to accept any alternative approach to training which excludes the practical application of new techniques.

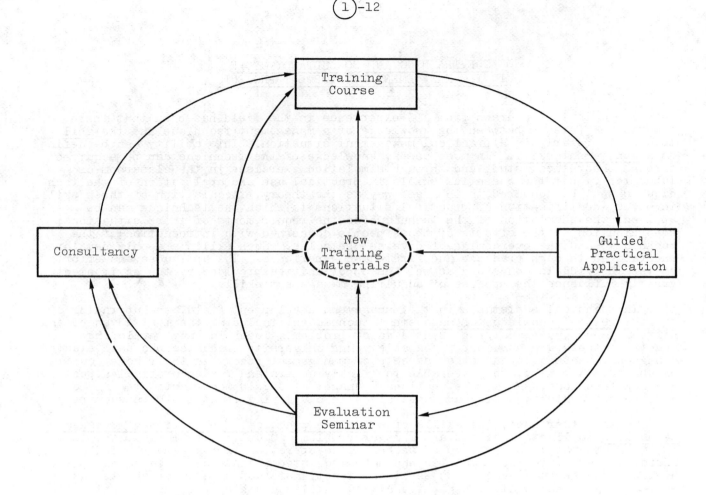

Figure 1: Training and Consultancy Cycle.

At the end of this practical in-plant application phase (whether part of a general course or follow-up phase after the completion of a course) participants return to the training centre for a few more days, so that each can present to the group the description of the problem he tackled, the methods used to solve it and the obtained or expected results. Through such "evaluation seminars" everyone has a further opportunity to learn about additional practical applications.

For many years the ILO programme of technical co-operation in management development has incorporated this in-plant training feature in virtually every training course. A subsequent and logical step relating to the improvement of management practice and to the building of national management development institutes is the introduction of management consultancy services of all types to enterprises and organisations. Several major advantages accrue from this key activity. First, training centre staff are able to provide direct beneficial assistance to enterprises and organisations where consultancy assignments are undertaken. Second, consultancy assignments provide a "feedback" of local knowledge and expertise to the centre, thus facilitating the acquisition of a national spirit and outlook for the centre and its staff. Third, consultancy assignments facilitate the maintenance of a practical orientation to the related training courses. Last, but not least, they originate demand for further training and stimulate its continuity. This additional training, whether provided in-plant or at the management institute, usually confers two additional important benefits; it prepares the staff of the enterprise to assume responsibility for a significant part of the implementation phase of consultancy; and it assists the enterprise in building up its ability to solve its own problems in the future.

It is considered that the combination of formal training with guided applications and regular consultancy work have been the key factors in the success of the ILO management development programme.

A very important feature of management methods and techniques is that most of them affect several departments in the enterprise and above all, more than one level in the management hierarchy. Techniques, which could be introduced and effectively utilised as a matter for a few specialists without involvement and support of general management, are rare and their real role in management is often marginal. Training in modern management techniques has to be provided, therefore, both to the specialists who will be actually working with a given technique and to managers responsible for the over-all operation of organisations, which includes the effective use of management techniques.

There are at least three very important reasons why managers, including those in senior and top positions, need - and appreciate - training in management techniques:

(a) to be willing to send specialists from the management staff to training courses in management techniques and to know where to send them;

(b) to understand the actual potential of each technique and to properly combine various techniques in the over-all process of management;

(c) to play a leading role in the introduction of appropriate management techniques and give personal support to colleagues in specialist and lower functions who are directly concerned with the introduction of new techniques.

If training in advanced management concepts and techniques should be effectively introduced in an enterprise, government department or any other organisation, it is essential to provide orientation training to top managers (preferably through short and very well prepared seminars).

The general manager, especially in a higher or top position, should receive training in management techniques which corresponds to the scope of his functions. He does not need to spend tens of hours to master the mathematical or other theory on which the technique is based or to study the equipment needed for certain techniques. He needs, however, to be familiar with conditions of use, areas of possible application, benefits to be drawn and his own role in the introduction and use of the technique.

Such training may be given in several ways, depending upon the techniques themselves, the level of management and the over-all situation in training. Advanced and top management programmes provided by management institutes and centres to managers from various enterprises include an appreciation of techniques appropriate to the main management functions, as well as to general management itself, in the enterprises from which the participants are recruited. Training programmes designed for a specific enterprise or group, i.e., adapted to its individual needs, deal in more depth with techniques which are to be introduced in the given enterprise.

Frequently the top and other general managers who have participated in orientation seminars, ask themselves for more training in the use of management techniques. This may be provided through simulation exercises, application projects or other training opportunities, in which the general manager handles the technique just as he would in his actual job and can, therefore, obtain help from specialists with the necessary mathematical, statistical, systems design, psychological or another specialised background.

The principles of the cycle on Figure 1 apply thus to all functions and levels in management and administration. The application of these principles will, however, be made with due regard to the possibilities and needs of these various functions and levels.

NOTE ON TERMS

"Management education" is most frequently used in two principal ways. In the first, narrower sense, it usually relates to a special area or field of professional (technical) education, given at certain universities and schools. It emphasises the understanding of facts, laws and principles governing economics and business, and the learning of general management methods and techniques applicable in a variety of concrete situations. "Management education is education in the basic principles and practices of management carried out in a school or university as a part of formal education. It is designed to provide the student with a general knowledge of management as a basis with which to start or in some cases continue his career in industry or commerce."[1]

The second use of the term "management education" is much broader. It covers not only education, which generally precedes practical work and is given at universities and schools, but also the further education, training and development of managers and their staff during their entire practical career. It is in this sense that the term "management education" is more and more frequently used today.[2] It actually means continuous, life-long education for management. When it is appropriate to show that this process has two major phases, management education used in this broad sense is broken down into "initial" and "further" management education.

"Management training" is sometimes seen in a very narrow sense only involving the development of practical skills in the use of management techniques and methods. However, it is now more recognised as the systematic and continuous development of that knowledge and those skills and attitudes which will prove beneficial both to the organisation and to the individual in achieving the objectives of the organisation. In such a concept, training is concerned with knowledge and attitudes in addition to skills in the use of techniques and methods. Both on and off-the-job training are included.

The term "management development" is used essentially as an indication of a complex process of "raising managerial ability in order to improve the effectiveness of management actions".[3] "Management development is the planned experience, guided growth and training opportunities provided for those who perform the management functions. This includes all members of management from the president through all supervisory levels and staff personnel".[4]

In management development, the training activities occupy a major place. Other endeavours and measures likely to enhance managerial competence in the short and long run are, however, also included. Management development, conceived in this broad sense, embraces career planning for managers, their rotation and promotion, motivation for growth, improvement of leadership and communication styles, the manager's self education, use of consultants and other measures helping managers to grow professionally and continuously improve their performance.

---

[1] ILO: The Effectiveness of ILO Management Development and Productivity Projects, MAN DEV Series No. 3 (Geneva, 1965), p. 74.

[2] See e.g. Management Education in the 1970s, proceedings of the Management Education Review Conference held in January 1970, British Institute of Management (London, 1970); and A.A. Zoll: Dynamic Management Education, Addison Wesley Publishing Company, 1969 (Reading, Mass.).

[3] A.R.B. Skertchly: Tomorrow's Managers (London, 1968), Staples, p. 1.

[4] L. Craig and L.R. Bittel (ed.): Training and Development Handbook (New York, 1969, McGraw-Hill), p. 363.

Handout I

<u>SESSION EVALUATION FORM</u>

SESSION NUMBER	RATING			
	Very Good	Good	Satis-factory	Poor
Usefulness of session content to your interests and needs				
Quality of Instruction (logic of presentation, depth, clarity, use of visual aids, etc.)				

What would have made the session more effective? _____

_____

_____

_____

_____

Signature (optional)

Objective

To present some of the more important factors influencing the learning process which should be taken into account when designing training programmes

Handout Material

I - Ten Simple Rules of Learning, p. 5

Background Reading

Some Aspects of Learning, pp. 1-4

Background reading for Session 3

Recommended Reading

Heyel, Encyclopedia of Management, pp. 408-413. Under "Learning Theory", the teaching-learning process is discussed as a human transaction involving teacher, learner and learning group in a set of dynamic inter-relationships

Craig and Bittel, Training and Development Handbook, Chapter 3, "The Learning Process" by J. Folley. Deals with learning in terms of stimulus and response

Lynton and Pareek, Training for Development

Bigge, Learning Theories for Teachers

Special Equipment and Aids

You may wish to record key words on the chalkboard, or prepare them on cards for the flannel board, e.g.,

          MOTIVATION   REINFORCEMENT   FEEDBACK
          PARTICIPATION/PRACTICE   TRANSFER

45 min.	**Session Guide 2**
	A study of the factors influencing the learning process is basic to the selection and evaluation of training methods (Session 3) and the design of training programmes (Session 19). The instructor should have a clear understanding of the material in all three sessions in order to co-ordinate the ideas in each.

10:30	Introduction. Learning can be assisted by –
	    improving the psychological conditions under which it takes place;
	    improving the material arrangements and methods of training.

	This session deals not so much with learning theories as with some general principles which are significant factors in all learning situations. Clearly, if we want to promote learning, we must understand those factors which will contribute most to learning. The teaching methods and learning experiences advocated during this course all capitalise on these principles, and we will be observing and evaluating how they do this throughout the programme.
10:35	Present and discuss with participants the aspects of learning as covered in the background reading, Some Aspects of Learning. Whenever possible, relate the principle under discussion to concrete examples relevant to local conditions. Draw from participants the various motivations they expect to find in their trainees; the nature of individual differences as they may meet them in their training context, etc. Record key words in front of the group as each is discussed.
	1. Motivation. Trainee attitudes. How to stimulate motivation. Types of motivation. Negative motivation.
	2. Reinforcement (stimulus and response). How to provide. Checking for correct responses.
	3. Feedback – knowledge of results. Its role as a motivator.
	4. Participation. Importance of active involvement for greater motivation, for the checking of response accuracy, for the purpose of practice, to facilitate transfer.
	5. Applicability – transfer of knowledge. Relevance to job, to individuals' background and experience.
	6. Individual differences. How to account for. Selection of participants for courses. Differences in rate of learning, in attitudes, in working habits, in expectations.
	7. Role of perception.
	8. Sequencing of material to be learned into meaningful wholes.
	You may wish to point out how certain teaching methods employ these principles to a greater or lesser extent. Material in Session 3 will be useful for this, especially Exhibit C, Application of Some Principles of Learning in Teaching Methods.
11:10	Summarise the session by noting that:
	– a major objective for the trainer is to create a learning situation which follows these principles;
	– when a trainee fails to learn, these aspects of the learning situation should be re-examined to see what may be hindering his progress.
	Distribute HANDOUT I, Ten Simple Rules of Learning.
11:15	Close the session.

SOME ASPECTS OF LEARNING[1]

Learning has been described as a relatively permanent change in behaviour that occurs as a result of insight, practice or experience. Learning may be simply an addition (new information); it may be a subtraction (unlearning a bad habit); or it may be a modification (adjusting new knowledge to old). Learning as change may be for the better or for the worse: we learn bad habits as well as good ones. Learning may be conscious or unconscious: we take courses in the English language but we unconsciously acquire styles of speech and gesture from family and friends.

Learning is such a complicated process that no one can really claim to know how it occurs. We do know that learning takes place more readily in some circumstances than in others, and that it can to a great extent be influenced. To facilitate learning, a teacher needs to understand the various factors which bear upon the learning process.

Motivation

Perhaps the most important factor in learning is motivation to learn. Experimental evidence indicates that little learning takes place in the absence of motivation. What motivates one person to learn may, of course, be quite different from what motivates another. For some people, it is the interest or challenge of the task (intrinsic motivation); for others, it is the anticipated reward or punishment (extrinsic motivation, e.g., money, certification);for still others, it is the need for recognition or status. Up to a point, the stronger the motivation, the more learning takes place, but beyond a critical level, the learner becomes too anxious and tense to learn effectively (some of the energy that has been aroused is spilling over in tension, which disturbs learning).

Perhaps we should consider the human needs to be satisfied in order to have a better understanding of motivation. It was the psychologist, A.H. Maslow, in his book Motivation and Personality, who described a theory of satisfaction of human needs extending in hierarchical form through five levels. He said that at the first level are the basic physiological needs: food, shelter, sex. The next level he described as safety or security needs, the need to protect oneself from threatening factors. The third level, he suggested, consists of the "belonging" needs, the need to have association with others rather than be isolated. He indicated the fourth level to be status needs, the need to have self-respect and a feeling of importance. The top level need, according to his theory, is that of achievement or self-fulfilment.

Maslow makes the point that when a need has been satisfied, it is no longer a need. Take the example of air. If one is deprived of air, then the human being is required to satisfy this need and he is not interested in trying to satisfy higher level needs. But once the need is fulfilled, it is no longer a need and the individual is motivated to try to satisfy the next level of need. After the basic and security needs are met, the higher level of needs play an important part in motivating the student to learn effectively.

Teachers and instructors should have an adequate understanding of the part that "needs satisfaction" can play in effective learning, from the basic problems of participant comfort (lighting, seating and ventilation) and fatigue (the timing of training) to an awareness of trainees' need to feel accepted and respected by colleagues and by the instructor. If these needs are met in large measure, participants will be more likely to try to satisfy their needs for creativity and self-fulfilment in the learning experience.

---

[1] Compiled from incidental papers prepared for ILO/Management Development Briefing Courses by J.D. Hounsell, P.D. Pereira, E.S. Phillips and K.F. Walker.

Stimulus, Response and Reinforcement

Motivation alone will not produce learning, however. Attention has to be given to the particular stimulus, to the checking of the accuracy of the response, in a rewarding situation. Rewarded behaviour is learned and tends to be repeated under similar conditions in the future, whereas non-rewarded behaviour tends not to be learned. Once we observe or discover the things that are reinforcing (rewarding) to a trainee, it becomes possible to shape his behaviour by reinforcing the desired responses.

Reinforcement and reward are always important aspects of the learning process. Evidence seems to indicate that the more frequent and prompt reinforcement is, the more effective learning will be. If the teacher has a genuine interest in the trainees, he will seek active ways of rewarding successful responses. A kind remark is a reinforcer, or a personal compliment, or sometimes, simply personal attention. Success is also a great reinforcer, perhaps the best. As the old adage says, "Success breeds success". In self-discovery techniques and programmed learning, success is a built-in reinforcer and motivater for learning.

Feedback, or Knowledge of Results

Of course, in order to learn effectively, the learner needs to know if he has been successful: this may be confirmed by the instructor, by the reactions of his colleagues, or by the learning situation itself. The more the learner knows about what he is doing, the more rapidly is he able to make improvements in his performance. This is the important principle of feedback, or knowledge of results, and it is the most common and probably the single most important source of reinforcement for the human learner.

For feedback to be effective, it should be given as soon as possible. We shoot at a target and observe the result: there is immediate feedback to correct and reinforce the learning. If feedback is delayed, it is more difficult for a learner to determine which of his actions led to a successful outcome.

If the learning situation can be arranged so that the learner is given a series of intermediate goals, and is provided with constant, precise feedback as to his progress, this helps to maximise the effect of this principle and helps avoid boredom. The case study, role play and discussion methods are good illustrations of learning by early feedback; similarly with business simulations where the results of decisions are fed back to participants immediately, providing useful information for new decisions. The best method for feedback is seen in programmed learning, where immediate reinforcement follows the participant's response to each new segment of information.

Participation and Practice

Experiments prove that the more a trainee participates in the learning situation, the more effective will be the learning, particularly where he is learning a skill. If the learner is not called upon to respond actively, there will be fewer opportunities to check the accuracy of the response and provide feedback for control and reinforcement. Participation also means practice or repetition of the behaviour to be learned, which is necessary for remembering and for transfer of the classroom learning to the real life situation.

Most trainees need to repeat the behaviour several times before they remember it. Repetition needs to be carried well beyond the first perfect performance - the principle of "overlearning" - to consolidate learning and offset the effect of forgetting. This need not mean a great deal of repetition all at once, but may entail a certain amount at intervals. Follow-up exercises, review and refresher courses also aid memory and transfer.

Transfer or Application of Knowledge

From experience, we know that learning is easier when we can see its relevance or applicability to our own situation. Wherever possible, there should be a close relationship between the training programme and the work to be actually performed. Obviously, if procedures for machine maintenance are being taught, they should be those currently used in the company. For management skills, business simulation, case studies and role-playing appear to be the best techniques for positive transfer, providing they are realistic and appropriate to the level of trainees.

The opposite effect is demonstrated when trainees return from a course full of ideas, only to find themselves prevented by top management from trying out the new procedures they have learned. Similarly, if human relations principles of the democratic variety are taught to students who will return to an autocratic situation, their learning will have been in vain. If we cannot apply what we learn, we tend to forget it.

Perception

Perception is what gives us our ability to observe the world, which is revealed to us through our five senses. We "perceive" when we:

- recognise (objects, sounds, tastes, smells, feel);
- discriminate (between colours, facts and fallacies);
- relate (parts to a whole, like objects to each other, a principle with its practice);
- select (what interests us or what we should focus our attention on).

Most important of all, perhaps, perception is what helps us to use the knowledge we have in an entirely different situation from that in which we learned it. For instance, I may have learned to use a knife to cut with, but I might subsequently use it to remove a cork from a bottle, open the lid of a tin, to turn a screw, or to paint a picture. Perception is such an important thing that many modern toys for children are designed to develop these qualities.

Perception operates from the most concrete to the most abstract levels and very often perceiving a relationship at one level will help us to perceive new material at another level. Thus, audio-visual aids, simplified models, graphic symbols, the use of examples and analogies all help to engage our perceptions and transfer/apply them to new situations.

A teacher also relies on the perception of the learner when he arranges the material so that it makes sense to the learner and allows him to build up a coherent structure easily. Research shows that to a surprising extent, better results are achieved by tackling a task as a whole rather than in a series of small sections that have little logical relation to each other. If the steps lead logically from one to another, and hang together in meaningful units, learning is facilitated. Instructional material may also be organised by:

- moving from the known to the unknown;
- progressing from the simple to the complex;
- relating the material presented to present tasks.

To influence the perceptions of other people, a trainer must attempt to understand their perceptions and relate the material to their understanding. Learning will be to no avail if the instructor is not realistic in discussing his subject in relation to the students' background and experience. Unless the learning is a meaningful experience in terms of their needs and aspirations, they will not learn as effectively and they will not make the effort to apply the knowledge and skills to their various jobs. Subject matter should be related to their:

- background (aims, fears, problems, satisfactions, social and economic needs, health, age, experience);
- education (level of education, knowledge of the subject or related subjects);
- abilities (capacity to learn - for instance, rate and amount of learning; capacity to do certain things, e.g., mechanical ability).

Of course, there are also individual differences with respect to trainees' skills, motivation, previous experience, intellectual capacity, attitudes and working habits, so that no two people will perceive information in exactly the same way. Self-instructional methods such as programmed learning, where the learner goes at his own pace, the discovery method, or individual assignments and projects are therefore very valuable in making individual learning more effective. However, it is frequently more expedient to give training to groups and in this situation, it is clear that learning will be more effective if the levels of previous skills, native intelligence, etc. are not too diverse. Proper selection of students for a course is necessary in this case.

As we grow older our perceptive processes become more and more complicated as we receive an ever-increasing amount of information. What happens to this information when we receive it? It is either stored or forgotten, depending on such things as whether it is interesting or necessary,   useful or not, understood or not, etc. High motivation or interest in learning, active participation in and sufficient practice of the learning, its relevance and applicability to trainees' current jobs will all act to offset forgetting and thus these various factors in the learning process become doubly significant.

Setting Training Objectives

In formal procedures of instruction, experiences are organised to accomplish specific learning (changes) within a restricted period of time. In this situation it is essential that a teacher clarify precisely what learning and unlearning he wants to facilitate, and let these objectives serve as a clear focus for his whole training programme.[1], [2] Specifically enumerated objectives (in knowledge, skills and attitudes) should indicate what material must be taught and will also affect the choice of teaching method. The trainee himself may learn more effectively when he has clearly defined goals toward which to work. A training programme should set forth goals or objectives in terms of:

- the job to be performed;

- the conditions under which it is to be performed;

- the level of proficiency required.

Summary

The more a trainer can arrange the learning situation so as to utilise these principles of learning, the more likely the learner is to learn. Thus, a training programme, or a teaching technique, will be judged adequate to the degree that it appears likely to:

- provide for the learner's active participation;

- provide the trainee with knowledge of results about his attempts to improve;

- promote by good organisation a meaningful integration of learning experiences that the trainee can transfer from training to the job;

- provide some means for the trainee to be reinforced for appropriate behaviour;

- provide for practice and repetition when needed;

- motivate the trainee to improve his own performance;

- assist the trainee in his willingness to change.

Learning is a life-long activity; we are never too old to learn, but we are frequently resistant to change. People often talk about problems as if they safe-guarded their position, e.g., "There are so many problems I cannot change". What they mean is, do not remove the problems or I might have to change. Learning is change.

---

[1] See the example cited in Handout II for Session 19, "A Systems Concept of Training" by Richard D. Miller.

[2] Some objectives for the learner:

Absorb knowledge	Make better decisions
Develop skills,(numerical, verbal, perceptual,critical,physical,social,etc.)	Communicate more clearly
	Understand others better
Arouse interest, motivate	Understand self better
Modify attitudes	Obtain feedback on his progress
Break down prejudices	Facilitate collaboration with others
Become more independent from authority	Improve clear thinking and behaviour under pressure
Adopt framework or concepts	
Develop own framework or concepts	Make concentrated attack on a problem
Ability to analyse complex situations	Ability to plan ahead increased
Ability to sift and evaluate information	Increased ability to conceptualise
	Incentive to develop self

TEN SIMPLE RULES OF LEARNING

1. <u>The capacities of learners are important in determining what can be learned and how long it will take.</u>

   The implication of this principle is that trainers should know their audiences. Bright people can grasp a complex message that is over the heads of the less bright ones. And they grasp significance of a simple message in less time.

2. <u>The order of presentation of materials to be learned is very important.</u>

   Points presented at the beginning and end of the message are remembered better than those in the middle. Thus, if four reasons "why" are given in a series of copy, the two most important points should be given first and last.

3. <u>Showing errors in how to do something can lead to increases in learning.</u>

   The effectiveness of a demonstration might be increased by showing not only "what to do" but "what not to do". Thus, to show how not to use a product and also how to use a product may be very useful.

4. <u>The rate of forgetting tends to be very rapid immediately after learning.</u>

   Accordingly, the continuing repetition of the training message is desirable. It usually takes a lot of repetition in the early weeks of a programme to overcome rapid forgetting.

5. <u>Repetition of identical materials is often as effective in getting things remembered as repeating the same story but with variations.</u>

   Psychologists term this identical vs. varied repetition. Using training films, they have failed to find significant differences in learning, after employing a lot of different examples versus repeating the same few over again.

6. <u>Knowledge of results leads to increases in learning.</u>

   If you are interested in teaching a given amount of material to people, knowledge of how well they are doing as they are learning leads to greater learning gains.

7. <u>Learning is aided by active practice rather than passive reception.</u>

   This point is of great importance. If you can get your audience members to "participate" in your presentation, they are much more likely to remember your points.

8. <u>A message is more easily learned and accepted if it does not interfere with earlier habits.</u>

   Thus, a training theme which draws on prior experiences of the audience will help the learning of the message.

9. <u>The mere repetition of a situation does not necessarily lead to learning. Two things are necessary - "belongingness" and "satisfaction".</u>

   Belongingness means that the elements to be learned must seem to belong together, must show some form of relationship or sequence.

   Satisfiers are real or symbolic rewards, as distinguished from annoying consequences that may be present in the learning process.

10. <u>Learning something new can interfere with the remembering of something learned earlier.</u>

    This is most important when the learner is being asked to change his habits or methods of work. For example, if you study French for an hour and then study Italian for an hour, your ability to recall the French will probably be less than it would have been had you substituted an hour's interval of rest in place of the hour's study of Italian.

Objective

To review the factors affecting the selection of various teaching methods and training materials

Handout Material

I - A Brief Guide to Teaching and Training Methods, pp. 11-13

HANDOUT I, Session 1, Session Evaluation Form

Background Reading

Principles for Selection of Teaching and Training Methods, pp. 1-10

Recommended Reading

Special Equipment and Aids

Overhead projector

Blank transparency to record a display similar to Exhibit A (p. 9) found in the background reading: Main Factors Affecting the Choice of Teaching Methods. This visual aid will be drawn in class as the lecture/discussion develops.

Exhibit B (p. 10) prepared on a transparency: Effectiveness of Participative Methods.

45 min.	**Session Guide** 3

From the learner, we turn to the management trainer and his particular set of considerations in selecting appropriate training methods to promote learning. The session complements Session 2 on the learning process, and is relevant to Session 19 since all the points bear on the over-all design of training programmes as well.

11:30

Introduction of the training methods which are key tools for the management trainer. As the person in charge of the learning situation, he must manipulate these tools skillfully. He must not only be acquainted with a variety of methods, but he must also know their strengths and limitations, their suitability under certain conditions, etc.

What factors will affect the selection of methods? Cover the main headings in the background reading. As points and sub-points are brought out, either in lecture or discussion, record them on an overhead projector transparency so that the display resembles Exhibit A:

- Principles of Learning (cover briefly, linking up with previous session)

- Human Factors - background of instructor and participants

- Objectives - knowledge, skills and attitudes (use Exhibit B to illustrate)

- Subject Area - methods which teach management techniques or show their use; especially methods which teach the inter-disciplinary approach to management problems

- Time and Material Factors - the resources of the training organisation; the availability of trainees.

Refer to the RCA case study (Handout I, Session 19, A Systems Concept of Training) which will demonstrate some of these factors at work.

12:10

Bring the session to a close by noting that the participants now have an over-all view of the different methods and aids, and some idea of the principles which affect their use. Each method will be treated in greater depth during the rest of the week.

Distribute HANDOUT I, A Brief Guide to Teaching and Training Methods. Ask participants to fill out the Session Evaluation Form.

12:15

Collect evaluation forms and close the session.

PRINCIPLES FOR SELECTION OF TEACHING AND TRAINING METHODS

by M. Kubr,
Management Development Branch
International Labour Office

I. INTRODUCTION

Until recently the armoury of teaching and training methods suitable for management education was quite modest. For years the case study was the only real participative method being used in addition to the more academic, classical methods. Although the Harvard Business School first introduced the case study as a teaching method in the 1920s, it was only much later that it began receiving recognition outside the United States.

Today we are still far from knowing exactly how managerial competence is best acquired and developed. But we do know much more about learning for management now than two or three decades ago. We have come to realise that both the education of potential managers and the further development of practising managers are extremely complex processes, in which formal education, practical experience and training opportunities play their respective roles, and hence, require co-ordination. Management education and training is endeavouring to see the manager's job in its entirety by taking into account the many factors which influence the operation of the enterprise in the contemporary world. This has emphasised the need for continuous improvement not only in the content, but also in the over-all organisation and methodology of management education and training programmes.

During the last fifteen years more than any other previous time, many new methods have been developed, tested, combined, and adapted to different learning situations. Some of the new methods have become irreplaceable tools in the teacher's and trainer's hands; others have remained marginal. Some are entirely new; others are more or less imaginative adaptations of older methods. Some are simple and can be used by virtually any teacher or trainer (or by the managers themselves) without any special preparation; others are fairly sophisticated, and it is not advisable to use them without extensive preparation of both teachers and course participants. A genuine process of innovation is occurring in teaching methods for management education and training. The recipients of training have also become more demanding on methodology; thus, it is anticipated that this innovation process will most certainly continue.

If we put aside the few cases of trainers and consultants who, for purely commercial purposes, want to amaze their clients with "miracle methods of training", we find that the overwhelming majority of those engaged in management education and training are seriously concerned about finding and using the most effective methods possible. Most teachers and trainers try to be realistic about the significance of each teaching method. They want to assess its advantages and disadvantages in relation to others. They try to match the correct method with the objectives of the education or training and with the specific conditions in which learning is to take place.

Exhibit A shows the main factors which affect the choice of teaching and training methods used in management education and training programmes, and which will therefore be discussed in the following sections.

II. FACTORS TO CONSIDER IN THE SELECTION OF METHODS

1. Human Factors

The Teacher

The teacher's knowledge, managerial and teaching experience, and personality are all factors of primary importance and are intentionally mentioned at the beginning. To put it bluntly: the teacher has to have a clear and significant message to pass, and his personality has to be acceptable to the students or trainees so that effective communication links can be established quickly and easily. If these conditions are fulfilled, a well-chosen and properly used method is likely to ease and stimulate learning. If they are not fulfilled, unfortunately the method may become an end in itself.

Teachers are advised on teaching methods by their directors of studies, by senior colleagues, in special "teaching methods" courses, through manuals, etc. But eventually each teacher has to assume personal responsibility for choosing the best methods for his particular teaching assignment. He ought to be able, therefore, to make a rational appraisal of his abilities and to try to employ methods likely to enhance - not reduce - the impact he hopes to make. Role playing, for example, is an exercise requiring some knowledge of psychology, a lot of experience with various types of human problems in management and the ability to react quickly in discussions. That is why a teacher who does not possess these qualities, but has an analytical mind and experience in solving business problems, might give preference to the case study method.

In training trainers one should encourage teachers to use a greater variety of methods, but certainly not impose upon them methods with which they would feel uneasy .

The Participants and the Environment from which They Come

Methods of teaching must respect:

(a) the intellectual level and educational background of the participants;

(b) the participants' age and practical experience; and

(c) the social and cultural environment.

For example, in training programmes intended for supervisors, middle managers or small entrepreneurs who have had only a basic education and who have been away from school for a long time, lectures should be replaced by short talks using visual aids extensively; concrete examples should be given and no high-level theories presented; simplified case studies should be used instead of long and complex cases; simple programmed books should be recommended instead of the usual textbooks.

In regard to the participants' practical experience, a distinction must be made between young people with little or no management experience, who first learn about management in a university or other type of school, and participants with practical experience, either from managerial functions or from specialist work in various functional departments.

In the former case, much of the information is new to the students, and it is difficult to link the teaching process with any previous experience. However, these students are open-minded and often more receptive to new ideas than the latter group. In training people with experience, only additional knowledge has to be imparted; and it is not only possible but absolutely essential to make an appeal to the participants' experience by relating the teaching to it. However, in this group some of the participants with practical experience may take the attitude of "knowing better in advance"; if so, the teacher's main problem may be how to change their air of self-complacency and make them aware of what they need to learn to do their jobs better. In such cases it is rarely sufficient for the teachers to talk about new methods and techniques of management. Practical assignments, case study discussions or simulation exercises are more likely to help the participants realise that they have gaps in knowledge and skills and that training may be the answer.

Experienced managers have the capacity to learn directly from each other, provided a favourable atmosphere is created and methods are used which stimulate this learning. Discussion groups, working parties, syndicates, consultancy assignments and practical projects carried out by groups of managers are well suited for this purpose.

The complexity of the problem is increased by social and cultural factors in the environment. It must be remembered that many of the participative teaching methods were developed in the United States - a country with its own particular social and cultural characteristics. High achievement motivation, little respect for formal authorities, priority given to action before contemplation - these and many other cultural factors may be absent in the country to which one or another teaching method is to be transferred.

Fortunately, educators are now aware of this problem and special studies are available on the question of transfer.[1] A number of experts with considerable experience in developing countries have also confirmed that, in general, any participative method may be used in any environment provided that it is instilled gradually, with foreknowledge of the environment, making the necessary modifications of the method and without hurting national pride.

2. Objectives of Teaching and Training

As a rule, training needs and objectives of educational and training programmes in management are defined in terms of changes to be effected in knowledge, attitudes and skills - which should afterwards lead to improved managerial action. Various training situations will be concerned with various types and levels of knowledge, attitudes and skills. A preliminary analysis of needs will help to identify what objectives a particular programme ought to have. Methods will then be selected with regard to their ability to impart new knowledge, influence attitudes and develop practical skills.

In this connection B. Hawrylyshyn[2] has developed a simple but interesting model based on the experience of the Centre d'Etudes Industrielles in Geneva (see Exhibit B). In this model six participative methods are related to the general skills which a manager should possess, whatever his special field of work or level may be in the hierarchy. Each method in the model can serve various purposes; however, a method reaches its peak of effectiveness only in connection with a specific purpose. This can be well demonstrated with the case method. Pertinent data are given to the trainee in the description of the case. He has to diagnose and analyse the problem, consider alternative solutions, discuss those solutions and modify them after hearing his colleagues' views. He does not have to make decisions or implement them; consequently, he is not trained in the skill of decision-making and there is no reliable feedback on the correctness of his solutions.

The main lesson to be drawn from this model is that if training is intended to improve multiple skills (which is usually the case), a combination of teaching methods must be used.

A similar type of analysis could be made to determine which methods are most likely to affect the managers' attitudes or impart a specific kind of knowledge.

Let us take the example of using specialist knowledge and experience in the preparation of management decisions on complex business matters. It is of little use to lecture about the value of specialists to a manager who overestimates his own individual judgment and is not willing or perhaps able to use the specialist services which are available to him. Team work in syndicates, participation in business games or practical projects might make such a manager aware of his drawbacks so that he will begin to change his attitudes towards team work and the importance of specialists. His interest in new knowledge and skills will undoubtedly be awakened.

On his leadership style, communication abilities, and behaviour in general, a manager may get more direct and stronger feedback from other participants in sensitivity training or as a member of a team working on a group project than in years of work in a managerial position.

─────────────

[1] See, for example, ILO: Social and Cultural Factors in Management Development, Man. Dev. Series, No. 5 (Geneva, 1966) or R.A. Webber: Culture and Management (Irwin, Homewood, 1969).

[2] B. Hawrylyshyn: "Preparing Managers for International Operations", in Business Quarterly (Canada, Autumn 1967), pp. 28-35.
The CEI is currently carrying out a research project, using this model. The main purpose is to assess the effectiveness of selected teaching methods on the basis of measured improvements in skills.

Obviously, knowledge, skills and attitudes are inter-related and this must not be overlooked when setting the objectives of training and choosing teaching methods. Furthermore, they are related to certain specific management functions or subject areas or, in many cases, to multi-functional situations and inter-disciplinary problems.

3. Subject Area

Various subject areas (finance, personnel, operations research, general management, etc.) have their own specific features. For example, operations research techniques are based on the extensive use of mathematics and statistics. It is usually taught through a combination of lectures (using audio-visual aids) and exercises during which the technique is practised. This may be supported by reading assignments. In certain cases lectures may be replaced or supplemented with programmed books. However, the main thing from the management point of view is not to know the technique itself, but to know when and how it can be used. This ability can be developed through practical projects, simulation exercises, business games, case studies, etc.

In programmes concentrating on the behavioural aspects of management, communication, leadership and motivation, training methods may be selected and combined in ways which give the participants numerous opportunities to analyse human behaviour, and at the same time directly influence the attitudes and behaviour of the participants themselves. These programmes use case studies dealing with the "human side of the enterprise", business games emphasising communication and relations between participants, role playing, sensitivity training and various other forms of group discussions, assignments and exercises.

It should be noted that it is often possible to choose from several methods, if we want to deal with a particular subject or problem. Thus, the analysis of a balance sheet can be taught through the case study method, a combination of case study with role playing, a lecture, as a classroom exercise or by reading a text or a programmed book on the subject. This is possible because the principal methods are versatile enough to be used in teaching a number of different subjects. Lectures, discussion and case studies are being used in virtually all subject areas.

However, in management education and training the principal problem is not how to deal with specific subject areas and functions. It is much more important to:

(a) explain the relationship between various sides and functions of the enterprise and show the highly complex character of the management process;

(b) help the participants to avoid a one-sided and oversimplified approach to multi-dimensional situations;

(c) promote general management skills, which essentially lie in an inter-disciplinary approach to management, and to combine and co-ordinate the various functions of management.

Once again, a sound use of participative methods can be of great help. A senior management seminar, for example, may start with a complex case study illustrating a business problem from multiple angles and arousing the participants' interest in specific subject areas, methods and techniques which, if properly integrated, will help them to take the right action in a complex situation. This may be followed in the second phase of the seminar by a more detailed study of these specific subject areas, methods and techniques. The final phase may be devoted to the integration of specialist knowledge and skills in general management through another complex case, business game or similar exercise or, if possible, through working on a practical project which requires this interdisciplinary approach.

4. Time and Material Factors

Decisions about the choice of teaching methods are not independent of time, financial resources and other factors.

- Preparation time (which affects the cost of the teaching material as well) varies for the different teaching methods. As a rule, complex case studies and business games require long and costly preparation, which includes testing with teachers or experimental groups, and making necessary revisions.

- The length of the course predetermines the kinds of methods which can be used. The longer the course, the better are the chances that the teacher will be able to use business games, complex cases and practical projects. This is not to imply that participative methods should be eliminated from short appreciation or survey courses, however, only methods which are not time consuming and are liable to quickly pass the message can be used in these courses.

- The time of day is more important than many course designers would imagine. For example, in the post-lunch period (14.00-16.00) it is more desirable to have enjoyable and attractive sessions which require active involvement.

- The teaching facilities may be a limiting factor in some institutes, or in courses given outside the institute, e.g. in small towns. Factors such as the number of rooms available for group discussions or syndicates or the accessibility of audio-visual aids should be anticipated and the methods altered in advance.

III. RELATIONSHIP BETWEEN THE PRINCIPLES OF EFFECTIVE LEARNING AND TEACHING METHODS

Education and training for management like any other educational process fulfils its role only by creating situations which are favourable to learning and in which learning actually takes place. That is why "all schemes for management education and executive development exploit or depend on the basic principles of human learning".[1]

Of course, principles of learning are not put into effect through the teaching method alone. Motivation to learn, for example, depends on a number of other variables, such as the challenge of the participant's present or future job, his own "achievement motivation quotient" or the stimulation provided by the environment. However, the methods used in teaching and training can influence motivation to learn and therefore should be examined and applied with this in mind.

Some selected aspects of the relationship between principles of learning and teaching methods are discussed in the following paragraphs.

1. Motivation

The motivation to learn is enhanced if the presentation of the material is interesting, emphasises applicability and shows benefits to be drawn from application. To some extent this can be obtained through any method, including a good lecture. However, many participative methods are directly concerned with applying theoretical knowledge to real life situations. The diverse ways in which they can be combined and sequenced can add to the enjoyment of learning and minimise participant fatigue.

2. Active Involvement

The principle of active involvement is perhaps the main "raison d'être" of participative teaching methods. As a rule, the deeper the involvement, the higher the motivation, the more the participants retain and the better they are equipped to apply it. It should not be overlooked, however, that the method itself, although considered as highly participative, does not assure that each person will be fully involved. Involvement also depends on organisation of case study preparation, leadership style and other factors. The participant may also be passive if he considers the material to be of poor quality or the performance of the teacher to be below his own professional level.

---

[1] T. Kelly: Organisational Behaviour (Irwin, Homewood, 1969), p. 548.

3.   Individual Approach

On-the-job training is a method which can be based on the training needs of one individual, with full regard to his present and future job.   It has, however, many limitations and that is why group training programmes should also involve work outside the enterprise.   They must take into account the fact that individuals have different capabilities and learn at different paces, have personal styles of study and application and should be subject to individual control of performance.   The over-all course design and methods of teaching have to provide, therefore, not only work in groups and teams, but also the opportunity for individual reading, thinking, exercising, and application of knowledge.

This can be done through:

- compulsory individual assignments (reading, exercises, projects, etc.);

- use of teaching aids for individual learning, like magnetic tapes, video-tapes, teaching machines, computer terminals accessible to individuals;

- the breaking down of group assignments and projects into assignments for each individual;

- voluntary additional work by the more capable participants.

4.   Sequencing and Structuring

Some methods are better suited than others for introducing new topics and ideas, for correctly sequencing them or for explaining the structure of a vast and complex area.   That is why in certain situations the teacher cannot do without lectures and reading assignments.

5.   Feedback

Different types of feedback are needed and have to be provided in learning:

- feedback on one's competence and behaviour (as seen by the other course participants, by the trainer and by the trainee himself);

- feedback on what was actually learned, and on one's ability to effectively apply it.

Direct feedback on the soundness of decisions is an integral part of business games, whereas in case discussions the only feedback on the individual's analytical abilities is the opinion of other participants and of the discussion leader.   Strong feedback on behavioural patterns is provided by participation in role playing, business games and sensitivity training (group dynamics). Practical exercises, consultancy assignments and application projects provide feedback on the practical usefulness of learning.

6.   Transfer

This principle requires that education and training help the individual to transfer what he has learned to live situations.   Some teaching methods, like lectures, study of literature or discussions do not pay much attention to this transfer.   On the other hand, in many participative methods the element of transfer is strong.   For this reason the methods of simulation and practical application projects are considered by some teachers as the most effective ones.

Exhibit C shows one way to rate the potential of some teaching methods to apply the above-mentioned selected learning principles.   A simple three-point rating scale has been used and rating is based on the author's personal assessment.

Examining teaching methods from the viewpoint of principles of learning shows the necessity to properly sequence and combine various teaching methods in order to secure the greatest impact on learning.   It also explains why there is a growing interest in certain methods;   those with high motivational feedback and transfer capabilities.   This, of course, does not eliminate other methods which are needed for different purposes.   Neither should it lead to an overestimation of a single method which, in fact, may fulfil its role only in combination with other methods (business games) or serve only very special purposes (sensitivity training).

IV. CURRENT TRENDS IN THE USE OF TEACHING AND TRAINING METHODS

In the preceding sections an attempt was made to show how many factors play a role in the choice of teaching methods and are therefore being increasingly considered by the directors of training and by the teachers and trainers themselves.

However, if one proceeds to an examination of various institutions and programmes with regard to the methods used, it is easy to find a number of differences. This, of course, is not surprising in view of the over-all present situation of management education and development in virtually all developed and developing Eastern and Western countries. Although the long-term trend towards professionalism in management is obvious and the standards of management education and training are constantly improving, we have not yet reached unanimous agreement on the best methods to use in attaining the various objectives of management education and training. On the contrary, the differences between institutions and their programmes are still important and in some cases go as far as complete rejection of certain methods.

Before talking about differences, we should first mention that the attitude towards classical academic teaching methods is now based on a generally recognised assessment of their benefits and shortcomings. Their use is decreasing not only in the training of practising managers, but also in university management education. Statements such as "the lecture method is useless and has to be completely eliminated from management development" can even be heard; such statements are, of course, extreme and lacking in realism.

The different approaches to the use of participative teaching methods are influenced mainly by the diversity in over-all concepts of management education and training and by an unequal appreciation of the value and potential of individual methods.

The case study method was first used to introduce an empirical approach to management education and training; emphasis was put on the study of typical cases of past practical experience. While today it is an exception to meet a trainer who considers the case study as the panacea for management education and training, it is fair to expect that the analysis of selected cases of practical experience and hence the case study method will continue to be important in the future.

During the last fifteen years the greatest progress has probably been made in simulation methods (games, exercises, simulation models, role playing, in-basket, etc.) which today are at the centre of the management teachers' interest. This is inter-related with the growing use of computers in management education and with the developments in operational research techniques for solving complex business and management problems. It is interesting to notice in this connection that there are now two fundamentally different schools of thought on the effectiveness of simulation in management education:

(a) the first one emphasises high motivation and transfer capabilities of teaching by simulation and therefore considers simulation as a very promising teaching tool which will be gaining importance in the future;

(b) the second one rejects simulation since to improve his performance the manager should know his own style and understand his own response patterns in actual, unstructured situations. For example, simulations of reality were not used at all in Belgium's Inter-University Advanced Management Programme started in 1968, as they "are always prefabricated in an intellectual world which is not the manager's own".[1]

---

[1] T. Houston: "Belgian A.M.P. is On-Line, Real-Time" in European Business (July 1969), p. 19.

In spite of the valid arguments put forward by the second school, simulation methods will continue to evolve and to be used in more and more educational and training programmes. Those programmes which concentrate on solving complex business problems, on decision-making and on quantitative methods use various types of business games (with emphasis on market research, economic forecasting and strategic planning problems), simulation exercises and model building, and promote the use of computer services by course participants. Of course, they also use complex case studies. Simulation methods and case studies are also being increasingly used by programmes which deal mainly with the human problems of management.

In order to enhance the practical usefulness of training and to make sure that the trainee will learn from solving practical management problems, some educational and training programmes give priority to the project method and to consultancy assignments used as a training tool. Curiously enough, this concerns training programmes in both developed and developing countries although the size and level of the practical projects done on courses might be different in these two cases. In the ILO Management Development Programme, which is basically concerned with the transfer of management skills to developing countries, practical assignments and consultancy work have been used as a method of training virtually from the Programme's inception. Some European programmes, like the Belgian one mentioned above[1] or the Top Management Programme at the Institute of Management in Prague, include complex projects which each participant has to work out and defend.

It should be mentioned, however, that a practical application project used as a training device will meet professional standards and fulfil its task only if prepared and supported by imparting the necessary knowledge. Furthermore, if a training programme claims to deal with the many facets of management, recourse may have to be taken in other methods likely to influence knowledge, skills and attitudes which are not sufficiently affected by the project method.

In the present and forthcoming period of rapid change, managerial obsolescence is a matter of major concern. Indeed one of the remedies to this is cyclical retraining of managers including those in senior and top positions. It is becoming clear, however, that retraining is not enough. Managers themselves must continue to learn, so that they can foresee and understand change, innovate and act correctly in completely new situations. This should be their principal skill which, again, is linked with a specific attitude – never to stop learning. The higher the level of management, the more urgent is this requirement, but it concerns all phases and levels of management education and training without exception.

That is why good educational and training programmes do not deluge the participants with enormous amounts of detailed information (which tomorrow will be obsolete) but help them to learn how to learn. Course curricula are consciously being designed to force the trainee to deal with new situations in a changing environment, from problem identification and analysis to the making and implementing of original solutions. This, again, calls for the use of participative methods – especially practical project methods, carefully chosen simulation exercises and models, case studies with a strong element of change, and various group assignments which build on the combined knowledge and expertise of all members of the group.

It is no exaggeration to say that the two above-mentioned features of management education and training – concern over their relevance to the continuously changing real-life situation and emphasis on learning how to learn – are becoming the determining factors in the selection, use, and further evolution of teaching and training methods. Since each method has its strengths and weaknesses, a mixture of methods based on the teacher's assessment of their potential and in certain cases emphasising one particular method around which the programme is built, is the predominant feature of management education and development activities today, and will probably continue to be in the near future.

---

[1] See R.W. Revans: "Le programme interuniversitaire de formation à la direction" in Synopsis (September-October 1969), pp. 39-54.

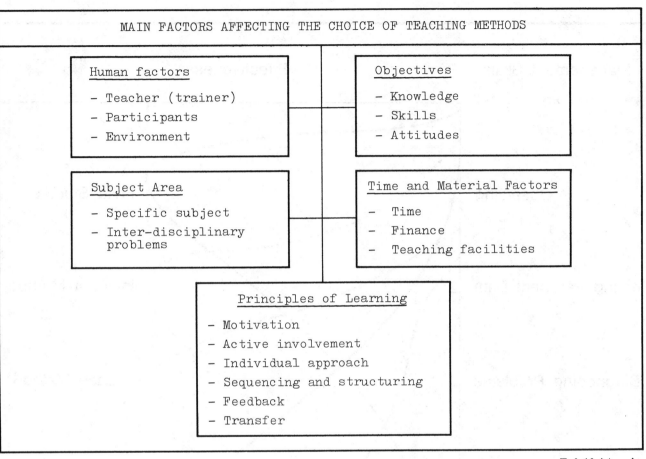

MAIN FACTORS AFFECTING THE CHOICE OF TEACHING METHODS

Human factors
- Teacher (trainer)
- Participants
- Environment

Objectives
- Knowledge
- Skills
- Attitudes

Subject Area
- Specific subject
- Inter-disciplinary problems

Time and Material Factors
- Time
- Finance
- Teaching facilities

Principles of Learning
- Motivation
- Active involvement
- Individual approach
- Sequencing and structuring
- Feedback
- Transfer

Exhibit A

APPLICATION OF SOME PRINCIPLES OF LEARNING IN TEACHING METHODS

Principle \ Method	Training on the job	Lecture	Group Discussion	Case Study	Business Game	Role Playing	Application Project	Reading Assignment
Motivation	Good	Average	Average	Average	Good	Average	Good	Weak
Active involvement	Good	Weak	Average	Good	Good	Good	Good	Average
Individual approach	Good	Weak	Average	Average	Average	Average	Good	Average
Sequencing and structuring	Average	Good	Weak	Average	Average	Weak	Average	Good
Feedback	Good	Weak	Average	Average	Good	Good	Good	Weak
Transfer	Good	Weak	Weak	Average	Average	Average	Good	Weak

Rating: ■ Good   ▪ Average   □ Weak

Exhibit C

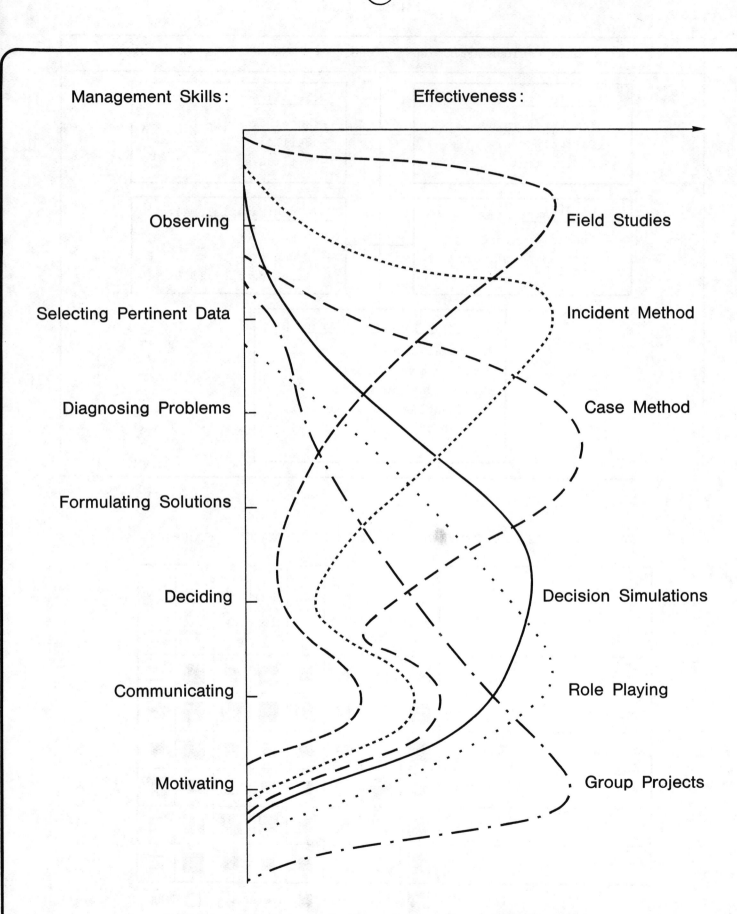

Management Skills:

Observing

Selecting Pertinent Data

Diagnosing Problems

Formulating Solutions

Deciding

Communicating

Motivating

Effectiveness:

Field Studies

Incident Method

Case Method

Decision Simulations

Role Playing

Group Projects

Effectiveness of Participative Methods

Exhibit I

A BRIEF GUIDE TO TEACHING AND TRAINING METHODS

	WHAT IT IS	WHAT IT WILL ACHIEVE	POINTS TO WATCH
Lecture	A talk given without much, if any, participation in the form of questions or discussion on the part of the trainees.	Suitable for large audiences where participation of the trainee is not possible because of numbers. The information to be put over can be exactly worked out beforehand – even to the precise word. The timing can be accurately worked out.	The lack of participation on the part of the audience means that unless the whole of it, from beginning to end, is fully understood and assimilated the sense will be lost.
Talk	A talk incorporating a variety of techniques, and allowing for participation by the trainees. The participation may be in the form of questions asked of trainees, their questions to the speaker, or brief periods of discussion during the currency of the session.	Suitable for putting across information to groups of not more than twenty trainees. Participation by the trainees keeps their interest and helps them to learn.	The trainees have the opportunity to participate but may not wish to do so. The communication will then be all one way and the session will be little different from a lecture.
Discussion	Knowledge, ideas and opinions on a particular subject are freely exchanged among the trainees and the instructor.	Suitable where the application of information is a matter of opinion. Also when attitudes need to be induced or changed. Trainees are more likely to change attitudes after discussion than they would if they were told during a talk that their attitude should be changed. Also suitable as a means of obtaining feedback to the instructor about the way in which trainees may apply the knowledge learned.	The trainees may stray from the subject matter or fail to discuss it usefully. The whole session may be blurred and woolly. Trainees may become entrenched about their attitudes rather than be prepared to change them.
Role Play	Trainees are asked to enact, in the training situation, the role they will be called upon to play in their job of work. Used mainly for the practice of dealing with face-to-face situations (i.e. where people come together in the work situation).	Suitable where the subject is one where a near-to-life practice in the training situation is helpful to the trainees. The trainees can practise and receive expert advice or criticism and opinions of their colleagues in a "protected" training situation. This gives confidence as well as offering guidelines. The trainees get the feel of the pressures of the real life situation.	Trainees may be embarrassed and their confidence sapped rather than built up. It can also be regarded as 'a bit of a lark' and not taken seriously.

WHAT IT IS	WHAT IT WILL ACHIEVE	POINTS TO WATCH
Case Study A history of some event or set of circumstances, with the relevant details, is examined by the trainees. Case studies fall into two broad categories: (a) Those in which the trainees diagnose the causes of a particular problem. (b) Those in which the trainees set out to solve a particular problem.	Suitable where a cool look at the problem or set of circumstances, free from the pressures of the actual event, is beneficial. It provides opportunities for exchange of ideas and consideration of possible solutions to problems the trainees will face in the work situation.	Trainees may get the wrong impression of the real work situation. They may fail to realise that decisions taken in the training situation are different from those which have to be made on-the-spot in a live situation.
Exercise Trainees are asked to undertake a particular task, leading to a required result, following lines laid down by the trainers. It is usually a practice or a test of knowledge put over prior to the exercise. Exercises may be used to discover trainees' existing knowledge or ideas before further information or new ideas are introduced. Exercises may be posed for individuals or for groups.	Suitable for any situation where the trainees need to practise following a particular pattern or formula to reach a required objective. The trainees are to some extent 'on their own'. This is a highly active form of learning. Exercises are frequently used instead of formal tests to find out how much the trainee has assimilated. There is a lot of scope in this method for the imaginative trainer.	The exercise must be realistic and the expected result reasonably attainable by all trainees or the trainees will lose confidence and experience frustration.
Application Project Similar to an exercise but giving the trainee much greater opportunity for the display of initiative and creative ideas. The particular task is laid down by the trainer but the lines to be followed to achieve the objectives are left to the trainee to decide. Like exercises, projects may be set for either individuals or groups.	Suitable where initiative and creativity need stimulating or testing. Projects provide feedback on a range of personal qualities of trainees as well as their range of knowledge and attitude to the job. Like exercises, projects may be used instead of formal tests. Again there is a lot of scope for the imaginative trainer.	It is essential that the project is undertaken with the trainee's full interest and co-operation. It must also be seen by the trainee to be directly relevant to his needs. If the trainee fails, or feels he has failed the project there will be severe loss of confidence on his part and possible antagonism towards the trainer. Trainees are often hyper-sensitive to criticism of project work.

WHAT IT IS	WHAT IT WILL ACHIEVE	POINTS TO WATCH
In-Basket (In-Tray) Trainees are given a series of files, papers and letters similar to those they will be required to deal with at the place of work (i.e. the typical content of a desk-worker's in-tray). Trainees take action on each piece of work. The results are marked or compared one with another.	Suitable for giving trainee desk-workers a clear understanding of the real-life problems and their solutions. The simulation of the real situation aids the transfer of learning from the training to the work situation. A valuable way of obtaining feedback on the trainees' progress. Also useful for developing attitudes towards the work, e.g. priorities, customers' complaints, superiors, etc.	It is important that the contents of the in-tray are realistic. The aim should be to provide trainees with a typical in-tray. The marking or comparison of results must be done in a way which will not sap the confidence of the weaker trainee.
Business Games Trainees are presented with information about a company – financial position, products, markets, etc. They are given different management roles to perform. One group may be concerned with sales, another with production and so on. These groups then 'run' the company. Decisions are made and actions are taken. The probable result of these decisions in terms of profitability is then calculated.	Suitable for giving trainee managers practice in dealing with management problems. The simulation of the real-life situation not only aids the transfer of learning but is necessary because a trainee manager applying only broad theoretical knowledge to the work situation could cause major problems. Also a valuable way of assessing the potential and performance of trainees. It helps considerably in developing many aspects of a manager's role.	The main difficulty is in assessing the probable results of the decisions made. Sometimes a computer is used for this purpose. The trainees may reject the whole of the learning if they feel the assessment of the probable outcome of their decisions is unrealistic. There is also a risk that the trainees may not take the training situation seriously.
Sensitivity Training (Group Dynamics) Trainees are put into situations in which: (a) the behaviour of each individual in the group is subject to examination and comment by the other trainees; (b) the behaviour of the group (or groups) as a whole is examined. (The trainer is a psychologist, sociologist or a person who has himself received special training).	A vivid way for the trainee to learn of the effect of his behaviour on other people and the effect of their behaviour upon him. It increases knowledge of how and why people at work behave as they do. It increases skill at working with other people and of getting work done through other people. A valuable way of learning the skill of communication.	Difficulties can arise if what the trainee learns about himself is distasteful to him. Trainees may 'opt-out' if they feel put off by the searching examination of motives. It is important that problems arising within the group are resolved before the group breaks up.

Objective

To demonstrate the use of the basic audio-visual training aids, with special attention to the use of local materials and low-cost, do-it-yourself adaptations

To stimulate trainees' ideas for the visualisation of their own material

Handout Material

I - Equipment Checklist for Visual Aid Presentations, p. 15

At the discretion of the instructor, selections from the background reading material, such as "Devices Available". See also the "Course and Conference Planning Sheet: List of Speaker's Requirements", annexed to HANDOUT I of Session 27.

Background Reading

Using Visual Aids, pp. 1-9

Projected Aids, pp. 11-13

Recommended Reading

Gould-Marks, Management Communication Through Audio-Visual Aids

Rigg, Audiovisual Aids and Techniques

Powell, A Guide to the Use of Visual Aids (BACIE booklet)

Powell, A Guide to the Overhead Projector (BACIE booklet)

Industrial Society, Using Sound Filmstrips (booklet)

Special Equipment and Aids

Film: Visual Aids or Using Visuals in Your Speech
16mm film projector, film screen, set up in a room which can be darkened

All aids to be discussed during the session, with appropriate accessories and prepared display material, e.g.:
- Flannel board and adhesive materials such as sponge, yarn, sandpaper, flannel, flocked paper
- Overhead projector with transparencies and writing pens (Exhibit A may be prepared as an overhead transparency in the absence of actual models of the various adaptations)
- Flip chart with writing pens
- Demonstration displays of these aids (could include those to be used in other sessions)

Tape recorder, slide or filmstrip projector, depending on the emphasis to be used in the presentation

60 min.	**Session Guide 4** (two versions)

To be truly useful,this session should be fully adapted to show the use
of <u>local</u> materials in visual aid production. As many of these materials
as possible should be on hand for demonstration and handling by the
participants. However, all aids and devices should remain "closed"
and set aside until the moment of their use during the demonstration.

14:00   Introduce the session with remarks based on "Why Use Visuals?" and
"Deciding Which Device to Use" from the background reading.

<u>VERSION I (with film showing)</u>

14:10   Introduce and show film, <u>Visual Aids</u>.

14:40   Have the overhead projector on hand, and proceed immediately to a
brief demonstration of the techniques of handling it.

14:45   Open the session for discussion, questions on the film and the various
aids. Have on hand materials about which you anticipate questions,
such as flocked paper or prepared appliqués for the flannel board,etc.

15:00   Close the session, suggesting that further discussion may be taken up in
Session 6. The types of aids just demonstrated have their greatest value
as supplements to a <u>lecture presentation</u> (liaison with next session).

<u>VERSION II (lecture and demonstration)</u>

Materials and displays must be arranged in advance. Timing will vary
with the prior experience and interest of the audience. Allow time
for questions or comments on each device before proceeding to the next
one. The main purpose is to <u>acquaint</u> participants with operation of
the aids, but the opportunity for putting across some ideas about
layout and design should not be lost. See "Designing the Visuals".

14:10   Chalkboard techniques –
Lettering aids, flipchart and other writing boards.
Show and compare the advantages and weaknesses of various lettering
devices (stencils, letter forms, ink pens).
Handling tips for flipchart.
For both chalkboard and flipchart, stress uncrowded, orderly layout,
proper size of lettering, use of colour for emphasis.

14:20   Flannel board and magnetic board –
Stress do-it-yourself construction and preparation of appliqués.
Show various appliqué materials: sandpaper,yarn,flannel,flocked paper.
Encourage use of simple symbols,e.g. symbols for people and appropriate
use of colour.

14:30   Overhead projector –
Explain operation, photocopying process of printing transparencies,and
construction of overlay displays (see Exhibit A).
Demonstrate various adaptations: flip-offs, flip-ons, "strip-tease".
Insist on readability of any reproduced material.
Stress ease of display preparation and storage;ease of use in classroom.

14:40   Sum up the preparation of displays by reiterating the importance of
simplicity, an effective use of colour, and pleasing, logical layout.

Then, <u>EITHER</u> open the session up for questions on the equipment and ask
for comments and suggestions from those members of the group who have
had experience in using some of the aids; <u>OR</u> devote another 10 minutes
to a demonstration of one or several of the more sophisticated aids,
e.g., slide projector, tape recorder, or film projector. The choice will
depend on the interest and experience of the group and the aids available.

15:00   Distribute HANDOUT I. Close the session with a bridge to Session 6 on
Using Films in Training.

USING VISUAL AIDS[1]

WHY USE VISUALS?

Research and experience have shown that audio-visual techniques can significantly increase and reinforce learning. Not only do they add interest to a presentation, but by engaging more than one of the senses, they also facilitate listening and remembering.[2] In the teaching of abstract concepts or unfamiliar subjects, visualisation can be essential to understanding.

Visual aids will not automatically increase teaching effectiveness however; they must be carefully designed to support a lesson and to suit a particular audience and situation. The planning and preparation of such aids requires time, thought and imagination, in:

- selecting the points to be visualised;
- translating ideas into suitably visual forms;
- choosing the most appropriate medium;
- designing layout and choosing colour;
- making the aid;
- evaluating its effectiveness and revising for future use.

A certain willingness to experiment and ability to improvise are especially important where aids must be hand made out of a limited budget and with a restricted set of materials.

What follows is a review of some of the basic visual devices, their strengths and weaknesses, and some tips on designing and handling visual displays. The comments are intended to be suggestive rather than comprehensive, as ideas for usage will come with practice.

DECIDING WHICH DEVICE TO USE

Proper use of visual aids requires a considerable investment of time and thought. It is better not to use any device unless you are prepared to give the time and attention that is required in designing your talk and the visuals which are to be used, and in adequate rehearsal and other preparation required to use the visuals properly.

No one device is the best answer to all visual aid situations. In choosing the best device for use in a particular presentation, the following are among the factors which must be considered:

Circumstances
To whom is the presentation to be made (one man, a class, a convention)? Where is the talk to be held (man's office, classroom, auditorium)? This will affect the size of the display.

Is it to be given once or many times? Most one-time presentations do not justify the time and cost of preparing elaborate visuals, but once in a while any expense is justified.

Will it be given in your own office building or in another location? That is, will you have to transport any of the display equipment and will you need people to help with this? Do you have portable equipment? Will electric power be available in the room chosen?

---

[1] Adapted from Visual Aids and Classroom Facilities by R.E. Reynolds, Man.Dev./Briefing Courses/3.

[2] It is said that people remember 20 per cent of what is heard; 30 per cent of what is seen, and 50 per cent of what is seen and heard at the same time. (See also the demonstration on the flannel board in the beginning of the film "Visual Aids".)

With what types of aids is the speaker already familiar?   Making due allowance
for experimentation, an instructor or lecturer will make a more effective presentation using visuals with which he feels comfortable.

Subject
Is any particular effect required in the presentation, such as realism?
surprise? shock?

Does the information demand a gradually built-up display?   Does it have segments
to be manipulated?   The flannel board and magnetic boards offer more possibility
of movement than the writing boards.   It is easier to build up a display on the
overhead projector than on the flip chart, etc.

Cost
Most of these devices cost considerable sums.   The overhead projector and its
screen are the most expensive;   followed by the flannel board and magnetic board,
which are roughly on a par.   Flip charts are least expensive but procuring suitable pens may be difficult.   The chalkboard, if one is available, requires no
additional expenditure.

Availability
If you don't have it and can't get it you can't use it.

DEVICES AVAILABLE

Chalkboard

■ Advantages:
Generally available and inexpensive - nothing to carry.
Requires no advance preparation of visuals (advisable, however, to carry your
  own chalk and eraser).
Especially helpful for such matters as demonstrations of the construction and use
  of mathematical and chemical equations, where much erasing occurs.

■ Disadvantages:
Requires speaker to turn away from audience.
Encourages speaker to talk to board and forget his audience.
Can be seen only a limited distance.
Dusty and messy to hands and clothing.
Dramatic, unusual effects not possible.

■ Handling tips:
Write for the audience, not for yourself.   Use print or block capitals for
  extra clarity.
Keep the work neat and tidy;   cut down to essentials;   don't overcrowd.
Clean the board when the work is no longer relevant.
Use coloured chalk for emphasis.

Flip Chart or Newsprint Pad

■ Advantages:
Can be used as blackboard, or as previously prepared sheets.
Especially suitable for one-time briefings which do not justify much time and
  money in preparation of more elaborate visuals.
Good for telling consecutive story with a number of points which need to be
  emphasised in outline fashion.
Quick.   Avoids mess and the time required to erase.
If sheets are just flipped over and not torn off, material is available for
  recapitulation and review.
Easily portable models are available commercially.

■ Disadvantages:
Pages have limited space.
Presents a transportation problem, though not a great one, to speakers who are
  travelling to place of talk.
Dramatic effects greatly limited.
Prepared drawings must be stored flat to avoid paper curling.

■ Handling tips:
Conceal the top of the chart with one or more blank sheets until you are ready
  for it.

Roll sheets smoothly over the top so as to avoid a crinkle which will become
    increasingly annoying as more and more sheets are turned over.   Stand to
    one side when displaying and turning the chart.
When the chart is merely a summary of the main points the lecturer is to make, it
    is a good idea to reveal them one at a time.   The "strip-tease" chart permits
    this.
Each heading is covered by a strip of white paper which is attached by paper
    clips or drawing pins and removed at the appropriate moment.   The process
    creates a certain amount of suspense and added attention.   It can also be
    applied to diagrams and drawings whenever it seems desirable to concentrate
    attention on one stage at a time.
When finished with the talk, roll up the pages "topside out" so that, when you
    next give the talk, the bottoms of the sheets will not curl out toward the
    audience and possibly conceal the bottom line of your chart or words.
If it is necessary to refer to special pages, mark them in some way such as
    folded corners, paper clips, etc.
Keep extra felt pens on hand as they tend to dry out.
Drawings can be prepared "invisibly" in light yellow pencil.

Plastic Writing Board or Whyteboard

■   Advantages:
Permits wide use of colour.
Less messy than chalk; writing smooth, clean and silent.
Bright, clean and pleasant to look at.
Electrostatic quality permits adhesion of thin papers and plastics for displays.
Light surface can also be used as a projection screen.

■   Disadvantages:
Expensive and not easily available in some regions.
Special pens difficult to obtain; if wrong pens are used (which happens fairly
    readily), stains are difficult to remove.
Some boards scratch easily.

■   Handling tips:
See under "Chalkboard" for writing tips.
Cut-outs of coloured plastic will also adhere.

Magnetic Board

■   Advantages:
Permits combination use of prepared visuals and as a blackboard.
Good for shaped props (often used by courts trying traffic offences to show loca-
    tion of streets, automobiles or pedestrians, lights).
Can also be used as a pin-up board, with magnets serving as drawing pins.

■   Disadvantages:
Board is very heavy, a factor if portability is essential.
Board is expensive, and unless it is needed to display heavy items or to be used
    as blackboard, it has nothing to offer that cannot be offered by a flannel
    board.
Suitable, cheap magnets sometimes hard to find.

■   Handling tips:
A dramatic effect can be achieved by lightly "throwing" the display items onto the
    board, making a sharp clicking sound.   Such a gesture needs to be rehearsed.
    Permanent outlines for recurring talks can be painted on the board.

Flannel Board

The essential parts of any flannel board visual are a <u>paper surface</u> seen by
the audience and flocked material on the side away from the audience.   It is
this flocked material which enables the visual to stay in place when it is placed
on a piece of flannel.   Sandpaper, blotting paper, felt or flannel can be used
in place of flock; foam rubber sponge, light balsa wood and nylon hook-and-loop
material (Velcro, Teazlegraph) will also adhere.

This combination of qualities (paper surface plus flocked back) can be
obtained in three ways: (1) by purchasing paper commercially prepared which has a
flocked back; (2) by using ordinary paper and purchasing commercially prepared
flock with an adhesive back which can be placed on the back of the other paper,
or   (3) by gluing on sandpaper or flannel as backing to ordinary paper.   Photographs, posters, illustrations from magazines, may all be mounted in the manner
described in (3).

■ Advantages:
Can be prepared beforehand and reused.
Permits quick back and forth adjustment of bits of the talk in preparation of revised talk for different audiences, and in answering questions during a talk.
Permits build-up of logical sequence.
Colourful.
Can use variety of kinds of visuals: words and phrases, lines, mathematical/chemical symbols; outlines, photographs or drawings of physical objects.
Permits dramatic effects (several-level visuals), thus adding the attention-generating factor of movement.
Do-it-yourself models easy to construct.

■ Disadvantages:
Unlike other boards, cannot be used as chalkboard for writing in front of class.
Visuals must all be prepared ahead of time.

■ Handling tips:
Plan in advance the exact appearance of the board at any one time, so as to determine where to place each visual on the board. Positions can be marked in light chalk.
Arrange the cut-outs in order before you begin.
Place the visuals exactly where you want them. Most visuals should be set on a horizontal plane. This takes some rehearsing.
Place the pieces on the board with a gentle downward movement so that the fibres engage. Brush the flannel occasionally to clean and roughen it.
Keep cut-outs flat in storage.

Overhead Projector

This machine, which comes in models of various weights, projects large-size transparent images onto a cinema screen under normal daylight conditions. Transparencies may be conveniently produced by drawing or writing directly onto transparent acetate sheets (up to 25 cm square) with grease pencils or felt-tip pens of a type suitable for working on glass or plastic surfaces. They may also be prepared using a photocopy process, in which case the drawing is prepared on an ordinary sheet of white paper. A piece of sensitised plastic is placed on top of the paper and the two are run through the Thermofax Duplicator. This produces a black on white visual. If a coloured image is desired, coloured adhesive film may be added, or a coloured pen may be rubbed lightly over the image area. When photocopying diagrams or excerpts from books in this manner, remember that typescript will generally be too small for the audience to read, even when projected.

Cardboard frames are available as permanent mounts for the plastic sheets. They also serve as a base on which to attach overlay sheets and tabs to be used in flip-off and flip-on displays, as illustrated in Exhibit A.

■ Advantages:
Speaker can always face his audience.
Speaker can work and write sitting down. He may also use more elaborate notes without it being so noticeable.
Permits use of a number of methods of visual presentation: prepared visuals (from elaborate, professionally-made, multi-colour, multi-effect to simple home-made visuals), and use of a roll of plastic to use as a "blackboard" in writing your own visuals in front of the class.
Easier to write on horizontal surface.
Permits elaborate effects: slides, flip-offs, and drop-downs.
Permits use of colour.
Is clean and quick.
Can be used without complete darkening of room - permits note-taking.

■ Disadvantages:
Some types of writing pens smudge easily or evaporate on plastic.
Requires heavy equipment: a projector and screen, and a source of electric power. (Always a problem when portability is a factor and often a problem even in moving from room to room in speaker's home building. Note that portable projectors and screens are available - but always carry a very long extension cord and an extra lamp.)
Light from the projection base can be hard on the speaker's eyes.
Device projects a keystone-shaped image unless top of screen can be tilted toward audience.
Sometimes difficult to place screen and projector with respect to windows, source of power, and other equipment already in the room so as to permit audience to see and speaker to talk.

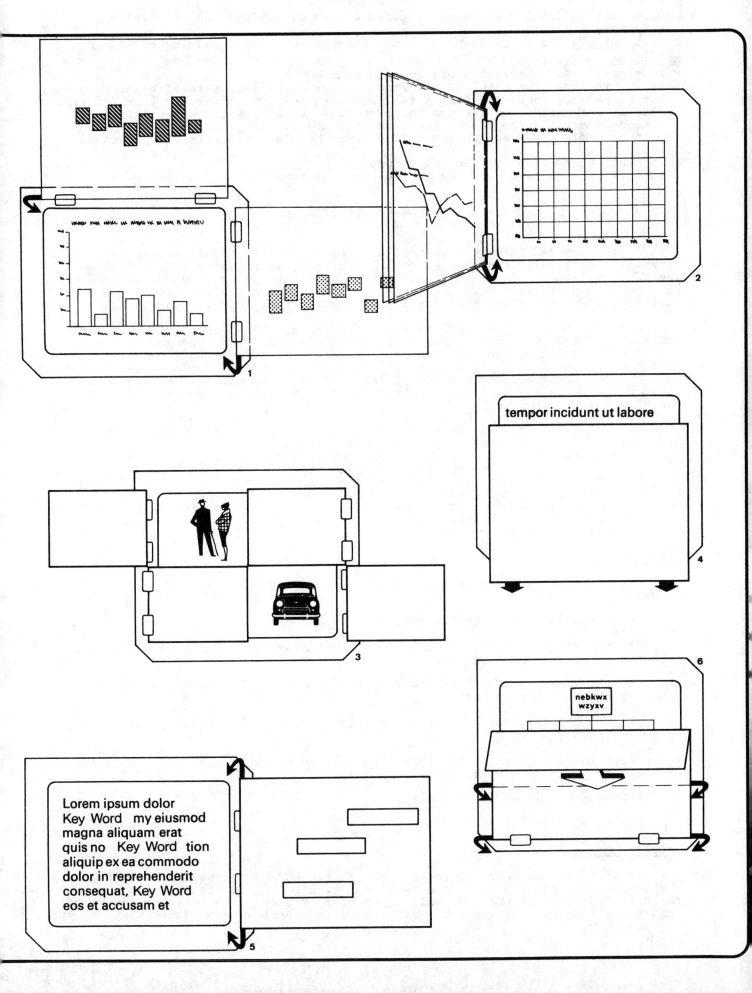

Cannot modify formal visuals in response to new situations and in answering
  questions.
Cannot <u>quickly</u> modify portions of handwritten visuals in answering questions.
■   Handling tips:
Have visuals (transparencies) in exact sequence.
Rehearse the use of special effect visuals such as slides, flip-offs and flip-ons.
  For flip-offs, make sure that a tab is raised for you to take in your fingers.
Fasten or mark guides on the projector so that visual frames can quickly be
  placed in exactly the proper position over the ground glass.
Top of projection screen must be tilted toward audience to eliminate keystone
  image.
Switch off the projector when not in use.
Test felt pens to make sure the ink does not evaporate.

DESIGNING THE VISUALS

A visual-aided talk is a composite thing. It is not just a talk with added
visuals. Many talks must be modified and simplified in order to make proper
use of visuals. Quite apart from the problem of designing visuals, this result
is a good thing because many talks are too complex or are organised in a confusing way, and the process of developing visuals will improve many talks.

When you have a first GOOD draft (after perhaps three or four rewritings)
you will probably be ready to start designing visuals. Go through your talk
sentence by sentence, idea by idea, and decide what needs to be visualised and
what can be visualised, and then start thinking of ways and means. The things
that can be visualised include ideas, concepts, relationships, processes.
Start with the belief that ANYTHING can be translated into visuals. Visuals
can be used:

- to bring out a series of facts and the conclusion to which they lead;
- to bring out points which need to be emphasised;
- to attract attention through unusual devices or colour;
- to present complex processes (industrial, mathematical, chemical);
- to introduce new and unfamiliar objects and concepts;
- to show relationships which exist among facts or objects;
- to show in outline form the growth of a complex idea, or the treatment of a
  subject so as to enable people to see readily which are the major and
  which are the subordinate points.

Methodology

Use pictures wherever possible - supplemented as necessary by words and
figures.

Use words (singly or in phrases) as a second choice.

Use the image area as a graph: to present statistics and statistical processes; to present mathematics.

Use the image area as a form: to present accounting reports, statistical
tabulations, and similar matters.

Use unusual devices: lines, arrows, elastic, movable ribbons, multiple-
layer images.

Use colour as often as possible (see section below on uses of colour) for
coding, stressing key facts, etc.

Use complex images as necessary.

Use your imagination!

Complex Images

It is often necessary during a talk to have an image area filled with a very
complex set of visuals. It is a fatal error, however, to present such a result
to an audience all at once. Build it up item by item. An audience can readily
absorb one idea at a time and be quite ready to accept a complicated final picture.

Thus: never present a blackboard full, or a flannelboard full of mathe-matical equations.   Put on one at a time, perhaps even broken into segments.

Thus: never present a complex industrial process as a completed matter. Show one piece of equipment at a time (or a portion thereof) and keep adding pieces or portions.   Different materials flowing through pipes can be shown by different coloured lines, added one at a time.

Thus: never present a statistical graph all filled in.   Show first the graph and explain the co-ordinates used.   Then add the figures or computed points a few at a time.

A flannel board is an excellent device for presenting complex final results a bit at a time, and is particularly suitable for use as a chart or graph.

The overhead projector is even more flexible for presenting complex results through three devices: (1) slides; (2) flip-offs; and (3) drop-ons.   A slide conceals all but that portion which is to be introduced and can be pulled out bit by bit as new portions of the image are to be revealed.   A "flip-off" can be used to accomplish the same result, especially for complex visuals in which odd-shaped portions can be revealed.   A "drop-on" is a visual in which items are added to a basic foundation.   For example, an accounting report can be presented in this manner, with the accounting form as the basic visual.   The entries in the columns or lines of the form can be "dropped-on" as needed.   Each part of the drop-on is on a separate sheet of plastic which is fastened to the top, bottom, or one side of the visual in the proper place so that, when the drop-on is flipped over on its hinge and lies on top of the basic visual, the image of the drop-on is in proper "register".   The number of drop-ons for a particular visual is limited only by the transparency of the plastic material: i.e. the addition of too many sheets of plastic transforms a transparent condition to an opaque one.   Many kinds of images can be presented through the drop-on tech-nique: charts, reports, mathematics, mechanical and chemical industrial processes.   These various arrangements are shown in Exhibit A.

Use of Colour

Colour can increase the effectiveness of almost any display by drawing attention to key points, coding (thus reducing to simpler terms) the functions represented in a complex diagram, improving visibility.

Contrast is best: black on white, white on black, black on yellow, yellow on black.   Avoid such combinations as light green or dark green.

Orange is a wonderful attention-getter, but people do not like it as a colour.   One investigator has found that colours rank in this order in terms of attention: orange, red, blue, black, green, yellow, violet, grey.   And that colour preferences were in this order: blue, red, green, violet, orange, yellow. Taking the two together indicates that red and blue are the best two colours. Apart from black on white, and white on black, the best combinations are dark blue on white, brown on white, and green on white.   Other acceptable combina-tions are cream on reddish-brown, light blue on dark green, yellow-orange on grey, orange on black.

Use of Symbols

Where ideas or objects can be symbolised rather than represented in words or in complex drawings, and providing the meaning of the symbol is clear, under-standing is more rapid and the display more concise and bold.   Consider the following symbols for persons:

Working out effective symbols takes time and imagination, but the end result can be well worth the effort. Here are a few examples:

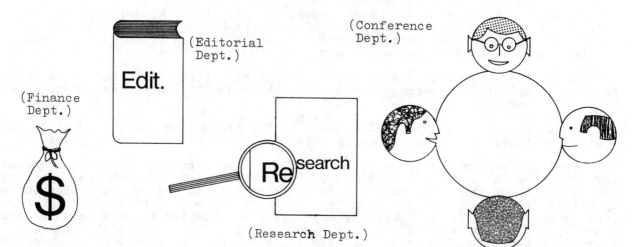

(Editorial Dept.)

(Conference Dept.)

(Finance Dept.)

(Research Dept.)

Simple, Bold and Clear

All visual aids, whether charts, graphs, models or diagrams, should aim to be:

Simple. Key phrases and words; full sentences are unnecessary and crowd the display. Uncrowded layout of displays. Simple design lines and shapes. A few well-chosen colours. Complexity can be distracting if not well handled.

Bold. Large enough to be easily seen by the audience for whom it is intended. Sections of the display show up clearly if colour, lettering style and size, and layout have been properly selected.

Clear. Is the display easy to understand? Does it reflect exactly the message of the lesson? Is it logically arranged, well-spaced and uncrowded? Do the main points stand out?

Lettering

Pre-cut letters in different types and different sizes can be procured commercially. High quality lettering can be done by yourself or by a graphic arts draftsman with the aid of the lettering guides made by commercial firms. Lettering can also be done freehand by the use of a felt-tipped pen (Magic Marker and similar products) through the use of a standard alphabet.

If the person doing lettering will look at his letters from a distance of 10, 20, or 30 feet he will quickly realise the need for LARGE letters WIDELY SPACED. Letters such as a, c, e, u, o should not be less than 2 cm. tall, and preferably should be 3 cm. Letters such as b, d, f, j, p, q should not be less than 3 cm. and preferably 4. The thickness of the line used for letters must be increased with the size of letter used. It cannot be emphasised too strongly that major errors in lettering are to make letters too small, and to crowd them too close together. Persons doing lettering think that because they can see the letters clearly, an audience will too.

Before doing any hand lettering, rule every line of letters on the visual lightly in pencil so as to guide your eye. Only in this way will your letters be sufficiently uniform in size, and the lines straight ... and plan ahead so that you don't run out of paper before your words are all on the visual. In making visuals using words, a useful rule is "the shorter the better" (even as short as one word).

PREPARING THE ROOM

Whenever possible visit the room where the talk is to be given several days in advance. If you cannot visit it, ask someone who knows the room. Inspect:

sight lines. Decide how to place the flip board, the flannel board, or the overhead projector and its screen with respect to the seats so as to avoid bad sight lines which interfere with the sight of the visuals by members of the audience;

seats. Decide whether it is possible or necessary to arrange the seats so as to improve sight lines or avoid glare from windows;

source of electricity. Overhead projectors and motion picture machines require electricity. Determine that it is available, of the correct type (AC or DC) and of the proper voltage. Ascertain how long an extension cord will be needed to reach from the source of electricity to the machine. Ascertain whether electricity will continue to be available when the room lights are turned off - that turning off the room lights does not also turn off the projector.

Go to the room early on the day of the talk to:

arrange the room (if you have the time or authority to do so). Place the seats so that everyone can see. If the seats are in rows and are moveable, try to stagger the seats in alternate rows;

place your equipment. Take with you an extra long extension cord and extra lamp for the projector if you plan to use such equipment. Take along a piece of chalk and an eraser if you plan to use the blackboard. Be sure you have felt pens (or other writing devices) if you plan to use the flip chart. <u>Place and test</u> all the equipment. Place the overhead projector in exact alignment with the screen and test the focus and size of the image, and the degree the screen must be tilted to avoid a "keystone" effect (an image wider at the top than at the bottom).

arrange all your visuals and other props so that they are as inconspicuous as possible but readily available to you. Be sure that they are in proper sequence.

An equipment checklist can be useful in completing your preparation. An example appears as Handout I for this session; see also a "Course and Conference Planning Sheet" annexed to Handout I of Session 27.

PROJECTED AIDS[1]

EPISCOPE OR OPAQUE PROJECTOR

This device is used for projecting small-sized opaque material onto a screen (maps, books, diagrams). It is especially useful for producing enlargements of diagrams, maps and illustrations from books - either for live presentation in the class, or for copying onto self-made charts, posters, etc.

In general, good blackout is essential for projection. Remember that the episcope tends to be very bulky, and because the lens usually has a short focal length, it has to be placed about twelve feet from the screen, at which position it can obstruct the view of the students. These disadvantages are being eliminated in some of the latest commercial models.

SLIDES AND FILMSTRIPS

Slides

There is an almost bewildering range of sizes. The one you are most likely to meet is the one known as the 35 mm.(this figure refers to the width of the film), although the size of the slide is actually 36 mm. x 24 mm. It may be mounted in glass, plastic or cardboard and the mount is always 2 inches square.

Slides constitute one of the easiest amateur means of bringing real-life situations into the classroom. Less expensive and simpler to operate than film, easier to edit and arrange for training purposes, they have great potential for adaptation to training needs. They may be organised into a complete lesson, accompanied by written notes or a tape-recorded commentary. Such a programme has the advantage of being easily adjustable to various training groups. See the notes on "Sound Filmstrips" below.

Filmstrips

Instead of cutting up 35 mm. film into individual frames and mounting them separately, they are often preserved in strip form. Filmstrips have a number of advantages - portable, quick and easy to produce, don't weigh very much, unbreakable, can't get out of order, easy to make extra copies.

Filmstrip frames may either be full-sized (36 x 24) or half size (22 x 18). Strips run through the projector either vertically or horizontally and it is important to check which way your filmstrip goes and ensure that it will fit into your projector.

Slide Projectors

Many models are now available, with different types of slide carriers (carrousel, tray and single slide changer) and storage trays. Some offer both manual and remote control systems, the latter offering great advantages to the instructor for carefully programmed material. Some makes also have timing devices for automatic slide changing.

Slide projectors with a filmstrip attachment are available but as a consequence, they lack the slide-handling conveniences of other models. If a sophisticated slide system is important to you, the only alternative is to buy a special filmstrip projector.

SOUND FILMSTRIPS (SLIDE-TAPE PRESENTATIONS)

A sound filmstrip consists of a length of 35 mm. film and a phonograph record or tape recording. On the filmstrip, a series of still scenes is arranged in a continuous sequence for sequential projection onto a screen.

---

[1] With the exception of the overhead projector, which is covered in the background reading, Using Visual Aids.

The record or tape contains a dramatised version of the story behind the pictures, sometimes in narrative form and sometimes as dialogue. Incorporated in the recording is a sound signal which tells the operator when to change the picture, or, in the most costly projection units, a device which changes the picture automatically.

This arrangement can be adapted in various ways: instead of a filmstrip, one can use a series of slides; home-made slides can be copied onto a filmstrip by a commercial laboratory at a modest price. Special projectors exist to operate tape and filmstrip simultaneously.

The Industrial Society in London[1] has produced a large number of sound film-strips, most of which are incidents or case studies suitable for human relations training and discussion. A few are more general training presentations, designed to provide a practical basis for discussion of techniques (delegation; leadership problems; communication).

Usually the scripts are based on incidents which have actually happened in factories, offices or department stores and have raised some difficulty, either in dealing with a human relations problem or in some detail of administration. Since their aim is to stimulate discussion, each filmstrip is accompanied by a set of notes for the discussion leader. These consist of a brief synopsis of the problem, followed by a series of questions for use during the discussion period.

A case study presented in this way lasts from five to ten minutes and can easily be replayed if necessary. In that brief period quite a complex situation - conflicting personalities, work attitudes and relationships, management problems - can be depicted in an engaging and lively manner.

This is a basically low-cost technique with maximum potential for adaptation to individual needs: slides can be photographed locally and native voices can be used in the recording to make the presentation seem as close to home as possible.

FILMS

Size of Film

Both 8mm and 16mm film is used in training; under the term "Super 8" 8mm film has been considerably improved and is now experiencing quite a revival. It is being used especially for technical training in cassettes and short loop films.

16mm film is that most commonly used for commercially distributed training films, and most management training films which you will use will probably be of this type. If the film is silent, it will have sprocket holes on both sides; if sound, the sprocket holes are on one side only.

Film Sound

This may be either optical - the majority of 16mm sound films are like this - or magnetic. A magnetically stripped film is one that has been converted by the addition of a narrow ferrous "stripe" of magnetic tape to receive a magnetic sound track. Some films carry both tracks, permitting bilingual versions.

A standard optical sound film projector cannot reproduce a magnetic sound track. Projectors which are equipped to reproduce either sound system usually come with accessories which permit the recording of a new sound track on the magnetic stripe.

On some projectors it is possible to switch off the existing sound track and plug in a hand microphone to the amplifier. In this way it is possible to provide your own narration to the film.

[1] The Industrial Society, Robert Hyde House, 48 Bryanston Square, London, W.1, UK. This organisation has published a 44-page booklet entitled Using Sound Film-strips which describes the technique and provides many ideas on how to present and follow-up the filmed case studies. It also gives information on production costs, script writing techniques, recording the commentary, and final editing.

Projection Screens

A <u>matt white</u> screen reflects at almost uniform intensity up to an angle of 50 degrees from centre. Of all the types of screens, it has the lowest maximum brilliance but is nevertheless the most versatile.

A <u>silver</u> screen gives a better image at the centre than the matt white screen, but there is rapid fall-off at angles greater than 20 degrees. It is less suitable for colour than the other two types. Used especially with overhead projection.

A <u>glass bead</u> screen viewed from dead centre has the greatest maximum brilliance, but there is rapid fall-off as the angle of viewing increases. At 20 degrees the image is poorer than that on the matt white. Very good for a long narrow room.

If funds are limited, fairly good results can be obtained by using emulsion paint on a section of the wall or on a sheet of hardboard.

The most versatile model of screen is probably the portable tripod type, and if only one can be bought this is the best investment. Pelmet type screens fixed above the chalkboard are very convenient, as are revolving chalkboards with a screen section. If the screen is also to be used for overhead projection, it should have the possibility of being tilted.

Rear/Back Projection

Usually films are shown in a dark room with the screen at one end and the film projector at the other. An alternative system known as rear, back, or daylight projection permits the room to be only dimmed and the projector may be placed in an adjacent room or cabinet where its running noise does not disturb the class.

The projector is placed at a right angle to the screen, and the picture is projected onto a mirror which reflects onto a translucent screen usually built into the wall and made of plastic or special frosted glass. The actual positioning varies with the size of the mirror, the projection lens, and the distances involved. There are television-like projector models which use this system to play cassette films. These are only suitable with small groups.

EQUIPMENT CHECKLIST FOR VISUAL AID PRESENTATIONS
(For Adaptation to Individual Needs)

When considering the use of visual aids equipment, **ask** yourself the following questions:

- What equipment do I need?
- Where is the equipment?
- When and where should it be put in the conference room?
- Who will arrange to put it in the conference room at the right time?

CHALKBOARD - white chalk, coloured chalk, eraser or sponge, pointer.

- Is the board large enough for the purpose?
- Is the board clean?
- Are the chalk and eraser at hand?
- Is the erasing sponge wet?
- Is there a ruler or other pointer available?

FLIP CHART - tripod or stand, paper pads, felt pens.

- Have prepared pages been securely attached to the pad?
- Are writing pens at hand?   In several different colours?
- Are pens full of ink (and not dry)?
- Is the stand stable?
- Have special pages to which you must refer been marked with a clip or folded corner?

FLANNEL BOARD - on tripod or wall, with prepared appliqués.

- Is the board slanted and positioned for easy viewing?
- Is the stand stable?
- Does the flannel surface need to be brushed up?
- Have you planned the arrangement of your appliqués?
- Are the appliqués arranged in the order they are needed?
- Do all pieces stick on?
- Are letters and figures clearly readable?

OVERHEAD PROJECTOR - roll of plastic, prepared transparencies, screen, grease pencils or felt pens, erasing cloth, alcohol for erasing if necessary, extra bulb.

- Where are the electrical outlets?
- Is an extension cord needed?
- Has the projector been prefocused and centred on the screen?
- Has the screen been tilted to avoid a trapezoidal projection image?
- Are the prepared transparencies arranged in order of use?
- Do the transparencies lie flat on the projector?
- Is there a supply of blank plastic sheets at hand?
- Are the pens full of ink?
- Do the pens write smoothly and darkly, without evaporation?

FILM PROJECTOR - SLIDE PROJECTOR - TAPE RECORDER - screen, extra bulb, extension cord, film reels and slides, tapes.

- Has someone been asked to set up and run the projector at the proper time?
- Have preparations been made for darkening the room?
- Where are the electrical outlets?
- Are the chairs well placed for viewing?
- Has the lens been focused on the screen?
- Is the sound control adjusted for the size of the room?
- Is the machine ready to run when it is turned on?   Must it warm up first?
- Is the loudspeaker, or the recording microphone, well placed?

Objective

To prepare participants for lecture practice by reviewing the characteristics, uses and limitations of the lecture method, and giving suggestions on how to make an effective lecture

Handout Material

I - Lecture Rating Form, p. 9

II - Lecture Presentation by Course Participants (to be adapted by the instructor), p. 11

Background Reading

The Lecture Method, pp. 1-5

Exhibit C, p. 6

Recommended Reading

Session 19, Handout III, Tips for Lesson Preparation and Presentation

BACIE, Tips on Talking, (booklet)

Powell, Lecturing to Large Groups, (booklet)

Special Equipment and Aids

Exhibit A (p.7) and B (p.8), (C optional) prepared for showing on one of the following: flannel board, chalkboard, flip chart or overhead projector

If a film is used, a 16mm projector and film screen must be set up in a darkened room

Films to demonstrate the lecture method:

Anatomy of a Presentation

How to Make an Effective Sales Presentation

The Lecturer and the Student

Successful Instruction

A Class of Your Own

The Lecture Method

Planning Your Talk

Unaccustomed as They Are

45 min.	**Session Guide 5**
	If the course leader desires to use a film, the schedule as presently laid down must be re-arranged.
15:00	Give a 30-minute lecture with visual aids on the basic points covered in the background reading on the lecture. Considerable detail has been included in this reading for the benefit of the instructor. He should select the points to be covered according to the needs of participants.

1. Begin by asking each member of the group to state what kind of experience he has had in speaking before groups. This will help you orient your remarks and allow you to call for comments from experienced members later in the presentation.

2. State reasons for reviewing lecturing technique. Refer to its place among other teaching methods and its role in classroom leadership. Planning techniques for lecturing are similar to those for general lesson planning. See also Session 19, Handout III Tips for Lesson Preparation and Presentation.

3. Planning and preparing the lecture.
   Use Exhibit A - the lecturer must consider four basic questions.
   Use Exhibit B to emphasise organisation of subject matter.

4. Delivering the lecture - tips on talking. Stress points on posture, manner, gesture and voice. Additional comments may be solicited from the participants who have had speaking experience. If Exhibit C is used, tailor the information to correspond with that shown in the display.

15:35	As a summary and transition, use HANDOUT I and go over this Lecture Rating Form which will be used in the evaluation of participants' lectures during the forthcoming lecture assignments.
	Give the lecture assignment: during Session 7 (evening study) each participant must prepare a 15-minute lecture on a subject of his own choice. Some of these lectures will be presented during Session 8. The length of the lectures and the number of actual presentations should be adjusted to the size of the group and their previous experience in this technique, e.g. longer demonstrations by experienced speakers versus short talks by as many members of an inexperienced group as possible. Instructions for the assignment may be written up and handed out as in HANDOUT II, Lecture Presentation by Course Participants.
	The seminar leader should indicate whether or not he wishes the lectures to be specifically instructional, and to what extent he wishes the lectures to incorporate audience participation, such as questions, discussion or practical exercises. Participants are responsible for the preparation of their own visual aids, but equipment and materials can be obtained from the instructor. Lecturers will be required to keep strictly to the 15-minute time limit.
15:45	Close the session.

THE LECTURE METHOD

We begin our study of training methods with one of the oldest and most basic - the lecture. Although experience and educational research show that the lecture is a relatively inefficient way to transfer knowledge, many instructors find themselves spending at least 30 to 50 per cent of their time lecturing. Why?

The use of lecturing depends on the subject matter, the teaching philosophy of the instructor or training centre, and the over-all learning situation. Formal lecturing has been used largely to build up basic theoretical knowledge which must be gained before practice or participative training sessions will be of any use. If there are large numbers of people to be trained, scarce teaching resources, or few hours available for instruction, lecturing may be the only alternative. A certain amount of informal lecturing is inherent in the conduct of any course, to set out the course objectives, motivate trainees, provide explanation and analysis relevant to study exercises.

Nevertheless, the lecture method has its limitations. Since it does not demand the active involvement of participants, it is largely unsuited to the teaching of skills, which require practice. It is also of limited value in pro-moting behavioural or attitudinal changes, which is a large part of management development. It is very difficult to convince anyone by merely talking at them; attitudes are changed best when people convince themselves. Participative methods are better for such purposes.

Apart from the fact that sixty minutes of unrelieved talking is not easily assimilated or remembered, the major disadvantage of the lecture comes from the fact that it is one-way communication. The listeners remain passive, for the most part. Unless the speaker is sensitive to his audience, he has no way of knowing whether or not they are taking in what he is saying. He has little opportunity to clarify meanings, to check on whether or not the trainees really understand what is being presented, or to handle the wide diversity of abilities and attitudes which they represent.

The lecturer, then, is bound to consider his communication problems before starting his lecture. He must study the nature of his audience, adapting his topic to their interests and level of understanding; must organise his material in the manner most likely to teach effectively, using aids where appropriate; must plan for variation in his presentation, including time for questions and discussion which will involve the audience and reveal what learning is taking place. What follows is a review of these basic steps in improving the instructional value of the lecture.

PLANNING THE LECTURE

Before starting to prepare your lecture, you must be able to answer four basic questions:

Who is your audience?	WHO	
What is the purpose of your talk?	WHY	(See
What is the time available?	HOW LONG	Exhibit A)
What is the subject matter?	WHAT	

The audience. Who are they? Civil servants, top managers, specialists? Is their attitude likely to be friendly? curious? indifferent? hostile (or sceptical)? Know the characteristics of your audience: their background, likes and dislikes, cultural features, level and nature of education. Are they used to listening to lectures? How fast will they be able to take in what you say? This may also involve their knowledge of languages.

What does your audience know about the subject? What can you assume that they know before you start your lecture? It may be helpful to start with a general discussion or ask questions to get opinions. This approach will give you some idea about the knowledge of the group and allow you to make some last minute adjustments if necessary.

Purpose of the talk. What is the end result you wish to achieve? What do you want the audience to do or understand better as a result of your talk? Your approach will certainly vary depending on whether you wish to:

- give general information on, or an appreciation of, a subject;
- gain acceptance for a new point of view;
- change basic attitudes;
- give detailed information;
- teach a particular skill.

With a clearly-defined purpose in mind, it will be easier to select appropriate material and to decide on the most effective way to present it.

Time available. What is the total time available? How much of it will be taken up by formalities? How much time will you leave for questions and discussion?

A good instructor respects the clock by narrowing down or adjusting his lecture to suit the time available. He knows that it is better to have an audience still interested and wanting to know more after a short and fully-used period, than to have them tired and uninterested after a talk that has been unnecessarily long. He also knows that a "sag-point" in the audience's interest occurs after about twenty minutes, and he plans his talk and his delivery so that interest is reawakened and passive listeners are reactivated from time to time, by the use of interesting examples, humour, rhetorical questions, audience participation through discussion or question period, etc.

Subject matter. Poor choice of subject or lack of sufficient knowledge about it may mean death for a lecture. It is important to speak from your own knowledge and experience, but at the same time your topic and approach must be relevant to the needs and interests of the audience.

Having set yourself a general title, which you can make more precise later on, and bearing in mind your objective, mark down a few basic headings under which you can list ideas. Do not worry about order at this point; the first step is simply to gather material together. Jot down everything you think you want to cover, consulting reference books and texts or previous lecture notes if necessary. Note down illustrative examples, anecdotes (as long as they are relevant) and quotes. Look up facts and figures. You may also think of ideas for discussion or quiz questions, for student exercises, or for visual aids, and these should be recorded alongside the points they will support.

After you have collected enough raw material, the next step is to sort it into "must say", "should say" and "could say" categories. What do you want the audience to remember at the end of the lecture? Put your emphasis on this and narrow down your subject accordingly, also bearing in mind the time available (see framework of Exhibit B).

There is plenty of evidence to show that people generally remember a greater percentage of a short talk than of a long one. If you try to cover too much ground you will only confuse your audience. Do a little well, rather than a lot badly. Remember the iceberg. Only about one-seventh of its total mass is visible above the surface of the water. So it is with the lecture. Only a part of the total mass of information at your disposal may "rise above the surface" in the lecture room. But this visible part is just as truly supported by the rest as in the case of the iceberg.

At this point you are ready to reorganise your notes into logical order and work out a more detailed outline, using the following basic structure (see Exhibit B):

1. The introduction, which should be brief and to the point, presents the theme and objective of the talk in a manner designed to arouse the interest and curiosity of the audience right from the start. Opening remarks need to be planned and rehearsed with some care, as it is very largely that first impression which will motivate the audience to go on listening or to "switch off". Above all, try to avoid beginning with an apology. It is seldom necessary or relevant and it will not really help you to achieve your objective.

2. In the <u>body</u> of the talk, the main theme is developed in logical steps so that the most important points will be remembered. One step should quite naturally stem from the previous one so that the listeners are carried forward. Add illustrative examples, related to the audience's experience where possible, anecdotes, and instructive demonstrations to substantiate the points being made. Use visual aids to help the audience understand and remember what is important. Put these up sequentially, as each new point is raised. You may also want to allow time for questions and discussion to clarify meanings. Keep an eye on the time so that audience participation does not prevent you from returning to your main points.

3. The type of <u>conclusion</u> you use will depend largely upon your objective, but at least give a brief recapitulation, in different words, of your main points (this is made easier when a visual display has been developed throughout the talk), plus some indication of "where do we go from here?" The quality of your conclusion may determine whether you achieve your over-all objective or not. For this reason, many speakers learn their conclusions off by heart.

PREPARING THE LECTURE

<u>Draft the talk</u>. Prepare the notes from which you will speak. Whatever type you use - cards, paper sheets - they should be easily readable (wide spacing, key words highlighted) and sequentially numbered to avoid possible confusion. Above all, notes should be notes and not a complete text. However, if you do write out sections of your talk in full, make sure that what you write is in the <u>spoken</u> language. You are not writing a book or an article, you are preparing something which is to be said out aloud so make sure that you write what you would say. If in doubt, say it aloud to yourself. Cut out the flowery phrases and long sentences.

Check that you will be able to cover the material you have selected comfortably in the time available. Try it out on a friend or with a tape recorder. Put approximate timings in the margin of your notes as a guide.

<u>Plan and prepare visual aids</u>. Various teaching aids may be employed to make the lecture more interesting and more easily assimilated by the listeners by engaging their sense of sight. The fact of having to make them often forces the lecturer to clarify and organise his thoughts. Charts and graphs may make quantitative data more meaningful. Photographs, drawings and diagrams may clarify the details of complex objects and structure; real objects or models may serve the same purpose. An outline of main points will help the listeners to remember the material.

The lecturer has many means for presenting these teaching aids. They may be distributed to the audience before, during or after the lecture. They may be displayed on racks or tables in the room. They may be projected as slides, filmstrips, or films. (See the sessions on audio-visual aids and training films.)

These training aids are double-edged tools that can cut both ways. They can gain the attention of the audience and help to provide information. But, unless they have been carefully selected and designed to support the lecture, they can actually distract attention from the points that the lecturer is trying to make. It might be better to use no aids than to work with the wrong ones.

<u>Rehearse</u>. Rehearsing the lecture is an essential step, even for most experienced lecturers. If a rehearsal audience can be recruited, the speaker has an opportunity to check his speech and his delivery of it. This may reveal points at which he is unintentionally unclear, transitions that are made too abruptly for his listeners to follow, and other errors that can creep into even the best planned lecture. Since the lecturer knows clearly what he means to say, he may be the worst judge of whether or not he has clearly said it.

Try out your visual aids, finalising plans for their arrangement, ensuring that they are readable and clearly visible in the training room.

The chief value of the rehearsal is in familiarising the speaker with his speech. Even experienced lecturers suffer from stage fright on occasions. One or two dry runs through a lecture can build a speaker's confidence in himself and in his material.

DELIVERING THE LECTURE

(Points about Speaking)

The written word can only be of limited help when it comes to advice on speaking technique. What is needed is practice followed by constructive criticism. Some of the essential points to keep in mind are set forth below.

Setting the scene. Make sure that you arrive at the appointed place a few minutes ahead of time so that you can check the physical arrangements which have been made for you, such as layout of the chairs and tables, lectern, teaching aids, provision of chalk and eraser. Try out any unfamiliar pieces of equipment you intend to use. You may also use the time to talk with your chairman and size up your audience if you haven't met them before.

Covering the material. Start punctually. Speak from your notes if necessary but do not put your nose into them; read a phrase, pause and look at the audience. If you get lost, stop, consult your notes without "flapping" and carry on. In any case, do not read all your lecture or you will have no audience left by the time you finish.

Leave time for questions at the end. If you have more than one main point it may help to pause at the end of each one for questions. If you don't know the answer to a question then say so without hesitation and without embarrassment. Ask if anyone in the audience knows the answer; if not, suggest where they may be able to find it, or offer to find out yourself.

Finish on time. When the scheduled closing time comes, if some people are still asking questions and seem to want to go on doing so, get the chairman to close the meeting formally. Those who wish to go may then leave and the others may stay and continue the discussion.

Posture. If you have a choice, speak from a position that is comfortable for you but appropriate to the situation. The main advantage of standing is that everyone can see you; it is also the convenient position from which to manipulate most visual aids. However, with a small group seated around a conference table, the informality of sitting may be desirable. Some speakers prefer to use a lectern because it holds notes at standing height.

Appearance. Have a look in the mirror. Speakers should make sure that there is nothing about their personal appearance which is out of harmony with the occasion or which is likely to irritate the audience or distract their attention. Clothes should be neat and suitable for the occasion. One should look confident and friendly (even if nervous) as audiences are very susceptible to first impressions.

Manner. Be poised. Any kind of leadership - talking before a group, organising a discussion - requires a certain confidence and dignity to gain and hold the attention of the group.

Be courteous. Careless choice of language or humour or a thoughtless gesture may create barriers to communication which will be difficult to overcome later.

Be sincere. Audiences are quick to judge speakers - they are not misled by cleverness and they don't like insincerity. Say what you mean and say it as if you meant it. Be yourself - don't try to imitate anyone else. Be enthusiastic, let your talk reveal and convince the audience of your own interest in the subject.

Establish eye contact with your audience. A speaker who is continually looking out of the window or down at his notes or visual aids is not doing his share in the communication process. Speak to all the audience and not just to the front row; if it is a large audience look first at one part and then at another. Don't fix on one particular person or group of persons; you end up ignoring the others.

Gesture.   Any actions and gestures must be natural and spontaneous; if
they are forced then it is best to do without them.   They should also be purpose-
ful and not just a flapping of the hands.   Mannerisms - jiggling coins, playing
with the chalk, walking about the platform for no apparent reason - should be
avoided, as they are distracting and sometimes extremely annoying.   Get your
weight evenly distributed on both feet and then anchor yourself.   Try to avoid
leaning on the table or the lectern or putting your hands in your pockets.   Consider carefully before smoking during your lecture.

Voice.   The tone of the voice can be altered to convey confidence, emotion,
emphasis and indignation.   Pace and volume should be varied occasionally to
avoid monotony.   Some people, probably due to nervousness, do lose some of
their normal expressiveness when they are in front of a group.   With a little
conscious effort, this can be corrected.   Rehearsal helps; it takes away some
of the strangeness and novelty of the actual lecture.

Speech should follow the rate of thought and remarks should be allowed
to tell upon the audience.   Don't be afraid of pauses and silences - they can be
very effective if employed to emphasise, to create suspense for what is to
follow, to allow an idea to sink in or to mark a question.   Don't gabble - it is
always better to speak slowly than to speak too quickly.

Remember that you are inviting the audience to listen to you.   Speak to
them as individuals and throw your voice to the back row so that all can hear.
This does not mean that you must shout.

Vocabulary.   It is best to use everyday language, avoiding slang, which
could be misunderstood, preferring short, familiar words and keeping sentences
short.   Be very careful with "funny" stories - especially if you are not a born
story teller, or if the audience is unknown to you.   Choose stories that are
relevant to the point you are trying to make.

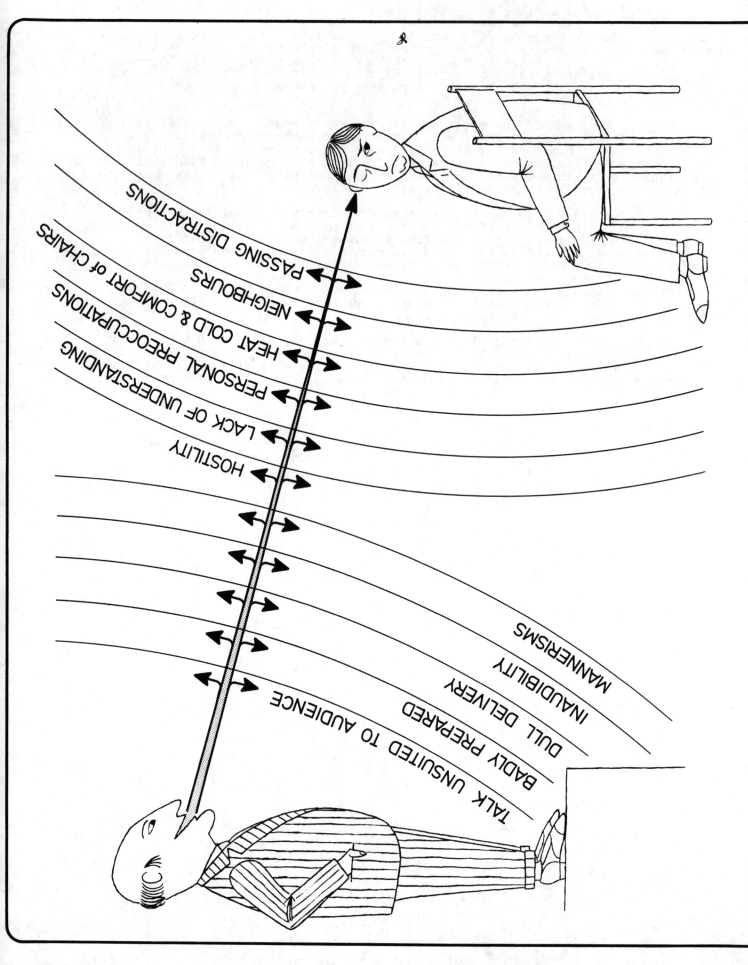

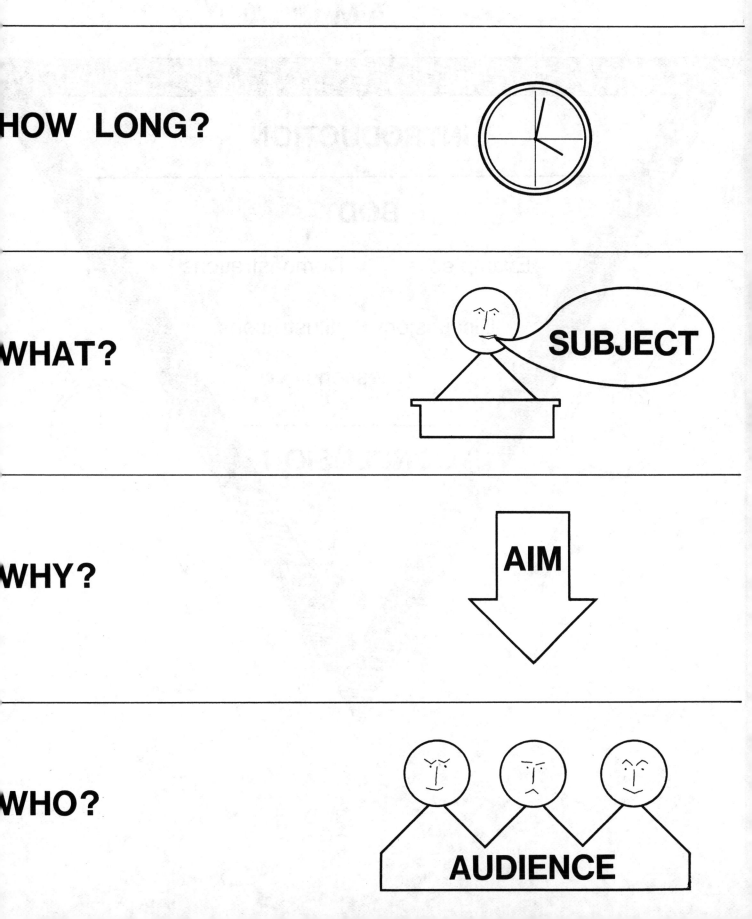

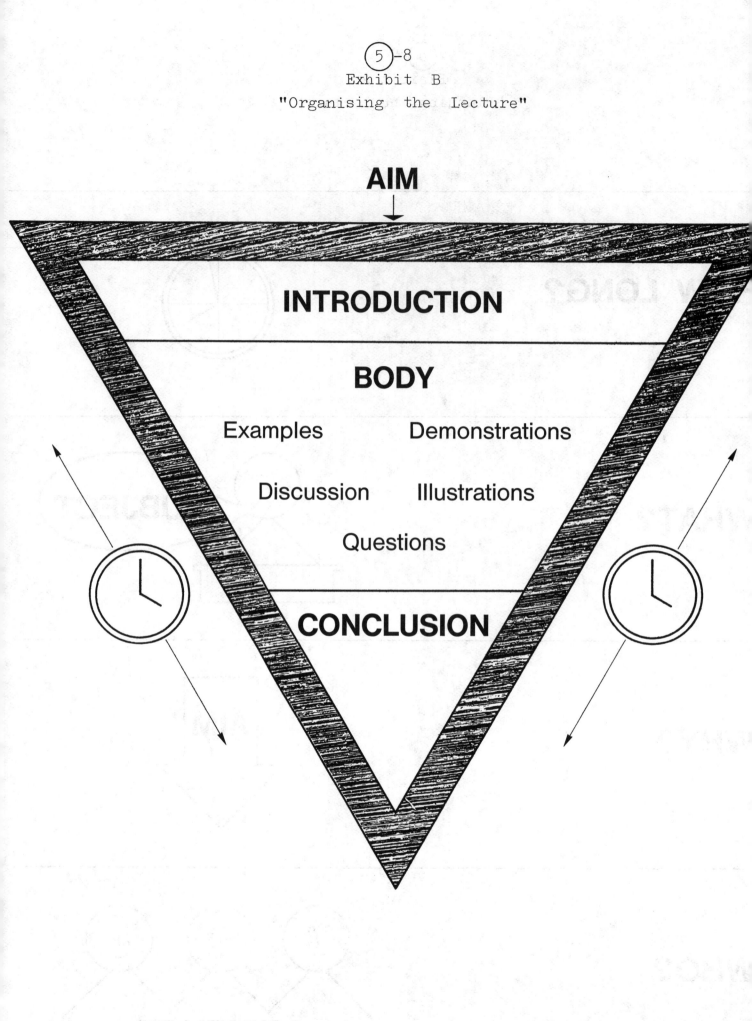

AIM

INTRODUCTION

BODY

Examples   Demonstrations

Discussion   Illustrations

Questions

CONCLUSION

LECTURE RATING FORM

Speaker: ....   Date: ....

Subject: ....

         ....

	Very good	Satisfactory	Weak
Organisation and Content			
1. Clear purpose	....
2. Appropriate introduction	....
3. Clear main points – principles	....
4. Development of points, theme (use of examples)	....
5. Conclusion	....
6. Adaptation to group needs and interests	....
7. Interest or novelty of topic or approach	....
Presentation			
8. Animation and directness	....
9. Use of voice (tone, expression)	....
10. Body and gesture	....
11. Use of notes	....
12. Total speaking ability	....
Other Methods (where applicable)			
13. Use of visual aids (comment if necessary)	....
	....
14. Handling questions/discussion	....
	....
15. Timing of session.	....
	....
Total handling of session	....

Remarks: ....

....

....

LECTURE PRESENTATION BY COURSE PARTICIPANTS
(A 15-minute lecture which you may be asked
to give to colleagues on the course.)

    Time limit. 15 minutes. A timer will be appointed to see that the time limit is observed. When the timer signals that time is up, the speaker - if he is not already or almost finished - is expected to move to his conclusion immediately.

    Subject. Draw on some part of your expertise or personal experience. In this case, you have limited time for outside subject preparation, so it is better to choose something with which you are already familiar and in which you are interested. Please note that a case study is not appropriate material for a 15-minute lecture. Above all, narrow down your subject so that it is suitable to the time limit.

    Title. Be simple and direct. Use the title to forward your aim of being understood.

    Visual aids. You are encouraged to use some visual aid(s) to clarify your presentation. Materials are available[1] but you are expected to prepare the display yourself (cutting, pasting, printing), and to make the necessary advance arrangements with the course director for setting up the necessary equipment.

    Evaluation. Each member of the audience will be given a lecture rating form on which he will evaluate the speaker's presentation. These will be handed to the lecturer at the conclusion of his talk. Participants are urged to note both strong and weak points and to make constructive comments where possible. Time permitting, discussion of these evaluations will be included.

---

[1]
    To be explained by the instructor.

Objective

To discuss and demonstrate the various ways of using film and photographic aids

To inform about local sources of films and photo equipment, including film hire and help with film/slide production

See NOTE below under "Special Equipment and Aids"

Handout Material

I - Specimen Evaluation Sheet for Films, p. 5

List of local sources for hiring or borrowing films, compiled by the instructor
Local film catalogues, if possible

HANDOUT I, Session 1, Session Evaluation Form

Background Reading

Using Films in Training, pp. 1-4

Refer also to "Films" section of Session 4 background reading entitled Projected Aids

Recommended Reading

ILO Man.Dev. Manual 15, Films - Management Development

Rigg, Audiovisual Aids and Techniques, pp. 8-21, 101-106

Gould-Marks, Management Communication Through Audio-Visual Aids, pp. 103-136

See also recent film reviews in industrial training journals

Special Equipment and Aids

Chalkboard or flip chart (to summarise discussion)

16mm film projector and screen. Films as selected by the instructor

Slide projector, slides and filmstrips

NOTE: It may be more appropriate to use this session to demonstrate a programme of locally prepared slides (with script or tape recording; see the heading "Sound Filmstrips" in the background reading for Session 4, Projected Aids). Discussion should cover ways of preparing and using slide-script presentations, which cost relatively little and can be tailor-made to training needs. Resources for local film and slide production should be mentioned. A photographic expert or enthusiast might be called in to offer tips on good photography and give general advice on technique.

45 min.	**Session Guide 6** (three versions)

This session should consist largely of demonstration and discussion, reflecting local resources for the use of films. An alternative approach is suggested in the NOTE under "Special Equipment and Aids".

16:00   DISCUSSION (Should take up where Session 4 left off)

Draw out from participants a discussion of the use of films in training; their strengths and weaknesses, advantages and disadvantages over other methods; local audience attitudes toward film. Refer to the comments about cinema film made in the movie, Visual Aids ,if you have shown it.

Comment on local sources of films for purchase, rental, or free loan (universities, schools, libraries, private firms, embassies, training centres). HAND OUT a list of these which you have prepared and display any catalogues you may have available.

Allow some discussion on equipment problems (including a proper room for film showings) and how to solve them, as this may be a major obstacle to using film. Tips on proper handling and projection may be mentioned (see the section, "Projecting Films" in the background reading) and time permitting, a period of hands-on practice for the participants. Allow for exchange of experiences.

DEMONSTRATION (Three alternatives are listed here to account for various possibilities of film supply and usage in the country and at the training centre.)

VERSION I

16:15   To summarise the material studied on the first day of the course, show one of the following films: Successful Instruction; A Class of Your Own; Pattern for Instruction.

16:35   In addition to discussing the content of the film as a review of the principles studied during the day, comment on the instructional strengths and weaknesses of the film itself.

VERSION II

16:15   Project a good industrial training film; if possible, one that is locally available. It should be appropriate for use by at least some of the participants in their work. Be prepared to answer technical questions about the film content afterwards.

16:35   In a follow-up discussion to the film, participants should consider what qualities make this a good film, what drawbacks it has, what type of audience it is appropriate for, and discuss various ways in which it could be used in training.

VERSION III

16:15   Conduct a demonstration lesson with film,using an open-ended case study or human relations film such as The Trouble with Archie or The Personal Problem.

      1.   Introduce the film, explain the purpose of viewing it and advise what to look for and what will be discussed afterwards.
      2.   Show the film (under as good conditions as possible).
      3.   Conduct a discussion on the problem posed by the film, based on a set of study questions you have prepared. Alternatively, the course participants may be asked to prepare this set of questions.

16:30   Once the demonstration lesson has concluded,there should be a follow-up discussion in which the participants analyse and evaluate the film's content,its suitability for training and with what audiences,the various ways they might use it in a training programme,what preparation they would make to use it (prepare supplementary handouts,their own guide questions,list of cast of characters written on a board or flipchart,etc.)

16:45   Before closing, ask members to evaluate the session.

USING FILMS IN TRAINING[1]

by B. Crowther,
Management Development Branch
International Labour Office

Why do most of us perk up when we know we're going to see a film?   We probably expect to have a chance to "get out" of the classroom, the conference hall or the movie theatre to explore new worlds: foreign countries, past centuries, battlegrounds, science laboratories, or maybe the world of nature.   And that film will probably take us far closer to the sights and sounds of the action than we could ever get by ourselves.   In a darkened room, our ears captured by the voice of the narrator and our eyes focused on technicolour images bigger than life, we easily forget about ourselves and enter into the lives of other people, other places, other problems.   No wonder a good film has such spellbinding power.

Such a medium clearly has a great deal to offer the instructor and his students, both by way of impact and range of possibilities.   Films provide variety and stimulate interest in a way that the instructor cannot.   In thirty minutes of filmed documentary the student may learn more about history than he could in three hours of reading - and he may remember it longer.   Film expands the reach of the ordinary classroom.   It brings the outdoors inside; it goes places it is either impossible or too dangerous for the ordinary human to go.   Compare showing a film of a factory to arranging a visiting tour for a hundred students.

In the industrial training context, we may cite the use of films for the study of human relations (labour disputes, disciplinary incidents, interviews, all brought up close for analysis); similarly, for making case study problems come alive; for demonstrating selling techniques; for revealing the intricacies of machines and industrial processes.   There are films which demonstrate and discuss everything from engineering techniques and leadership skills to management philosophy.

As with any other type of training material, the quality of films varies. Their effectiveness as training aids will depend largely upon the instructor's imagination and skill in selecting the films and integrating them into his training programme.   The following sections are a review of the main factors involved in using films in training.

Sources of Film

Outside of the United States and the United Kingdom, films produced especially for management training are scarce.   A word about some of the possible sources of films, both local and international, may be helpful in the search for appropriate material.

Specialists in the production of management training films are such firms as Roundtable Films and BNA Films in the United States, and the British Productivity Council, Rank Audio Visual Ltd., and S.B. Modules Ltd., in the United Kingdom. Some of these producers have long experience in the field and their technical material is well organised for training purposes.   A few firms have specialised in making films for a particular area, like salesmanship or industrial engineering. More recently, management consultancy groups and industrial training specialists are starting to produce their own films.   All of these are of course designed mainly for the "home" audience of managers.

Private manufacturing firms prepare films for public relations, sales or staff training purposes.   Despite their product orientation, they contain good technical material and are often high quality productions.   Films from IBM, oil companies like Shell, and the airlines are good examples.   Many of these internationally-based firms prepare multi-lingual versions of their films.

---

[1] Summaries of most of the films referred to in this article may be found in the ILO Management Development Film Library Catalogue, Man.Dev./Manual 15.

Government agencies, in particular the departments of defence and education, are likely to have large film collections suitable for training. Government information services in foreign countries make films available for public information purposes. Utilities companies - power (British Coal Board), transport (British railways, SNCF), communications (Bell Telephone) - often make their own films and have large lending libraries.

Educational materials firms sometimes go into the production of films to supplement textbooks. McGraw-Hill is an example.

Education centres, national education offices, universities, and training institutes usually have film libraries and sometimes produce their own films.

Television networks collect documentary film material for their programmes. The British Broadcasting Corporation has recorded several of its programmes on management subjects on film for public distribution.

International or bilateral aid agencies prepare their own public information films and collect training films suitable to their fields of work for distribution on loan.

When searching for an appropriate film, it is best to have a fairly open mind as to subject and source. Church organisations, for example, might have access to films in the human relations area. Private companies, as mentioned above, may have useful films on industrial processes and products. Despite the promotional nature of such films, they are usually good quality productions and contain up-to-date technical demonstrations. As to the choice of subject, films prepared for use in one context can often be adapted to use in another - especially in the field of human relations and communications. "How to Make an Effective Sales Presentation" or "Visual Aids" can be used for salesman training, instructor training, or even for executive development (public speaking). "The Engineering of Agreement" and "Styles of Leadership" would be useful to discussion leaders, supervisors, personnel managers and administrators.

Selection of Films

Considerations of length, content and over-all quality will figure in the selection of any film for a particular training purpose. When using foreign-made films, instructors should be especially sensitive to those features which might be culturally unacceptable or simply misunderstood by the audience. A few of the points to consider:

Length
Is it appropriate to the subject treated, and to the time available in the programme? Can it be used in parts?

Condition
Is the film copy in good condition (not scratched or broken)? How old is it? Will old-fashioned styles (clothing, hair-dos, automobiles) or outdated machinery create the impression that the message is old-fashioned too? Can something be done to counteract this impression?

Content
Is the objective of the film in line with the objective of the training session? If not, can it be adapted to the teaching purpose? Is the technical information up to date? Appropriate to the audience level? Applicable to the local situation or sufficiently similar to it? Is the subject dealt with at an appropriate level? Are there any attitudes or concepts which will be confusing or objectionable to the audience? Is the narration clear and unaccented? Choice of vocabulary understandable and appropriate to the audience?

Style
Will humour (if any) be understood and appreciated by the audience? Is it appropriate to the subject? Will cartoons, drawings and charts be understood? If animated drawings of people are used, will they be taken seriously? Is the acting convincing? Will the attitudes portrayed be accepted as realistic by the audience?

If you are going to make a habit of using films, it is advisable to keep some sort of record, such as a card index, of the films you have viewed and used.

Each film notation should contain information on the source and subject of the film, as well as comments on its use and effectiveness. An example of an evaluation sheet for this purpose is shown as Handout I.

Techniques for Teaching with Film

There is much incorrect use of films, for by their very nature they offer the trainer a tool which may, at first sight, seem so efficient that it needs no support. However, no film can introduce itself, and in most cases a follow-up discussion will prove valuable.

To decide how best to use a particular film, it is clearly necessary to preview it, noting the main points and any special features you wish to emphasise or explain, and to prepare a list of study questions for a follow-up discussion. It may be useful, as well, to prepare supplementary handouts or visual aids, such as charts and diagrams, to help recapitulate and to eliminate the need for note-taking by trainees.

The introduction to a film should make clear the purpose for which the film is being shown and suggest points to look for or questions to be answered after the film showing. For a case study film or documentary, it may be helpful to introduce the characters in advance. Some background to the film - why it was produced and for what original purpose, special terms which are used, any unusual cultural features or technical faults - is likely to help the audience understand the film better at the first showing.

Research experiments have shown that stopping the film at an appropriate point and asking participants to analyse or summarise events up to that point, is effective in increasing learning. Some films have this type of pause for review built into the scenario (see "Successful Instruction", "A Class of Your Own", and "Get Organised"). A film may be stopped after a question has been posed to allow participants to discuss the problems so far, work out an appropriate solution and anticipate the next set of events. This approach is particularly valuable in the study of human relations. In films where a management expert comments on a case study, stop the film before his remarks and require the audience to carry out their own analysis and discussion first (see "Avoiding Communication Breakdown" and "Person-to-Person Communication").

A follow-up discussion or question-and-answer period is essential to obtain full value from a film. If the group is large, or the film poses a case study type problem, it may be useful to break up into small syndicates for this purpose. In the case of a technical exposition, a question period may be necessary first. A blackboard or flip chart should be available for review notes. When the film is being used to teach a skill, then a practice exercise may be the most appropriate follow-up.

There are many good training and documentary films which are complete in themselves, so that the film by itself may be the focus of attention for the entire class period. Some of the newer films series dealing with management psychology (the Gellerman "Motivation and Productivity" series) or with the expertise of management consultants ("Management by Objectives", "The Effective Executive") are of this type. Producers of these films generally supply study guides and background material to support a film-centered programme. Such films are usually full of much more information than can be readily absorbed during one period. An instructor should consider showing the film twice, once as an introduction and later on for review. This type of film could also be used to refresh peoples' memory on a subject prior to going on to new material. The film "Visual Aids", for example, covers the theory and use of the traditional aids, leaving the class instructor free to move on to the demonstration of more sophisticated equipment.

A film which, because of length or level of the technical material, may be inappropriate for showing to trainees, may nevertheless be used by the instructor as a reference in preparing his own lesson. Lecture films on general management subjects issued by the American Management Association will provide useful guidelines. The same is true for "Pattern for Instruction" (where the analogy to American football might be inappropriate for some audiences) and for "Successful Instruction" (which is very long).

Of the films which can be used as case study material, some are open-ended ("The Personal Problem", "How's it Going?") and others must be stopped before the analysis is given on the film ("Avoiding Communication Breakdown"). Study and discussion of these films is conducted just as any other case discussion, the only drawback being that participants may find they wish to re-examine the facts of the case, which will involve reshowing the film. Wherever possible the instructor should make provision for this. Follow-up to such a film could ultimately include a role play, re-enacting events and incorporating changes which have been suggested by the participants.

Projecting a Film

If a film is to teach properly, it should be shown to its best advantage. Breakdowns, poor sound reproduction, bad film focus, a stuffy atmosphere and unnecessary background noises will all limit the impact of even an excellent film, and may well damage it for future use by others. The following is a review of the essential steps to good projection:

Arrange the room for good viewing comfort. Seats should be staggered, with a good distance between the front row and the screen (about two widths of the screen).

Check to see that the room is sufficiently darkened, that there is ample ventilation and a supply of ashtrays if necessary.

Position the loudspeaker in front of and slightly above the audience, pointing toward the centre. Place extension cords out of the way of the audience or fasten them down.

Set the projector on a stand at a suitable height in line with the centre of the screen. Ensure that it is set up firmly so that it does not shake or produce undue noise.

Check to see that all necessary equipment is on hand: extension cords, film spools of the right size, and an emergency kit containing spare projector and exciter lamps, fuses, and repair tools. Ensure that the voltage is suitable for the projector.

Check the film to see that it is correctly wound and in condition for showing.

Clean the lenses and the film path of the projector thoroughly. Particular attention should be paid to the gate, where dust and celluloid particles may be removed with a fine brush.

After threading the projector, test run to adjust the focus, volume and framing.

SPECIMEN EVALUATION SHEET FOR FILMS

[The following is intended only to be suggestive of the type of information which might be recorded in the evaluation of a film. Trainers should eliminate those categories which do not suit their needs and add others which do.]

Language ....

Title of film .... Length ....

..... Black and white .... Colour ..... Optical ..... Magnetic ..... Silent
                                         sound   sound

Producer .... Date of production ....

Local supplier ....

CONTENT

Subject

Type of treatment (lecture; documentary; humour; case study; etc.)

Intellectual level

Depth of coverage

Synopsis

Picture quality (cartoons, diagrams)

Sound quality (voice, accent, vocabulary)

Condition of film (if not new copy)

UTILISATION

Appropriate target audiences ....

Type of course .... Section of course ....

What supplementary aids or materials are needed to get the most out of
the film?

Recommended follow-up activity (discussion, role play, practical exercise)

Lecture Method II (Preparation)

Objective

To give participants time to prepare a 15-minute lecture

Handout Material

As for Session 5

Background Reading

As for Session 5

Recommended Reading

As for Session 5

Special Equipment and Aids

As required by course members

Session Guide 7

Evening Study.

The main part of the evening will be spent on the lecture preparations.
Be available to answer any questions or discuss ideas, as needed.
Make sure that course members have no special difficulties with their
lecture presentation and preparation, such as inability to obtain
reference material or supplies for the preparation of simple visual
aids.

Objective

To give as many participants as possible an opportunity to:

- practice the lecture method and receive feedback on their performance
- listen to and evaluate short lectures, with a view to improving lecturing skill

Handout Material

HANDOUT I, Session 5, Lecture Rating Form (4 copies per participant)

Background Reading

As for Session 5

Recommended Reading

As for Session 5

Special Equipment and Aids

As may be required by members, e.g., lectern, standard visual aids

Two meeting rooms if the group is split in two

90 min.	**Session Guide 8**
	All of the following arrangements - the number of presentations, their length - should be adjusted to the size of the group. Longer individual presentations are desirable if time permits. If the group is large, split it in two to allow more speakers to participate. In this case, appoint a leader for each group to be responsible for conducting the evaluation discussion after each lecture. The instructor himself should divide his time between the two groups.
	Choose four participants (or four in each group) to present their lectures and decide on the order of presentation. Appoint a timekeeper for the group and make him responsible for strict adherence to the programme.
	HAND OUT an adequate number of Lecture Rating Forms. Each member of the audience should fill out one of these forms for each speaker at the conclusion of his talk. Alternatively, the instructor may prefer to conduct evaluation without these, using the rating form only as a guideline for comments to be raised in discussion. Filled-in forms should be passed to the speakers at the end of the session.
	If necessary, help with comments after the presentations, but aim to let suggestions come primarily from the group. Normally, speakers will show different strengths and these should especially be brought out in summarising the session. If marked weaknesses have been demonstrated but participants have been reluctant to comment on these, they can sometimes be brought out in the final comparison and summary.
8:30	First presentation
8:45	Comments on first presentation
8:50	Second presentation
9:05	Comments on second presentation
9:10	BREAK (at discretion of the instructor)
9:25	Third presentation
9:40	Comments on third presentation
9:45	Fourth presentation
10:00	Comments on fourth presentation
10:05	Comparison, review and summary of practice lectures
10:15	Close the session

Objective

To have participants discover the characteristics of programmed learning
by working through part of a programme and discussing it afterwards

---

Handout Material

I - How to Read a Balance Sheet (excerpts), pp. 9-14

Handout I, Session 1, Session Evaluation Form

Background Reading

Programmed Learning, pp. 1-8

Recommended Reading

ILO Man.Dev. Manual 25, Introduction to Programmed Learning. Includes a
       bibliography of programmed books and reference works on this technique.
ILO Man.Dev. Manual 26, Programmed Learning - Book Reviews
ILO - How to Read a Balance Sheet
ILO - Creating a Market

Special Equipment and Aids

Chalkboard or flip chart

Some samples of programmed books (see ILO books above) which illustrate
the linear and intrinsic (branching) forms of programming

If available, one of the more sophisticated teaching machines
(e.g., Aututor, Bristol Tutor) would be interesting to demonstrate

Films about programmed learning:
       Programmed Learning
       Teaching Machines and Programmed Learning (UK)
       Teaching Machines and Programmed Learning (USA)

45 min.	**Session Guide 9**
10:30	Give a very brief introduction to what programmed learning is – a method whereby the trainee teaches himself by working through a series of steps all leading to carefully defined goals or objectives. Refer to background reading, "What is Programmed Learning?"
10:35	Issue HANDOUT I, excerpts from How to Read a Balance Sheet. Ask members to work through these pages. Be sure to provide a mask (a sheet to cover the answer column) with each handout.
10:55	Stop individual work.

Allowing maximum participation by members so that they can use their recent experience of working through a programmed text, explain the basic features of programmed learning. As each feature is discussed, write it down on the chalkboard or flipchart. At the end, you will have a summary of the basic features which will look like this:

1. Trainee works at his OWN PACE
2. Through a series of LOGICAL STEPS
3. All leading to pre-defined goals or OBJECTIVES
4. By ACTIVELY RESPONDING
5. And by MASTERING EACH STEP
6. He receives FEEDBACK information (or knowledge of results)
7. Which MOTIVATES (or encourages) him to continue
8. The programme is thoroughly TESTED before it is printed.

Many of these features are related directly to principles of learning which were discussed in Session 2, and reference should be made to that discussion. Programmed learning is a method which can cope especially well with individual differences in learning.

If time permits, give a brief explanation of the three best known forms of programmed learning:

> Linear Programming – the members are already familiar with this kind from the exercise
>
> Intrinsic (or Branching) Programming
>
> Adaptive Programming – if possible, a teaching machine

11:05	Demonstrate a teaching machine if you have obtained one. Although programmes can be presented in machines, it is important to stress that, unless the subject matter warrants this, they can be very successfully presented in books.
	Discuss some ways in which trainers may use programmed learning. Show sample texts, if available, and indicate (local) sources of programmed learning material.
11:10	HAND OUT a content summary if you have prepared one (optional, to be taken from background reading). Ask members to evaluate session.
11:15	Collect evaluation forms. Close the session.

PROGRAMMED LEARNING[1]

by P.D. Pereira,
Management Development Branch
International Labour Office

WHAT IS PROGRAMMED LEARNING?

Programmed learning (or programmed instruction, as it is also called) is one of the training methods developed in recent years from extensive research and laboratory tests. It is a teaching method which places the emphasis on communication - if the student or trainee fails to learn, then it may well be the fault of the "teacher" rather than his own.

Programmed learning is a method whereby the trainee teaches himself by working through a series of steps all leading to carefully defined goals or "objectives". He cannot go on to the next step until he has mastered the preceding one and so on to the end. To ensure that he is really learning the information in each step, he must answer "questions" correctly. He has immediate knowledge of results at each step (after he has replied) so that he can check to see how well he is doing.

The information to be taught is presented in a form known as a PROGRAMME, the person who writes the programme is known as the PROGRAMME WRITER or PROGRAMMER, and the people for whom the programme is written are known as the TARGET POPULATION. Programmes can be presented either in book form or in machines but whatever the form of presentation, the basic principles remain the same.

BASIC THEORY OF PROGRAMMED LEARNING

The three best known and most popular forms of programmed learning are: linear, intrinsic (or branching), and adaptive.

Dr. Skinner is the originator of what is known in programmed learning as linear programming. Every student works through all the sequences of the book in a straight path as it were, from page 1 to the end. At the end of every step he is called upon to reply and then given the correct answer. If he is right he goes on to the next section; if he is not he rereads the information until he understands it.

Dr. Crowder became the pioneer of intrinsic (or branching) programming. The trainee is presented with a piece of information and called upon to make a reply; he selects the correct answer from among several possible answers. If he is correct he is presented with some more information and another question. If he chooses the incorrect answer he is told that he is wrong and why; sometimes he is sent to reread the information and to try again; sometimes he is given extra explanation and a differently worded question. In this way the student works through the programme by one of several paths or "branches" according to which responses he chooses. Different students would work through the programme by different paths. Since the student's choice of reply determines which path of learning he would take through the programme, this form of programming is known as "intrinsic".

Gordon Pask, a British electronics engineer, developed a form of programming known as adaptive programming. This form of programming makes allowances for more variations in student ability. These programmes can only be presented in machines which "adapt" to the trainees, hence the name.

---

[1] Adapted from ILO: Introduction to Programmed Learning, Man.Dev./Manual 25 (Geneva, 1967). Available in English, French and Spanish.

Naturally, there are certain differences between these forms of programming, but they are all to some degree based on a theory of

STIMULUS (information and "question")	RESPONSE (reply)	FEEDBACK (knowledge of results)

The "stimulus" is a limited item of information plus a "question" of some kind. When this has been absorbed, i.e. when the student has read the information and question, he is then called upon to reply or "respond". As soon as he has done this, he is presented with results, or feedback information, which appears immediately after the learning piece to which it refers.

This process of STIMULUS, RESPONSE, FEEDBACK is repeated as often as is necessary for the trainee to learn the information. How often this "triangle" needs to be repeated will depend on the level of trainees, and the subject matter and will be shown up at the testing stage.

BASIC FEATURES OF PROGRAMMED LEARNING

Programmed learning is a self-instructional method of training stressing MOTIVATION to learn. It places the emphasis on COMMUNICATION with the trainee - if he fails to learn, then it is probably the programmer (the "instructor") who is at fault. He may not have explained properly, or in a vocabulary which the trainee understands, or may not have given him enough information. It is therefore up to the programmer to make sure that his trainee is learning.

Own Pace (or rate)

Most people are familiar with the problem of the "slow" learner, the trainee who needs to have things explained to him several times while his "brighter" colleagues seem to sail ahead. Recent experiments suggest that intelligence is really measured, at least in part, by the rate at which the trainee or student learns. Within limits, most students are capable of learning - some merely take longer than others. Programmed learning takes account of these differences by allowing each trainee to work at his own rate. The material to be learned is presented in the form of a PROGRAMME, which the trainee works through at his OWN PACE.

Logical Series of Steps

A PROGRAMME consists of a series of steps or FRAMES (pieces of information + a "question" = stimulus). Here is what a frame looks like. These two are actually taken from a linear programme.[1] Frames might be a few lines long, or a page long.

102. Until manufactured goods have actually been sold, can a company be quite certain that it will make a profit on them?

(answer) No

103. A company can never be absolutely certain in advance that it will make a profit on the sale of its goods. It would therefore be unwise to value its inventories at greater than their original cost. Suppose, however, that the market value of the inventories at the date of the balance sheet is less than cost. In this case, a cautious management will value its inventories at (cost/market value).

(answer) Market value

[1] ILO: How to Read a Balance Sheet, Chapter 2, p. 19, Geneva, 1966. Available in French and Spanish.

The learning material or process is carefully broken down into sections because of the theory that trainees or students are better able to grasp the subject if they are led gradually, by reasonably-sized steps, through some logical sequence which affords continuity of ideas.

To take a simple practical example with which most people are familiar; let us suppose that you want to teach your son to ride a bicycle: he has never been on a bicycle before. Unless he were an unusual child, he would not be able to ride a bicycle first go. You might teach him to ride by following a sequence something like this:

Preliminary: Demonstrate riding, with simple manoeuvres, at the same time mentioning some of the benefits to him of being able to ride (motivation).

1st Step: Hold bicycle, get him on, walk with him, teaching him how to balance: until he can balance unaided at slow speed, starting from the astride position.

2nd Step: Teach him how to pedal: until he can balance and pedal at slow speed.

3rd Step: Have him gradually work up pedalling and balancing: until he is confident at medium speed.

4th Step: Teach him to make turns of progressively tighter turning radius, to use brake and bell: until he can carry out all normally required manoeuvres up to a medium speed.

5th Step: Teach him to mount and dismount in motion.

The ability of the child, the nature of bicycle riding (there are some steps which MUST be taught before others), and to some extent your own views of how this should be taught, would determine the best sequence of teaching the steps, as well as their length. For example, one child might learn the first three steps in one hour, while another might need several days to master the first step only.

In programmed learning you would not write a programme for one trainee but for several having the same characteristics and/or training needs. In general, programmes start with something that the trainee already knows and gradually build up to new information; or they may start with the concrete and build up to the abstract. The reverse situation is also found, of course: what really matters is that it should be logical to the trainees using it.

Objectives

But these series of steps do not exist in a vacuum. They are all carefully designed to lead to predefined goals or "objectives". The first thing that a programmer does is to study the characteristics of the group of trainees for whom he will write the programme: their knowledge, abilities, interests. He then analyses the subject matter or job to be taught deciding which points are important and which are not. When this has been done, he must decide in detail what it is he wants his trainees to know or to be able to do when they have finished the programme.

For example, using the bicycle illustration just quoted: your reason for teaching your son to ride a bicycle might be any one of the following:

(a) exercise and pleasure;

(b) so that he can earn pocket money by doing local delivery of light goods and newspapers;

(c) so that he can participate in cycling competitions;

(d) because you own a bicycle factory and you want him to become familiar with bicycles so that he can develop different types of bicycles.

Every one of these reasons would demand a different treatment, greater/less emphasis on and accuracy in one or more aspects. If he is going to compete in races to see who can cycle the fastest, then obviously the accent will be on speed; if he is going to enter endurance competitions then the accent will be on building up his stamina; if he is going to develop bicycles for different purposes, for example, racing, small children, ladies, then the accent will be on the mechanical characteristics and performance of bicycles.

Not only is it necessary to decide what goals will be achieved, but it is also necessary to state under what conditions they are to be achieved, how achievement is to be measured and what will be accepted as "passable" achievement. Taking item (c) above to illustrate this, your objective might read: "will be able to ride a bicycle at not less than (specified) miles per hour, for distances of (specified), on (even/uneven) surfaces, in competition with other cyclists. Initial success will be achieved if a prize is won, ultimate success if the competition is won". As the subject or skill becomes more complicated the number of objectives and sub-objectives would be multiplied.

The programmer, then, presents his learning material in a LOGICAL SERIES OF STEPS so that the information leads up to the achievement of these carefully predetermined OBJECTIVES.

Active Responding

The difficulty of retaining attention is well known to anyone who has been concerned with trainees or with students in general. How easy it sometimes is to read through a paragraph or more of a text and find that one has not really been paying attention at all. This problem of holding the reader's attention is even more acute for anyone writing a programme - he will not be around to supervise what is going on, but he still wants to make sure that the trainee is learning.

In order to make sure that the trainee is paying attention to the information contained in each frame, the programmer calls on him to do something. When he knows that he will be called upon to participate at each step, he is more likely to pay attention to what is going on. Instead of reading or listening passively, he takes part actively.

So as not to bore the trainee, and to cater to the needs of different subjects and trainees, the programmer varies the type of action he wants him to perform; he may ask him to solve a problem, construct or complete a diagram, interpret a picture, work a machine or set it up, check a measurement or use a slide rule. For this reason, the term "responding" is used and not the word "answering" - the trainee works through the programme by ACTIVELY RESPONDING.

In a well constructed programme, responding is not a guessing game (it may be deductive, of course). The programmer is not interested in outsmarting the trainee - he gives him all the help and information he needs to master each step, and he makes sure that his explanations and language are suitable for his audience.

Masters Each Step

However, progress in programmed learning depends on success at each step, or mastery of each piece of information. Only when he has shown that he has thoroughly mastered the information by making the correct response can he go on to the next step. In this way, a programme is able to do what the instructor of a large group very often cannot do - make sure that each trainee is MASTERING EACH STEP.

Which raises the question "How does the programme make sure that the student is mastering each step?"

(a) Reasonably-sized Steps

First of all, the information is put into reasonable steps, according to the difficulty or type of material and the level of the particular group for whom the programme is written. Obviously, what is a small step for an experienced engineer would probably not be small enough for a first-year apprentice and would serve only to frustrate and discourage him. Conversely, too small

a step might well result in boredom and loss of interest. Steps must be correctly tailored to the trainee's ability. They should keep him sometimes
working at his best, challenge him sometimes and help him at other times. As
a general rule, there is a <u>tendency</u> for linear programmes to consist of relatively small steps and for <u>intrinsic</u> programmes to contain larger ones, but it is
more usual now to find a mixture of both in a good programme.

(b) <u>Prompts</u>

    However, putting the information into reasonable steps might not be suffi-
cient to obtain the correct response, so prompts or hints are used. For
example, consider this frame or step:

> 17. Look at the above balance sheet carefully and compare it with
> the one preceding Question 11. This new balance sheet has two
> things missing. These are ....

There are two obvious prompts operating in this frame: the first is the word
"two", which immediately tells the trainee that there are not three or four
things missing, but <u>two</u>. The second prompt is the "dotted" line of the last
sentence which tells the trainee that there is not just one word missing but
several (he will know this from the instructions issued at the beginning of the
programme). There is a wide choice of the type of prompt which can be used.
These include pictorial, sequential, thematic and grammatical prompts, which
are removed or gradually faded out until the student is able to respond correctly without prompting. Whether prompts are used or not and to what extent
is determined by the level of the group for whom it is written, type of subject
matter and the end result required.

(c) <u>Testing</u>

    At this point, one might well say, "So, the programmer puts his informa-
tion into reasonably-sized steps and uses prompts to obtain the correct response
from the student, but how does he <u>really know</u> that his programme is teaching and
that his trainees are learning?" The programmer finds out if his programme is
teaching by TESTING it. This is the important difference between programmed
learning and conventional textbooks. When the author of a conventional textbook publishes his work for the first time, he very often has no proof that it
will teach, although he may well be convinced in his own mind that it will.
The proof that a conventional textbook teaches more often than not comes after
the book has been published. In programmed learning, a good programme is
thoroughly tested <u>before</u> it is printed by a large number, perhaps a hundred or
often more, members of a sample group (a group having the same characteristics
of the group for whom the programme is written).

<u>Immediate Feedback</u>

    The programmer knows that the trainee is mastering each step but, since
this is a self-instructional method of learning and the trainee can work in his
own time, it follows that he too should have a way of finding out if he is
mastering each step. This "knowledge of results" is provided after each step
and is called FEEDBACK. Notice that we have not said knowledge of the "correct" reply. This is due to the fact that very often (particularly in intrinsic programming), the trainee has a choice of two or more answers out of which
only one can be correct. If he chooses any of the others, therefore, he will
be told that he is <u>not</u> correct and given an explanation.

    This principle of feedback might best be explained by the diagram below,
which represents what might happen in one step of a programme.

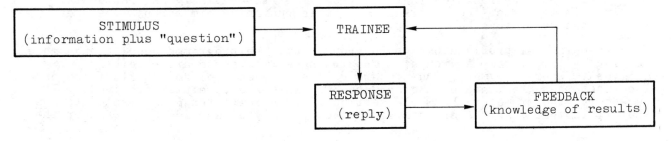

The trainee is presented with information and called upon to take part actively (stimulus); he replies (response); and he is then informed of the results (feedback). What happens then? This feedback will cause the trainee to CHANGE his behaviour or knowledge previous to the stimulus. If he is informed that he is correct then he will prepare to repeat the correct action or knowledge when faced with the same stimulus. If he is told that he is not correct then he will alter his response to that particular stimulus until it approaches the correct response (he will often be helped in this). This is, of course, a very simplified explanation of an extremely complicated process.

One of the theories of learning is that the sooner the trainee receives knowledge of results and the more specific this knowledge is, the more effectively he will learn and the better motivated he will be. In conventional examinations, for example, in certain trade tests, the trainee is usually told after some time has elapsed (often weeks) that he has passed or failed; more often than not he is not given details of any error in the test piece or examination paper. By the time he does know the results, his interest has waned. With programmed learning, however, the trainee knows immediately after each response whether it is correct or not. This is analogous to the situation in industry where incentive schemes work best when the operator knows as soon as possible what he has earned (be the reward monetary or otherwise) in a given period. This FEEDBACK has the effect of:

Motivation (or encouragement)

Motivation in this sense is the desire to learn or the desire to acquire a certain skill. Some trainees have a greater motivation to learn than others, and it is a well-known fact that (with rare exceptions) the greater the desire, the greater the learning. The object of programmed learning, therefore, is to maximise this desire to learn. This is achieved in large part by knowledge of results (or feedback) which encourages the trainee; because he finds that most times he has made the correct response (which means that he is mastering the information), he is encouraged to continue. The times when he will make an incorrect response will be few and will not normally discourage him. Indeed, some programmers believe that trainees learn by their mistakes provided, of course, they are not too many. When faced with the same stimulus again (question or situation) he knows which is the correct response (reply) and will make it.

Why people are motivated to do things is, of course, not always very evident or even due to one particular characteristic, and marketing specialists are only too aware of this. Whether the programme is dull or interesting for the student depends on the skill of the programmer, to some extent the subject and presentation and many other less discernible reasons. However, it is generally agreed that knowledge of results (and more often than not, of success) plays a major part in MOTIVATING or encouraging trainees to work through programmes.

Testing

When the programme has been written, it is finally tested by a "sample" group similar to those for whom it is written. There are several stages in the testing of a programme, the first stages covering one trainee at a time; the programmer tries to find out from him which words or frames are not clear or where he is having difficulty. In most cases, the trainee himself has a pretty clear idea of why he did not understand something; this might have been due to ambiguity, the keyword of the frame not being understood, material being taught in the wrong sequence or an idea several frames before which might not have been explained properly or repeated often enough for him to have retained the information. For this reason, when programmes are being tested, it is important that the trainee should be told that it is not he who is being tested but the programme: when he realises that the programmer is genuinely interested in helping him to master the material and not in punishing him for his mistakes, then he can be of invaluable help.

When initial problems have been ironed out, the programme goes through more testing by larger sample groups. The trainees' responses are carefully analysed; where too many students are getting the same or an important response incorrect then the frame or the sequence of frames is carefully examined. If necessary, the frame or the whole section is then rewritten and retested to see that it is teaching. Responses are not only analysed according to whether they are right or wrong.   Some responses are obviously more important than others. For instance, the trainee getting a response wrong after he has just worked through several explanatory frames, or after it has occurred the third time is obviously misunderstanding the material, while the trainee who makes an incorrect response through not paying attention may well have understood the information. Not until the sample population has measured up to a certain predetermined minimum requirement is the programme finally printed.   The minimum requirement is set by those who arrange for the programme to be written.   This might be 95 per cent accuracy of 90 per cent of the target population, or it might be 80 per cent accuracy of 80 per cent of the target population.   The reason for which the programme is written will, of course, have some bearing on the degree of accuracy required.

Testing is not only done when the programme is finished - it is being done throughout the programme.   This may take the form of revisions, summaries, sub-tests and post-tests.   These tests do serve to show the student how he is doing but they are also there to show the programmer, instructor or person administering the training that the programme is teaching.   Many programmes carry a pre-test which is done by the student before he works through the programme in order to find out his exact entering knowledge and skills.   This is then compared with the post-test done after he has finished the programme so that a better idea can be obtained of how much the programme has taught.   When the learning process is a purely mental one and not easily observable, these tests also serve as a guide to the instructor of how well his trainee is mastering the subject. In observable skills, of course, the problem of measurement is less acute.

In summary, then, the basic features of programmed learning are:

1.   Trainee works at his OWN PACE
2.   Through a series of LOGICAL STEPS
3.   All leading to predefined goals or OBJECTIVES
4.   By ACTIVELY RESPONDING
5.   And by MASTERING EACH STEP
6.   He receives FEEDBACK information (or knowledge of results)
7.   Which MOTIVATES (or encourages) him to continue
8.   The programme is thoroughly TESTED before it is printed.

Difference between Programmed Learning and Other Methods

There are four major differences between programmed learning and other methods of teaching.

(1)   It is self-instructional.

(2)   The subject matter and/or task is thoroughly analysed, and each sequence carefully designed to reach predetermined objectives.

(3)   Trainees are called upon to take part actively at each step and they receive immediate knowledge of the results.

(4)   Programmes are thoroughly tested and proved to teach what they are intended to teach.

SOME WAYS IN WHICH IT IS ENVISAGED THAT ILO EXPERTS WILL MAKE USE OF PROGRAMMED LEARNING

Programmed learning (both programmes designed for presentation in books and in teaching machines) is designed for self-study; however, for many subjects additional training is also needed - discussions, case studies, films, text-books, and so forth - where the "trainee" is given the opportunity of using the information with expert guidance.   At the moment, it is envisaged that ILO experts might profitably use programmed books (ILO-produced, as well as suitable ones available on the market), in the following ways:

(1)   for bringing the members of courses, conferences, etc. up to a certain minimum entering level from which to start discussion or to build up knowledge;

(2)   for doing the "donkey" work of teaching facts, thus affording more time for
      adaptation, orientation and further work in the subject(s), including prac-
      tical application of knowledge;

(3)   for "fixing" the main points of a lecture or course after the terms and
      meanings have been explained;

(4)   for teaching secondary subjects or skills which are essential or helpful for
      understanding the main topic. For example, the use of the slide rule in
      connection with production management;

(5)   as a starting point for the use of other more elaborate books on the various
      subjects;

(6)   as a self-teaching device for those who are unable to attend formal lectures
      and courses but who are interested in learning the subject(s) in their own
      time;

(7)   for spreading the knowledge of certain basic principles of various aspects
      of management to a greater number of people especially those who are unable
      to attend other types of training (e.g. because of geographical isolation).

-9

Handout I

HOW TO READ A BALANCE SHEET[1] (Excerpts)

HOW THE PROGRAMME WORKS IN PRACTICE

1. Place a cardboard mask over the left-hand column of this page.
2. Read question A carefully and fill in the missing word.
3. Move the mask down to check your answer.

CHECK	QUESTION	YOUR ANSWER
Is your answer right? Check below.	A. In this programme you will often be asked to fill in missing words as you go along. Sometimes you have to write one word, and sometimes more than one. Where there is one dash you write _____ word.	
A. one.	B. Where there is one dash you write one word. Where there are two dashes you write _____ _____. Sometimes these two dashes may be joined by a hyphen to indicate a hyphenated word.	
B. two words.	C. Just occasionally you will have to fill in more than two words. In this case there will be a row of dots. Where there is a row of dots you write......	
C. more than two words.	D. Going back for a minute: one dash calls for _____ word; two dashes call for _____ _____; and a row of dots means that you have to fill in	
D. one; two words; more than two words.	E. When square brackets containing two or three words or phrases are separated by oblique strokes, you should select the right word or phrase. For example: This book is [a conventional textbook/a new type of textbook].	
E. a new type of textbook.	F. Before you start on the programme itself, note that you don't have to guess to get the right answers. Read the questions carefully and they will give you the information which you need to get the r_____ answers. In this case the r before the dash means that the missing word which you have to fill in begins with r.	
F. right.		

---

[1] ILO: How to Read a Balance Sheet, Geneva, 1966, pp. 1-8. Also available in French and Spanish.

CHECK	QUESTION	YOUR ANSWER
	G. Don't hesitate to write a word because you think that it is too simple or obvious. The whole idea of this programme is that it moves in easy steps. You never have to g_____ the answers.	
G. guess.		
H. one; two words; more than two words; choose the correct word or phrase.	H. A reminder: Where one word is wanted there will be _____ dash. Two dashes mean that you should write _____ . A row of dots means that you should write... .... Where there are square brackets containing two or three words or phrases, you should [choose the correct word or phrase/simply read them].	
I. (a) one; two words; more than two words; correct; (b) right; (c) question.	I. Finally, the correct way to go through the programme is: (a) read the question and fill in the missing_____word, _____ _____, or ...., or choose the [correct/incorrect] word or phrase; (b) move the mask down so that you can read the r_____ answer; (c) go on to the next q_____ .	
	Now start working through the programme itself.	
	Read each question carefully before writing anything.	
	On turning over each page, remember to cover up the left-hand column with the mask before going on to the next question.	

CHAPTER I

WHAT A BALANCE SHEET IS ABOUT

(Don't forget to cover up the left-hand column of each page with your mask and to move the mask down to check your answer before going on to the next page.)

CHECK	QUESTION	YOUR ANSWER
Is your answer right? Check below.	A balance sheet may look rather complicated but basically it is a simple statement about a business enterprise. Most business enterprises produce statements at regular intervals showing what they own and what they owe. 1. A balance sheet is a statement of what an enterprise _____ and what it _____ at a particular date.	
1. owns; owes.	The things an enterprise owns are called its assets, and the various sums of money that it owes are called its liabilities. 2. Would a company's buildings and manufacturing tools be classed as assets or as liabilities? _____.	
2. assets.	3. Assets include land, buildings, manufacturing equipment and anything else an enterprise o_____ that can be given a value in terms of money. Can the stocks of raw materials held by a manufacturing company be given a value in monetary terms? _____.	
3. owns; yes.	4. Stocks of raw materials (or finished goods) are things owned by an enterprise that can be given a value in _____. They are classed as _____.	
4. monetary terms; assets.	5. Now, to acquire its assets an enterprise must obtain money from various sources, for instance it may borrow from loan companies or banks. It therefore o_____ this money.	
5. owes.	6. The various amounts of money owed by an enterprise are called its _____.	
6. liabilities.	As well as borrowing from banks and other sources, many companies obtain a good deal of the money that they need from their shareholders. 7. The shareholders of a company generally subscribe, or make money available for the life of the _____.	
7. company.	8. Because the money subscribed by shareholders is provided for the life of the company it will be repaid to them only if the company is wound up. Nevertheless, this money is still o_____ to the share holders.	
8. owed.		

CHECK	QUESTION	YOUR ANSWER

9. The money subscribed by share-holders is _____ to the shareholders, and it is therefore part of the company's [assets/liabilities].

9. owed; liabilities.

10. Balance sheets may be set out in different ways, but however they are set out they always show the _____ and _____ of the enterprise concerned.

10. assets;
    liabilities.

--- Here is a very simple balance sheet ---

HANDICRAFTS LTD.

Balance Sheet at 31 December 1964
(expressed in "world money" units)

ASSETS		LIABILITIES	
Raw materials, etc.	3,460	Bank overdraft.	2,150
Land, buildings, etc.	8,750	Long-term mortgage loan, owed to loan company.	7,000
		Money subscribed by shareholders.	3,060
TOTAL ASSETS		TOTAL LIABILITIES	

11.
(a) This balance sheet shows the assets and liabilities of _____ _____ (whom?) at........(date).
(b) Both the assets and the liabilities are expressed in m_____ terms.
(c) Fill in the missing totals in the balance sheet.
(d) Are these totals the same or different? _____ .

11.(a) Handicrafts
    Ltd.31 Dec.1964;
   (b) monetary;
   (c) 12,210;12,210;
   (d) same.

12. The name "balance sheet" comes from the fact that the total _____ always equal the total _____. In other words, they b_____ each other.

12. assets;
    liabilities;
    balance.

Let us see why the total assets and the total liabilities are in balance. Look at the balance sheet of Handicrafts Ltd. again. The bank, the loan company, and the shareholders have all made money available to the company.
13. In other words, the [assets/liabilities] on the balance sheet show what money has been made available to the company from various sources.

13. liabilities.

Now, an enterprise obtains money with the object of employing it: for instance to buy raw materials, etc.
14. We can see how an enterprise has employed or used its money by looking at the _____ on the balance sheet.

14. assets.

CHECK	QUESTION	YOUR ANSWER

15.available;
   employed or used.

16. liabilities;
    assets.

15. The liabilities, then, show what money has been made_____to the company, and the assets show how this money has been_____.

16. The total assets and the total liabilities will be equal because the _____ show the money that has been made available to the enterprise and the _____ show how this money is employed by the enterprise.

— Here is another simple balance sheet —

BALANCE SHEET
(expressed in "world money" units)

ASSETS		LIABILITIES	
Raw materials, etc..	6,000	Bank overdraft	3,600
Land, buildings, etc. . . .	10,400	Long-term mortgage loan owed to loan company . .	5,000
		Money subscribed by shareholders	7,800
TOTAL ASSETS	16,400	TOTAL LIABILITIES	16,400

17.The name of the enterprise, and the date of the balance sheet.

18.name; date.

17. Look at the above balance sheet carefully and compare it with the one preceding question 11. This new balance sheet has two things missing. These are..............................
....

If you are looking at a balance sheet in order to assess the current position of a particular enterprise, it is important to make sure that you have the balance sheet for the right enterprise. You will also want to know whether you are looking at the most recent balance sheet.

18. The first two things to look for on a balance sheet, then, are the _____ of the enterprise and the _____ of the balance sheet.

CHECK	QUESTION	YOUR ANSWER

─────── Now look at the following balance sheet ───────

HANDICRAFTS LTD.

Balance Sheet at 31 December 1964
(expressed in "world money" units)

ASSETS		LIABILITIES	
Raw materials, etc.	3,460	Bank overdraft	2,150
Land, buildings, etc.	8,750	Long-term mortgage loan owed to loan company . .	7,000
		Money subscribed by shareholders.	3,060
TOTAL ASSETS	12,210	TOTAL LIABILITIES	12,210

19. Yes.

19. Does the above balance sheet give you the same information as the balance sheet preceding question 11 on page 4?_____ .

20. assets;
liabilities.

20. Balance sheets can be set out in many different ways. However they are set out, they should include two main groups of figures: the_____ and the _____.

SUMMARY

21. at a particular date.

21. To sum up so far, we can say that a balance sheet is a statement of the position of an enterprise [over a period of years/at a particular date].

22. assets;
liabilities;
balance.

22. A balance sheet gives two main groups of figures, the_____ and the _____. The two totals b_____ each other.

23. liabilities;
owes

23. The_____indicate what money has been made available to the enterprise from different sources. The enterprise o_____ this money.

24. owns; employed or used.

24. The assets are what the enterprise _____. They show how the enterprise has_____the money available.

25. enterprise
(or company);
date.

25. Every balance sheet should include the name of the_____and the _____.

26. No.

26. Before finishing this section we should note that there are many factors which affect the position of an enterprise but which cannot be expressed in monetary terms. For instance a company might be fortunate in having a highly trained and stable labour force. Are factors like this indicated on a balance sheet?_____ .

27. monetary terms.

27. A balance sheet can show only those assets and liabilities which can be expressed in_____ _____.

Objective

To explain why and how discussion techniques are used

To provide guidelines for structuring and leading discussions

---

Handout Material

I   -   Discussion Planning Sheet, p. 3

II   -   Discussion Leading, pp. 5-8

III -   Discussion Leading - Evaluation Sheet, p. 9

Background Reading

Syndicate Work, p. 1-2

Debenham, A Training Officer's Guide to Discussion Leading (BACIE booklet)

Recommended Reading

Special Equipment and Aids

Freehand drawings of diagrams for the overhead projector showing seating arrangements and patterns of discussion (see BACIE reading)

Films about the discussion method and conference leadership:

All I Need is a Conference   Meeting in Progress

How to Conduct a Discussion   Running a Meeting

Let's Discuss It   A Shift of Opinion

45 min. | **Session Guide** 10

If a film is used as a basis for this session, this outline must be revised to bring out the main techniques demonstrated in the film.

11:30 | Highlight differences between lecture and discussion. (Refer to the BACIE Introduction).

11:35 | Cover the following points: (BACIE, pp. 4-21)

- the role of the leader

- preparing to lead a discussion (use HANDOUT I, Discussion Planning Sheet)

- handling/controlling the discussion

- the use of questions (BACIE, pp. 22-24)

- physical arrangements (possible visual aid)

- patterns of discussion (possible visual aid).

Many of these points will be illustrated further during the practice sessions.

Distribute HANDOUTS II and III and use them to summarise the points covered.

12:00 | Explain what syndicates are and discuss when they may be used. (Refer to background reading and BACIE, pp. 26-27)

12:10 | Brief members on their preparation for discussion practice sessions, 13 and 15, scheduled for the following day:

1. During Session 12, each participant is to select and prepare a subject for a 20-minute discussion (length at the discretion of the instructor) which he may be asked to lead in Session 13. He must also prepare appropriate visual aids or handouts if he requires them.

2. In Session 15, the group will be divided into (four) sections for the first 25 minutes. Each small group will discuss the question, "What learning principles are most neglected by management trainers and why?" After the initial discussion, the groups will come together to present their conclusions. Members should give the topic some thought during the preparation period in Session 12.

12:15 | Close the session.

SYNDICATE WORK

Any method of working which a small group may use to achieve a particular purpose might fairly be described as a syndicate method. The essence of the syndicate method is that men should learn from each other and should contribute their own experience to the fullest. The main task of the tutorial staff is to organise the work so that this mixture of experience takes place to the maximum extent possible within the duration of the course.

A syndicate can either be designed to include in its membership the widest possible variety of experience or members may all be specialists of one type usually under the chairmanship of a non-specialist. On general management topics, the first type is advisable since members acquire an interesting and continuous contact with the viewpoint and way of thinking of other specialists or men of other kinds of experience while discussing topics which are of general interest to all. But where a course consists of several syndicates, the other kind of constitution is often useful, partly as a variation to give members a change of company and voice, and partly for the preparation of material on specialist subjects for other members of the course without any particular knowledge of specialist terminology.

A normal subject might proceed as follows: the chairman and secretary receive the relevant documents at the start of a subject for which they are to be responsible. They get these ahead of other members of the syndicate to enable them to prepare a scheme of work for their colleagues. After the chairman and secretary have had a preliminary glance at the papers, they go into private conference with the tutor in charge of the syndicate. He satisfies himself that the scope of the subject to be handled and the arrangements made for its treatment are understood by the chairman and secretary. As much responsibility as possible should be thrown upon the group member; the tutor in charge of each syndicate assists in the background.

The chairman and secretary next examine the books and pamphlet material which will have to be shared among the syndicate if the work is to be done effectively and within the time allotted. The chairman then holds the first organising meeting for his subject. He should explain to the syndicate the task they are undertaking and make his proposals for carrying it out. Apart from knowledge and experience within the syndicate and the information derived from books and pamphlets, supplementary information from outside may be acquired both by visits to outside organisations and by conference with visitors. Where the former source is to be tapped, the chairman's documents should inform him of suitable organisations to be visited. (Arrangements may have been made by the tutorial staff for such visits beforehand. One or more members of the syndicate should be sent to such organisations after briefing to observe and report back upon what has been seen or discovered.)

The visitors might include men of practical experience either in industry or public life, or men with specialist or academic qualifications. They may either lecture to the course as a whole or they may visit the individual syndicates, sitting with the members at a table, and either taking part in their discussion or in some cases being treated as consultants from whom the syndicate will try and extract information upon specific points thought out in advance. It is one of the chairman's responsibilities to see that proper preparations are made to secure full value from these consultations.

It may happen that the course includes a member with some specific knowledge and experience not available in each syndicate, and it may be useful for each member to act as a specialist and visit other syndicates who will treat him in the same manner as an outside visitor.

Each syndicate exercise should lead to the accomplishment, within the time fixed, of a definite task, usually the completion of a report of specific maximum length, or particular aspects of the problem studied. This is normally drafted initially by the secretary and the syndicate must agree that it is a fair description of their views which may not be unanimous. The preparation of such a document and its passage through the syndicate is often difficult and time consuming. (Experience has shown that members do learn a surprising amount about drafting and particularly the drafting of other persons' opinions from the preparation and criticism of such documents.)

This document, together with the parallel reports from other syndicates, would then be duplicated and circulated to each member of the course and all syndicates should review all the reports.

The chairman's last duty is to present the work of the syndicate to the course as a whole for critical examination. He is required, with his syndicate sitting around him, to give an account of his stewardship and to call attention to points of interest or difficulty that have arisen. In doing so, he gains experience of one very difficult part of a senior executive's work - the expression to a wider audience of views with which he does not necessarily agree personally. After the chairmen of all the syndicates have presented their reports, the main issues, particularly those upon which differences have emerged, can be discussed by the course as a whole.

DISCUSSION PLANNING SHEET

1. Overall objective of the discussion

2. Topic

3. Equipment and materials required

P L A N

Introductory remarks   Time allowed: ___ min.

Main Phase of the Discussion	Key Points	Timing

Phase
  Opening question:
 	
  Intermediate summary		

Phase
  Opening question:
 	
  Intermediate summary		

Phase
  Opening question:
 	
  Intermediate summary		

Final summary		
Closure		

DISCUSSION LEADING

HOW TO PREPARE TO LEAD A DISCUSSION

1. Determine the overall objective

    Why are you going to lead this discussion?
    What is the end result you want to achieve?

2. Define the topic clearly and concisely

    Collect facts and information about it.
    Arrange your material in a logical, usable order.

3. Consider the group

    What are they likely to know, feel, think, about this subject already?
    What are the possible objections and conflicts?

4. Prepare a detailed discussion outline

    Decide which aspects of the subject you want the group to consider.
    Decide how much time is available for each aspect.
    Prepare your introductory remarks carefully.
    Have a well thought-out opening question.
    Set intermediate objectives.
    Frame appropriate questions for each phase of the discussion.

5. Have everything ready

    See that members of the group are informed in good time about the date, time,
        and place of the meeting.
    Arrange the accommodation satisfactorily - lighting, heating, seating,
        ventilation, etc.
    Make sure that all necessary materials, handouts, equipment, audio-visual aids
        are ready in time.

HOW TO LEAD A DISCUSSION

1. Get off to a good start

    Start the meeting on time.
    Try to make the group feel at ease.

2. Lead in to the discussion

    State the general purpose of the discussion.
    Announce the topic clearly and concisely.
    Explain the discussion procedures and define its limits.
    Introduce the topic.

3. Guide the discussion

    Encourage participation by all members.
    Control the over-talkative member.
    Draw out the shy member.
    Don't allow one or two members to monopolise.
    Deal tactfully with irrelevant contributions.
    Avoid personal arguments.
    Keep the discussion moving.
    Keep the discussion on the subject.
    Summarise frequently.
    Use audio-visual aids.

4. <u>Summarise the discussion</u>

    Review the highlights of the discussion.
    Review the conclusions which have been reached.
    Make clear what has been accomplished by the discussion.
    Re-state any minority viewpoint.
    Get agreement for any action proposed.
    End on a high note.

QUESTIONS AND THEIR USES IN DISCUSSION LEADING

<u>The Uses of Questions</u>

To get all members of the group involved in the discussion.
To draw out quiet, shy or backward members.
To start people thinking.
To awaken interest.
To find out what previous knowledge of the subject members may have.
To keep the discussion moving.
To keep the discussion on the subject or bring it back to the subject.
To recall a 'wandering' mind.
To stop private conversations.
To prevent monopolisation by one member.
To draw out members' experience which may be relevent and helpful.
To get each member to hear a range of opinions all different from his own.
To put a 'difficult' member in his place.
To highlight important aspects of the subject.
To check on the group's assimilation of the subject matter.

<u>The Types of Question</u>

    Broadly speaking, there are two types of question:

1) The <u>general question</u> (sometimes referred to as the "overhead" question) is addressed to the group as a whole. The discussion leader wants to stimulate thinking by <u>all</u> members of the group. If he names the person who is to answer before he asks the question he is simply encouraging all the other members to go to sleep while the "victim" tries to answer. If he puts the question to the group as a whole, every member of the group has to rack his brains. In addition, by using a direct question too early in the discussion, he may embarrass members of the group by asking them questions which they are not yet ready to answer.

2) The <u>direct question</u> is addressed to an individual by name. It has definite advantages in certain circumstances but it must be used with care. It could, for example, put the person to whom it is addressed in the very uncomfortable and embarrassing position of having to reply when he just does not have anything to say. On the other hand, if there is an acknowledged "expert" on the topic under discussion in the group, the direct question can be used to draw upon his experience. It can also be used to draw a shy member into the discussion, but in this case the question should be carefully chosen and one which he is pretty sure to be able to answer. It can also be used to break up private conversations or to interrupt a "monopoliser" (i.e., by asking someone <u>else</u> to comment).

    Note that it is a useful technique to phrase the question as a general question first, pause to allow all the members of the group to think, and then name the individual who should answer; e.g., "What do you consider the basic reason why this situation arose - (pause) - Mr. Smith?"

    Another form of the direct question is what is sometimes described as the "pick-up" question. This is used to refer back to a contribution which got passed over in the 'heat' of the discussion. This frequently happens with a contribution from a shy member who may speak rather quietly and be interrupted by a more aggressive or more vocal member. The important thing is that the leader should make a mental note at the time and come back to the point later if only to give recognition to the contributor. Here is an example: "I believe that you were saying a few minutes ago, Mr. Smith, that you had found a new way of dealing with this particular type of problem. Would you like to tell us a little more about it?"

We have said that every question is either a general question or a direct question. In addition, questions can be further divided into a number of categories. A few are described below.

An open question is expressed in very broad terms and is capable of a wide variety of answers. It is usually prefixed by who, what, when, where, how, why.

"Who ought to be responsible for taking action in this type of situation?"
"Why is it important that a company should have a sound induction scheme?"
"What are the advantages of apprentice training schemes?"

A factual question seeks facts, information data, etc.

"How many members of the group have attended a previous supervisor training course?"
"Which of you have previous experience in the steel industry?"

A re-directed question is used when members of the group put specific questions to the discussion leader. He should, wherever possible, re-direct them to other members of the group. This keeps the group active and prevents a dialogue between the discussion leader and one member.

In the case of a rhetorical question, the leader does not expect the group to answer and the group know this. They know that either no answer is required or the leader will answer himself, e.g., "In these circumstances what else could I do but go along with the crowd?"

In a leading question, the answer is implicit in or suggested by the question, e.g., "This sort of behaviour is quite unacceptable isn't it?"

One comes across many other categories of question in the literature on the subject including, for example, imperative, exploratory, provocative, controversial and ambiguous. But the categories dealt with above are the most important in the industrial discussion group situation. Of the five categories, the last two, rhetorical and leading, have no value in discussion leading. They do not provoke the group members to think and they do not stimulate further discussion. In any case, the leading question is usually considered slightly "improper". If you have the choice, try to pose questions most frequently in the "open" or "neutral" or "non-directive" form.

General Hints on the Use of Questions

1.   Questions should be brief, clear and simply worded.

2.   Direct questions should be distributed at random. A fixed order, e.g., clockwise around the group should be avoided at all costs. They should also be well distributed among the various members of the group.

3.   Questions should, as far as possible, cover one point only.

4.   Questions should, where possible, be related to the ability and experience of the person to whom they are addressed.

5.   Having asked the questions, give the members of the group time to think before expecting an answer.

6.   Don't use rhetorical or leading questions to try to get out of a difficult or awkward situation in the group. This is more likely to make the situation worse.

<u>Using Questions to Establish the Right Pattern of Discussion</u>

Finally, on the use of questions, here are two diagrams which give us a bird's eye view of the pattern of discussion we are trying to achieve.

<u>Not this</u>   <u>But this</u>

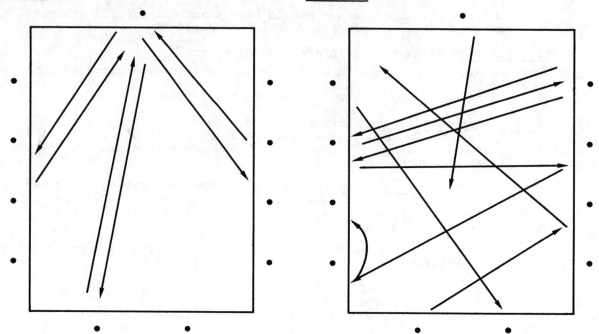

DISCUSSION LEADING - EVALUATION SHEET

Leader _____

Topic _____

_____

		Poor	Fair	Average	Good	Excellent
		1	2	3	4	5
1. Preparation	How satisfactory were the 'physical' preparations (accommodation, materials, etc.)?					
2. Opening	Did the discussion get off to a good start?					
3. Objective	Was the general purpose of the meeting clearly stated?					
4. Topic	Was the topic announced clearly and concisely? Was it introduced well?					
5. Atmosphere	Was there a relaxed, friendly atmosphere?					
6. Participation	Did the leader achieve all-round participation?					
7. Keeping to the subject	How well did the leader manage to keep the discussion on the announced topic?					
8. Questions	Were they well-designed? Were they well-distributed around the group? Did they stimulate discussion?					
9. Leader's own contribution	Was the leader careful not to pose as an expert?					
10. Pace of discussion	Did the discussion keep moving and making progress?					
11. Control of group	How well did the leader control personal arguments, private chats, irrelevant material?					
12. Intermediate summaries	Did the leader make adequate intermediate summaries?					
13. Chalkboard or chart work	Was it well planned? Was it well executed?					
14. Final summary	How adequate was the final summary?					
15. Closure	How adequate was the closure?					
16. Achievement of objective	Was the objective of the meeting achieved?					

Case Method I

Objective

To explain the features of the case method and why and how it is used

To have course members participate in a case discussion

To demonstrate how to lead a case study

To provide guidelines for the selection and writing of case studies

Handout Material

I   -   Case Study: Union President and Works Manager, p. 7
II   -   Writing a Case, pp. 9-10
III -   Questions for Case Study Analysis, p. 11
Handout I for Session 17, Case Study: The Plywood Factory
Handout II for Session 17, Case Study: The Northern Cement Factory
Handout I, Session 1, Session Evaluation Form

Background Reading

The Case Method, pp. 1-2

Notes on the Case Study Method, pp. 3-4

The Incident Process, p. 5

Instructor's Guide to Union President and Works Manager, Instructor's Notes, p.8

Recommended Reading

BACIE, BACIE Case Studies. See especially the introduction by A.I.S. Debenham.

Craig and Bittel, Training and Development Handbook, pp. 180-189

Pigors, Case Method in Human Relations - The Incident Process

Towl, To Study Administration by Cases

Special Equipment and Aids

Chalkboard or flip chart may be useful for explaining certain points.

One of these films will demonstrate a case:

        The Personal Problem
        The Trouble with Archie
        The Case Method of Instruction - Part III

16mm Projector - and film screen, set up in a room which can be darkened

90 min.	**Session Guide** 11
	Timing of this session must be adjusted according to the film used and whether or not the instructor chooses to cover the incident method.
14:00	The following review of the case study method can either be a short presentation by the instructor, or a discussion which brings out the key points. The choice will depend on the previous training experience of the group.
	Explain the case study: What is a case? (use a film or set of films to show an example of a case and draw out its identifying features in discussion). What is the case study method? (see background reading).

14:25	Direct attention to the case study, HANDOUT I, Union President and Works Manager. Allow participants a few minutes to read the case and consider: - what are the relevant facts;
	                              - what is the central problem;
	                              - what are some possible solutions to the problem.
	Then conduct a discussion on the case.

15:00	BREAK (at the discretion of the instructor)
15:15	Following up this immediate experience, discuss what makes the case study a valuable method for management training. Ask for participant views on advantages and limitations.
	Touch briefly on the task of the case discussion leader (demonstrated especially in The Case Method of Instruction series of films). Distribute HANDOUTS II and III, Writing a Case and Questions for Case Study Analysis.Handout III should be kept at hand for guidance during the evening case discussions.
15:35	In summing up, emphasise that the method introduces trainees to the analysis of a situation from various perspectives and shows them that there is very often more than one solution to a problem. Some pointers on its use, based on experience in developing countries, are:
	1. Know the technical knowledge level of your group before introducing the case method. 2. Do not introduce the case method too early in the course. 3. Use simple cases in the beginning and more complex towards the end of the course. 4. Use simple cases for short courses (2-3 days) and complex cases (if desired) for longer courses. 5. Practise writing your own case studies since you will probably want to use locally developed cases.
15:40	Briefing for Sessions 17 and 18:
	HAND OUT the cases to be discussed, The Plywood Factory and The Northern Cement Factory (HANDOUTS I and II, Session 17). Participants should read and make a preliminary study of these cases in advance of the evening study period.
	Divide the members into (four) small discussion groups and explain that they will meet on the following evening to discuss the two case studies. Each group should elect a reporter/spokesman who will present its conclusions and solutions at the general course discussion in Session 18. (Consult Session Guide 17 if you wish to give further instruction at this time on the procedure to be followed in discussing the cases.)
	Appoint two members to be observers (possibly those who would be assigned to do the role play - see note on Session Guide 12) during the subsequent case sessions. They are to circulate, observe how the groups approach the cases and prepare summary comments for Session 18.
15:45	Close the session.

THE CASE STUDY METHOD

Apart from the knowledge he has to acquire, one of the fundamental tasks of a manager is to make and to implement decisions. These decisions are, for the most part, based on analysis of such facts and other information as may be available. Rarely, however, can the manager have access to unlimited information and he often has to make decisions on incomplete information and under conditions of uncertainty. One of the foremost tasks of any effective management education, therefore, must be to improve the ability of managers and embryo managers to take wise decisions and make plans for their successful implementation.

In essence, this is what the case method in management education aims to do. The use of cases in training for business is not primarily to help students accumulate a store of knowledge or to acquaint them with current business practice although it also does these things. Rather the prime purpose is to help students develop their skill in discovering and defining the vital questions that need to be answered and then to learn how to set about finding the answers. Almost inevitably the businessman is compelled to decide on a course of action before he can obtain all the facts he would like to have. The student of a case acts in a like manner.

The case study technique is based on the belief that the trainee can best attain managerial understanding and competence through the study, contemplation and discussion of actual situations. The rigorous analysis required, especially in the longer cases, is said to develop habits of logical thinking and searching for as complete information as possible before reaching conclusions. Experience in arguing a viewpoint before one's peers also develops ability to communicate clearly.

A case study has a different meaning depending on how it is used. To some people, it will mean the same as a legal case, a precedent that can usefully be followed; to the researcher, a case may appear as a vehicle for testing hypotheses. We are concerned with the form of case study most suited to our objectives in management education. This form of case study will present the student with an authentic management problem. It will present reports, facts, and even opinions, but will not evaluate. It will have been gleaned for the most part from research in the field and will have been put together in a conscious effort to ensure accuracy and reality. The aim throughout is to train the student in analysis and decision-making. This aim is ensured by facing the student with a whole series of case situations designed to give him as wide an experience as possible.

The "classic" or "Harvard" approach uses very detailed case reports. These sometimes run to forty or fifty pages of text, with supporting charts and documents. The material is usually in the form of a running narrative. Anything (some say almost everything) that might bear upon the situation is included: the history of a company; biographies of key persons; information about finances, marketing, production, and other functions. This type of case includes not only data that is pertinent to the problem, but also a tremendous amount of information that really has little to do with it.

Study of these cases requires considerable time. Not only does it take time to read the material once, it may be necessary to go back over portions of the case repeatedly. This is because the problem is not identified as such, nor is the pertinent information necessarily presented in the best sequence for logical analysis. A student must determine what the problems are, which is the most important, and what facts bearing upon it are available. Then he attempts to determine just what can be done.

After students have studied the case individually, they meet to discuss their analyses. Various aspects of the case may be suggested as the major problem, or different attacks upon the problem may be suggested. Each contribution to the discussion is supposed to be a closely reasoned argument, with supporting evidence drawn from the case. The leader keeps the discussion moving along lines that will encourage healthy debate. Since there is no "right" answer to a classic case, the leader does not have a mould into which he must try to force the discussion (other than clear exposition of a reasoned analysis and proposal for action).

Another variation of the case method utilises short cases. These may be only a page or two. All extraneous information is removed, leaving only the information pertinent to one problem.

Still another version uses recordings or films to present the case. This adds the element of drama which can be achieved with acting, sound effects, and other aids to realism. It usually precludes presentation of much background information, however, and thus is closer to the short case than to the classic in this respect. On the other hand, the dramatic scene may portray the emotional overtones of a situation more effectively than is generally possible with written material, particularly if the case problem is essentially one of human relationships.

Finally, there is the Incident Process. This variation was developed by Paul and Faith Pigors of the Massachusetts Institute of Technology. (See the background reading for this session, "The Incident Process".)

Case material, drawn from actual business situations and presented with only a necessary minimum of disguise, seems to have a strong appeal to managers, and the realism of the case material makes many managers relate what they are learning to their own situations. They use their own experience in analysing the cases and derive management principles from the discussion of their analyses.

The case method is, however, time consuming. The task of gathering all the pertinent facts, arranging them, and then putting them into effective writing is a long and often tedious process. Time is also required of the knowledgeable managers who supply the facts.

In addition to the time and talent involved even before the first trainee reads the case, the actual use of the case method is time consuming as well. Because general principles are derived from the detail of numerous specific instances, a fairly large number of cases must be studied. This requires a lengthy programme if real benefits are to be attained. Each session requires time for advance preparation as well as for group discussion of the case.

The "classic" cases have been criticised for being needlessly long, with too much extraneous information. Students, particularly younger ones, may have so much trouble deciding just what is important that the discussion may not lead to useful learning; yet complicated financial, investment, production, or marketing problems frequently cannot be treated without supporting documents and statistical tables that require intensive study. If the inter-relatedness of management functions is the emphasis of the case, a long write-up may be needed to show how decisions in one area affect operations in others.

Short cases limit the depth to which the student can probe, and can be attacked for making everything "too easy". In real life, ask the critics, how many management problem situations arise in which the major problem is self-evident and in which all the necessary evidence is neatly tied up in logical order? What is the value of using cases unless trainees learn to dig beyond the obvious symptoms of trouble for the information they need to diagnose and solve real problems?

This was part of the thinking that led to the Incident Process. Problems come to management's attention as incidents. The job is to decide what information is needed and to find it. The fact-finding phase of the approach is intended to give students practice in hunting for the data they need by thinking and questioning, rather than merely recognising its importance when they read it.

The case study method takes getting used to. Trainees who have not had previous experience with this method can become quite frustrated when they find that there is no "right" answer to the case problem and that there even may be a question as to just what the problem is. "How can I learn to manage," they ask, "if no one is sure of what is wrong or what should be done about it?" Most trainees pass through this stage successfully; they learn eventually that management situations often are ambiguous and that there frequently is no single best solution.

NOTES ON THE CASE STUDY METHOD

by J.D. Hounsell,
Management Development Branch
International Labour Office

Case Study and Simulation

First of all, let us take care to avoid confusion between a case study and a simulation. The two are quite different training techniques. The case study samples real life through incidents or cases for the primary purpose of study. Simulation, role play and the business game deal with real events played out largely for the purpose of providing "controlled" experience. In the case study, the action is about doing something; in a simulation we actually start action. In the case study trainees are witnesses to rather than participants in the events.

Advantages of the Case Study

1. A case study presents a sample of business life in slow motion, so that it may be studied in detail. Trainees learn to get the most out of sometimes limited data by asking effective questions. They develop the habit of taking a greater number of factors into account than usual. The objective diagnosis of causes and alternative solutions broadens participants' understanding and provides an improved guide to action. Learning is likely to occur to the extent that a trainee's colleagues evaluate and reinforce his conclusions and the way in which he arrived at them.

2. Case study analysis and debate, as well as exposure to the experience and opinions of other trainee-managers, help participants to realise that there are several ways of looking at, thinking about and acting in a particular business situation. Thus they are encouraged to develop flexibility in their approaches to organisational problems. They learn to recognise that for most cases, there is no single "right" solution. There may be degrees or shades of right and wrong, but the problem has to be seen as a whole in its total context.

3. The method develops a systematic way of thinking about business issues and managerial decisions. Through examination and diagnosis of situations comparable to their own, participants may be drawn to re-examine their own attitudes and relationships.

4. In the course of studying and making decisions on a number of cases, participants will discover some of the underlying principles of management.

5. Using case studies is a convenient means of exposing participants to a diversity of business situations and problems during a training course.

In sum the case study method accomplishes several objectives of management development programmes:

- it distributes knowledge and facts;

- it improves participants' skills in problem analysis, communication and decision-making;

- it affects attitude formation and particularly brings home to the participant that nothing is absolutely "right" or "wrong" in the field of human behaviour.

Applying the Case Study Method

The case study provides a learning situation which depends on involvement and participation in group discussion for its success. It is essential that those using the method have a thorough knowledge of discussion leading techniques. Discussion should be focused yet free and informal.

Gauging the proper time and the way to draw trainee's attention, now to their own experiences, now to other people's, now to specific issues, now to general principles, is the instructor's most difficult task.   Provided he sees his role as that of a developer, a changer of attitudes, he is not likely to fail.   He must stimulate discussion, but not upset it;   must intervene when he feels it is necessary but not so that members "freeze";   "he must listen to other people's feelings instead of the din of his own".

No two trainees will view a given case in exactly the same way;   although they will generally agree on the existence of certain issues, their interpretations are likely to be very different.   The implication for the case leader is that he cannot be too dogmatic, that there is no one right answer, etc.

Good case discussion also generally requires conscientious preparation by the participants.   Only with a thorough knowledge of the data can the group avoid abstract arguments and concentrate instead on a meticulous consideration of available data.   The accent must be on study, by means of which the participant is able to explore details of motivation and action which he might otherwise ignore.

To select the right case at the right moment the instructor needs a good understanding of his group, for it is primarily the members that he is teaching, not the case.   He should have several cases from which to choose, and they should be suitable for the needs of the group.

THE INCIDENT PROCESS

There are several differences between the Incident Process and other forms of the case method. For one thing, only a bare "incident" is reported to the group. It may involve merely a statement that a foreman saw two workers involved in a dispute and then saw one strike the other. Other information relevant to the incident is known only to the discussion leader. This may include company rules, union agreements, or biographical information about the characters. The group gets this information only by asking for it specifically; if no one is astute enough to ask the proper questions, key information is withheld. On the other hand, the proper question might elicit a copy of the union contract, an organisation chart, or a prepared statement of the limits of authority delegated to the managers involved in the incident. Such hand-outs are given to each member of the group, when and if someone requests the information.

After this fact-finding stage, the group attempts to determine the major issue to be resolved and whether or not minor issues must also be considered. When the issues have been clarified, each member writes his own solution, then joins in a short period of general discussion of all the proposed solutions. Next, those with similar solutions meet to iron out their differences and select a spokesman to argue the merits of their approach in debate with other viewpoints. Finally, the leader reports the "real life" solution. Since the cases in the Incident Process, like most cases, are drawn from actual events, it is possible to report the solution that a management or an arbitrator actually reached.

It has been suggested that the conventional case method has a basic limitation in that it cannot readily reproduce the unfolding quality of actual events. If the student does not perceive and respond to the quality of the process when he thinks about a given case, the case is not real to him and he will therefore not put enough into its discussion to learn much from it.

Paul and Faith Pigors claim that it is virtually impossible to capture the living quality of a case situation by reading about it and that the process of case reporting can be far more illuminating than the product.[1] The Pigors believe that people pick up the idea that change is characteristic of every situation more readily when they re-construct the case orally - by asking questions - than when they first get their information by reading a full length report. In the Incident Process, all the student receives is a thumbnail sketch of a precipitating incident. This is followed by the first spate of questions concerning the WHAT, WHEN, WHERE and HOW of the case - at the time of the incident - and WHO was immediately involved. This questioning leads into full scale discussion and lively analysis because people find it easier to THINK and FEEL that the situation is happening now and that they are taking part in it.

---

[1] Paul and Faith Pigors: Case Method in Human Relations: the incident process (McGraw-Hill, 1961).

CASE STUDY:
UNION PRESIDENT AND WORKS MANAGER

The new Works Manager had originally joined the company about three months previously to design and implement a complete retooling and partial automation of the company's main production lines. Two weeks prior to the date of the conversation noted below, he had accepted the post of Works Manager following a violent disagreement on policy between the previous incumbent and the President of the company.

One hot afternoon, the Works Manager encountered the company's Union President in the local village after work and invited him to have a quiet beer in the local restaurant-tavern. The following conversation ensued after some preliminary non-company small talk.

WM: Joe, in several of our conversations you have emphasised that the company union is generally composed of pretty straight characters with reasonably high ethics and morals ...

UP: Well, we don't pretend to be angels, but they're a pretty straight bunch ... why?

WM: Well, Joe, talking as two chaps off the job ... I'd like to know how you personally justify ... ethically and morally ... the high percentage of idle time amongst the men?

UP: Saw you wandering around making notes ... suppose you found we average about 30-35 per cent idle ... a bit higher in the forge shop ... uh?

WM: Well ... as a matter of fact, the over-all figure is nearer 37 per cent ...

UP: (Took a long and thoughtful pull at his beer and ordered another before replying) ... 37 per cent ... um! ... it's crept up a bit ... Tell me, Shorty ... I suppose you checked on other time losses too? ... suppose you found lost time due to layout and all the other management delays was about 45 per cent of what we left over, didn't you? ...

(WM did a small recalculation in his notebook ... and nodded ...)

WM: Yes Joe ... you're within a percentage point or two ... why?

UP: (After another long and thoughtful pause ...) Well ... I guess that if they can afford to waste about 45 per cent. ... we're not too bad sticking around the 35 per cent mark ... What do you think Shorty? ...

(not to be distributed   INSTRUCTOR'S GUIDE TO
to participants)   UNION PRESIDENT AND WORKS MANAGER

     This case study has been used to stimulate thinking and discussion in the area of labour-management relations. Two of the key points that will normally emerge are:

- the importance of some informal channels of communication;

- the way in which discussion based on facts is usually more productive than discussion based on opinions and assumptions.

     Here are some suggested leading questions:

1. Could somebody explain what this case is all about?

2. What is the actual problem that exists between the Union President and the Works Manager?

3. How would you define the cause of this situation?

4. Describe the type of relations between the Works Manager and the Union President.

5. Are the percentage figures an important element of this case?

6. Why does the Union President call the Works Manager "Shorty"?

WRITING A CASE

Five steps are normally involved:

1. <u>Select the type of problem and the enterprise from which the material will be obtained.</u>

The type of case required will normally determine the kind of enterprise in which to seek the material. Within this range, it is preferable to select an organisation in which the case-writer is already known and accepted, particularly when it may be necessary to dig deep and to obtain confidential data.

There is some evidence that mature students in particular learn more from problem situations in industries <u>other</u> than their own. While they may be more interested and find it easier to deal with a case written about a problem in a familiar environment, students often display 'blind' spots working with such material; consequently, learning is slowed down.

2. <u>Observe and collect the data.</u>

The fundamental need is for objectivity. By the time you start collecting data, you know what you <u>want</u>. Once you get into the collecting process, you will almost certainly find that the facts vary from any preconceived pattern you may have formed. In fact, you may find that the data will not serve as useful teaching material in the area you had envisaged, but could be valuable in another area. Irrespective of such findings, the facts, situations and events must be observed and recorded objectively and as completely as the situation warrants. They must not be forced to fit your anticipations.

A good case is well documented and contains all the information which is available to the executive concerned. Accordingly, the case writer must make detailed notes and collect statistics, operating statements and other exhibits containing information about the organisation he is studying. In some situations the case writer may include some data which, in his opinion, is somewhat irrelevant.

It is, of course, impossible to observe and record a total picture, even if you are on the spot as the events happen. (If you are in this last happy position, try to record as many of the <u>facts</u> as possible immediately afterwards and before the abstraction process commences in your own memory system). The general rule is, within the practical limitation, make notes or collect exhibits of every situation or event bearing on the case and then arrange these in a logical structure and order for examination and selection before writing the case.

3. <u>Write the case.</u>

The sole criteria in selecting what you will or will not use from your observations, and how you will write it up are:

- objectivity;
- the practical usefulness of the product in the envisaged training situation.

Length, structure, detail, method of presentation, literary standards and style, should be subordinated to these criteria.

Within the above, and once you have obtained permission to prepare the case from the appropriate executive, the following notes may assist:

(a) <u>Select the detail:</u> you originally set out to write the case for a particular purpose. The data revealed as you made your observations may have changed your viewpoint. Before you start writing:

- clarify your objective in relation to the particular purpose or purposes for which you wish to use the case;

- decide whether you have actually obtained material for two or more cases, each having different applications. Failure to separate out such cases clearly first in your mind, and then in the write up, may result in presenting a confused picture that produces no clear-cut training result. Remember that in some training situations a series of cases all drawn from one enterprise, allows the 'students' to progress quickly from one aspect to another without wasting time absorbing new background in each segment.

(b) <u>Set the scene quickly</u>: the first few sentences should enable the student to paint his own mental picture of the situation, and of the type of problem involved, in a few broad brush strokes. This should ensure that, as he absorbs each new fact, he can start adding this detail to the right part of his painting.

(c) <u>Write in the past tense</u>: if your case is a useful one, it is likely to be used over a long period.

(d) <u>Decide on disguises</u>: most executives will be reluctant to have the mistakes that they and their colleagues made exposed to others. For ease in writing, however, it is usually better to develop your case to the final draft stage using the real names, places and figures. It is essential that alterations made in the interest of disguise shall not alter the basic facts and relationships. Large changes of scale are particularly dangerous. For similar reasons, changes in the type of industry or product should be avoided unless use of the real one would break the disguise. If such changes are made, the replacements must be selected with great care so that essential relationships are not destroyed.

4.   <u>Clear the case.</u>

Review your observations from time to time with the appropriate executive of the enterprise concerned. Using true names and figures, review the final draft and finalise the question of disguise with him.

5.   <u>Confirm the usefulness of the case as teaching material.</u>

This involves conducting a full-scale discussion of the case in realistic circumstances. For this purpose, a trial with a group of staff members is rarely a good indicator. However, this may be useful as a device before trial in a normal conference. The trial run should be observed carefully for:

- correct visualisation of the broad picture and understanding of the details by students;

- data which could be omitted without reducing effective teaching, or data which should be added (re-clearing the case as required);

- subject matter which should be discussed prior to or following the case;

- improved methods of conducting the case; more, or less time in preparation or discussion, the desirability of syndicate work, the need for charts or diagrams, etc.

Finally, the case writer and case leader (preferably the same person) should prepare "leader's notes" which will guide others who wish to use the material in the future.

QUESTIONS FOR CASE STUDY ANALYSIS

- What is going on here?

- Is there a problem at all?

- What precisely is the problem?

- What has caused it?

- Are we looking at causes or symptoms?

- What are the main issues?

- Why are these issues important?

- Whose problem is it?

- What precisely are his objectives?

- What should he try to do now?

- What possible courses of action are open?

- How realistic is each of the actions/solutions proposed?

- What are their possible effects?

Objective

To give participants the opportunity to prepare a 15-minute discussion

Handout Material

As for Session 10

HANDOUTS I and II, Session 17: The Plywood Factory, The Northern Cement Factory(case studies)

Role Play Exercise selected from Session 15, given to two participants assigned to the Role Play

Background Reading

Recommended Reading

As for Session 10

Special Equipment and Aids

As required by course members

Session Guide 12

Afternoon Study.

16:00   Course members will do individual preparation for Sessions 13, 15 and if time permits, 17 (case study). Two persons will also prepare for Session 14 (role play).

For Session 13:

Each participant should select and prepare a subject for discussion-leading in Session 13. The handouts from Session 10 should help them plan and structure their discussions. Provide assistance to those who need reference material or supplies for simple visual aids.

For Session 15:

Participants should think about the discussion topic planned for this session: "What learning principles are most neglected by management trainers, and why?" and make preparatory notes if necessary.

For Session 17:

Participants should begin studying the cases, The Plywood Factory and The Northern Cement Factory, in preparation for analysis and group discussion the following evening.

For Session 14:

Select two or three persons to prepare for the role play exercise planned for this session (it might balance the study load slightly if the two people nominated as observers for the case study sessions, 17 and 18, were to do this). Issue their briefs for the exercise and give them enough background about the technique and the plans for the session so that they understand and feel confident about the assignment.

Objective

To give as many participants as possible an opportunity to:
- lead and take part in short discussions
- evaluate participation in and leadership of the discussions

Handout Material

Handouts for Session 10 should be available as checklists

Background Reading

Recommended Reading

As for Session 10

Special Equipment and Aids

As required by course members

50 min.	**Session Guide** 13

Select two members to lead the discussions in this session. Remind the whole group that they are expected to take a full part in each discussion, as well as to comment critically on the conduct of the discussion at the end of each. For this, Handout III from Session 10. Discussion Leading Evaluation Sheet, may be useful.

8:30   Begin first discussion

8:50   Comments on first discussion

8:55   Second discussion

9:15   Comments on second discussion

9:20   (The following instructions may be given at the end of Session 14, if preferred.)

Before closing the session, divide the group into four (depending upon the number of participants) small sections which will discuss separately for the first 25 minutes of Session 15. Indicate the rooms in which they are to meet.

For each group, appoint a discussion leader and a reporter; the latter will be the spokesman for the group in the plenary session.

Select a chairman for the plenary discussion in Session 15.

Role Playing

Objective

To discuss and demonstrate the role play method
To give some participants experience in role playing
To discuss the use of role playing in management training

Handout Material

I - Role Playing as Teaching Aid, pp. 7-9
II - Role Play Exercise/Role Briefs (selected by the instructor), pp. 9-16
HANDOUT I, Session 1, Session Evaluation Form

Background Reading

Role Playing, pp. 1-4
Trainer's Notes on Role Playing, p. 5

Recommended Reading

ILO, Man.Dev. Manual 4, Human Relations - Case Studies and Role Playing

Craig and Bittel, Training and Development Handbook, Chapter 11, "Role Playing", by Malcolm E. Shaw

Special Equipment and Aids

None, unless a few props are wanted for the role play, such as a desk and two chairs, a foreman's working coat, an interview report form, pencil and paper, etc.

90 min.	**Session Guide 14**
	Select one of the role play exercises in HANDOUT II, or prepare your own. Assign two or three participants to prepare for this role play <u>in advance</u> (e.g., during Session 12, a preparation period). Each player should receive a written brief for the role he is to play.
9:30	Introduction.
	This is the first methods session based on simulation, where there is an opportunity to learn by doing; to experiment with alternative ways of behaving without incurring the risks of real organisational life; to gain practice in reacting to conflict situations. Role-playing allows for learning by observation, feedback and imitation as well, since observers tend to identify with the characters and become as involved as participants through the follow-up analysis and discussion.
	Explain the technique of role-playing and its purposes. Compare its features with the case study; role-playing can often be introduced in the context of a case study discussion.
9:45	Brief participants on the role play exercise they are about to witness, and suggest what they should especially watch for to discuss in the follow-up period. (This will depend on the concepts which the role play is designed to teach.) If you wish, assign certain members to concentrate on observing particular aspects of the role play.
9:50	Begin role play. It should be performed briskly; if it is dragged out, the attention of participants will lag. If the players have difficulty in taking their roles seriously, stop the role-play and re-explain the technique.
10:15	Stop the role-play. BREAK (at the discretion of the instructor).
10:30	Follow-up analysis and discussion of the role-play should concentrate on how the characters handled the conflict or problem situations. Participants should consider alternatives to the action that was performed – how would <u>they</u> act in this situation? If the discussion warrants it, ask other members to take the roles to demonstrate their views.
10:55	To summarise and conclude, review the technique from the trainer's point of view: when and how role-playing can be used, its advantages and limitations, possible adaptations. Distribute HANDOUT I, Role Playing as a Teaching Aid.
11:10	Ask members to evaluate the session.
11:15	Collect forms and close the session.
	Give instructions for the discussion meetings to be held in the next session if you did not explain the procedure at the end of Session 13.

ROLE PLAYING

Prepared at the
United Nations Institute for Training and Research (UNITAR)[1]

Definition

Role playing is a training technique in which participants assume an identity other than their own, to cope with real or hypothetical problems in human relations and other areas. "Role-fitting" and "role-taking" are other terms sometimes used to describe this process. Though it is a technique often used within the laboratory context, it is a sufficiently independent methodology to warrant separate treatment and analysis. One of the features that makes it such a useful teaching device is indeed that it can be employed in almost any training context, even as an adjunct to a primarily didactic design.

In playing their roles, participants undertake to act out behaviour patterns they believe are characteristic of those roles in specific social situations. For example, two trainees might act out an interview, one taking the role of manager, the other of a subordinate, in which the manager is responsible for evaluating the job performance of the subordinate. Major variables, thus, include the role itself; the role requirements, that is, the specific behaviour patterns the player builds into the role; the social situation presented to the person playing the role; and the participant's own personality as it infuses the role during the playing.

Major Aims

Role playing allows a player to practise reacting in conflict and other stressful situations. Simulation of reality, in this way, eliminates many of the risks and accountability inherent in real life while retaining many other aspects of the interaction. Mistakes can thus be made and observed, and alternative responses tried. In other words, role playing permits experimentation with different ways of behaving in a given situation.[2]

Roles can be selected which are in contrast to the real-life situations of the player so as to provide vicarious experience and widen the insight of the trainee into the real meaning and possible implication of the behaviour of other persons with whom he comes into contact. The social situations which are presented to the participant playing a given role can be varied, to exploit a wide range of reactions which the trainee may believe to be appropriate to the role.

Since the role-playing exercise permits practice in reacting to conflict situations without the risks normally inherent in real organisational life, mistakes can be tolerated.

In addition to the general insight into human interactions made possible by the activity, the trainee can be helped to modify his own behaviour patterns by getting feedback from others who have watched him play a role. When successful, this may open up communication channels and release some of the inhibitions which may otherwise hinder resolution of conflict situations.

---

[1] From a draft manuscript by Sidney Mailick and Nancy A. Bord, "Experience in the US with Newer Techniques for Training Managers", UNITAR, December 1970.

[2] The "instrumented learning" exercises of Prof. B. Bass and others are examples of new "role-taking" approaches.

Design and Methodology

Practically speaking, effective role playing can take place in almost any setting, since no specific physical arrangement or special equipment is required. In fact, very simple, ordinary materials can be used to simulate a real-life situation.

The problems that are used should, of course, be relevant to the participants in the group, so that motivation to learn will be generated from the members themselves. Although the development of roles and situations may take many forms, either of two approaches is generally used:

Structured role playing: In this type, a leader selects both the situation and the roles to be enacted, and specifies the goals of the activity. This type of pre-planned role playing provides, in some cases, very elaborate written materials that describe the roles and situation, and elicit complex responses from the observers. In more simple cases, if, for example, the goal for the group is to study different leadership patterns, the trainer might assume the role of the leader in the role-play, and orally assign the other roles.

A variation of this approach consists of having the role playing planned in advance by members of the group itself rather than by the leader. This would be appropriate when trying to communicate information, setting and studying a social problem, or interpreting a report. The simulated situation is presented to the group first, followed by the enactment. The leader or group planning the exercise may determine the degree of spontaneity desired and adjust how much the players should or should not be told in advance.

Spontaneous role playing: This approach relies on the problem situation arising from the group discussion, without advance planning by the group or leader. In this instance, the enactment itself serves as the "briefing" to the group on the problem and situation.

Both structured and spontaneous role playing relate to learning through (a) doing, (b) imitation, (c) observation and feedback, and (d) analysis. As is the case with the T-group, role playing represents a form of experiential learning.

In addition to these two approaches, there are also two major orientations to role playing. The two orientations are not confined to either of the two conceptual approaches but work within both a structured and unstructured framework, and involve the focus on either a situation-centred or human relations-centred problem.

In a situation-centred problem, the roles of the actors are defined, and the situation is left open to allow the group the freedom to explore a problem. The second orientation focuses on how individuals function; therefore, the roles are left more flexible and the situation is well defined. The emphasis in both orientations and approaches is to analyse, evaluate, and suggest improvement in the interaction skills of participants.

A role-playing session begins with a preparation period during which the participants and the audience are given as much information, written or oral, as necessary to create a reality situation. Players must be given time to fix their characters in their minds and the audience is usually oriented to what they are to watch for.

The simple role-playing design calls for the enactment of the role playing, followed by discussion. The analysis and discussion centre around criticising the character's handling and reaction to the conflict situation. In order to maintain the illusion and the low-pressure atmosphere, role names rather than real names are usually used. The audience can be divided into listening or watching sections or as special observers, who are chosen in advance, to form a panel to discuss the role playing. In addition, devices such as tape-recorders and closed circuit television are, at times, used to refer back to key incidents during evaluation sessions which follow a role-playing scene.

The advantages of "single-group" role playing before an audience are that the audience can observe and discuss the details of a particular action, the participants can benefit from the observers' comments as they are often unaware of the effect of their actions on others and, the observers can develop a sensitivity to the feelings of the participants. Another technique, referred to as "multiple role-playing", divides the entire participant group into role-playing subgroups and everyone role plays simultaneously. The advantages of this method are that it maximises opportunities for all group members to try out new attitudes and behaviours; it provides data from each subgroup so that comparisons between subgroups are possible; and it gets all group members involved in a problem and may thus more quickly dispel feelings of shyness and self-consciousness. Following multiple role playing, there is a discussion of mutual experiences led by the trainer.

Assessment of Effectiveness

Whatever the particular variation used, much of the effectiveness of role playing as a training technique is dependent upon the group's initial understanding and acceptance of the concept and utility of role playing as well as effective execution of the role playing itself. This requires a trained leader who can control the group interaction. The leader must also provide constant stimulation for the group to evaluate its behaviour. He must know when to interrupt or stop the role playing, where to ask questions, who should play a particular role, how to summarise the remarks and issues brought out in the role playing, and how to maintain a proper tempo to prevent boredom and yet still allow the analysis to be thorough. Conducting a role-playing session requires a high level of discussion leadership. The trainer needs to be able to personally demonstrate as well as to tell what and how things should be done. Finally, it is the task of the trainer to choose or advise about the situations which are to be acted out and these situations generally need to be planned anew for each new role-playing group.

Because role playing is, in a sense, a case study in action, one way of looking at effectiveness is to compare the two. A research study which compared the particular benefits of role playing with the case study as discrete training mechanisms concluded that each technique may provide a number of meaningfully different experiences.[1] (refer following page) For example, the following distinctions were suggested as representative of the kinds of training experiences which exposure to one method as compared with the other might be expected to provide:

Case Study	Role Play
1. Presents a problem for discussion.	1. Places a problem in a life-like setting.
2. The problem is derived from previous events.	2. The problem involves ongoing processes.
3. The problem typically involves others.	3. The problem typically involves the participants themselves.
4. Emotional and attitudinal aspects are dealt with in an intellectual frame of reference.	4. Emotional and attitudinal aspects are dealt with in a similar frame of reference.
5. Emphasises the importance of facts.	5. Emphasises the importance of feelings.
6. Discussion is typically from a psychological position "outside" of the problem situation.	6. Participants are psychologically "inside" the problem situation.
7. Facilitates intellectual involvement.	7. Makes for emotional involvement.
8. Furnishes practice in analysis of problems.	8. Provides practice in interpersonal skills.
9. Provides for development of ideas and hypotheses.	9. Provides for testing ideas and hypotheses.
10. Trains in the exercise of judgment.	10. Trains in emotional control.
11. Defines action or solution.	11. Provides for execution of action or solution.
12. Consequences of action are usually undetermined.	12. Allows continuous feedback.

The data suggested that role-playing procedures quite effectively perform functions of examining feelings and provide opportunities for skill practice in a realistic manner. Thus, while new principles and concepts can be provided to the trainees by means of such information-giving procedures as lectures, reading, etc., role playing of a problem can then be used to bring about the "experiencing" of the feelings involved as well as furnishing opportunities for continued skill practice. In addition, in post-play discussion of the role playing or in the feedback period, insight can be given into the process of conceptualisation of the problem-solving process.

There are, however, a number of drawbacks to the method, which may or may not be serious depending on the situation:

1. Much of its effectiveness depends on the skill of the leader, the importance of whose role has been indicated earlier. In the US, role playing has become such a popular device at meetings and educational sessions of a wide variety, that many groups use it without much serious planning or leadership; under these circumstances it tends to become merely a way for a group to ventilate its feelings.

2. Role playing is time consuming, and necessarily restricts the number and complexity of problems that can be dealt with at one time.

3. Some feel that it is too artificial, resulting in little transfer of behaviour change to real situations, and that the very theatricality that makes it engrossing for participants may lead them to forget the problem they are supposed to be dealing with.

4. On the other hand, if the problems used lack sufficient conflict or variety, participants may find it boring.

5. Of considerable significance is the place of spontaneity in the culture of the community or group concerned; it is much more likely to be successful if the group is accustomed to the informal, game-like atmosphere required.

There have been efforts at improving real-life transfer by having individuals who are involved in a real-life conflict situation undertake role playing together, often playing each other's roles. In the ideal case, there can be startling improvements in the resolution of conflict between members of subgroups in organisational settings.

In general, while the above-mentioned criticisms can and have been made regarding the effectiveness of role playing as a management training technique, general opinion would tend to indicate that the advantages and positive factors associated with role playing far outweigh the negative ones, provided that the technique is properly used and directed.

---

[1] Allen R. Solem, "Human Relations Training: A Comparison of Case Study and Role Playing", Personnel Administration, September 1960, pp. 29-37.

TRAINER'S NOTES ON ROLE PLAYING

From the trainer's point of view the first role playing is crucial. It is at this time that the group's attitudes to the technique will be determined and their future performance as role players will be settled. The role-playing session should start by the trainer briefing all the participants. He should outline the situation that is to be the basis of the role playing and he should give a concise description of the characters involved in the situation. This being done, the group then acts out the situation making up their lines as they go along. At the end of the scene the actors and the audience discuss what has taken place during the scene, the motivations of the people involved and why the scene developed as it did.

In a role-playing situation that is effectively handled not only the actors but also the audience become involved and this involvement often carries over to the discussion thereby enriching and enlightening it.

If the trainer wishes to involve the audience further he may give members of the audience definite tasks to carry out during the scene. For instance, one member of the audience may be required to note the gestures and mannerisms of the actors, another may be briefed to listen for significant remarks and yet another may be asked to try and spot focal points of the drama. Another useful way of involving the audience is to ask certain members of the audience to act as under-studies or prompts for the actors.

Role playing can be elaborated by the use of several associated techniques. Most obvious is role reversal, the change of character from, for instance, shop steward to supervisor. This can be further elaborated so that roles are changed several times during the scene thus providing the actors with different viewpoints from which to observe and become involved in an on-going sequence of events. If required a scene can be repeated several times with the actors changing roles at the completion of each scene.

The main advantages of role playing are:

1. Role playing provides an opportunity for developing insight into what is happening when it is happening.

2. Role playing emphasises the importance that feelings and emotions play in many problems, especially problems associated with human relations.

3. Role playing enables the manager or supervisor to see a situation from a perspective different to his own.

4. Role playing, successfully handled, develops the interest of the learner, thereby providing a dynamic situation during the course of which attitudes can be modified and new attitudes developed.

ROLE PLAYING AS TEACHING AID

by R.B. Macdonald,
Management Development Branch
International Labour Office

When developing or revising your training programme you may ask yourself:
"Which method or technique or aid should I use to illuminate my ideas on
organisational behaviour, or to drive home controversial principles of human
relations on the work site?" Without doubt you will use the lecture method to
explain the various principles involving people on the job. You may even wish
to supplement your lectures and class participation by showing a well chosen film
on the subject in question. Yet you may still find something missing from your
programme. Perhaps the class has remained somewhat detached from the whole
session because they have not become adequately involved in the teaching process.
Furthermore, the very nature of human relations, i.e. the value judgments involved,
tend to make it difficult for even the most effective educator to get some of the
more abstract principles and ideas across to the class.

Some business educators have solved this problem by supplementing their
lectures, discussions and films by adding role playing sessions to their programmes. It is important to note in passing that in using role playing as a
tool, emphasis should be placed on supplementing other techniques and methods at
your disposal. Role playing is not an end in itself.

What is role playing, and how can it help you in your teaching task?

As the name implies, role playing is simply a teaching situation whereby
participants act out brief roles, a process somewhat akin to the short stage skit
familiar to all of us. There is one difference however; for the purpose of
business education, role players do not follow detailed scripts. Rather, they
are given brief written situations or problems with enough supporting facts about
the personalities to be portrayed to be able to project themselves into the particular roles. It might be worth while mentioning at this point that most role
players partly depict themselves in the given environment without realising it.
And with this in mind you may be interested to learn that role playing got its
start with psychotherapy. It was first used by psychiatrists to induce patients
to act out past situations, thereby helping to produce catharsis and to develop
in the patient a deeper insight to his basic personality problems.[1]

Almost everyone agrees with the principle that the ability to get along with
people is a personality trait which is needed to be successful in business — at
least in the organisational sense. But you have seen, I am sure, the supervisor
who has given lip-service to this most important principle, yet who at the same
time feels that he has nothing to improve in his relations with his subordinates
and therefore he is excluded from the need to perfect himself in this most difficult function. Role playing can help correct this, since once the supervisor is
actively engaged in a role playing session, he should soon notice where improvements could be made. One of the greatest difficulties in getting supervisors to
participate in role-playing sessions is in convincing them that role playing is
not a theatrical experience but that it is designed to help them become better in
their jobs as supervisors. You should always emphasise that point and explain
to the participants that they should act as natural as possible.

It is true that role playing will not change a person's basic personality.
Nevertheless with proper guidance from the instructor, it can help a timid supervisor learn how to be more confident in himself, or it can help an overly dogmatic executive to realise where he might improve his personal relations with
others. And if nothing else, role playing can be used as a medium to promote
animation in a class which otherwise would remain dull and uninteresting. You
will soon see in using role playing as a teaching aid that it has a tendency,
because of its dramatic personal aspect, to involve actors, observers and
instructors alike.

---

[1] J.L. Moreno: Who Shall Survive (Beacon House, Inc. Beacon, New York, 1953).

In planning for a role playing session you should keep clearly in mind the basic principle, the problem to be covered or the message to get across to the others. Keep this idea foremost in your mind when you develop the roles for specific participants. Try to reflect a natural situation common to all participants - role players and observers alike. When you prepare your plan it is important to start from the known, as far as the participants are concerned, and proceed to the unknown - a most important principle in teaching. Use terms, names, localities familiar to each and every participant. For instance, if you were to use the role playing technique to teach managers how to chair conferences when some of the participants may not have participated in conferences, you might find it appropriate to start first with simple roles involving committee meetings. After one or two sessions you could then advance to the more complex and difficult conference situations.

You will not want to use role playing until you have had a very comprehensive discussion of the issues to be covered. You will want to explain what role playing is and what it is not. For example, before having a role-playing session on employee evaluation you should spend ample time discussing the primary principles behind the need for and use of employee evaluation. You may wish to outline to the class (or better still to have the class outline briefly) what the ideal employee evaluation situation involves.

Roles should be designed so that the session of role playing itself lasts only 15-20 minutes at the most. Participants must be given ample time to prepare for their roles and observers should be given instructions on what to look for. At the start of your sessions you may find it helpful to emphasise the "total participation" aspect of role playing, i.e. observers must understand that they are not just passive onlookers who sit and watch but that they too will be required to participate in the final critique.

Another important factor to keep in mind is the physical arrangements of the room where the sessions are to be held. You should strive for an informal friendly atmosphere. It has been found that the best arrangement of chairs assures that all participants face each other as close together as possible for comfort. A blackboard should be placed in such a way that it is clearly visible by all present, as this will permit you to have basic instructions or information in view at all times. Chairs or desks for those who play the roles should be set in the front of or slightly to the side of the group.

At one time or another all of us have participated in role playing, perhaps without realising it. For instance, when you applied for your first important job you had in your mind an idea of how you, the applicant, should act. You then tried to play this role, or in other words to adjust your personality to correspond with the image in your mind. You certainly tried to use your most convincing manners. If you did not get the job you may have chided yourself for the improper (in your mind) response to the interviewer. What you did was to undergo a self-analysis of your performance during the interview - of the role played by you. There are two strong objections to this type of role playing - it is uncontrolled and the only evaluation is through self evaluation, at its best most misleading. Many more examples could be given of how we play roles in everyday life.

Role playing as used by business educators helps correct this because it permits controlled situations and objective analysis or evaluation by others. Participants should have no fear of committing errors. Certainly in some situations the instructor may intentionally ask the players to commit errors in order to clarify a point through comparison with the correct action.

A number of role-playing situations are available. These range from the simple single role as used to teach sales clerks how to sell merchandise to the multiple complex role session where supervisors learn to deal with group problems. Roles can be reversed to give everyone the chance to see the other person's side of the story. One time Bill can play the role of Jack the supervisor who is counselling his subordinate. Then Jack and Bill can change roles. The result can be quite edifying for players and other participants in the session.

After each short role-playing session it is important to hold a critique. This is when the observers actively participate. To emphasise a point you may want one or two of the observers to play the role themselves.

But role playing is not suitable for each and every teaching situation. You will find that it cannot be used with much success to teach purely technical subjects. It can hardly be used to teach mathematics, chemistry or geography, for example. The time-honoured lecture method supplemented by audio-visual aids perhaps remains best in those disciplines.

Finally, the results obtained in using role playing as a teaching aid are almost always directly proportional to the time and effort invested by the instructor in planning and developing his sessions.

ROLE PLAY EXERCISES[1]

Role-Playing Exercise No. 1

Brief for John McKay

You are John McKay and you are a centre lathe turner employed by a well-known engineering company. Apart from three-and-a-half years in the Royal Navy all your working life has been spent with the company. You started as an apprentice in 1925 and are now 48 years old.

The company is a good employer and you like your job. You have the reputation of being the best turner in the works and you are usually given the most difficult and responsible jobs to do. For skill and ability you know you are among the most highly rated hourly employees in the company.

You are not too popular with your work mates and it is with some reluctance that you were persuaded to join the Union. In the main you consider them to be a clock watching, snivelling lot with little interest in their jobs or the company.

Jack Hardy is your foreman and you have known him from your apprenticeship days. You think a lot of him; he was a good craftsman and always conscientious and reliable as a mate. You feel that he has merited his promotion and is doing a good job. On the other hand you dislike Simmons, your chargehand, whom you consider two-faced and a tale carrier. He was a trouble maker as a shop steward and has not improved as a chargehand. He was also, in your opinion, a very moderate craftsman. You feel annoyed that you should have to take orders from him.

This clocking-in business annoys you. Why should you, as a first-class craftsman, be treated in just the same manner and subjected to the same discipline as a new start? You feel the firm should in some way recognise the service and ability of their best men. Clocking offends your sense of dignity as a craftsman.

You have had several arguments with Simmons about time keeping and this morning as well as being late you lost your temper with him. In any case you feel that if you lose a quarter of an hour it is your loss and not his, and that you will do much more work than those who clock in before time but don't get their machines running until 7.40 a.m.

Jack Hardy has sent for you. What are you going to say to him? Will it be wise to tell him you have to take your wife to the flourishing little shop you have set up on the other side of the town? Or will you leave him to take action?

---

[1] Extracted from Human Relations - Case Studies and Role Playing, Man. Dev. Manual 4 (Geneva, ILO). Case studies and role-playing exercises made available to the ILO by the Management and Supervisory Training Section of the Bristol Aeroplane Technical College.

Role-Playing Exercise No. 1

Brief for Jack Hardy

You are foreman of the Machine Shop, a post you have held for almost ten years. All your working life has been spent with the firm; you started as an apprentice in 1926. The Machine Shop is an important section of the company, vitally affecting the work programmes of all other departments. The men in the shop are a good crowd, loyal, conscientious and turning out a good volume of work of pretty high quality. While a number of the men are not time-served apprentices they have had many years of experience with the company and are "green card" members of the AEU. While the company will not accept the principle of a "closed shop", there is 100 per cent union organisation.

John McKay is one of your problems. You and he were apprentices together and from the start he possessed marked mechanical ability and today is really an exceptional tradesman. He is the highest-rated man in the shop and had he any ambition in that direction might have been foreman. You have always found him loyal, co-operative and obedient. He is also absolutely trustworthy about his work, the quality of which is of the highest standard. He can best be described as having "green fingers" and is at his best when a job is a challenge to his initiative and ability.

However, John dislikes taking orders from anyone but you. He has a naturally independent nature and is rather quick tempered. He and his charge-hand, George Simmons, have never co-operated and there is obvious mutual dislike. Incidentally, McKay caused some trouble during the strike by refusing to come out and, although still a union member, has let it be known that this is only under compulsion. Simmons, on the other hand, was shop steward prior to his promotion.

Simmons has again reported to you that McKay is consistently late in the mornings and upon being warned has been abusive. He has strongly recommended that disciplinary action should be taken. He adds that some of the better young turners are already tending to imitate both McKay's attitude and his unpunctual habits.

You have sent for McKay to come up to your office. While you are waiting for him you read a memorandum from the Chief Engineer to the effect that a proto-type will be in the shops within the next two weeks. This will involve a great deal of turning work which, until jigged up, will be of an extremely difficult nature. As you reflect on this information there is a knock at the door. McKay is waiting to see you. What are you going to do?

Role-Playing Exercise No. 2

The Case of the Karbits Company Limited

The Karbits Company is an organisation specialising in the manufacture of accessories for the motor car, motor cycle and caravan trade.

The case involves John Marsh, the young General Manager of the subsidiary company in the West Midlands.

The branch factory employs about 400 people; 300 male, semi-skilled press hands, welders, drop-forging hands and simple assembly fitters. There are 30 skilled men engaged in tool room and maintenance work. The rest are male and female office workers. The family tree of the company is as follows:

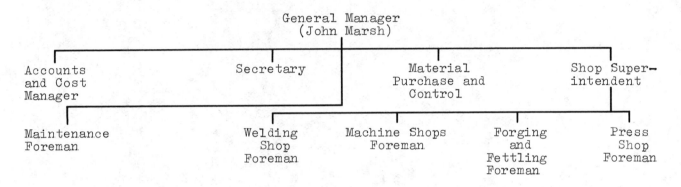

Marsh was appointed manager of the factory in March 1956 and was then aged 29. During the ensuing period the labour force has been raised from 180 to its present figure. Production has trebled but much of this is due to the introduction of the latest press tool, welding and forging plant.

Individual incentives based on measured work — standard minute performances — have been introduced and have contributed to the success of the organisation. In March 1957 an additional monthly departmental bonus system was introduced which was related to set target figures. These were prominently displayed barometer-fashion in each shop. An interesting innovation was that of paying a monthly bonus to Departmental Foremen based on the above scheme.

At the end of each month Marsh meets all his foremen and staff and examines in detail their production figures. This is in no sense a disciplinary meeting but rather tends to an attitude of "how can we do better?" The foreman of the Press Shop, Bob Keen, has been the most successful since the introduction of the Staff Bonus Scheme. He is constantly improvising and adapting his equipment and in this he works very well with the Maintenance Foreman, Bill Sharpe. Marsh thinks he has observed signs of unrest — jealousy perhaps — amongst the other foremen but has not been able to pin it down. However, this month, Keen has again made the greatest increase and at the monthly meeting March read out a letter from the Managing Director of the parent company, congratulating all on their efforts but specifically mentioning Keen by name.

After the letter had been read there was a silence and then Tom Mann, Machine Shop Foreman — a good, earnest, dependable type of person — expostulated with some anger, "We could do the same if we flouted factory regulations and ignored safety precautions." Marsh questioned this statement and was really surprised to find that Mann was supported by the other three foremen. Further, they accused Keen and Sharpe of conniving at these practices and challenged Marsh to "go and see for himself".

Accompanied by the Shops Superintendent, Marsh has visited the Press Shop and found that press guards are not being properly used and that pulleys have been changed to give higher speeds. The operatives admit altering the guards to earn more piecework and justify themselves by saying "Well, Bob Keen knew all about it".

Marsh is very perturbed.   He has always found Keen to be one of his most energetic and successful foremen and consequently there has been little direct intrusion in the administration of his department.   On checking accident rates he finds that the Press Shop has the highest figure in the works.   The Shop Superintendent is even more worried, for as he says: "If the Factory Inspector had seen what has been done we would be in real trouble."

Marsh has asked Keen and Sharpe to come up to his office.   What action should he take?

Role-Playing Exercise No. 3

The Case of Harry Peters

The Problem

News spread rapidly through the factory some days ago that a large airliner, which we manufacture, almost came to grief with a full load of passengers. A Class 1 component in the flying control system had failed just before take-off, but fortunately not before the pilot had run out of runway. Tragedy was very narrowly averted.

An investigation into the fractured component showed that it had failed because of fatigue. It should not have done. Originally fatigue tests on this type of material had proved the properties were more than equal to the task. Further investigation into the offending component showed that the original cast from which it was made was at fault. The batch number of the component was taken, and an instruction issued to ground all aircraft having components made from the same batch of material.

Examination of Inspection Records indicated that ten such batch numbers existed, and showed the ten aircraft in which they were installed.

Indications were that ten aircraft would be grounded, the components removed and replaced.

But the investigation had triggered off an incident in the memory of Harry Peters, the inspector who had finally passed the components in the machine shop just over a year ago. Not ten, but thirty such components had been passed together. Ten of them had been made from each of three different batches of material, and the operator had failed to keep them separate for batch numbering. They were inseparably mixed - all thirty of them.

As always, the Production Foreman had been in desperate need of them and had pointed out to Peters that these parts were perfect in every respect, worth £600 and short of nothing but a number.

Peters had recently been transferred from Production to Inspection and was unfortunately receptive to the argument. He verified the accuracy of the components, had them crack detected, divided them into three groups of ten, <u>used his discretion and allocated one of the three batch numbers to each group.</u>

Now that the rogue batch had been discovered Peters was faced with two alternatives:

1. To remain silent.

2. To confess that he had used "discretion" when it was <u>not</u> his to use.

If he remained silent, at least some of the grounded aircraft would have sound components. <u>What was worse, certainly some of the other twenty flying aircraft would have components belonging to the rogue batch - and these could be expected to fail tragically.</u> A brief chat with a mathematician friend revealed that there was only one chance in 30,045,015 of the ten components being correctly numbered in these circumstances.

If he confessed, not ten but thirty aircraft would have to be grounded and penalties met by the company for loss of revenue on all of them, to say nothing of the cost of twenty new components <u>more than was necessary</u>, had each one carried the correct batch number.

A chat with the Production Foreman revealed that "he couldn't remember the incident at all".

Harry Peters made his decision. He confessed to Dick Burte, the Foreman Inspector, last night at 5.25 p.m. Dick Burte sprang into action to pass the information on to the Chief Inspector so that the 20 additional aircraft could be grounded. Peters was told to report to him at 8.30 a.m. the following morning.

It is 8.30 a.m.

Role-Playing Exercise No. 3

Brief for Dick Burte

You are Dick Burte and you are Foreman Inspector in the Machine Shop. You have been involved in machine shop work in this aircraft factory for twenty years, and have been a foreman on Inspection for eight years.

When Harry Peters came over to your staff from Production eighteen months ago you were very pleased indeed. You had known him ever since he started for the firm fifteen years ago, and you had nothing but respect for him as a worker and as a man.

Recently you heard of an aircraft narrowly averting tragedy because of the failure of a flying-control component - a Class 1 part. You were very concerned about it until yesterday morning when the laboratory was able to confirm that the material itself was at fault, and that no blame fell on the manufacture of the part. It was obvious that all aircraft carrying the same batch of components would be grounded.

The records were consulted and the Chief Inspector advised that there were ten aircraft involved, the serial numbers of which were supplied.

Then came the shock. At 5.25 p.m. yesterday Harry Peters came timidly into your office and confessed that just over a year ago he had accepted as satisfactory thirty of these Class 1 parts when they were, in fact, three different batches all mixed inseparably together. The components were identical, but made of three different casts and three different batches of material.

He pointed out to you that it was impossible to tell which of the components belonged to each batch but he had inspected them, had them crack-detected and split them up into three groups of ten. To each group he had allocated one of the three batch numbers.

You grasped the point immediately. It was impossible to tell which of the other twenty-nine components originated from the defective cast. All thirty aircraft had to be grounded. Peters was told to report to you at 8.30 a.m. in the morning and you set the wheels in motion to avert further failure.

Last evening you gave the whole thing a lot of thought. You have met the problem of mixed batches before and experienced the inevitable fuss which followed. You know that such a decision was not even within your terms of reference, let alone those of Peters, and you know he must be called to answer for what virtually is an inspection failure. He should not have used discretion in this matter because discretion is not his to use. Only the Chief Inspector or his Deputy is allowed discretion, and this decision should have been theirs.

You intend to deal with it in as firm a manner as you think necessary, but knowing this man's almost uncanny appreciation of machine shop practice you know it will have to be handled with some delicacy. Furthermore, you are not at all sure who failed in this - you or him. It was clearly your duty to enlighten him on inspection procedure, but you had rather assumed that he would know all that. It now occurs to you that he had no way of knowing, for whilst he had been a brilliant operator his inspection experience was only four months at that time. Since then he has developed into a first-class inspector.

You face this man with this on your mind. You are also aware that he was probably technically equipped as well as anyone could be to take such a decision and that he is going to be very upset at any implications to the contrary. He is not a violent man, but he is sincere and sensitive.

The news had spread very quickly, and Peters had taken it very much to heart. You know that the decision he took was within his rights as far as he knew at that time. Should he be discharged?

In the back of your mind you wonder whether Peters did this out of sympathy for one of his ex-colleagues on Production, and whilst you hesitate to believe it, it is a factor you must consider and eliminate.

You see him approaching your office, and for the first time in your experience of him he looks harrassed.

Deal with him.

Role-Playing Exercise No. 3

Brief for Harry Peters

Fifteen years ago when you first walked into the machine shop you felt the great thrill of realisation of your ambition. You had always been a calm, unruffled type, and you tackled your apprenticeship in just that way. Your interest in machine shop work seemed to make it all easy for you, and you quickly grasped all of the techniques. You have always got along well with people, and throughout your very successful career on a wide variety of machines you have always been willing to help others who were less gifted.

You welcomed the opportunity to go into Inspection 18 months ago, for whilst you were aware that it would mean finding faults with the work of your ex-colleagues, you rather felt they would not mind that from you. You also had a strong sense of vocation for Inspection, believing that the respect which your old colleagues held for you would make them think twice before submitting faulty work for your inspection, and had hoped in your own quiet way to improve the quality of machine shop work in general.

When you had been on Inspection four months, a young operator brought thirty identical components for final inspection. He had made them from three different batches of material, and had got them mixed together. They were Class 1 components which should have been kept separate for batch numbering, but now it was too late. You were suitably severe in dealing with the young operator – but you felt the problem was yours to deal with. You thought about it through the lunch time, and decided that it would not be necessary to worry your foreman with it. After all – what could he do about it? He could not separate them into their right batches any more than you could, and as the Production Foreman had said, it seemed a piece of folly to scrap thirty perfectly satisfactory components because of a mere batch number. The thing that mattered was, were they right or wrong?

You had satisfied yourself that they were correct to drawing and you had sent them for crack detection and found them defect free. Here were thirty components. Perfect – and worth £600. All they were short of was a number. Certainly they had to have a number – and any one of three could have applied. You decided to use your discretion and split them into three groups of ten, allocating one of the numbers from each card to each group.

The components went on their way and you forgot about the job until yesterday when you heard that one of the components had failed on an airliner and that all aircraft carrying components of the same batch were to be grounded for fear of tragic failure.

You froze when you realised that this was one of the thirty components concerned with the mixed batches, for you knew that the numbers you had allocated meant nothing. To be safe, aircraft carrying components belonging to any one of three batches had to be grounded – and that meant thirty money-spinning airliners. There would be compensations involved, and you dreaded to think of personal consequences.

But if you said nothing there would be failures in flight and hundreds of lives lost. That was clear, for these were vital flying-control components and there could be no doubt that all of the rogue batch would fail – and shortly! The chances of the right ten aircraft being grounded were so slim that it was not worth hoping for. When you talked to the Production Foreman he "couldn't remember a thing about it".

You decided to confess yesterday at 5.25 p.m. and the Foreman Inspector, Dick Burte, had hurled himself at the phone yelling to you to see him at 8.30 a.m. in the morning.

It is now 8.30 a.m. You tossed and turned all last night. You feel every eye in the shop burning holes in your back as you walk toward Burte's office. You are not a violent man, but for the sake of your good name you propose to do everything you can to defend yourself. Your big point is going to be that you had sufficient know-how to make your own mind up on this, and no matter who had been consulted he would have arrived at the same conclusion.

You see Dick Burte's face frowning through the office window, and you realise you are about to endure criticism for the first time in your life. You wonder how long your inspection career is going to last. In fact - you have already considered throwing it in, and at the last resort you are prepared to do just that.

Now, in you go - and <u>have</u> a go.

Objective

To give members an opportunity to work in small groups, discuss a topic and present their conclusions at a plenary session

Handout Material

As reference, any handout material or personal notes made during Sessions 2 or 3

HANDOUT I, Session 1, Session Evaluation Form

Background Reading

As for Session 10

Recommended Reading

As for Session 10

Special Equipment and Aids

Meeting rooms for the four discussion groups

A chalkboard or flip chart should be available in each room

45 min.	**Session Guide** 15
11:30	Discussion sections meet in their rooms for a 25-minute discussion of the topic:
	"What learning principles are most neglected by management trainers, and why?"
	Each group has a discussion leader and a reporter, assigned during Session 13. The members should bear in mind that they are expected to bring some conclusions from their discussion to the plenary session. The reporter and/or the leader should attempt to summarise the group's ideas at various points in the discussion.
11:55	Participants return to the main course room and reporters present the conclusions of their groups. A general discussion should follow, under the leadership of the chairman nominated in Session 13.
12:15	Summarise this experience and ask members to evaluate the session.
	Collect evaluation forms and close the session.

Objective

To acquaint members with the business game technique through explanation, discussion and actual practice in playing a game

Handout Material

I - Business Game: Ilo Control - Instructions for Participants, pp. 15-16

II - Ilo Control: Decision Sheet (two per participant), p. 17

HANDOUT I, Session 1, Session Evaluation Form

Background Reading

The Management Game, pp. 1-5

Technical Notes on the Use of Business Games, pp. 7-13

Business Game: Ilo Control - Instructions for the Umpire, pp. 19-22

Recommended Reading

Craig and Bittel, Training and Development Handbook, Chapter 14, "Management Games", by C.J. Craft. Includes bibliography

ILO, Man.Dev. Manual 27, An Introduction to Business Games

Graham and Grey, Business Games Handbook

Special Equipment and Aids

Chalkboard and chalk, graph paper, slide rules (desirable but not essential), notepaper, pencils

150 min.	**Session Guide** 16
	The time available for this session is only sufficient to allow participants a brief glimpse at what business games involve, since most business games take several hours minimum to complete. You may wish to play only a part of the one-hour game scheduled below, and take more time to explain gaming techniques.
	Optional: Appoint an observer who reports his observations to the group during the evaluation and discussion period which follows the game.
	On meeting a game for the first time, it is advisable for the umpire to have a practice run with a few colleagues before using the game with students.
14:00	Introduce the business game by differentiating it from other training techniques, especially from decision-making in a case study and from role-play simulation.
	Explain how gaming became a management training technique. Describe the main characteristics of a management game and its purposes.
14:15	HAND OUT a copy of Instructions for Participants and the Decision Sheet for Ilo Control to each member. Go over these as outlined in the Instructions for the Umpire.
14:30	Once you are sure that all participants understand what is expected, announce the start of the game.
15:30	End of game, and BREAK.
15:45	Carry out the evaluation session according to Instructions for the Umpire.
16:15	Continue with your earlier description of the business game, explaining in greater detail:
	- the types of games, their variations;
	- the job of the instructor;
	- the evaluation discussion;
	- the problem of team organisation and co-operation on more complex games;
	- the uses, advantages and limitations of business games.
	See "Assessment of Effectiveness" in the background reading, The Management Game.
16:40	Summarise the key points concerning simulation techniques such as the business game:
	- allows the student to actively participate in the learning process;
	- brings the classroom closer to practice;
	- requires (in some games) teamwork;
	- provides immediate feedback.
	Ask members to evaluate the session.
16:45	Collect evaluation forms and close the session.

THE MANAGEMENT GAME

Prepared at the United Nations Institute for
Training and Research (UNITAR)[1]

Definition

This is a training technique in which participants, grouped into teams, consider a sequence of problems and organise themselves to make decisions. It is a form of simulation, which may be defined as a sequential decision-making exercise structured around a hypothetical model of an organisation's operations, in which participants assume roles in managing the simulated operations. Its most crucial aspect is the attempt to reproduce the social-psychological and economic dynamics of organisational behaviour in an artificial setting.

Using a set of relationships built into a skeletal model of an organisation, the decisions which are made by the participants are processed to produce a series of hypothetical actions in the form of performance reports. The decisions and reports on their results pertain to a specific time period, which may be a day, a month, a quarter, or a year.

Most games concentrate on general management principles, such as long-range planning, decision making, and effective utilisation of time, men and materials. Other games aim at teaching very specific skills and techniques, particularly those games which are built around the production, marketing and financial functions.

There are many different management games in existence; the variety of games and the many different ways they are used indicate the flexibility of this training tool. Various industrial, military, educational, governmental and professional organisations have developed their own games and other organisations use existing games. Management games are also used in colleges and universities and in various departments of the military.

Games can be incorporated into training courses in many ways. They can be used at the beginning of training courses as an orientation device. They can be used more than once, perhaps before and after a particular management principle or technique has been discussed. However, for greater effectiveness, games should be used only with a clear understanding of the objectives to be attained.

Games may be differentiated according to the level of management for which decision making is simulated. By and large, most general games are also top management games, whereas functional games are more likely to aim at middle management and the more specialised sub-functional games aim at the middle and junior management levels. In some games, each team may be given freedom to decide exactly what parts of the management structure of the organisation the team should include, when such discretion is in line with the purpose of the game.

Major Aims

The purpose of management games is to increase a person's understanding of (1) specific organisational problems (marketing, production, etc.); (2) the inter-relatedness of the functions and parts of an organisation and its relation to its environment; (3) the problems of organisation policy and decision making; (4) the problems of working in a team.

---

[1] From a draft manuscript by Sidney Mailick and Nancy A. Bord, "Experience in the US with Newer Techniques for Training Managers", UNITAR, December 1970.

Design and Methodology

Games may be extremely simple or complex and of considerable depth. In some cases computations are made manually, perhaps with the aid of desk calculators; in other cases the complexity of the model demands the power of modern electronic computer equipment. Some games may be played in a few hours, others span several weeks. Some games have only a few participants; other games can accommodate several dozen participants.

Most games, notably at the functional and sub-functional levels, are designed for each participant to represent an individual decision-making unit. In other games, group decision making is the rule. Very often the internal organisation of the group may be prescribed; even where it is not, the instruments provided to the players may assume a particular structure.

The number of teams in a game is largely predetermined by its purpose. Manual games are generally restricted to a dozen teams or less, due to the computational problems encountered with great numbers of teams. The maximum number of members per team depends largely on the complexity of the game and the time available for an effective organisation effort and intra-team communication in decision making. Four to seven members is the usual size of teams though some games have teams as large as fifteen members.

The number of decision activities in a game run should be great enough to permit the teams to establish a working organisation, to become involved in planning and to see the results. Presumably, the optimal number of activities tends to vary with the characteristics of both the individual participants and the game being played.

The time available for making decisions within each period of play during a game run is normally related to the complexity of the game. In practice, one finds in use periods ranging from a few minutes to two hours or more. In order to digest voluminous data, gain an over-all perspective and acquire a sense of the inter-relationships between the whole and its parts, the average participant needs time for personal and unhurried reflection. This encourages the use of a pattern of several play periods, separated in time.

At other times, the games are played to provide quite deliberately too little time for participants to analyse the situation and to assess the information available to them before reaching the next decision. This can produce a situation of strain and tension between members of the group which not only adds to the general excitement of the session, but produces what in some quarters is regarded as an approximation of the actual strain which is involved in the real world in making administrative decisions.

There is less objection to continuous play in quite simple games. There are no firm criteria on how long the period should be between decision meetings. However, even in highly complex games it is probable that teams are capable of formal decision meetings once or twice a week without strain, provided that the administrators of the game can furnish output data a day or two in advance of each session.

Post-play evaluation sessions are important, and continuous review of decisions is usually a component of the game. In addition, provision may be made for periodic review sessions involving comparison with other teams as a part of the game.

Although there is a wide variety of management games, there are certain practices which appear to be part of the operation in most of the games.

First, the game managers brief the participants about the objectives and the rules of the game. Second, the participants are grouped in teams, representing an organisation. The teams are provided with starting information about the status of the organisation , its competitors, and the environment. Next, the teams are required to analyse the information and to reach certain decisions within a given period of time. The decisions are recorded by the teams on special forms.

This cycle of receiving current information, making decisions and obtaining feedback about results continues for several time periods. At the end of the game an over-all critique session is usually held, in which the teams and the game administrators discuss the performances.

Assessment of Effectiveness

Despite their increased utilisation there is a considerable amount of discussion and debate regarding the specific merits and shortcomings of management simulation as a training device for managers. Since most of the support for management simulation is impressionistic, consisting primarily of intuitive judgments based on personal experience, its proponents as well as its opponents are generally dissatisfied with the existing empirical evidence. Surprisingly little empirical research has been undertaken to determine the educational value of this new approach to management training. The task of testing the educational value of games is indeed difficult and there have been relatively few controlled experiments that really get to the heart of the matter.

The principal criterion used to evaluate games has been player reaction, which has been generally enthusiastic. One US corporation's business simulator was given a rating of 4.88 out of a possible 5 by participants who used it in training session. A game played at Indiana University was scored 8.66 out of a possible 10 by the participants, one-third of whom called it the most valuable educational experience they had ever had. And, in discussing the University of Chicago's international operations simulation, one authority suggests that while the educational and research potentials of the game have as yet been only superficially explored, participant enthusiasm and preliminary observations as to the capabilities simulation exercises are sufficiently strong as to warrant much further application and analysis.[1]

Somewhat more substantial evidence comes from a large US industrial corporation which devised a laboratory test to measure both cognitive and attitudinal learning in its industry game. The results were positive in terms of the increase in the participants' understanding of company policies and their awareness of how their actions contribute to company efficiency.[2]

In the absence of any further empirical evidence one can only examine the theoretical claims made for gaming and the reservations suggested by some observer-critics. A number of arguments in favour of the use of management games as a training device have been advanced. The first is involvement; all trainees participate and not only the motivated or especially bright ones. A second is practice; the opportunity to make mistakes is afforded and, in doing so, also the opportunity to lose the fear of making mistakes. A third factor is the exchange of ideas; games provide an opportunity to compare one's own action with those of others, usually peers, who are faced with the same problems, at the same time and under the same circumstances. A fourth reason is that games provide "learning through exposition", i.e. the manager must defend his own point of view and explain his position. This may help stimulate careful thought processes which are vital to effective learning. A fifth factor is that of "instant experience". By tackling a series of situations that would normally be encountered over a longer period of time, the participant may gain greater awareness of cause-and-effect relationships. A sixth consideration is that games may provide executives, who may have become overly concerned with their own spheres of management, with a new perspective on over-all organisation operations as they observe the interaction of men, money and materials. A final reason is "decision replay". The players can return to a previous point in the game, proceed with an entirely new set of decisions and see how the outcome is altered.

There is little question about these potential benefits of gaming in theory. A more modest assessment of practical outcomes appears to include the following:

---

[1] Hans B. Thorelli, "The International Operations Simulation at the University of Chicago", Journal of Business (July 1962), p. 297.

[2] American Management Association, "Simulation and Gaming", 1961, p. 24.

1.   General management games probably do not teach anything very specific about the business enterprise or the management of the firm. However, they may serve to demonstrate some very broad facts of organisational life such as that all areas of an enterprise are inter-related, or that they have to be co-ordinated, or that each of them is important.

2.   Experienced executives probably learn little that is absolutely new to them from gaming, although the experience may affect some of their long-held attitudes. Gaming may, for example, make a functional executive more tolerant of his co-workers in other departments and more aware of their problems.

3.   The emotional impact of gaming probably does make it a suitable technique for changing attitudes, provided the game situation is sufficiently clear-cut to pinpoint the attitude to be changed.

4.   Although gaming can hardly be said to teach organisational decision making per se, it does provide experience in learning from experience, particularly in the application of statistical and analytical methods.

5.   Games undoubtedly do provoke interest which may lead the participant to additional reading and study. They may change attitudes and they do seem to give some sort of "feel" for organisational problems.

Serious criticisms of the management game generally, aside from such questions as its higher cost in both money and personnel and the requirement, in some cases, of such exotic equipment as computers, focus on three issues. One is that some of the very things that make gaming engrossing and exciting may diminish their lasting educational effectiveness. The competitive aspects of a management game, for example, may arouse motivation and may help sustain effort. But they may also detract from long-term learning by leading participants to play "conservative" strategies instead of experimenting with new approaches, by teaching participants to emphasise short-term "profits" within the game context instead of building and trying to achieve long-term strategic plans, and by influencing participants to let anxieties about relative performances interfere with their efforts to learn.

Further, the involvement and excitement of the game raises a central problem inherent in all simulation processes of the tendency for participants to attempt to "win the game" by approaching the task as only a game rather than as a realistic business situation. If the model underlying the game does not include the necessary attributes of reality, the training in the simulated environment is less likely to be successfully transferred to real-life organisational behaviour. Although most games are based on simplified models of reality, the degree to which they represent the actual processes of organisations varies considerably.

Participation in management games often tends to be a pleasant experience; thus, there is a tendency to devote too much time to play and not enough to a careful analysis and critique of the games' results. Many game administrators emphasise that games should be used in conjunction with more conventional teaching devices. Lectures, discussion sessions and other techniques can alert the game player to the artificiality of the assumptions in the model and help him to discriminate wisely between what can and cannot safely be applied to real-life situations.

A second major focus of criticism is on the way in which teams are often organised. Keeping groups together simply because they have worked together before does not necessarily enhance what they get from the experience. Organising them so that they are homogenous in ability or prior performance may also prove to have drawbacks. On the other hand, it may be detrimental to both satisfaction and performance to have teams which reflect obvious differences in potential compete against one another.

Third, some critics point out that many management games involve only quantitative variables and ignore human elements of organisation almost completely; they question how such games can truly provide a realistic training ground for management. They tend to applaud, consequently, those games in which the human factor is not neglected and in which group processes and dynamics of one of the teams are considered by the other team or by the team itself. This represents one method by which management games can be used to study inter-group and decision-making problems on the psychological dimension.

One such human relations refinement involves the use of videotape cameras which record both image and sound on tape for replay through ordinary television receivers.   The discussions of teams can be recorded and then played back after the end of the game in order to analyse what has taken place in making their decisions.   The obvious advantage of videotape is that human behaviour can be captured live and presented as factual data to be observed and even measured, encouraging participants to become aware of subtleties in their interactions and reflect upon the way in which they have worked together.[1]

In sum, games appear to be a valuable training device in emphasising the importance of long-range planning as well as the need to operate on the basis of established policies rather than expediency.   Most games are planned so that opportunism brings only temporary advantages;   the real pay-offs accrue to those companies which devise an effective long-range plan and stick to it with only minor modifications.   The players are encouraged to be concerned not with one functional problem but with the agency's over-all strategy.

---

[1] Cf. the ERGOM exercises in groups and organisational development problems developed by Professor B. Bass of the Management Research Center of the University of Rochester.   This series contains at least one exercise dealing specifically with problems of developing countries, has been translated into a dozen or more languages and used extensively since 1967 in Latin America, India and (though on a more limited scale) Africa as well as Europe, Japan and North America.   These exercises are also being used as the basis of a major cross-cultural research project into managerial attitudes.

<u>TECHNICAL NOTES ON THE USE OF BUSINESS GAMES[1]</u>

I.   WHAT IS A BUSINESS GAME?

A Business Game has been defined as a "Dynamic Sequential Management Decision Simulation Exercise" and whilst this is a frightening title it is fully explanatory. We shall return to this full title later but in these notes shall use the shorter title "Business Game".

The business game is perhaps the most powerful teaching technique available to us and like all other powerful things it should be used correctly to ensure a power for good rather than ill. The game is also a logical step in the development of teaching techniques which started with the time honoured lecture, enlivened eventually by exercise and discussion. The main disadvantage of the lecture is that students must for the most part adopt a passive role, the lecturer indulging in a one way "exchange" of knowledge.

A break-through in teaching method came with the use of the case study where students are forced into a more active role as exchanges develop in three directions: lecturer to student; student to lecturer; student to student (most important).   Variants on the case study theme followed in the form of In-Basket Exercises, Role Playing and the Incident Process: each of these variants being designed to increase the participation of the student in the learning process, whilst at the same time bringing realism and practice into the classroom.   A vital aspect of the case method and its variants is that it puts the student in a decision making situation and so gives him practice in this vital management field which is so difficult to "teach" by more traditional methods.

How does the business game become the next logical step, as claimed above? Perhaps a disadvantage of the case method and its variants is that while students learn to make a decision, they do so in a static environment - this falls very short of practice.   At the end of a case study a student may make his decision and sit back and praise himself on a good job of work - in practice he will eventually find out by bitter experience, and only in retrospect, whether that decision was 'good' or 'bad'.   Moreover, in practice he must frequently reach his decision in the presence of a very severe time constraint and whilst the situation is changing (perhaps by the hour.)   The business game attempts to bring these elements of practical decision-making into the classroom by requiring the student to make a decision in a given situation; the outcome of this decision affects this situation, and the student is then called on to make further decisions in sequence in this continuously developing situation ..... hence the full title "Dynamic Sequential Management Decision Simulation Exercise."

II. A SHORT HISTORY OF BUSINESS GAMES

Business games clearly have their roots in War Games which were devised to develop the strategy of warfare and to train serving officers in such strategy by simulation of military situations.   The war game itself was developed in Germany - the 'Kriegspiele'; it journeyed westwards through England - the 'Tactical Exercise Without Troops (TEWT)'.   Eventually it found application in the United States where, on a visit to the US Naval Academy, a member of the American Management Association witnessed a war game and realised its implications for management training.

Thus it was that in the late 1950's the American Management Association published their "Top Management Decision Simulation" which was the first business game and which the A.M.A. hoped would lead to the formation of a 'war college' for business managers.   Shortly afterwards G.R. Andlinger of McKinsey and Company published his well known Harvard Business Review article "Business Games - Play One" and the "Andlinger Game" - the prototype of many to follow - was born.

---

[1] Extracted from ILO: <u>An Introduction to Business Games</u>, Man.Dev. Manual 27, (Geneva).

Business Games as such therefore, have a very short history and consequently there is constant development and expansion, which is taking place in many countries as the 1960's progress.

III. CLASSIFICATION OF BUSINESS GAMES

There are of course many case studies dealing with every facet of business activity. As has already been described, the business game is much younger than the case study, and so there is not the same wide choice here.   However, because a business game is constructed around a mathematical model of a business environment, one can be devised for almost any situation. Consequently, as with cases, there are also games dealing with every facet of business activity.   To assist selection and specification therefore, it is convenient to adopt a classification and the following has been suggested:-

(a) by coverage:

1. company game (or 'total enterprise' or 'top management')

a game linking different functions in the simulated company so that participants are able to see how these functions are integrated when making decisions affecting total company policy.

2. functional game

a game covering one specific function in the simulated company so that participants may experience problems of the simulated function - e.g. production control, inventory control, sales promotion.

3. other specialist areas

games have been devised for instance, to test out government economic policy.

(b) by competitive element:

1. interacting game

the fortunes of a team of participants are affected not only by its own decisions but also by the decisions of its competitors - as in a game of tennis where a player's performance is directly affected by the actions of his opponent.

2. non-interacting game

whilst still competitive, in this type of game each team is largely in command of its own performance: or at least its performance is affected only by its own decisions - as in athletic track and field events.

(c) by processing of results:

1. computer game

the more 'realistic' a game aspires to be, the more complex becomes the computational task of the umpire; because a computer can handle vast amounts of detail at speed, this type of game will therefore tend to be more complex - i.e. more variables can be built into the underlying mathematical model.

2. non-computer game (or 'manual')

> all the calculations are performed by hand or with the
> aid of simple calculating aids; whilst necessarily less
> complex than a computer game, a non-computer game is
> certainly more flexible and far less costly to run.

This basic classification will help to identify the design features of a
game e.g. a game can be described as a company, interacting, non-computer
game (this describes the original Andlinger game) or perhaps a functional,
non-interacting, non-computer game (this may describe say a dynamic inventory
control exercise.)

Games have also been classified by nature of model (e.g. whether
abstract or based on fact) and by purpose (e.g. whether for training or
research purposes.)

IV. CONSTRUCTION OF A BUSINESS GAME

It is difficult to present any formal rules entitled "How to write
a business game" because this is to a certain extent a creative process –
this section must therefore be regarded as descriptive rather than
instructive.

Naturally, it is first necessary to have some object in mind when a
game is constructed, i.e. what is the principal lesson or lessons one hopes
to put over in a game (participants will always learn in addition, some other
lesson peculiar to their own needs – this is one of the bonuses which come
with the use of this teaching method.) For example, a game which intends
to instruct in the use of a technique will be relatively simple, whereas a
game designed to test intra group reaction will be more complex, embracing
several functional responsibilities.

The core around which a business game is constructed is a mathematical
model of a business environment. In this model the inter-relationships
between functional areas of a business are translated into mathematical
relationships, and it is therefore possible to evaluate activity in one
area in terms of its impact upon another area. This naturally implies
mathematical computation in the use of business games and the degree of
functional inter-relationship which can be built into a game is controlled
by the computational facilities available (see section on computer and
non-computer games above). However, it must be stressed that no matter
how complex the mathematical model appears to be, nor how powerful the
computational assistance, the game will always be a drastic over-simplification
of a real life situation. This point, which must never be overlooked by the
supervisor, is taken up again in the section on Evaluation.

The model may be completely deterministic (i.e. react only to decisions
by participants) or may be stochastic (i.e. react also to some outside
influences in a completely random manner.) A stochastic model can cause
bitterness amongst participants but the element of chance <u>does</u> enter into
real life business situations and therefore must be faced.

It is customary to give certain relationships within the model as 'rules'
of the game; however, the larger part of the model will clearly be hidden from
participants – <u>one of their objectives in playing the game will be to discover
what makes the underlying model react the way it does</u>.

V.   OPERATING A BUSINESS GAME

A typical presentation follows the pattern set out below:-

1.   Introduction and briefing.

This part of the exercise must never be hurried.   Participants must fully understand all that is expected of them before the game starts, or confusion will quickly develop.   It is a good idea for the umpire to read through the instructions with participants to ensure that all matters are understood.   Ensure also that participants understand how to fill up any forms which must be completed and if necessary arrange a demonstration or practice run.

2.   First decision by participants.

Again, this should not be hurried because participants are feeling their way in a strange situation.

3.   Umpire calculations followed by feed back of first results.

This must be accomplished as quickly as possible in order to maintain tempo.   The umpire will be wise to have at hand whatever charts, tables, ready reckoners or other computational devices will speed up his calculations.

4.   Publication of information on results achieved.

There may be time delays in the publication of certain information in an attempt to reproduce real life circumstances.   (Some information may be available for 'sale' to participants.)   This aspect of a game helps to generate a spirit of competition but should also test the ability of participants to handle and interpret published information.

5.   Repeat of 2, 3 and 4 for a series of simulated time periods.

Participants should be encouraged to adhere to a strict time-table (for inter-acting games this is essential to the completion of umpiring computations.)   It is only now that pressure should be brought to bear on participants as the pace is speeded up.

6.   Announce the end of the game.

To avoid 'end game' tactics it is advisable not to give advance warning of the end of a game.   Announce the end as final results are returned to participants.

When should the game end? How long should a game last? These are difficult questions to answer, but generally speaking a halt should be called when the purpose of the game has been fulfilled: a game should not continue to the boredom of the participants, nor should they be seen to be literally 'playing' with no educational interest.   If participants plead that they have now got the measure of the thing, and if only there were another decision they would demonstrate their success ..... the umpire has chosen well his time to close!   At the end of the game, participants may be required to perform certain concluding tasks - it is wise to give instructions on such tasks at this stage rather than in the introduction.

7.   The evaluation.

This is most important because it is here that the umpire brings out the lessons learned.   A later section is devoted to this matter.   Evaluation should never be hurried or skimped.   If time is short, savings should be made on the actual running of the game rather than on evaluation.

A perusal of the above 7 items will indicate that a business game is a time-consuming operation. A game should not be contemplated unless the teaching programme permits the luxury of such use of time. On the other hand, the teaching value is so high that it is worth making time available at the expense of something else.

Layout of the room is an important factor in successful operation of a game. Participants will normally operate in teams, and each team should have its own working surface of adequate size to accommodate all members of the team. Teams should be located so as to permit quiet discussion amongst team members without being overheard by other teams: however, a separate room for each team is a luxury not a necessity. Similarly, the umpire should have adequate working surface, but it is imperative that participants are not permitted access to this area or they may discover the mysteries of the underlying mathematical model. Adequate visual aids should be available to accommodate any necessary demonstration, presentation of information or summary of results.

VI. ROLE OF THE UMPIRE

It cannot be over stressed that the conduct of a business game is not an excuse for not teaching. The business game is a teaching technique, and must be used seriously for teaching a pre-planned lesson as with any other teaching technique. In fact, far from the umpire having an easy time, he may work harder in a game than in a lecture or case study. However, the pressure of work in a game is erratic: the umpire must be prepared to work quickly and accurately under extreme pressure for brief spells, interspersed by holding a watching brief. At the end of the game when perhaps he is tiring, he must conduct an evaluation session which is the most important part of the whole game.

There are two reasons for this pressure on the umpire:

1. the backwash of pressure which the umpire places on participants.

2. the involvement of participants and their all consuming interest in the situation. This point requires further comment:

Of all teaching techniques, without doubt a business game generates the greatest involvement and enjoyment on the part of students. Even if they approach the game in frivolous or apathetic mood, this quickly changes as the effects of competitive effort make themselves apparent. A game quickly becomes 'real', decisions are made in a very serious mood, and each participant is keen to become personally involved in every aspect of the game. Moreover, participants enjoy this experience (which may be new to them) of learning by actually doing something in the classroom. The umpire therefore finds himself in charge of a tremendously enthusiastic, interested and deeply involved group of students. He must share and reflect this involvement, and keep up the pace if he is not to send students away angry and frustrated.

The following will help the umpire in this task:

1. He must fully understand the game and be familiar with the situation and constraints, so that he can both deal immediately with any question raised, and carry out his calculations promptly. On meeting a game for the first time, it is advisable for the umpire to have a practice run with a few colleagues before using the game with students. This is the surest way to understand the game.

2. He must take pains to ensure the participants understand the game before it gets under way. Not to do so, is to court confusion.

3. He must constantly 'expect the unexpected' and so be able to handle any new development quickly and calmly. It is impossible to forecast every question and action of participants in this type of situation, but if the umpire has prepared himself as indicated, he will be able to handle such new developments. Clearly the umpire becomes more adept at this as he gains experience.

4. He must maintain momentum by feeding back results quickly. Wherever possible participants should have a task to perform whilst the umpire is making his calculations. It is death to a game to have participants sitting around whilst the umpire works ponderously through calculations. Participants should be kept busy throughout the game.

5. He must have a planned timetable for conduct of the game itself, and a clear plan for conducting the evaluation session.

6. He must demonstrate confidence and be seen to be in complete command of the dynamic situation which is certain to ensue.

VII. THE EVALUATION

Frequent reference has already been made in these notes to the importance of the evaluation session. This is where acknowledgement can be given to lessons learned (notice that lessons will be learned, not taught for 'wisdom cannot be told.') This is the denouement, long awaited by participants. There will be no lack of audience participation in this session, the main problems of the umpire will be giving everyone a fair hearing, and steering the discussion into the most profitable channels.

An evaluation session might usefully begin with a review of the final results of each team in the light of policies and objectives which each team set for itself. (With advanced groups it is often interesting to ask for a written policy statement before the first decision is made.) What must be avoided in this economic type of evaluation is an attempt to declare a winner. The winner is he who has learned most from the exercise - and this is only in the minds of the participants. There is a parallel here which should be developed: how does one assess economic performance in real life - how does one declare a winner? Is it by share of market, profits, size of assets, cash balance, ability to continue trading, customer satisfaction ... or what? Some of these measures may be inconsistent, thus a company with a large share of the market may have low profits.

Wherever possible comparisons must be made with real life situations because the game is an over-simplification, and must embrace certain unrealities and artificialities. These artificialities are certain to be seized on by unsuccessful participants, and on first sight might appear to be a disadvantage of the game technique. However, this can be turned to advantage. First explain that only in such a refined situation can the game become manageable and moreover, this way no one participant has the advantage of having experienced this situation before - all decisions must therefore be empiric. Then invite the participant who raised the matter to lead a discussion on how the situation would develop in real life without the artificiality, and how he would deal with the situation. Other participants may have a different view on what happens in 'real life.

Patterns of behaviour within teams; difficulties of establishing a working organisation and in reaching a co-ordinated decision at the right time; problems of delegation and responsibility ..... these are topics which must feature to a greater or lesser degree in an evaluation. (If the umpire wishes to make a special feature of this aspect he should use large teams, and present a lot of information for digestion by each team.)

Form and extent of any records maintained over and above the necessary decision forms might also be discussed with advantage. The application of any technique recently discussed in the teaching programme should also be pursued: e.g. statistical forecasting, costing or charting techniques.

At some stage during the evaluation session, participants will expect the umpire to reveal the secrets of the underlying model or otherwise reveal how he computed the results of their decisions. It is not advisable for the umpire to discuss in detail the mathematical relationships which have been built into the model, as this might steer discussion in a difficult and unnecessary direction. Rather should he describe in general terms how the model reacts to decisions, and explain in general terms the constraints underlying the model. This is all that is necessary to enable participants fully to evaluate their performance.

Naturally the actual content of any evaluation will be determined by the teaching objectives of the business game and the stage of advancement of the participants. Clearly the same business game will not give rise to the same pattern of evaluation after each use. The game should be used as a springboard from which an evaluation session can be developed to any depth desired. Towards the end of an evaluation session, it is sometimes interesting to ask participants what lessons they have learned, and to compare their answers with the teaching objectives of the game. It is not unusual to find that participants have learned valuable lessons which the umpire did not have in mind!

VIII. EDUCATIONAL USE OF BUSINESS GAMES

Reference has been made previously in these notes to benefits both for teacher and participant, arising from the use of business games. Reference has also been made to the use of the game as a teaching technique. However, it should be stressed that the business game must find its place in a teaching programme alongside other techniques referred to in the opening section of these notes. The game is another weapon in the teacher's armoury, and in no way completely replaces other teaching techniques: no one technique can ever be the complete answer, a well designed teaching programme will make use of all techniques in their place. Perhaps the game particularly comes into its own for demonstrating a functional technique or for demonstrating the problem of functional inter-relationships.

Games naturally have their disadvantages. Amongst these might be mentioned: the matter of artificiality referred to above; the danger that participants feel that they have learned a general lesson universally applicable, when perhaps it might be applicable to the simulated economic environment of the particular game; as in any 'learning by doing' situation, there is the danger that participants may learn bad habits as well as good. These disadvantages must be guarded against by careful supervision by the umpire.

How effective is the business game as a teaching technique? Who can answer this question? How effective is any teaching technique? Those who have participated in business games certainly claim that they have derived benefit from the experience, and that they have found the experience stimulating and a first class environment in which to learn. Perhaps more than this cannot be claimed until further research is carried out into controlled group reactions and results.

Perhaps a final advantage that can be claimed for the game is its flexibility and versatility. With a little experience, the enthusiastic teacher will be able to adapt and develop any game to meet the differing requirements of disparate groups of students. Some refinements and developments are mentioned in the Umpires Instructions in the individual games in this series but these should not be regarded as exhaustive: an enthusiastic teacher will take the germ of an idea from a game, develop this to his own requirements, and then use it to his personal satisfaction and success ..... and to that of his students.

BUSINESS GAME: "Ilo CONTROL"[1]

INSTRUCTIONS FOR PARTICIPANTS

1. Situation

You are now to assume that you are in charge of a factory which produces only one product - the Ilo.

In your assumed capacity you will have to make a series of decisions concerning the number of Ilos to be produced each month. Your task has been simplified because you can also assume that:

    (a) once you decide on the number to produce, this has immediate effect, i.e. there is no time lag between making your decision and bringing machines into production.

    (b) Ilos are immediately available for sale in the month in which produced.

    (c) there is unlimited production capacity and storage space.

Your factory receives orders for Ilos in the demand pattern outlined in section 2 below. Normal trading terms are such that the customer expects his order to be met from stock. All prices and costs are expressed in a mythical currency unit - the UN.

2. Demand Pattern

The following information is available concerning potential demand from customers, i.e. the orders you can expect to receive in the coming year:

    (a) there is no seasonal pattern.

    (b) demand fluctuates but appears to average around 200,000 units per month.

    (c) the highest demand in any one month over the past few years was 260,000 units whilst the lowest was 140,000 units. However, these extremes were experienced not more than once or twice per year - well over half the time demand varied between 160,000 and 240,000 per month.

As stated above, the customer expects his order to be met from stock. However, demand which cannot be met due to shortage of stock can be carried forward and receives priority for delivery as soon as sufficient stock is available .... but additional cost is incurred should the customer be inconvenienced in this way. (See section 5(c) below).

3. Production Level

You are to assume that at the commencement of the exercise your factory is producing at the rate of 200,000 units per month. You may decide to alter this, up or down, in the first or any subsequent month.

However, the production process is such that production level can only be changed in steps of 10,000 units.

Once you have made a decision on a level of production, your factory will continue to produce at this level each month until you change the level by subsequent decision.

4. Stock Level

You commence the exercise with 50,000 units of finished Ilos in stock. The amount available for sale in the first month will thus be this figure plus whatever you decide to produce in the first month.

---

[1] Extracted from ILO: An Introduction to Business Games, Man.Dev. Manual 27, (Geneva).

5. Costs

The following costs will be incurred as a direct result of the decisions you make each month:

(a) UN 100 for every 10,000 unit step up or down in production level.

(b) UN 3 for every 1,000 units in stock at the end of each month.

(c) UN 25 for every 1,000 units of Ilos which cannot be delivered in any month due to shortage of stock - this is payable to the customer as compensation for inconvenience caused.

You may, if you wish, keep a cumulative total of costs incurred each month, but in any case these costs will be computed in total at the end of the year.

6. Sequence of Operation

This simple Business Game will adopt the following sequence:

(i) You will decide your production level for month 1 and record this on lines A and B in month 1 of the Decision Sheet. This will automatically determine the amount available for sale in month 1, having taken into account the opening stock of 50,000 units. Month 1 on the Decision Sheet is thus completed as far as line D.

(ii) As soon as each participant has completed line D the umpire will announce the demand for month 1, this you will record on line E of the Decision Sheet.

(iii) You are now in a position to calculate your closing stock at the end of month 1 - or your stock shortage as the case may be; record this on line F or G of the Decision Sheet and carry forward to line C of month 2.

(iv) You will now decide your production level for month 2 and record this on line A and B in month 2 of the Decision Sheet. An adjustment of the opening stock, or stock shortage as the case may be, will again enable you to determine the amount available for sale - Month 2 is now completed as far as Line D.

(v) As soon as each participant has completed line D the umpire will announce the demand for month 2, this you will record on line E of the Decision Sheet.

(vi) Sequence (iii), (iv) and (v) is repeated until the end of the year.

(vii) At the end of the year you will compute the grand total costs incurred as a result of your decisions in accordance with section 5 - this will be recorded at the right hand end of the Decision Sheet.

(viii) The exercise concludes with an evaluation session when points brought out by this Business Game will be discussed.

Ilo Control:
DECISION SHEET

Line	Description	Source	Month O	1	2	3	4	5	6	7	8	9	10	11	12	Total No.	Cost Each UN	Total Cost UN
A	Change in Production Level (10,000 unit steps)	Decision															UN 100	
B	New Production Level	Last Month B Amended by This Month A	200															
C	Add Opening Stock or Deduct Stock Shortage	Last Month F (+) or G (−)		+50															
D	Available for Sale	B + or − C																
E	Sales Demand	Given By Umpire																
F	Closing Stock	D − E (Positive)	50														UN 3	
G	Closing Stock Shortage	E − D (Negative)	−														UN 25	

Grand Total Cost   UN

Note: For convenience omit '000s in all quantities

BUSINESS GAME: "Ilo CONTROL"

INSTRUCTIONS FOR THE UMPIRE

(Not to be distributed to participants)

1. Outline of Game

     This is a non-interacting functional game.   Participants must plan
production into stock to meet a fluctuating demand from customers, there is
a penal charge for inability to meet demand from stock but there is also a
cost penalty every time the level of production is changed or stock is carried
over from one decision to the next.   The Game is designed to bring home the
problem of operating production, stock and sales policies within a minimum
cost structure.

     The product - Ilo - is fictitious and created from the initial letters
of International Labour Office.

2. Organisation and Timing

     Due to its simplicity and speed, participants may operate individually
rather than in teams for this Game.   The umpire has little to do and therefore
there is no limitation on numbers.

     The whole exercise, including evaluation, can be completed in one to
two hours.

3. Equipment Required - Participants

     A set of Participant's Instructions.

     One Decision Sheet each.

     A sheet of notepaper.

     A pen or pencil.

4. Equipment Required - Umpire

     A set of Participant's Instructions and Decision Sheet.

     Blackboard or other visual aid.

     Notepaper and pen or pencil.

     Umpire's Instructions - particularly Appendix "A".

5. Detailed Operating Instructions

     (a)   Hand out Participant's Instructions and Decision Sheet, read through
the instructions with the participants - amplifying and explaining any necessary
points - the game must not be started until each participant fully understands
what it is all about.

     (b)   Ensure that participants understand how to use the Decision Sheet -
draw up and demonstrate its use on the blackboard, for example:

	Month			
	1	2	3	4
A	+10	-10		
B	210	200		
C	+50	+40	-10	
D	260	240		
E	220	250		
F	40			
G		-10		

(c)   Announce the start of the Game and instruct participants to make their first decision and complete Month 1 of the decision sheet as far as line D.
    Walk round and quickly inspect each decision sheet to ensure that each participant has completed it correctly.

(d)   When satisfied on item (c) above, announce the demand for month 1 by reading the first figure off Appendix "A", first year.

(e)   Instruct participants now to complete the month 1 column of the decision sheet and bring forward the closing stock, or shortage as the case may be, to line (c) of month 2.   Walk round and quickly inspect each decision sheet again to ensure that each participant has completed it correctly - if there is no problem at this stage the rest of the game can follow quickly as each participant clearly understands the routine.

(f)   Instruct participants now to make their decision for month 2 and complete the month 2 column to line D again.   When all are ready announce the demand for month 2 from Appendix "A".

(g)   Continue in this manner through to month 12, announcing each month's demand when all participants are ready.   Clearly the speed will be governed by the slowest participant.   It is advisable to score a pencil line through each demand figure as it is announced to avoid any error when announcing a subsequent figure.

(h)   On conclusion of twelve months instruct participants to compute their grand total cost by adding across lines A, F and G and carrying out the necessary calculations.   Note that in adding across line A it is the total number of 10,000 unit steps, irrespective of whether these are plus or minus, which form the basis of the calculation - impress this upon participants.

(j)   An evaluation session is now carried out (see below).   However, participants may claim that they have just got the "feel" of the situation and may wish to run a second year - this will take very little time.   If so, hand out a further decision sheet each but this time ask participants to substitute their own opening stock (or shortage) for the 50,000 units at line C, month 1. The "2nd Year" figures in Appendix "A" are for each second year.

6.   Publication of Information during the Game

    None.

7.   Summary of Information on conclusion of the Game

    The following information is useful during the evaluation session and should be tabulated on the blackboard either for each participant or for a selected range only.   If two years have been simulated, the figures for each year should be ranged in adjacent columns to demonstrate any improvement:

    Grand total cost

    Number of production changes

    Number of times out of stock

    The maximum and minimum stock balances

    Individual groups, or umpires, may feel that other information is useful as a basis for discussion.

8.   Evaluation Session - suggested points for discussion

    Review summary of information (see 7 above) and observe if there is any improvement, if two years have been simulated.   What were the actions which produced the highest and lowest grand total cost figures?

What policy of control was adopted by each participant? In balancing the conflicting objectives of different sub-systems, one item must always be left to take up the slack - it is not possible to control or stabilise every one. Was stock allowed to fluctuate - or production?

How did participants interpret the demand pattern? In fact the description in section 2 of the Participant's Instructions is the description of a random incidence but with a normal distribution. If this statistical fact had been established the decisions would have been easier (in fact quite a low grand total cost will be incurred if no change is made to production level).

Were participants able to forecast demand? Because the distribution is normal, it becomes easier to forecast on a cumulative basis as the months pass by.

General discussion on the realism of the game - in reality it becomes infinitely more complex because there are many more variables to balance and the whole is overlaid with other human and technical problems. However this is a very real practical problem in any industry. The game demonstrates that here is an area of decision making which has its direct effect on the cost structure of the organisation and for which we must strive for a solution.

Whilst the game is simple, it can be used as a springboard from which to develop a series of later lectures, discussions or readings, for example;

The use in industry of various statistical techniques in the area covered by this game.

Practical problems in planning and control and the balancing of sub-systems.

The problem of carrying buffer stocks at various stages in a production process, who makes the decision, the costs incurred.

The much wider implications of this type of problem i.e. the field of Industrial Dynamics - see for example: Management Controls: New Directions in Basic Research, edited by Bonini, Jaedicke and Wagner. (Chapter 6 is contributed by E.B. Roberts). McGraw-Hill Book Company 1964. ..... but this last paragraph relates to material which one should not attempt to cover in evaluating the game within the time schedule indicated at section 2 above!

9. Possible Developments

The umpire may wish to further develop the game to meet particular participant requirements. Some suggestions are noted below:

The game could be played with teams rather than individuals to observe how a planning policy was evolved within a team.

A time lag could be introduced, e.g. a decision on production level made in month 'n' can only be implemented in month 'n + 3' due to problems of arranging a labour force.

Stock could be made perishable - say, valueless if unsold within two months, of completion.

The demand could be made seasonal and/or put onto a rising or falling pattern instead of the static pattern of this game.

See "Oli Business" business game,[1] which is in fact a development of "Ilo Control".

---

[1] ILO: An Introduction to Business Games, Man.Dev. Manual 27 (Geneva).

BUSINESS GAME: Ilo CONTROL

(For Umpires Only - not to be distributed to participants)

Customer demand for Ilos each month:

Month	1st year	2nd year
1	216,000	172,000
2	248,000	240,000
3	172,000	236,000
4	234,000	200,000
5	156,000	148,000
6	206,000	172,000
7	144,000	238,000
8	184,000	144,000
9	260,000	250,000
10	224,000	190,000
11	180,000	176,000
12	192,000	238,000

For interest only:

Total 12 months	2,416,000	2,404,000
Average per month	201,333	200,333

Case Method II (Preparation)

Objective

To analyse two case studies in small group discussions

Handout Material

I - Case Study: The Plywood Factory, p. 1

II - Case Study: The Northern Cement Factory, pp. 5-6

HANDOUT III, Session 11, Questions for Case Study Analysis

    (You may prefer to use locally developed case studies for this session, or choose another case from ILO Man.Dev. Manuals 4, 20, 21 or 30)

Background Reading

Instructor's Guide to The Plywood Factory, p. 3

Instructor's Guide to The Northern Cement Factory, pp. 7-10

As for Session 11

Recommended Reading

As for Session 11

Special Equipment and Aids

Additional meeting rooms for the discussion groups

Chalkboard or flip chart in each room

Session Guide 17

Evening Study.

Briefing instructions for this session were given to participants in Session 11.

Four separate discussion groups meet to study and discuss the cases, The Plywood Factory and The Northern Cement Factory, which members have read in advance (during Session 12). Each group elects a reporter who will present the conclusions of the group to a plenary discussion in Session 18. The group may also wish to name a discussion leader for each case.

To analyse the cases, the groups should ask themselves the Questions for Case Study Analysis printed on Handout III from Session 11, e.g., What is going on? What is the problem? What has caused it? What solutions should we consider? A good case discussion depends on rigorous analysis by participants along these lines.

With two cases to study, the groups should set themselves a time limit for the two discussions, e.g.:

10 min.   Individuals re-read the case and make notes.

30 min.   Group discussion of the case.

10 min.   Formulation of conclusions which the group will
            present to the plenary session.

BREAK

Repeat for second case.

Two observers will circulate to see how the groups approach the problems; they will report their observations in Session 18.

The course leader should circulate, assist the groups in discussion and comment on their work as appropriate.

CASE STUDY:
THE PLYWOOD FACTORY[1]

In May 1965 the Plywood Factory was concerned with ways and means of improving its marketing operations. Recent improvements in the factory had created a situation where available output exceeded actual sales by 30 per cent.

During the previous year, ILO experts had introduced work study into the factory. The results of this study together with technical improvements had resulted in a 30 per cent increase in productive capacity. Sales of product, however, were rising at a much slower rate. In May 1965 the sales volume achieved from "new business", that is, orders from other than previous customers, was averaging 10,000 UN[2] per month. In order to match the rising productivity it was calculated that new business sales of 80,000 UN per month were required.

A survey of the organisation and methods of the company's sales function disclosed several basic weaknesses. Little attention had been paid to market research and no systematic approach had been made to provide a calculation of market potential. The most unorganised segment of the marketing function was the sales force itself. Cases were found where several of the nine salesmen called on one customer within a brief period. It seemed that a system of laissez-faire existed wherein salesmen acted as independent messengers of goodwill and the salesmen reported to the supervisor verbally whenever they happened to contact him in the office. It appeared certain also that many potential customers were neglected.

A survey of the prospect system disclosed an informal prospect list. Each salesman was expected to contribute names to this list which was then made available to all of them. If a salesman thought a prospect was a good one he would call upon him. There was no restriction on the areas wherein salesmen could operate and this meant that more than one would call upon all the good prospects.

Another aspect of the sales function was the handling of orders. Each salesman collected a proportion of orders from old customers and each salesman was responsible for the clerical work involved in processing that order. Clerical work, however, was kept to a minimum because there was no analysis of orders or record of sales against calls made.

One problem which was mentioned by salesmen was the absence of a statement of stocks of products available. The production department objected to issuing such a statement on the grounds that it would quickly become out of date and incorrect. The production manager also held the view that it was the sales department's function to sell the products in the types[3], finishes[4] and sizes fixed by production. At this time no documentation had been made of the detailed elements of types, finishes, qualities and sizes which could form a basis for rationalisation and standardisation of production. Nor had a detailed study or possible end-uses of products been carried out.

In May 1965, Mr. Excel, a marketing expert, was assigned to the job of improving the company's marketing function. Mr. Excel saw immediately that many aspects needed attention. He listed market research, sales promotion, advertising, territory penetration, compensation plans and price-volume studies as aspects which needed attention. In the first place, however, he felt that certain basic weaknesses of the sales function should be corrected before attention was given to the more sophisticated aspects of marketing.

Accordingly, he set about preparing a plan for the reorganisation and improvement of the sales function.

QUESTIONS

1. How would you go about reorganising the sales function?
2. What specific training would you give?
3. What control data would you require?
4. How would you plan to maintain the new system?

---

[1] Extracted from Man.Dev. Manual 21: _Case Studies for Management Decisions_ (ILO, Geneva, 1966).

[2] An international monetary unit (UN) made up of 100 centimes (c).

[3] Types included marine, outdoor and indoor-only plywoods.

[4] Finishes varied from plain plywood to costly veneers.

(not to be distributed
to participants)

INSTRUCTOR'S GUIDE TO
THE PLYWOOD FACTORY

To reorganise the sales function the following steps are necessary:

1. Collation of data on the product, end-uses and the potential end-users.
2. A training programme for salesmen.
3. Organisation of salesmen's duties.
4. Establishment of sales quotas.
5. Organisation of sales reports and control statements.

1. Collation of Data

This involves a detailed study of the types, finishes, sizes and quality of the products manufactured. It should provide a basis for rationalisation and standardisation of production. A listing of possible end-uses of each type, finish and size should provide a basis for future production. Lists of possible end-users should be compiled from directories and other statistical sources.

Similarly specifications, advantages and disadvantages, prices, discounts and types of competing materials are needed. This information can form the basis of a product knowledge manual which can be used for training salesmen.

2. Training Programme for Salesmen

This should be a continuing process. Initially, the impetus should be given by a course covering the following aspects:

(a) selling techniques and methods;
(b) company policy;
(c) product knowledge;
(d) competitors and their products;
(e) organisation and sales reports.

It would be worthwhile testing salesmen's product knowledge before and after the course with a series of true/false questions on the subjects listed above.

3. Organisation of Salesmen's Duties

The first need is to bring the salesmen under strict control. Each man should be given a standard number of calls per day and a monthly target for orders. The service of old customers can be carried out by one or two salesmen, the others should then be used exclusively on selling to new prospects.

The prospect list should be controlled. One man can be assigned to the job of finding prospects by consulting trade lists and advertisements, by talking with friends and business associates and by touring the sales area by car.

From the prospect list and the record of calls made, a daily calling list can be prepared for each representative. This should cover a reasonably compact geographical area and should give the names, types of business and other data for a standard daily number of prospects. For each call the salesman must fill in a simple, largely pre-printed call report which must be returned to the office, together with his orders, at the end of each day. At that time, the salesman picks up his call list for the following day. A sales meeting is held once a week. There is something to be said for meeting early Monday morning.

The clerical work of processing orders and maintaining an analysis of orders should be assigned to a clerk in the office.

4. Establishment of Sales Quotas

Sales quotas for new business should be set on the basis of the number of calls per day, the probability of getting an order and the probable average size of order. These targets can be varied in the light of experience.

5. Organisation of Sales Reports and Control Statements

Simple sales control statements should be prepared for each salesman and in total for the sales manager. They should show weekly and monthly:

(a) performance against target of each salesman in calls made, the number of orders and value of orders;
(b) sales of each type of product against target;
(c) sales by type of end-user.

The maintenance of the new system will depend upon the sales manager. This man must be selected with care, either from among the salesmen or from outside the company. He should be thoroughly indoctrinated in marketing and management.

CASE STUDY:
THE NORTHERN CEMENT FACTORY[1]

Problem on whether to manufacture or purchase
paper pockets for containing cement.

The Cement Factory manufactures 500,000 tons of cement per year, and packs it in double-lined paper pockets. Each pocket contains 42,638 kilogrammes of cement. The pockets are bought from a nearby factory at a price of UN24 each.[2] The following charges are incurred each year in buying the pockets:

1. Buying	UN 000
Stationery for orders and correspondence	4
Telephone calls	1
Portion of Purchasing Manager's remuneration	16
Portion of Purchasing Office expenses	150
Total	171

2. Storage and Handling |
---|---
Labour of handling and transporting pockets | 5
Labour of inspecting, sorting and accounting for pockets | 20
Portion of storage charges | 50
| 75

Five per cent of all pockets are lost or damaged.

The Cement Factory has been offered machinery for manufacturing the pockets. The machinery will cost UN15,000,000 and has a capacity of 9,400 pockets per hour. A building to house the machinery will cost UN6,000,000. The factory can borrow the total amount needed to buy the machinery and erect the building, on the following terms:

Interest payable 10 per cent per year, repayment of capital sum to commence after four years, and to be paid in 10 equal half-yearly instalments.

The machinery is expected to have a life of 25,000 productive hours, or 15 years, whichever is the shorter. At the end of its life, it will have a scrap value of UN1,000,000.

Pockets are manufactured from Kraft paper, which can be bought at a price of UN75,000 per ton from a nearby paper mill. There are 280 grams of paper in each pocket. Ten per cent of the paper fed into production is spoiled or is cut off in unusable pieces and can be sold as scrap at UN15,000 per ton. The following costs will be incurred in buying the paper each year:

Stationery and telephone calls	UN 3,000
Portion of Purchasing Manager's salary and of Purchasing Office expenses	100,000

It is estimated that UN30,000 should be allocated to the paper as part of the costs of storage charges. The handling, transport and inspection of the paper will be performed by the staff of the pocket factory.

In addition to Kraft paper, the following material costs are incurred for each cement pocket:

UN0-35 for staples and UN0-20 for adhesives

Labour required for operating the pocket manufacturing plant is estimated as follows:

2 supervisors at UN16,000 per month;
2 inspectors at UN12,000 per month;
1 clerk at UN10,000 per month;
12 machine operators at UN350 per day;
6 porters at UN250 per day.

---

[1] Extracted from Man.Dev.Manual 21: Case Studies for Management Decisions (ILO, Geneva, 1966).

[2] A world monetary unit (UN) made up of 100 centimes (c).

The factory allows workers 15 paid holidays each year and two weeks' leave on full pay. The company contributes 15 per cent of workers' remuneration to pension, social security and retirement funds. Welfare services cost the company UN30,000 per worker per year.

It is estimated that the following costs will be incurred in operating the pocket manufacturing plant each year.

		UN 000
1.	Maintenance - Fixed	2,300
	Variable UN250 per operating hour.	
2.	Re-allocation of expenses of maintenance administration and workshops - Fixed	1,150
	Variable UN70 per operating hour.	
3.	Power UN80 per operating hour	
4.	Re-allocation of expenses of power reticulation - Fixed	150
	Variable UN20 per operating hour.	
5.	Insurance of inventories of materials, building, plant and machinery	700
6.	Sundry supplies	1,000
7.	Heating	500
8.	Water	300
9.	Portion of factory and general administration costs	1,000

INSTRUCTOR'S GUIDE TO

THE NORTHERN CEMENT FACTORY

PURCHASE OF POCKETS
(direct costs only)

Number packed	$\dfrac{500,000,000 \text{ Kgs.}}{42.638}$	=	11,726,629
Number purchased	$\dfrac{100}{95} \times 11,726,629$	=	12,343,820

	UN 000
Cost at UN24 per pocket	296,252
Plus variable costs of buying, handling and storage	30

Stationery for buying	4	
Telephone calls	1	
Labour 5 + 20	25	
Total		296,282
Per pocket		UN24.002

		UN 000
1.	Maintenance - Fixed	
	Variable UN250 per operating hour	2,300
2.	Re-allocation of expenses of maintenance, administration and workshops - Fixed	1,150
	Variable UN70 per operating hour	
3.	Power UN80 per operating hour	
4.	Re-allocation of expenses of power reticulation - Fixed	150
	Variable UN20 per operating hour	
5.	Insurance of inventories of materials, building, plant and machinery	700
6.	Sundry supplies	1,000
7.	Heating	500
8.	Water	300
9.	Portion of factory and general administration costs	1,000

MANUFACTURE OF CEMENT POCKETS
Cost of Direct Material per pocket

1. Kraft paper:

280 gms. x $\frac{100}{90}$ = 311 gms. at UN75,000 per ton =		23.325
Less scrap 31 gms. at UN15,000 per ton =		0.465
Net cost of paper		22.860

2. Staples   0.350

3. Adhesives   0.200

Total material cost   23.410

Production Plan and Depreciation

Number of pockets required   12,343,820 pockets
   at 9,400 per hour requires   1,313.2 hours

Number of hours available :

Calendar days		365
Less: Sundays	52	
Holidays	15	67
		298
At eight hours per day =		2,384 hours
Less 20 per cent non-productive		477
Productive hours		1,907

Maximum output on one shift: 1,907 x 9,400 =   17,925,800
Surplus to company's requirements   5,581,980

Depreciation

1. Working 1,314 hours per year, the life of the asset will be
   15 years x 1,314 hours = 19,710 hours and depreciation is:

   $$\frac{UN15,000,000 - 1,000,000}{19,710} = UN710 \text{ per hour}$$

2. Working 1,907 hours per year, life is 25,000 hours and depreciation is:

   $$\frac{UN15,000,000 - UN1,000,000}{25,000} = UN560 \text{ per hour}$$

Interest at 10 per cent per year in UN

Year	Capital	Interest For half year	Interest For year
1	21,000,000		2,100,000
2	21,000,000		2,100,000
3	21,000,000		2,100,000
4	21,000,000		2,100,000
5	21,000,000	1,050,000	
	18,900,000	945,000	1,995,000
6	16,800,000	840,000	
	14,700,000	735,000	1,575,000
7	12,600,000	630,000	
	10,500,000	525,000	1,155,000
8	8,400,000	420,000	
	6,300,000	315,000	735,000
9	4,200,000	210,000	
	2,100,000	105,000	315,000
	Total		14,175,000

Over 15 years = per year	945,000
Over 25,000 hours = 13 years = per year	1,090,385
1907	

Labour Cost in UN per year

Day Workers - pay days

Calendar days		365
Less Sundays		52
Earning days		313
Less paid holidays	15	
Less paid leave	12	27
Working days		286

2 supervisors at UN16,000 per month	384,000
2 inspectors at UN12,000 per month	288,000
1 clerk at UN10,000 per month	120,000
12 machine operators at UN350 per day	1,314,600
6 porters at UN250 per day	469,500
23 Total salaries and wages	2,576,100
Pension contributions 15 per cent	386,415
Welfare 23 x UN30,000	690,000
Total labour costs	3,652,515

DIRECT COSTS OF MANUFACTURING CEMENT POCKETS IN UN 000

	12,343,820 pockets per year (1,314 hours)			17,925,800 pockets per year (1,907 hours)		
	Total	Fixed	Variable	Total	Fixed	Variable
Material at UN23.41	288,969		288,969	419,643		419,643
Labour	3,653	3,653		3,653	3,653	
Depreciation 1,314 x 710 / 1,907 x 560	933		933	1,068		1,068
Interest	945	945		1,090		1,090
Purchasing charges	3	3		3	3	
Maintenance - Fixed	2,300	2,300		2,300	2,300	
Variable at UN250	328		328	477		477
Variable workshop costs at UN70	92		92	133		133
Power at UN80	105		105	153		153
Variable reticulation costs at UN20	26		26	38		38
Insurance	700	700		700	700	
Sundry supplies	1,000	300	700	1,317	300	1,017
Heating	500	500		500	500	
Water	300	300		300	300	
Total	299,854	8,701	291,153	431,375	7,756	423,619
Per hour in UN	228,199	6,621	221,578	226,206	4,067	222,139
Per pocket in UN	24.292	0.705	23.587	24.064	0.432	23.632
Sell 5,581,980 pockets at UN24 each				133,968		
Remainder for 12,343,820 pockets				297,407		
= per pocket				24.094		
Purchase of 12,343,820 pockets at UN24 each plus charges	296,282					

Case Method III

(18)

Objective

To give course members the opportunity to present and discuss their solutions/proposed action on the two cases they have studied in small groups

Handout Material

As for Session 17

Background Reading

As for Sessions 11 and 17

Recommended Reading

As for Session 11

Special Equipment and Aids

Chalkboard or flip chart

90 min.	**Session Guide** 18
8:30	Ask the four group reporters to present concisely the views of their groups for the case study, The Plywood Factory.
8:50	General discussion will follow the presentations.
9:10	BREAK
9:25	Ask the reporters to present their group's views on The Northern Cement Factory. Follow with a general discussion of the different solutions proposed.
10:00	Ask the two observers to give their evaluation of Sessions 17 and 18:
	- the different group approaches;
	- the approach to the two different case studies;
	- the value of the case study as a teaching method.
10:15	Close the session.

Designing Training Programmes I

Objective

To inform participants of what is involved in designing management training programmes

Handout Material

I - A Systems Concept of Training, pp. 11-27

II - Designing Training Programmes, pp. 29-38

III - Tips for Lesson Preparation and Presentation, pp. 39-41

Instructions for Designing a Course Programme (prepared by the instructor; see Session Guide 22)

Background Reading

The Determination of Training Needs within an Enterprise, pp. 1-5

An Extract from the Management of Learning, pp. 7-10

Recommended Reading

Craig and Bittel, Training and Development Handbook, Chapter 2, "Determining Training Needs" by R.B. Johnson. Includes a bibliography on training needs. See also Chapter 29, "Planning and Scheduling" by James H. Morrison.

Special Equipment and Aids

Overhead projector, film screen

Prepare the following to be displayed on the overhead projector:

Exhibit A (Figure 1, "The Traditional Conception of the Training Model", from Handout I, A Systems Concept of Training), p. 13

Exhibit B (Figure 2, "Conception of the Training Model as an Integrated Process", from Handout I, A Systems Concept of Training), p. 14

Exhibit C (Figure 1, from the background reading, An Extract from the Management of Learning), p. 10

90 min.	**Session Guide** 19
	This session should be an informal talk in which participants have ample opportunity to ask questions and report on their experiences with the design and implementation of training programmes. The instructor should draw on the background reading to prepare a more detailed list of points he wishes to cover.
10:30	Present an over-all view of the five major phases in the design and implementation of training programmes. As an outline, use Exhibit A showing the traditional training model:
	- determination (identification, assessment) of needs; - setting of objectives for the programme; - selection and preparation of programme content, methods and organisation; - implementation; - evaluation (to be dealt with more fully in Session 21).
	Turn to Exhibit B to show the systems approach to training, to the design and perfecting of training programmes. We are dealing with a dynamic, cyclical process in which each phase has many relationships to, and is therefore integrated with, every other phase. In this process continuous improvements are needed to keep training programmes up to date.
	Exhibit C (optional) shows a more detailed view of the steps in the design process.
10:45	Explain the content and major problems involved in each phase, building on participants' experiences and ideas in each area. Stress that there will, of course, be differences between training situations, and it is necessary to be highly creative and adaptable to devise and carry out an appropriate range of training programmes.
	When dealing with the selection and preparation of programme content, methods and organisation, differentiate between decisions on the over-all concept of the programme (subject areas to be covered, organisational pattern of the programme, proportion of classroom instruction and practical applications, etc.) and operational decisions concerning particular lessons.
11:15	BREAK
11:30	Continue as above. The discussion will no doubt touch on the differences between more sophisticated training situations found in developed countries and in some of the more advanced enterprises in developing countries, and the "less than ideal" training situation which still prevails in most developing countries. Warn against mechanical transplanting of successful training programmes from industrialised to developing countries, and emphasise the need to adapt the programmes to the socio-economic and cultural setting of each country. (This point is likely to come up again in the later discussion on the RCA training programme.)
12:00	Summarise, issue HANDOUTS I, II and III, and lead into the study assignments. In Session 22, members will read HANDOUT I, a case history of a leadership training programme conducted at the Radio Corporation of America. They will prepare individual comments on the RCA approach and present these during Session 25. You may wish to ask a member to prepare to lead the discussion on the case.
	For the rest of the evening study period, participants will design course programmes to be discussed in Session 26. Divide members into groups for this assignment, forming two homogeneous groups to construct special subject courses, and two heterogeneous groups to draw up general management courses. Detailed instructions may be printed on a HANDOUT; consult Session Guide 22.
12:15	Close the session.

THE DETERMINATION OF TRAINING NEEDS
WITHIN AN ENTERPRISE

by

Rex Strayton,
Associate Professor of
Personnel Administration,
International Centre for Advanced
Technical and Vocational Training, Turin

Introduction

There is a great difference between the way in which we would set about deter-mining training needs and organising training activities in a perfect world and an ideal company, and the way in which we often have to do it in the circumstances in which we happen to find ourselves working.

On the one hand, we may have a progressive company with highly-organised central personnel and training departments, and a plan for integrated manpower development. At the other extreme, we may have a company where the personnel and training responsibilities are not very clearly defined, and where the function, if it can be identified at all, is one of a number of general responsibilities carried out by an official whose main responsibility is something quite different.

In the first type of company, the determination of training needs is something which is constantly being carried out and reviewed as circumstances, policies, markets, and company objectives change. This work is probably done by a central training committee of which the heads of all major departments are members, and of which the training manager is usually secretary.

In the second type of company, the training is much less likely to be planned 'globally' for the company as a whole. The initiative is often left to one particu-lar department manager who happens to realise the potential benefits of training and is keen to do something about it. He may nominate one member of his staff as training officer and activities may be launched which are related only to the specific needs of that particular department at that particular time. They may even conflict with the needs of the organisation as a whole.

So we find, at the one extreme, training needs carefully analysed and reviewed and, at the other, a piecemeal approach, unplanned, unsystematic, and often not related to the needs of the company as a whole. In between these two extremes there are, of course, all the permutations and combinations imaginable. We must, there-fore, discuss this subject in fairly general terms. I shall make a large number of suggestions from which you must select according to the situation in your company at a given moment.

1.   A word of warning

First, a word of warning. If we compare training in the industrial situation with other situations where training is extensively carried out as, for example, in the armed forces, we are bound to recognise a fundamental difference. In the armed forces the need for training is universally accepted - it is considered a first priority. In industry it is not the same. There are many different views about what should be the primary purpose of an industrial enterprise, but few, if any, would say that its primary purpose is to train.

There are still many boards of directors who do not accept the need for training, and even in companies which 'officially' accept the need, there are often departmental managers within that company who are far from sold on the idea.

If you are lucky, you may find yourself working in a company where the training function is firmly established and where it is quite natural to talk about long-range manpower planning. If you are not so lucky, you may find yourself working in a company where you still have to 'sell' yourself and your function. It is more likely that, in the short term, most of us will find ourselves in the latter situation.

2.   The ideal situation

Let us say a word or two about what we might reasonably call the 'ideal' situation before we go on to talk about the situation which we are more likely to find.

In the ideal situation the company will have an integrated manpower development programme. Much could be said about this subject but, in a nutshell, the objective of such an integrated programme is to make better use of our existing manpower and to make whatever preparations are necessary to ensure that we shall have, short term and long term, enough of the sort of people we are going to need at all levels and in all departments of the organisation. One of our major concerns is, of course, to ensure that suitable people are going to be available to fill key posts in the organisation as needs arise.

Such a systematic programme for manpower development is, unfortunately, still the exception rather than the rule but the number of companies using it is growing.

The introduction of such a programme implies an examination of existing personnel policies and practices and especially those relating to selection, recruitment, performance appraisal, 'development' and promotion.

The approach of each company will vary from that of other companies and so it should, but fundamentally there are a number of common basic steps.

A.   We have to take an inventory.   We take stock of our present manpower, both quantitatively and qualitatively, and naturally we shall tend to begin with our supervisory and management people and those we consider as potential supervisors and managers. A good deal of the information we need will already be available to us in the personnel department, i.e., information about qualifications and previous experience and training already given by the company. To this we have to add information about how effective these people are in their present jobs and about their promotability, and this implies an effective performance appraisal scheme.

B.   We have to make forecasts of future requirements. Here we consider normal 'wastage' through retirement, transfers, resignations, etc. and the possible effects of changes in the company's policies and objectives, e.g., expansion, re-organisation, contraction, etc.   There are many ways of recording the information collected in this way but a simple one which is frequently met and which gives a fairly clear picture of the situation is built up on ordinary departmental organisation charts. The chart shows the jobs and job titles and will include new posts to be established during the review period. Under the job title is the present holder's name and under this a box. The corners of the box are used for symbols which record some of the key factors about the present holder, e.g., length of company service, service in the present post, promotability, etc. and the box is frequently shaded to show age. A particularly good example of this type of departmental situation chart will be found in Management Development by F.I. de la P. Garforth. Then we must prepare job descriptions of the vacancies we foresee and 'man' specifications of the sort of people we are going to need to fill those vacancies.

C.   We now need to decide where we are going to find the people we need. We may get some of them from within the organisation but not unless we have a well-planned scheme for 'spotting' talent. It is in this third step that we try to combine the results of steps one and two. Step two forecasts all future requirements but in particular it highlights key jobs which will need to be filled during the review period. Step one has told us what type of people we have and what their potential is. We now try to match the two by allocating people to 'target' jobs. If it is unlikely that we shall be able to fill all vacancies from within the organisation, we shall have to decide which of the many sources outside the company we are going to try to tap.

D.   We finally have to decide what we are going to do to develop our manpower - both those we already have and those we plan to recruit - in order to help them to be fully effective in their present posts and to prepare them for their 'target jobs'. In practice it is a good idea to prepare people wherever possible for two target jobs. This is because some personnel development programmes are quite lengthy and in the meantime company objectives - and therefore organisations - may change. The 'two-target-job' approach will give us greater flexibility.

This, in a nutshell, is the raison d'etre of the training officer's job.

If a scheme of this nature has been introduced in a particular company, it will probably be co-ordinated by a central committee of which the training officer will be a member. The training needs, both short term and long term, will be spotlighted by the development programme. The training officer's task will be to advise on what is to be done within the company to meet these training needs and also what use, if any, is to be made of 'external' facilities offered by training institutions, consultants, technical and commercial colleges, universities, etc. In order to do this, the training officer needs to keep himself well informed about the work of these organisations and its quality.

In the past, a good deal of time and money has been spent unwisely and unproductively in sponsoring people for 'external' courses. This has been due, in part, to the fact that industry and commerce have been very slow in making up their minds about what they really wanted. The initiative has therefore been with these 'external' institutions, many of which have welcomed clearer specifications from industry and commerce of their requirements. And because they did not have an integrated manpower development plan, industrial and commercial sponsors have been working the wrong way round - they have been looking for people to fit courses rather than courses to fit people.

These, then, are the major steps in the operation of an integrated manpower development scheme. The subject is clearly an extensive one and the reader is recommended to read widely in the professional journals.

3. The 'less than ideal' situation

If an integrated manpower development scheme of the type we have been discussing is not operating in the company, the training officer will have to base his strategy on a number of other factors.

A. Consider your terms of reference

Above all, make sure that you fully understand them. You may be required by your company president or managing director to make detailed recommendations for the company as a whole. In this case, you must be careful to work at all times in close co-operation with the company personnel manager. You may, on the other hand, be required initially to confine your activities to a specific department or group of departments or a specific problem within a department. Often training begins this way and slowly expands until all departments of the company are involved and the last thing that happens very often is the thing which those with the theoretical approach would say should happen first, i.e., the establishment of an over-all company training policy.

B. Consider the situation within the organisation

A vital step in the process of determining needs is to find out, right at the start, what training is already being done by the various departments of the company. There may be some fairly formal training schemes already well established in some sections of the company where perhaps a particular manager is enthusiastic about the potential benefits of training. Much more frequently you will find 'informal' training schemes already in operation. These schemes can often be 'discovered' in departments which outwardly make very little fuss about what they are doing and put very little down on paper, but nevertheless are doing a very good job. It is vital that the training officer who is about to begin operations within a company should find out all there is to know about these formal and informal schemes and tread very carefully. Those managers or supervisors who have been doing a good job perhaps for years, may well resent the appearance of a 'new broom' and may well feel that the appointment of a training officer is an implied criticism of the quality of the work they have been doing up to now.

Obviously, the company president or managing director can do much to prevent such misunderstandings if he carefully explains to a meeting of his managers what the new appointment is all about and stresses that the function of the training officer is essentially to help managers to carry out their training responsibilities and not to take the job away from them. Training is and must remain the line manager's responsibility.

The training officer will need to do his own 'appreciation of the situation' and, bearing in mind his terms of reference, determine his objectives and his strategy. On the whole, production managers are down-to-earth, practical people, and it is usually better to help them at first with a problem which they recognise and understand, and show that training can contribute to the solution of their problems than it is to press for long studies and detailed reports right at the beginning. One successful job on the training of crane drivers or slingers or fork drivers may sell the training function throughout that whole department. And one 'satisfied' department manager will be your best salesman as far as other department managers are concerned.

C. Consider the information already available

(i) New employees

Some indication of the need for further training is available from the notes taken at the initial selection interview. However well you may have done your job description and your 'man' specification, you very often discover that the most suitable applicant available does not measure up in every detail to your specification. He may have a number of qualities or skills surplus to your requirements, but he may also be deficient in some areas. Clearly, if the company has engaged the man, it was believed that these deficiencies could be made good by means of training. So this is the starting point for new employees.

(ii) Existing employees

If we have, on the one hand, job descriptions coupled with some form of performance appraisal then the difference between the two is the need for training in order to fit people to carry out their present jobs satisfactorily. Sometimes, of course, the performance appraisal may reveal deficiencies which cannot be remedied by training. Perhaps selection procedures need to be evaluated and overhauled.

If we have simple replacement tables showing who is to be groomed for the key jobs in the organisation by what dates, then we have a fairly reliable source of information about training needs to prepare employees for promotion.

The first two items in this section are more related to those aspects of training which are usually planned and co-ordinated centrally and concern key jobs. Training within the primary working group is frequently left to the section supervisor and he may have a training timetable of the type recommended in traditional 'job instruction' programmes. If the section supervisors do not have such training timetables, the training officer may offer help with their preparation. If training timetables do exist, the training officer may offer to help the section supervisors to carry out the training needs they reveal.

D. Consider the problems which arise within the organisation

Training needs can often be identified by an analysis of the problems which arise within an organisation. There are many 'signals' which can guide us in this type of investigation. Appendix A lists some of the more common ones.

Remember that the existence of one of these problems within your organisation is only prima facie evidence of the existence of a training need. The problem may have its roots in several causes, one of which may be bad training or no training at all. The important thing is to analyse the problem before we prescribe a remedy.

Sometimes it is possible to estimate the direct cost to the company of bottlenecks, the cost per hour of having a rolling mill standing idle, the extent to which these things were due to deficiencies in knowledge and/or skills of employees and therefore the cost of not training.

If you calculate the time it takes at present for a new operator to reach optimum output, or what is often called 'experienced worker performance standard', and the average cost of materials wasted during this period, you can calculate the potential saving to the company by a reduction in this initiation period, including a reduction in the cost of wasted materials. Information of this type will help the training officer to 'sell' training programmes. You can also calculate the loss of earnings to the operatives because they took an unnecessarily long time to reach experienced worker performance standards. This sort of information helps to sell training schemes to operatives and workers' representatives.

E.   Consider other possible approaches

(i) There are eleven techniques for determining training needs in a list
prepared by the Research Committee of the American Society of Training Directors.
They are:

(a) Observations   (f) Questionnaire surveys
(b) Management requests   (g) Tests or examinations
(c) Interviews   (h) Merit or performance ratings
(d) Group conferences   (i) Personnel records
(e) Job or activity analysis   (j) Business and production reports
                                     (k) Long-range organisational planning

(ii) Some people believe that indications of training needs can often be
obtained from a study of the sort of things people say at the exit interviews. The
writer believes that such interviews should continue but we must be very careful
about accepting all that is said by employees at an exit interview at its face
value. If the employee and the circumstances which led to his or her leaving the
company are personally known to the person conducting the exit interview, we are on
safer ground. But the information which is given at an exit interview is usually
highly subjective, often so incomplete as to be worthless and sometimes untrue.

(iii) Questionnaires are sometimes used to help in the determination of
training needs. Some users place great faith in them, others dismiss them as a
waste of time. The truth is probably somewhere between these two extremes.

We must face the fact that there is a great deal of evidence that questionnaires and opinion surveys can be extremely unreliable and misleading. People
often really do not know what they think or believe and there is much evidence to
show that even if they know it, they will not always tell you. The reasons are
many and complicated. If you want to use questionnaires you are strongly recommended to do some serious study of the literature available. H.J. Eysenck and
J.A.C. Brown are well worth reading on this subject.

(iv) Tests of various types are often used for this purpose. This is a highly
specialised field. Test must be valid, reliable, objective and standardised.
It is sad, but true, that many 'tests' are used which fail to meet one or more of
these basic requirements. Those who have not been trained in the administration
of tests and the interpretation of test results and who cannot get professional
advice from someone who has, would be well advised not to use them.

APPENDIX A

Problems Check List - Most enterprises, at one time or another, suffer from most of
                      the problems listed below. Often these problems are the result
                      of bad selection or bad training or the complete lack of a
                      systematic approach to either.

1. Customer's complaints
2. Delays caused by errors and mistakes
3. Excessive time taken to finish
    jobs or orders or supply parts
4. Low output
5. Excessive absenteeism or
    unpunctuality
6. Excessive number of applications
    for time off
7. High labour turnover - and
    especially during the new worker's
    first 6 months
8. High accident frequency
9. Excessive maintenance costs
10. Frequent bottlenecks in production
11. Excessive holdups through slow
    paperwork or procedures
12. Errors resulting from instructions
    not clearly understood
13. People receiving instructions from
    more than one person
14. Poor communications generally
15. Ignorance of safety rules by employees
16. Failure to observe known safety rules
    or use safety equipment
17. Neglect of minor injuries
18. Untidiness of work area
19. Ignorance of company rules and/or
    department rules
20. Inadequate information about company
    organisation and policy
21. Excessive wear and tear on equipment
22. Employees' difficulty in mastering
    new job or new equipment
23. New employees who take too long to
    reach experienced worker (standard)
    performance in quantity and/or quality
24. Lack of flexibility in labour force,
    no substitutes for absentees
25. Too much waste, scrap, or work which
    has to be put right
26. Specifications not followed
27. Standards of quality not met
28. Errors caused by careless measuring
29. Employees' lack of interest in the
    work
30. Employees' failure to realise
    importance of minor jobs or details.

AN EXTRACT FROM
THE MANAGEMENT OF LEARNING[1]

by I.K. Davies

Although many teachers and psychologists would disagree as to the exact nature of the learning process, there are certain principles of learning upon which most educationists would agree.

- Whatever a student learns, he must learn for himself - no one can learn for him.

- Each student learns at his own rate, and for any age group the variations in rates of learning are considerable.

- A student learns more when each step is immediately strengthened or reinforced.

- Full, rather than partial, mastery of each step makes total learning more meaningful.

- When given responsibility for his own learning, the student is more highly motivated; he learns and retains more.

Until now, the design of an educational course has ordinarily involved a combination of expert judgment and known principles of learning - with a seasoning of commonsense. However, it may well be that the problem lies less in an acceptance of the learning principles involved than in putting them into effect in the actual learning situation. At the same time, the difficulty is intensified by the three problems of "Who, ought to teach what, and to whom?"

When we consider what qualities a good teacher should possess or what qualities make for a successful teacher, the answer is fraught with difficulty. Qualities such as sincerity, efficiency, courage, resolution, energy, tact and personality all spring to mind: however, the list is seemingly endless, and even after having compiled it no one really is sure of how it can be used. A more useful approach is to consider what a teacher actually does; in other words to adopt a functional rather than a qualitative approach, and then to make sure that these functions are carried out in the most efficient, effective, and economical manner possible.

Basically there are but two kinds of activity in which a teacher can engage; teachers either manage learning resources or else they operate as a resource.

When a teacher deliberately creates a learning environment in his classroom with a view to realising predefined objectives, he is acting as a teacher-manager. When the same teacher physically teaches in that classroom, he then becomes one of his own resources and takes on the role of a teacher-operator. He is saying, in effect, that he is the most appropriate resource available, more appropriate for realising the objectives than any textbook, workbook, programme, film, tape or record obtainable. On many occasions this will probably be very true, but too often a teacher decides to engage in talk-and-chalk because he enjoys teaching: the decision to be a teacher-operator is taken on the basis of personal preference, rather than on the needs of the learning situation.

Since the time available and the capacities of teachers must always be limited, it follows that they should concentrate, as far as possible, upon doing that work which stems from their unique organisational role as managers of resources for learning. Viewed in this way it is possible to isolate and identify the four functions of the teacher-manager:

Planning	Leading
Organising	Controlling

---

[1] Reprinted by permission of Industrial Training International. See I.K. Davies, "The Management of Learning" in Industrial Training International (Pergamon Press Ltd. Oxford), June 1967.

When the teacher-manager "plans", he attempts to forecast future requirements, define the objectives which will have to be realised, write a syllabus of instruction, determine the order in which topics will be learnt, allocate the time available, and budget the resources involved. Organising is a far more simple and straightforward activity. It involves the deliberate creation of a learning environment, and delegation of responsibilities. At the same time, the most effective relationships must be established amongst the people involved in the educational system.

Probably the most skilled work that the teacher-manager performs, and certainly the most personal, lies in the guidance, encouragement and inspiration which he communicates to his students. In this way, the teacher makes decisions as to how the objectives can best be accomplished, communicates them to his students and then motivates them sufficiently so as to get them to accept responsibility for their own learning. This leadership function provides for the inner needs of students since well-led students do learn without plans and organisation, but - backed by good plans and organisation - well-led pupils become outstanding. The controlling function is concerned with the need to check performance against previously established criteria, with a view to determining whether or not the objectives have been realised.

These four functions are separate and disparate activities, but together they make up the whole of the educational management process.

Now that the functions of the teacher-manager have been considered, it is possible to consider how the resources that are available to him can be most effectively utilised. For a very long time, most efforts were concerned with polished and elegant attempts to mechanise the process of teaching through the production of teaching and learning aids. Such devices, however, ought to be considered less as aids and more as part of the new technology, promising to transform the present-day concepts and methods employed by the teacher.

The decision, however, on whether to use a particular learning or teaching resource can only be based upon an analysis of its characteristics, and how far they are likely to be useful in realising the objectives of the system.

In the design of a learning course, all these requirements must be taken into account; the teacher must consider not only the resources which he has available, but also the personal functions which he himself must fulfil. Figure 1 attempts to show how such a course can be developed. It will be seen that course design involves an orderly sequence of twelve activities, some of which represent the basic framework, while others - no less important - are concerned with the validation of the system once it has been installed.

Viewed in this way the successive stages in the development of a learning system are:

(1) <u>Analysis of over-all system.</u> This analysis consists of a study of the environment in which the learning will take place.

(2) <u>Analysis of task or job.</u> The particular topic is studied in order to determine exactly what the student is required to <u>do</u> when he has achieved mastery. On occasions, such analysis can demonstrate that no teaching is needed whatsoever.

(3) <u>Specification of required knowledge, skills and attitudes.</u> This consists of a statement of what the student must learn.

(4) <u>Definition of target population.</u> The trainees are identified in terms of their intelligence, aptitudes, and abilities. The statement also includes the assumptions that can be made about them in terms of the learning task.

(5) <u>Statement of training need.</u> Although goals can sometimes be met without training, formal instruction is usually required. This will need to be stated in concrete terms as an educational problem.

(6) <u>Analysis of objectives in behavioural form</u>. Now that the educational need has been identified, the target population defined, and the knowledge, skills and attitudes specified, it is possible to state the objectives that the course is to realise in precise enough terms so as to be capable of observation and measurement.

(7) <u>Course construction</u>. This step involves the selection of the specific material to be used, its structuring into appropriate learning sequences and the determination of the most effective strategies and presentation modes available.

(8) <u>Development of measures of job proficiency</u>. This criterion measure, usually written concurrently with the course materials, is developed in order to determine whether the student has or has not acquired mastery of the subject.

(9) <u>Validation of proficiency measures</u>. In order to ensure that the measures are valid, they are tried out in a variety of situations.

(10) <u>Field testing and evaluation</u>. The course is now tried out with a sample of students representative of the population for whom the course was designed. The measures of proficiency are then used in order to evaluate the success of the learning system in realising its objectives.

(11) <u>Revision</u>. If the course fails to meet the objectives, the material is re-written and revised until the necessary standards are achieved.

(12) <u>Implementation</u>. This final step involves the introduction and integration of the new course into its educational environment. It also includes gaining the teacher's acceptance of any new and unfamiliar ideas and techniques.

Activities 1, 2, 3, 4, 5 and 6 are primarily concerned with the teacher's PLANNING function, activities 7 and 12 with his ORGANISING function, and activities 8, 9, 10 and 11 with his CONTROLLING function. The LEADERSHIP function is, of course, personal to the teacher himself.

1. The Development of a Learning System

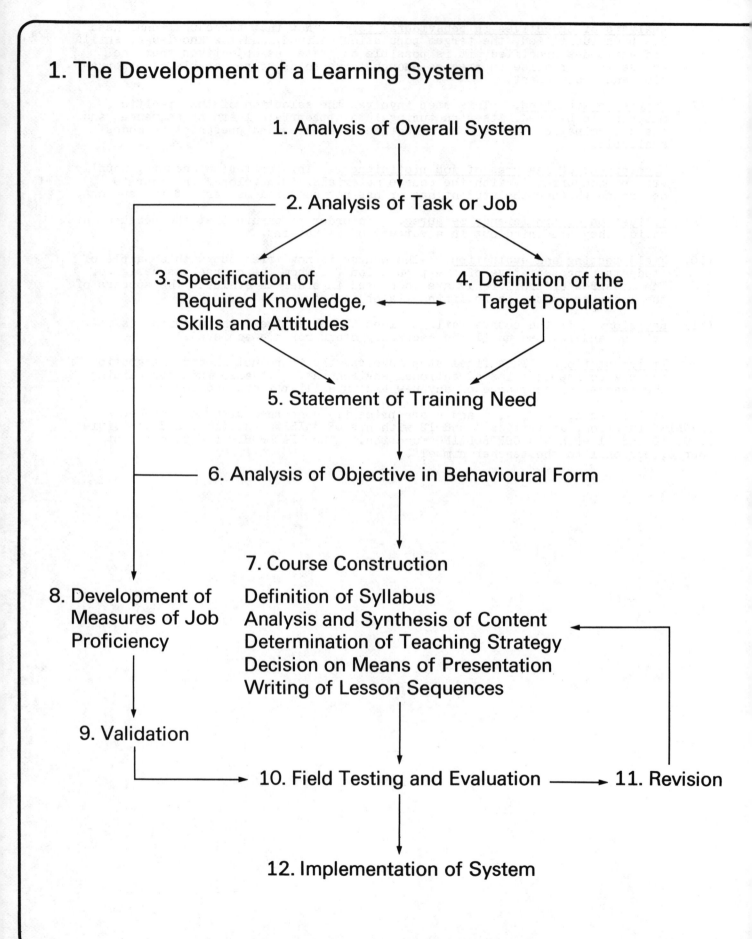

1. Analysis of Overall System

2. Analysis of Task or Job

3. Specification of Required Knowledge, Skills and Attitudes

4. Definition of the Target Population

5. Statement of Training Need

6. Analysis of Objective in Behavioural Form

7. Course Construction
Definition of Syllabus
Analysis and Synthesis of Content
Determination of Teaching Strategy
Decision on Means of Presentation
Writing of Lesson Sequences

8. Development of Measures of Job Proficiency

9. Validation

10. Field Testing and Evaluation

11. Revision

12. Implementation of System

A SYSTEMS CONCEPT OF TRAINING[1]

by

Richard D. Miller
Training Specialist,
Memory Products Division, RCA,
Needham, Massachusetts

The training literature frequently refers to a particular model which is commonly used in training. This model is the traditional model composed of the phases assessment, objective setting, design, implementation and evaluation. The training model is said to have a professional value. Rarely is the model said to have functional value or utility. This may be due to several factors. One factor is that the use of this model has not been subject to critical scrutiny and/or research, possibly because it is frequently conceived as being composed of five discrete phases connected sequentially with each phase standing independently. The findings and results of these phases are generally conceived as final statements. This particular conception of the training model is diagrammed in Figure 1.

This particular way of thinking about training tends to lead to several particular consequences and results: (1) needs assessment data are prematurely organised and stated as training needs which results in (2) objectives stated in very general and unmeasurable terms and not closely related to the real training needs which leads to (3) programs designed and implemented which are only slightly related to real training needs or "real life" circumstances faced by trainees. This, then, has a large effect on trainees' motivation, involvement and learning. In general, this conception of training leads to increasingly more general and less precise training efforts.

Another way of conceiving the training model is to view it as an interdependent and interrelated process in which the five phases form subprocesses which are highly interrelated and interdependent on all other subprocesses as well as on the total process. This way of thinking about the training model is diagrammed in Figure 2.

The conception of the training model as an interrelated process leads to a set of consequences quite different from those of the traditional conception. The consequences which result from using it as a process are in general (1) the results of each subprocess   do not become final statements but are continually reworked and reconceived, resulting in (2) increasingly specific questions, answers, and actions in each subprocess which results in (3) a functional utility in terms of training results.

A Leadership Training Study

This article reports on a leadership training program conducted at RCA in which the training model was used in a precise and integrated process manner. Part of the results of that training program could only be explained as outcomes affected by this specific and concrete use of the training model. If the evidence and data are correct, this would be a very useful research study of the functional value of the integrated training process. As such, the implications for training and development (industrial and otherwise) would be widespread.

Before beginning, it would be helpful if some key assumptions and concepts were stated. First, the traditional training model (assessment, setting objectives, etc.) can more appropriately be conceived as an integrated process. Secondly, each phase of the total process is a subprocess to the entire process. The relationship of the total process is systemic in nature; i.e., the subprocesses are interdependent, interrelated, stand individually but, when connected, form more than the sum of their parts.

[1] Reproduced by special permission from the April 1969 Training and Development Journal; Copyright 1969 by the American Society for Training and Development, Inc.

The author wishes to express his special gratitude to Mr. William J. Underwood for his most helpful comments and criticisms in the writing of this article as well as the key role he assumed in the development of this program. The author also wishes to express his gratitude to Dr. Robert F. Maddocks for his constructive criticisms in the writing of this paper.

Some evidence exists to support the belief that a key variable affecting how much functional value the training process has on trainee learning, involvement, etc. is the degree of specificity, completeness, and comprehensiveness to which the process is carried out. It should be cautioned that causality is not ascribed to this variable, but a correlation was experienced with results which were otherwise unexplainable. There was no control of groups or variables due to the clinical nature of the study.

In this article we will be working at several different levels at different times. The general format of the article will be to identify all subprocesses of the training model. Next, an operational description of how each subprocess was conducted will be presented. This material will be described to demonstrate the key points and evidence which exist. This descriptive material will then be analyzed to show how and in what ways the actual conduct of the phases of the program was handled as a process. The analysis will also deal with the consequences and utility of using the training model in a process manner.

The Assessment Process

The project itself was initiated at the invitation of top management of one of RCA's divisions who felt the need for training of some sort for lower levels of management. An assessment was initiated which consisted of depth interviews with all levels of management. In almost all cases, the initial interviews were non-directive and set within the general context of the manager's job and himself and how he saw and felt about each of these. The direction of the interview was to focus and refocus continually on how he perceived the job, how he perceived his boss' behaviour and expectations, what he said he did in his job and how he behaved as a supervisor. The shortest of these interviews lasted 40 minutes and in most cases complete notes were taken.

From the interviews, considerable data were gathered on how lower level managers said they performed their jobs, how they felt about their job, how they perceived their boss's behavior, feelings and expectations and some data regarding "the way things are around here" - i.e., the organization's "culture." From the first-level supervisors' managers, almost the same data were derived about that level plus pertinent data about how he (the second level manager) perceived and appraised the first-level supervisor's job and his performance in that job. Despite the large amount of data gathered, the process of assessing the training needs was only partially completed. Throughout the data gathering, no effort was made to work with or organize the data in any way.

Key Findings

Following the first run of data gathering, the data were reduced and organized to be meaningful and useful. Several key findings resulted. In general, the findings were that the first-level supervisor saw:

1. Leadership or specific leadership acts as comprising a small part of his job (leadership being seen as 15 percent of the total job).

2. Leadership and leadership behavior as being peripheral rather than integral to his job and his responsibilities.

3. Control of subordinates as being his prime, if not sole leadership responsibility.

4. Leadership as a means of maintaining control or stability more than as a means of building work group productivity, competence, etc.

These findings were relatively consistent but several inconsistencies were significant, and the findings did not yield much evidence as to the cause of these phenomena. It was necessary, therefore, to begin a second phase of data gathering to (1) make the first set of findings more specific and (2) account for inconsistencies, as well as (3) gain more evidence as to causal reasons.

A second interview effort was begun especially with those supervisors where inconsistencies had been noted. In addition, observations were made of supervisors' behavior to determine how accurate their verbal reports had been as well as to gather more specific data.

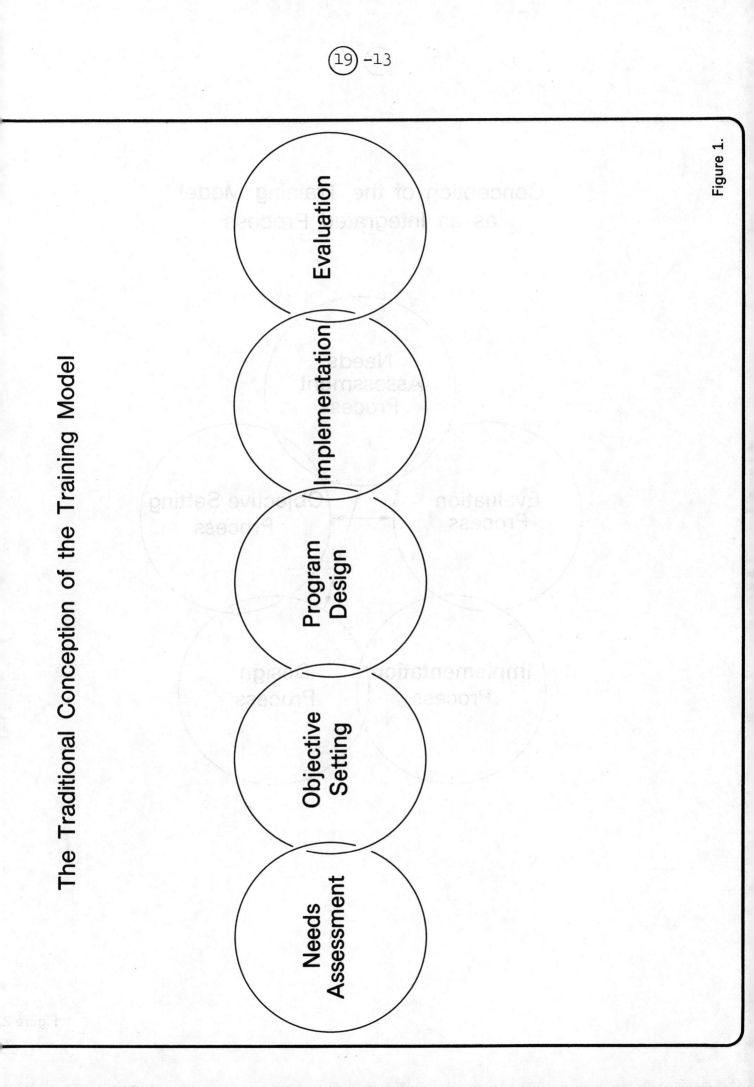

The Traditional Conception of the Training Model

Needs Assessment

Objective Setting

Program Design

Implementation

Evaluation

Figure 1.

Conception of the Training Model as an Integrated Process

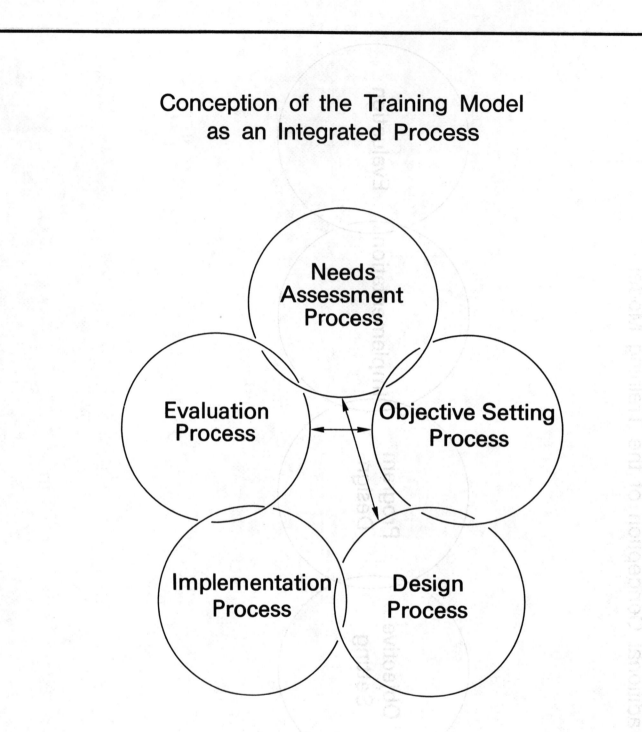

Figure 2

Leadership Patterns

From the further interviews, it was found that supervisors' perceptions of their jobs did differ. These differences tended to form consistent patterns. The patterns are based on attitudes, reported behavior and observed leadership behavior of these supervisors with subordinates. These patterns of leadership behavior tended to fall into styles. That is, the patterns which emerged formed into three styles of leadership. The styles or categories were called A, B, and C. The data gathered indicated that almost all managers could be appropriately categorized into one of these three styles.

Style A supervisors saw the leadership parts of their jobs in the following ways:

1. Simple and peripheral to their job.

2. Capable of being performed by means of -

    a. techniques and methods used primarily to control subordinates' behavior;

    b. addressing technological rather than leadership issues.

3. Fixed and constant in nature; that is, they felt as though there was little quality differentiation in the act of leadership and that leadership was to be used primarily for controlling and disciplining subordinates.

4. This category yielded a tendency on supervisors' parts to see maintenance of the status quo (production) as being an important end result for their work groups.

Style B supervisors tended to:

1. Be less concerned with control of subordinates as a means of performing leadership responsibilities.

2. See leadership as a more important and integral part of their jobs.

3. Differentiate symptoms from causes: i.e., they tended to speak of behavior and motivation problems as leadership issues rather than technological issues.

4. Provide more functional leadership than Style A or C managers although adequate knowledge and skill of leadership issues and behavior was still weak.

Supervisors categorized as Style C were typified by managers who saw their job as that of a task specialist. That is, a Style C supervisor was one who saw his job almost solely in terms of technological problems. One example of a Style C supervisor would be an accounting manager who had six clerks and two accountants reporting to him but saw his job as requiring almost no leadership responsibility. Rather, he saw his job solely in terms of handling accounting problems.

Training Implication

The findings to this point strongly indicated that leadership was the general area in need of development. The inconsistencies found in the first data gathering effort were accounted for by the findings of the second data gathering and data reduction process. That is, further data indicated that the inconsistencies were a result of different styles of leadership used by managers. The styles themselves (A, B, and C) appeared to be internally consistent.

These data had several implications. First of all, it suggested that the lack of highly-developed leadership knowledge and skill could not be solely caused by the organization or its "climate," for there were significant differences between the three styles. The data indicated that the lack of highly-developed leadership knowledge or behavior was probably individually determined. This conclusion was a critical one, for, had the findings indicated that the development needs were caused by the organization's management system or "climate" alone, a training effort for the first-level managers would have been pointless. Under such conditions, transfer

of learning from the program to the job would have failed to be significant.[1]
Thus, there were significant indications that the phenomena were caused and controlled at least partially within the individual supervisor. By training him,
change was at least possible.

Training Needs

Another implication was that the supervisors who might be trained were found
to be significantly different in their knowledge, attitudes, and behavior regarding
leadership. Would they all need further training? Would it make sense to have
them attend the same program? In the same group? Such questions might tempt
trainers toward answers at this stage of working the data if the training model
were being used in its traditional sequential conception. Under an integrated
conception, however, such questions put the cart before the horse. As of yet,
the training needs had not been formulated. To this point, only diagnostic and
assessment data of the characteristics of the managers had been determined. Thus,
the next task was to express specifically the training needs of each category of
manager. From the diagnostic data the following training needs were formulated:

Category A's Training Needs

1. Explore leadership as an integral aspect of supervision.

2. Explore various types of leadership behavior such as the leader dealing with:

   a. group phenomena;

   b. people's needs, values, and expectations.

3. Explore the need for control.

   a. other aspects and heretofore unconceived consequences of various types
      of control;

   b. alternative means of control and results and their consequences.

4. Assess the relationship between leader behavior, control, subordinate's
   nature, values, and expectations and the results which can be expected.

5. Assess their present level of functioning in relation to alternatives and
   assess their future paths by testing newly presented alternatives against
   their past experience.

6. Express and deal with dissonance which may result.

Category B's Training Needs

1. Assess their present level of functioning consciously and explicitly.

2. Express whatever feelings of frustration and dissonance due to lack of
   organizational support, sanction, and/or reward.

3. Explore other aspects of supervision such as:

   a. other aspects of leadership than presently conceived;

   b. group phenomena and group leadership concepts;

   c. people's needs, values, and expectations as factors affecting the
      accomplishment of work.

---

[1] It should be pointed out that additional data did indicate some organization
support of a particular style. Appraisal reports for the preceding year for each
category of style indicated that, on the average, managers categorized as Style A
received higher ratings than did managers categorized as Style B or C who received
about even ratings on the average. No statistical analysis was done. Also, interview data indicated some incidence in Style B managers of feeling little support
or understanding from their bosses regarding how they (the Style B managers)
performed and/or led their subordinates. This indicated a development need at
other levels and perhaps some organization development needs.

4. Explore other criteria of leader effectiveness and group performance beyond production and discipline such as:

   a. teamwork-cooperation phenomena;

   b. building group competence, resources.

5. Explore and assess the relationship of leader behavior and the functions he performs with the various results which can be expected to occur.

6. Assess these cognitive concepts and theories against their past experience for validation and integration in their thinking.

Category C's Training Needs

1. Exposure to the concept of leadership as an integral aspect of supervision.

2. Explore various aspects and methods of leadership.

3. Search and explore issues of people's needs, values, and expectations relevant to the accomplishment of work.

4. Search and explore other result criteria beyond production and discipline.

5. Assess the relationship between leadership behavior and methods; people's needs, values, and expectations; and the results which can be expected.

6. Assess their present level of functioning and assess their future paths.

Assessment Process Analysis

This final formulation of the training needs concluded the assessment process. To help keep the central thesis of this article clear, let us look back over the assessment process and restate it in terms of the central notions being presented.

First of all, it was stated earlier that it would be useful for training people to think of the training model as a total, integrated process, systemic in nature and composed of subprocesses rather than phases. The assessment process which was just described appeared to be a complete process composed of subprocesses. The first data gathering might more appropriately be called the exploratory subprocess, for the finding of this subprocess did not yield final diagnostic data nor complete training needs. Rather, the findings indicated initial findings and the general direction of inquiry along with some disturbing inconsistencies. Further work was obviously needed.

Thus, the second data generation activity began which could be called the diagnostic subprocess. This subprocess resulted in findings which were more specific in nature than those of the exploratory subprocess. It also resulted in validation of the original findings as well. These findings accounted for inconsistencies and gave indications of causality of the phenomena which helped answer the question of whether or not further work with this level of manager would be functional. And yet the training needs had not been stated.

The third and final subprocess was the formulation of hypotheses specifying training needs by category. This process might be called the hypothesizing of training needs. This way of measuring the needs assessment process gives some insight as to the systemic nature of the process for each subprocess is inter-related and interdependent on each other subprocess. In addition, each subprocess is very closely connected to and flows from the results of the preceding subphase. Had the process been ended at the diagnostic subprocess, as is frequently done in training efforts, the findings would not have been sufficiently specific or accurate to build precise and meaningful objectives.

The needs assessment activity has been described as being a subprocess of the entire training process. In turn, the needs assessment subprocess has been further described as being composed of further subprocesses which were called the exploratory, diagnostic, and hypothesizing training needs sub-subprocesses. The interdependence and interrelated nature of these sub-subprocesses is diagrammed in Figure 3.

Objective Setting Process

The final needs statements stated earlier were pointless unless carried towards further action. The needs statements only indicated what was needed and did not define what would be striven for. The interest here is to demonstrate the relationship between the objective setting subprocess and the needs assessment subprocess and how close that relationship can and should be.

In this process, several crucial questions were raised. First of all, are the needs of each style category comparable with the needs of the other categories? And secondly, if the needs of each category are comparable with each other category, would it be meaningful to compose one generalized set of objectives?

To answer these questions, it was necessary to return to the findings of all three subprocesses of the needs assessment and look at these findings from a different perspective. The findings needed to be reviewed to answer several questions, such as the following: What common needs were there among categories A, B, and C? What common characteristics did each category of supervision have? What disparate characteristics did each category have and could these disparities be in fact commonalities manifested at different levels? What, if anything, could be generalized to all supervisors from the findings?

The answer to these questions began to affect the objective setting process, for only in the answer to these questions raised about the findings of the needs assessment could meaningful objectives be found. In reviewing and reconceiving the exploratory and diagnostic findings, commonalities began to be evidenced. For example, it became evident that all supervisors, except perhaps those classified as Category C supervisors, were indeed providing leadership for their work groups. The quality and quantity of leadership varied by category, but the indications were that leadership was being provided.

In addition, the diagnostic findings indicated that each supervisor was practicing a particular style of leadership and that each of the supervisors (1) was not aware that he was practicing a particular style and (2) was not aware that there were several styles (with specific characteristics and predictable consequences) from which he could choose to practice. These findings indicated that the managers were behaving in their environment under conditions of limited awareness of alternative behavior and limited choice. The difference or disparity of characteristics between different categories were differences in level more than differences in basic characteristics.

Category Differences

Conceived in this way, the differences between categories of managers could be seen primarily as differences in the awareness of and knowledge about various leadership modes or styles on the part of these managers. Thus, several key factors of the objectives finally fell together. The findings indicated that almost all supervisors needed increased knowledge and awareness of alternatives of choice.

The prime purpose of the program, then, would be to increase cognitive knowledge rather than to change behavior or attitude. The general knowledge area would be leadership styles, their characteristics and consequences. The objectives were that as a result of the program the trainees would (1) know the characteristics of several styles of leadership and their resulting consequences, (2) have knowledge of factors affecting subordinate motivation and productivity, and (3) see leadership as an integral part of the total job of managing. (This is, of course, an attitude change objective rather than a knowledge change objective.)

Objective Setting Analysis

In looking back over the description of how the objectives were set to see how they fit into the central thesis as can easily be seen, the major activity in this process was that of continually reconceiving the data and findings of the needs assessment. The findings of the needs assessment were not taken or used as final statements to determine objectives, but, rather, were used in a dynamic interrelated way with the setting of objectives. The needs statements were continually reworked and reconceived until they made or had "new " meaning in terms of what objectives would be most meaningful.

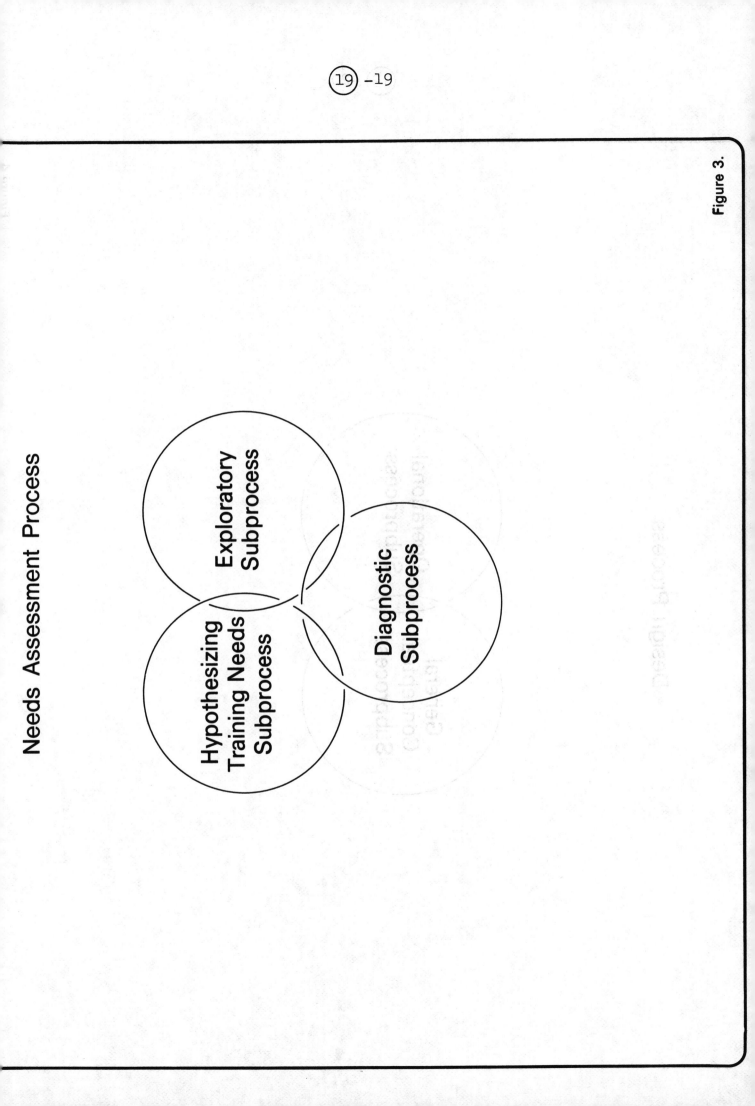

Needs Assessment Process

Exploratory Subprocess

Hypothesizing Training Needs Subprocess

Diagnostic Subprocess

Figure 3.

Design Process

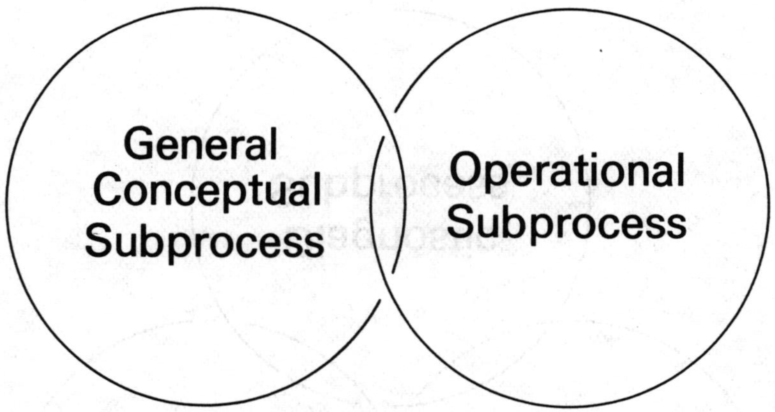

Figure 4

General
Conceptual
Subprocess

Operational
Subprocess

This way of processing the data and findings helped to determine the domain (knowledge change) and content of that domain (leadership style characteristics and consequences). The key aspect of working through the process of determining objectives was that the findings of the needs assessment were highly interrelated with and used in a process manner to the determination of objectives. The key is the interrelation of the two processes, for, had the setting of objectives been done in the more traditional manner, which is to begin working sequentially from the assessment findings and conceiving the findings as final statements rather than by dealing with the objectives and the assessment results coordinately or in an interrelated manner, it would not have been possible to arrive at objectives so meaningfully related to the actual training needs.

Design Process

The design process, as it was carried out in this training effort, was composed of three subphases which might be called development of a general training concept, feedback and proposal presentation, and operational design and detail. Only the first and last subphases will be discussed. The feedback and proposal presentation has been excluded, not because of its lack of importance, but, rather, because of the fact that it is somewhat unique and has been the subject of independent study. The two subphases (Conceptual and Operational Design) differ not only by level (general or abstract vs. specific or operational) but also in general nature.

The first subphase (most appropriately called the development of a general concept) is an activity in which the needs and objectives are begun to be operationalized in a general way. That is, questions along very general dimensions need to be answered such as what general trends or patterns should develop? Along what dimensions should these trends develop, such as trainee participation, trainee involvement, dealing with increasing personal or non-personal issues, etc.? In this subprocess, both the needs and objectives should be worked with as well as outside tools such as learning and development theory and research. These needed to be closely interrelated, for, had the needs and objectives dealt with how to live with a computer or how to discipline subordinates, learning research and theory as well as experience would tell us that a lecture and slide program would have been most effective. But as was the case in this effort, dealing with very central personal issues such as one's behavior and self-concept requires a much more extensive and intensive conceptual design effort.

Concern For Climate

The findings of the exploratory and diagnostic subprocesses of the needs assessment indicated that these managers typically did not deal consciously and explicitly with such issues as their behavior or leadership styles. This, then, meant that the design of the program must take into account the particular training environment or "climate" needed to facilitate dealing with these new and difficult issues. The findings of the needs assessment also indicated that the managers had experience in leading other people (as well as being led) but had little exposure to the research or theory regarding leadership. Theory and research findings in training and development,[1] indicate that high levels of trainee participation and involvement would be the most (if not only) effective mode of operation for dealing with such complex and difficult personal and interpersonal issues.

Thus, a general program model could be expressed. The program needed to be designed and conducted in such a way that the dimension of trainee participation would continuously increase. Secondly, since the needs statement indicated that the trainees would need to deal with relatively personal issues, the amount of trainee involvement and the extent to which he felt responsibility for his own learning would be generally increasing as the program progressed. This meant also that the content of the course would go from relatively non-personal to increasingly

---

[1] Lombard, G.F.F., Behavior in a Selling Group: A Case Study of Interpersonal Relations in a Department Store. Harvard University Press, 1955.

Orth, C.D., Social Structure and Learning Climate. Harvard University Press, 1964.

Zaleznik, A., Foreman Training in a Growing Enterprise. Harvard University Press, 1951.

personal for each trainee. In addition, the cognitive concepts which would be dealt with and related to the personal issues faced by the trainees would need to become increasingly complex. The program model, then, was that trainee participation, involvement, and the extent to which he felt responsibility for learning would increase as the program progressed. In addition, the content of the course would go from simple to complex and would begin by being non-personal from the trainee's point of view and become increasingly personal.

Operational Design

The final subprocess of the design process was the operational design and detailing necessary to address the training needs, meet the objectives, and fulfill the general design concepts which were needed as well as to set appropriate beginning and ending points. The first step needed to be the design of the beginning program activities. The diagnostic findings indicated that all the trainees, regardless of categories, frequently saw human and leadership issues and problems as being technological problems and addressed them as such. This, then, marked an appropriate point of departure.

In the first session, several issues needed to be dealt with. First of all, a point of departure was needed. Secondly, the "ground rules" of trainee participation and trainee responsibility for his own learning needed to be made clear. Thirdly, the first session, like all sessions, needed to be tied into "on-the-job" situations as closely as possible. And, finally, a general overview and explanation of why the program was being conducted and what would be dealt with needed to be included.

As a result of these considerations, it was decided that prior to the session the trainees would be asked to formulate a complete and comprehensive list of all the duties that they performed on their jobs. The session would begin with the trainees formulating a composite list as a group. Then, the trainer would present a model of the supervisor's job composed of three parts (technological, administrative, and leadership). This model would be described and explained and then the trainees would classify their duties into the three categories. This would meet several of the criteria stated earlier.

By attempting to make explicit and to clarify the manager's role, a meaningful point of departure would be set as well as introducing trainee participation as a mode of operating. In addition, clarifying their role was very closely tied to "job" situations. And, finally, this activity laid the necessary definitives and groundwork for explaining what would be dealt with in the program (leadership) and why. A specific explanation of why the program was being conducted, what areas would be dealt with, and what the trainer's expectations were in regard to the trainees' behavior and performance would be included. A brief lecturette on some expanded notions of leadership and preparation for a homework assignment would conclude the first session.

Second Session

To design the second session, it was again necessary to return to the exploratory and diagnostic findings. The finding that human and leadership problems were frequently seen and addressed as technological problems by the trainees would be a meaningful focus for the second session as well as the first. This issue seemed to be the approximate content of the second session.

It was decided that a case would be an effective means for the participants to begin to acquire knowledge and skill in understanding and handling just such an issue.[1] A search of the literature uncovered the "Hovey and Beard Company" case.[1] This case reports a problem faced by a foreman. The case is presented in four sequential parts. In the first part, the problem faced by the foreman appears to be a technological one. The second part adds more data with some leadership issues brought to bear on the problem. Action is taken to address the leadership issues at the end of Part 2. Part 3 reports the results of the action taken. Part 4 reports on the results of revising the action taken in Part 2.

---

[1] Lawrence, P., et al., Organisational Behavior and Administration. Richard D. Irwin, Inc. and The Dorsey Press, Inc., 1961.

This particular case was decided upon because of the dramatic nature with which it illustrates how human and leadership problems can appear on the surface to be solely technological in nature. The case also introduces several other leadership issues. One of these issues is the results which occur when workers have control over some of the decision-making, about how their job will be done. Another key piece of data illustrated in this case is the low effect that wages and incentive programs can have compared to non-monetary factors. The case not only would establish with the trainees the process of working with case situations but also would address two training needs and objectives. Those were to see leadership problems as such and to learn of factors affecting subordinate motivation and productivity.

Third Through Fifth Sessions

The third session was designed to begin dealing with particular styles of leader behavior, their characteristics and consequences. To do this, the "Century Company" case[1] was to be used. This case demonstrates two particular styles which could be called "autocratic" and "laissez-faire." In a very complete and detailed manner, the case studies the two leaders' behavior, the effect on subordinates' sentiments, motivation, and the emergent social system as well as work group productivity.

The next session was designed to deal with a third style of leader behavior which might be called "situational." The "American Radiatronics Company" case[1] was decided upon. This case demonstrates just such a leader's behavior and its effect on the work group's development, workers' motivation, sentiments, and productivity, again in very close and fine detail. These two cases, then, would meet the needs of the trainees to know the characteristics and consequences of particular modes or styles of leadership behavior.

The diagnostic study had found that many managers felt that leadership acts should be used to control their subordinates' behavior. To address this situation, it was felt that practice in working under such a condition - i.e., one in which the trainees did and did not have control of the planning and decision-making about how they would work - might be valuable. It was decided to use Bernard Bass's "Exercise Organization."[2] This exercise gives participants an opportunity to operate two different plans on the same task - one plan which they had devised and a plan which another group had devised. Attitudinal and productivity data can be gathered for each operation and discussed following the session.

Sixth Session

In the sixth and next-to-last session, it was felt that the trainees should have an opportunity to assess their own leadership styles so as to have some central and independent awareness of how they actually behaved with subordinates. This would be a key and critical factor if the trainees were to become fully aware of the possibilities of choice - i.e., where they were in relation to where they might want to go. It was decided to use the Leadership Opinion Questionnaire.[3] The questionnaire would be handled in the following ways to assure that the trainees had as meaningful data as possible.

First of all, the trainees would take the test twice, answering the questions from two frames of reference. The first frame or set would be "How would the ideal leader answer as you see it?" The second frame or set would be "to answer the questions as they best describe you and your feelings." Following this, the two dimensions measured on the test (consideration and structure) would be defined and explained. The next step would be to have the trainees estimate on a grid made up of these dimensions where they felt the ideal leader would fit and where they, themselves, would fit. On the two dimensions, these estimates would tell them where they thought they were on the two dimensions and where they would like to be in terms of them.

---

[1] Lawrence, P., et al., op cit.

[2] Bass, B., "Exercise Organization," Management Development Associates, Inc., 1967.

[3] Fleishman, E.A., "The Leadership Opinion Questionnaire," Science Research Associates, Inc., 1967.

Following this, the scoring key would be explained and they would score and chart their actual test results compared to their estimates. This, then, would give them a measure of where they really were versus where they had guessed they would be versus where they would like to be in terms of two dimensions of leader attitudes.

Final Session

The final session was one in which debriefing and counselling would be necessary following the previous experiences, particularly the LOQ results. To assist in translating program learning to on-the-job behavior changes, it was decided that an assignment would be given to the trainees. The assignment would ask what, if any, ideas had been dealt with in the program with which the trainee would like to experiment on the job as well as what means of implementing and what difficulties the trainees would experience in attempting to do things differently. This tool would also be part of the evaluation.

Design Process Analysis

In terms of the central thesis of this article, the design activity can be seen as a process of extending the objectives closer to action. The process of designing the program began with extending and expanding the objectives into a general training concept composed of several key dimensions and parameters. These dimensions and parameters defined general conditions and trends which would need to develop if the objectives were to be met. This general concept then needed to be expanded into a complete and detailed program. By working within the parameters of the general training concept as well as turning to the findings of the needs assessment process and to the objectives, the operational design and detailing process was worked through. The interrelatedness of the subprocesses of the design activity are shown in Figure 4.

The content of most sessions was determined directly from the findings of the needs assessment and the objectives. There again the interrelationship and the interdependence of the design process with the previous processes can easily be seen. It is in this subprocess that the results of using the training model as a process begin to be obvious. The specificity of the findings in the previous processes allows for content material to be drawn on which will handle specific training needs with great precision.

Implementation Process

Due to the fact that much has been written about the conduct of programs, it is not necessary to dwell on this aspect of the total program other than to mention that 16 hours of training time were used, spread over one month. In addition, the primary concern in this article is to demonstrate and provide evidence to support the notion of the functional value or utility of viewing the training model as an integrated process, for, if the results of the needs assessment, objectives setting, and design processes are valid and not "abnormal" levels of trainer skill and if trainee competence could be assumed, the conduct of the program should result in the objectives being met.

Evaluation Process

Prior to the program, several evaluational tools were designed to measure whether or not or to what extent the objectives were met. The objectives of the program once again were that as a result of the program the trainees would (1) know the characteristics of several styles of leadership and their resulting consequences, (2) have knowledge of factors affecting subordinate motivation and productivity and (3) see leadership as an integral part of the total job of managing.

The first two objectives were of increasing knowledge while the third was an attitude change objective. The program purposely did not attempt to change or alter the trainees' behavior, styles or ways of functioning.

There were several reasons for not setting a behavior change objective. First of all, it was felt that if training was to attempt to change leadership styles, the fundamental decisions as to the direction and nature of change should be made by the division's top management and that this should be based on a more extensive assessment and data feedback effort than time had allowed. Secondly, as was mentioned earlier, the diagnostic findings and the needs statement indicated that fundamental changes in cognitive knowledge were needed and were possible to attain whereas behavior changes may not have been possible. And, finally, limited program time conditions precluded the opportunity to attempt behavior change efforts on the trainees' part.

Testing for Objectives

To measure the degree to which the objectives were met, a test was devised for the trainees to complete. The test itself was composed of 25 questions, 23 of which were designed to measure the amount of factual knowledge retained. In addition, two opinion questions were included in the test, one of which was to determine the attitude change objective. The 23 knowledge questions were of the short essay type. The test had many general questions regarding characteristics and consequences of three leadership styles as well as factors affecting subordinate motivation and productivity and required relatively specific answers. The test was designed to make it inordinately difficult to receive a score above 50 percent correct. The essay type questions and the inordinate difficulty were designed into the test in order that the amount of knowledge acquired could be differentiated by level.

Bloom's Taxonomy of Educational Objectives[1] provided a hierarchy which was used to differentiate levels of learning. In addition, the test's difficulty would allow room for demonstration of large variations in under- and over-performances. Although the objectives had been set at a level of acquired knowledge of specific facts,[1] there was also interest in how deep the learning had been.

The tests were returned by 70 percent of the trainees. The average over-all score of the tests returned was 70 percent. Individual scores ranged from 43 per cent to 95 per cent. Only three individuals scored below 50 per cent while six individuals had scores of 85 per cent or better. No scoring above 80 per cent had been anticipated. An analysis of those tests with scores of 85 per cent or better indicated that not only had the trainee acquired and retained a large amount of the information dealt with in the program, but also indicated deep levels of comprehension of the issues dealt with. In addition, tests with scores of 85 per cent or better indicated analysis and synthesis of relationships not dealt with explicitly in the program. In terms of measuring the test scores against the objectives, it can be generalised that the program's objectives were met and exceeded. Of the tests returned, 40 per cent had scores of 85 per cent or better, indicating results well beyond the level set in the objectives.

Attitude Change

The opinion question on the test measured the importance of the leadership component (as compared with the technological and administrative components) of their total job as the trainees saw it. Prior to the program, opinions were solicited in interviews conducted with the trainees. At that time, they saw leadership as comprising 15 per cent of their total job. Following the program, the 70 per cent of the trainees returning tests indicated that they saw leadership as comprising 39 per cent of their total job. It is interesting to note that after the program, the trainees, as a group, felt that leadership was the most important aspect of their total job. Individually, 64 per cent of the trainees indicated that leadership was the most important part of their total job; 82 per cent of the trainees indicated that leadership comprised at least one-third of their total job.

This data gives some indication of a possibly significant attitude shift. It should be mentioned that the data cannot be stated firmly as an authentic, significant attitude change for several reasons. First of all, the before and after data were not gathered by the same tool. In addition, no control groups were used to assure control against multiple contamination of the variables. And, finally, the after measure may have been contaminated or distorted due to the possible stimuli condition of its being contiguous with the course itself. Nonetheless, it is felt the data is worthy of being reported.

---

[1] Bloom, B., ed., et al., Taxonomy of Educational Objectives: The Classification of Educational Goals - Handbook I: Cognitive Domain. David McKay Company, Inc., 1956.

The table below indicates the average perceived importance of the three components of a supervisor's jobs by the first level supervisors measured before and after the program.

	Leadership	Technology	Administration
Before the Program	15%	50%	35%
After the Program	39%	31%	30%

From the test results it was determined that all three objectives had been met.

Carry-over to Job

There was also curiosity about the transfer of learning from the classroom to the job. Although it is quite early (perhaps too early) to expect on-the-job changes, and recognizing that job behavior change was not a program objective, there was curiosity nonetheless about two things: (1) what the trainees might want to do differently on their jobs and (2) what changes their supervisors might have observed. To measure these we handed out two additional questionnaires. One of these was given to the trainees. They were asked what, if any, ideas had they dealt with in the program that they would like to experiment with on their job. They were also asked what difficulties they foresaw in implementing these changes. Sixty-five per cent of these questionnaires were returned.

The responses were judged on the following criteria: (1) the height of the motivation to experiment with new ideas or set of ideas on the job, (2) the depth of the understanding of the ideas with which they wished to experiment and (3) the degree of interest or effort shown as to how these ideas might be implemented. After evaluating the comments, the questionnaires were sorted into three categories called substantial, moderate, and low motivation to do things differently on the job. The results are shown below.

	Level of Motivation to Do Things Differently on the Job
Substantial	20% of trainees
Moderate	33% of trainees
Low	47% of trainees

No predictions can be made about what, if any, changes will actually be made, for this depends on too many other factors. Nonetheless, the trainees have indicated an interest and motivation to experiment with some changes in the way they lead their subordinates.

Supervisors' Evaluation

The final part of our evaluation data was derived from the trainees' supervisors. The supervisors were given a questionnaire which asked them to help us evaluate the program by observing whatever changes they saw in their subordinate(s) who attended the program. They were asked to list whatever changes they saw which they felt could reasonably have resulted from the program.

The changes were classified into three different categories: (1) changes in knowledge, ways of thinking, or attitudes, (2) changes in behavior when the trainee related with his boss or with other supervisors, and (3) changes in the way the trainee led or dealt with his subordinates. The supervisors' observations were then classified into three categories: (1) substantial, (2) some, or (3) no change in the trainee.

NUMBER OF TRAINEES OBSERVED TO CHANGE
AS A RESULT OF THE PROGRAM
AS OBSERVED BY TRAINEES' SUPERVISORS

	Substantial Change	Some Change	No Change
Knowledge and Attitudes	1	5	13
Behavior with Boss or Other Supervisors	1	2	16
Behavior with or the Way He Leads His Subordinates	1	5	10

Eighty-three per cent of the questionnaires were returned. The results are shown above. The results show moderate changes observed to this point. Neither this questionnaire nor the questionnaire given to the trainees (measuring motivation to change) can be considered as a highly accurate means of assessing changes but, rather, as some indication of on-the-job changes in behavior of the trainees.

Evaluation Analysis

The results of the program are difficult to express succinctly in terms of the functional ability of implementing the integrated training process model. Nonetheless, they do need some comment. In the best judgment of the author and other trainers associated with this program, significant learning was evident based upon extensive data. The amount and depth of learning was beyond expectations of what could be accomplished in 16 hours of trainee participation based on past experience. The results of the test scoring began to raise the question of why the wide positive deviation from expectations. Various variables and sets of variables were looked at and finally discounted. The only variable which could meaningfully account for the data was the way in which the entire training process was conceived and conducted – that is, as a system conception.

Conclusion

As we have attempted to show, the conduct of the entire training process was dealt with in a systemic manner. The needs assessment and objective setting subprocesses were particularly significant in the effect they had on other parts of the program. The results of each of these subprocesses were extensively used in all of the following activities. These findings set the initial parameters of what the program covered and what it should and could accomplish.

As questions of design, implementation, and evaluation arose, the results of the needs assessment and objective setting processes were continually referenced. By means of working through and reconceiving the data and findings of these processes, the questions raised in later processes became clearer and more capable of being answered. The initial use of these findings set general parameters, but further use was invaluable in "honing in" on and allowing both questions and answers to be handled in an increasingly specific manner. Thus, the findings and results of the needs assessment and objectives setting activities did not become final statements or final answers. The findings were continually re-examined and reconceived to fit the context and needs of designing, conducting and evaluating the program itself. An integrated conception of the training process results in the ability to become increasingly specific, precise, and concrete, to answer questions raised, and to restate questions and decision issues in more specific, concrete, and meaningful ways. This is the very essence of the functional value of conceiving and dealing with training as an integrated process.

DESIGNING TRAINING PROGRAMMES[1]

PRELIMINARY STEPS

These are as follows:

1. Enlist support of all concerned.
2. Examine the job.
3. Describe the job in simple terms.
4. Analyse the job-training requirements by -

(a) identifying skills and knowledge broadly,
(b) breaking down skills and knowledge in detail required,
(c) summarising job training requirement in a syllabus (i.e. a broad statement, under main headings of the material to be covered in the training programme).

Knowledge (and attitude)

When identifying the knowledge element of a job it is important to take into account the attitude of the employee when he comes to apply that knowledge. For example a programme on "Safety" may provide full knowledge of the work hazards and the rules to be observed but if it leaves trainees with the attitude that "It will never happen to me", then the programme will have failed.

There are many other examples where the attitude induced in trainees is crucial to their success at the job. A salesman, an interviewer, a receptionist, a supervisor, a welfare officer, a manager - all of these and many others must have the right attitude to the job they do or they will not do it successfully.

It is hard to think of anybody in any organisation of whom it could be said, "His attitude to the job does not matter". Where the attitude is crucial to job performance the written training programme must take this into account. In this paper the word "knowledge" is used in the wide sense of meaning not only what the trainee needs to know in order to be able to do his job but also the attitude of mind he will bring to bear when using this knowledge.

CONTENT OF THE TRAINING PROGRAMME

1. A statement of objectives, including the stages at which the trainee is to be tested and the standard to be attained.

2. A statement of the material to be learned (the syllabus), broken down into stages, in the order in which it is to be presented to trainees and indicating the skills and knowledge (including attitude) to be learned.

3. The place where the training is to be given.

4. The job title of the person who is to do the training.

5. The training techniques to be used.

6. The time allocated to each stage (although this can be flexible within the over-all time for the programme).

STATEMENT OF OBJECTIVES

The objectives of the programme must be clearly set down. This will help to ensure that only those items are included which help the trainee to achieve the learning or the standard required.

---

[1] Extract reprinted by permission from Ceramics Glass and Mineral Products Industry Training Board: Information Paper 5 (Harrow, Middlesex). Copyright remains the property of the Board.

The statement should include the following:

1. for whom the programme is written (Training Specifications);

2. what the trainee is expected to be able to do at significant stages of the programme;

3. the standard of performance to be achieved (e.g. fully experienced worker);

4. how this standard will be tested (e.g. formal written test, on-the-job performance);

5. the situation in which these standards will be tested (e.g. in classroom or at place of work).

PRACTICAL CONSIDERATIONS AFFECTING THE DESIGN OF TRAINING PROGRAMMES

Once the objectives have been set the training programme must be designed to meet those objectives.

It is sometimes impossible to provide the necessary facilities to run the desired training programme. Where limitations exist the programme should first be written to the highest possible standard and then adjusted to meet the practical situation.

This approach has the following advantages:

(a) A standard is set. The effect of the limitations can be seen. Management has a target to aim for.

(b) The programme designer is dealing with one thing at a time. First, the elements of a training programme; second, the limitations. It is very difficult to consider both aspects at once.

(c) Future adjustments, to meet changing conditions, are more easily made.

The most common practical considerations which may limit the training programme are cost, urgency, availability of space, availability of instructors and availability of training material.

Cost

For the smaller firm this can be a particularly difficult problem. Sometimes the best appears too expensive and second-best is accepted. A word of warning is appropriate. The cost of trainees' time, the cost of trainees' mistakes (waste), the cost of accidents, the cost of labour turnover all have to be taken into account when deciding what is "too expensive".

Urgency

In the same way that money may be wasted, so time, in the long run, may be wasted by what appears at first sight to be a saving.

If the trainees do not reach the required standard further time will be taken up with more training. If the trainees feel any sense of failure this additional time may exceed the time originally "saved".

For many small companies this is a problem which may affect the implementing of the training programme.

There is no real substitute for a well equipped training area or centre for off-the-job training. However, imaginative use can be made of such places as the foreman's office or a corner of the workshop. Off-the-job training can be successful in these places if every possible effort is made to create the right conditions for learning (e.g. minimum distractions, light, air, cleanliness, availability of visual and other aids).

Training done in a part of the workshop set aside for the purpose can be most effective. It can often be far enough "removed" from the pressures of production to give trainees the best learning opportunity without giving them a false impression of the work situation.

Availability of Instructors

If there are not enough trained instructors available it will be impossible to run a full training programme to the desired standard.

There is no substitute for a trained instructor, but a lot can be done to help a man who has to give instruction before he can be booked on an instructors' course.

Availability of Training Material

"Training Material" covers everything from manuals to large machines.

Manuals and other written reference material - Much of an instructor's time that is spent talking may be saved if suitable written material is available for study by the trainee. Manuals and simple job cards (like training programmes) must be designed specifically for a particular type of trainee. If they are not available the training programme will suffer. There is no quick or easy solution. The written material must be produced at the earliest possible date.

Written material for exercises, case studies, etc. - There is a lot of written material of this sort available but it is often hard to find the one which meets the specific training need. An experienced trainer can usually amend existing material or, better still, write his own. If this is not possible, the next best solution is to look for another method to meet the training need rather than to "make-do" with something that does not quite fit the programme.

Films and film-strips - These offer variety in a training programme, but like exercises and case studies it is often hard to find the "right" one. It is sometimes difficult to choose between the benefit to be gained by way of variety, which helps maintain the trainees' interest and the knowledge that the particular film (or film-strip) is not ideal for the training purpose. The guideline is that it is never worth putting items into a training programme just for the sake of variety. If the item does not help to meet the over-all training need it may confuse.

Visual aids - A large proportion of what people learn is learned through the sense of sight. Good visual aids are, therefore, an important element of training programmes. If these aids are not available, they can usually be made quite easily. It is not necessary to produce elaborate "works of art". Some of the best visual aids are simple to draw or make.

If the instructor is not very good at preparing them, there is usually somebody employed by the company who can help.

Machinery and other manual aids - A workshop may contain a very large machine. The logical ordering of the programme may indicate that an apprentice should learn to strip it down in the second month of the third year of training. If the machine is the only one of its kind, to strip it down would stop production.

In these circumstances the only time the apprentice can learn to take it apart is when it breaks down. The programme must take account of this fact. Much can be improvised on a small scale perhaps, to take the trainees as nearly as possible to that full understanding which will come from stripping the machine.

Small-scale models of parts of the machine may be reasonably easy to make - it could be part of the apprentices' training to make them. The principles of the machine may be explained during routine maintenance and from what can be seen of the machine in action. The manufacturer's booklet may help.

None of this effort will be wasted. The logical learning order will be largely maintained. The apprentice will take less time to learn the remaining details when the machine does break down. He will be more useful than would otherwise be the case at the moment of crisis.

ORDERING THE MATERIAL TO BE LEARNED

The material to be learned has been identified during the preliminary analysis and preparation of the syllabus. The objectives of the programme have been stated. The next step is to look at the breakdown of skills (what the trainee must be able to do) and knowledge (what the trainee needs to know to be able to do his job) to see in what order they should be arranged to best meet the needs of the trainee (i.e. the logical learning order).

The "logical learning order" means that each item of the programme makes sense to the trainee because of what has previously been learned.   To take a simple example it would be illogical (and dangerous) to tell a trainee, "Attach the positive wire to the left hand terminal" if he does not know how to identify the positive wire.

START by setting down the items to be learned according to what common sense suggests is the logical order.

CHECK by starting at the end of the programme and working back to the beginning to see that each item will make sense to the trainee in the light of what he has already learned.

This check takes us back to the beginning of the programme.

Programmes start at the point of existing knowledge and skill of the trainee. This must be carefully assessed or the logical ordering of items will be wasted.

Relationship Between Knowledge and Skill

When the training material is being put in the order in which it will be presented to the trainees, account must be taken of the relationship between knowledge and skill.

The trainee is given knowledge to enable him to do his job.   As soon as possible after he acquires the necessary knowledge he should have the opportunity to put it to practical use.   Practising the job skill will help him to remember what he has learned.

The principle applies equally to all levels of trainee from operatives to managers.   (A manager learning the skill of selection interviewing needs to practise as soon as he has acquired sufficient knowledge.   This will reinforce what he has learned.)

The Need for a Pattern

It is important that the subjects covered by the programme are developed to a pattern which helps the trainee to learn.

Broadly, there are three ways of structuring a training programme:

(a) The whole of the material to be learned is first covered in broad out-line and then each item or subject is dealt with in depth.   (This is the most common pattern.   It is used when there are no special considerations which make an alternative pattern more appropriate.)

(b) The whole of the material to be learned may be covered several times over, each time at increased depth.   (This is appropriate when each complete part is so large or complex that the relationship of one part to another may be lost if each part is dealt with separately in depth.)

(c) Each item or subject may be presented separately and the "parts" brought into a "whole" at the end of the programme.   (This is suitable only when each item or subject is in itself a complete piece of learning.   It is used when it is important for the trainee to discover for himself the relationship between what they different items or subjects, e.g. supervisory training.)

Whatever the pattern adopted make sure it is understood by the trainees. This understanding of the structure will help them to learn and remember what they have learned.

THE PLACE WHERE THE TRAINING IS TO BE CARRIED OUT

Depending on the type of job for which the trainee is being prepared, there will be elements of the training which are best done off-the-job (either in-company or externally) and some which are best done on-the-job (either super-numerary or as part of the normal labour force).   The mixture will depend on the nature of the job, the in-company facilities and the availability of external courses.

Handout II

The final learning, in whatever sphere of production, takes place on-the-job. It is, therefore, important that all off-the-job training is planned to help the trainee to meet the on-the-job situation.

The choice of where each part of the training is best carried out must be made from the following:
- in-company, on-the-job (part of the normal labour force),
- in-company, supernumerary,
- in-company, off-the-job,
- external courses.

In-Company, On-The-Job

The proportion of the programme devoted to this type of training is largely determined by the type of job to be learned. It will occupy the major part of the programme when the job to be learned is relatively simple and is mainly a matter of skill development rather than acquisition of knowledge. On-the-job training may be applicable to more complex jobs which can be broken down into a series of simple steps but it is usually difficult in the production situation to keep the steps in logical learning order. The tendency is to deal with each step as it arises in the production situation. This can confuse the trainee.

This training can be fully effective only when:

(a) the person giving the instruction is trained to instruct;

(b) those parts of the job best suited to off-the-job training are not dealt with on-the-job;

(c) there is full induction of the trainee into the work situation.

A point of difficulty with on-the-job training is that the trainee is surrounded by, and therefore involved in, all the pressures of production. Experienced workers easily forget how difficult it is for a newcomer to adjust to this situation. It is, therefore, important for the person giving the instruction to be available whenever needed by the trainee.

In-Company, Supernumerary

This training is suitable when off-the-job training (in-company or external) is to be followed by a period during which the trainee will develop skill at the place of work.

This need arises:

(a) when further off-the-job training results in less learning in a given time than is possible with supernumerary training;

(b) when the transfer of learning from the off-the-job training situation is difficult because:

(i) it is some time before the trainee can contribute much to production. This is a particularly difficult point if the production situation demands team-working (the trainee may feel incompetent if he is expected to do his full share of the work),

(ii) the logical learning order developed during the off-the-job training period is hard to relate to the job itself. This problem is minimised by ensuring the techniques used during the off-the-job training period assist the transfer of learning to the place of work (i.e. simulation techniques).

Supernumerary training is also suitable when the trainee needs broad experience of several types of work. For example, a management trainee will need a knowledge of a number of jobs and the environment in which they are performed.

It is important that:

(a) the supernumerary trainee follows a carefully prepared training plan;

(b) the person supervising the learning is available whenever needed by the trainee;

(c) the off-the-job and supernumerary elements of the training programme are phased to aid the transfer of learning from the off-the-job to the production situation.

In-Company, Off-The-Job

Off-the-job training is used:

(a) to establish the self-confidence of the trainee before he is introduced to the production situation;

(b) when the tasks which the trainee will face in his job do not occur in any coherent order (i.e. when there is no logical learning order possible at the place of work);

(c) when some of the tasks the trainee will be required to perform occur only infrequently at the place of work (i.e. it could be a long time, possibly years, before the trainee sees every part of his job);

(d) when the slow speed at which the employee can, at first, perform the job would disrupt production;

(e) when the trainee needs a lot of knowledge to be able to do the job (it is hard to put over information at the place of production);

Maximum benefit is obtained from off-the-job training when:

(a) sufficient account is taken of the problem of transferring what has been learned to the production situation;

(b) instructors are trained to use the full range of available training techniques;

(c) the training environment is suitable (the ideal is carefully planned training accommodation).

External Courses

The training facilities of external bodies are used when:

(a) the skills and knowledge learned internally need to be supplemented by external courses;

(b) the company has no comparable facilities internally to give the training required;

(c) the company does not have suitable lecturers or instructors available;

(d) there are too few trainees to warrant the setting-up of an in-company course;

(e) there is an advantage to be gained by the trainees in mixing with the employees of other companies.

A point of difficulty with external courses is that they will generally cater for a wide range of trainees from different companies and cannot, therefore, be "tailor-made" to meet the exact requirements of an individual company. (This is not always the case, e.g. courses run by a group training association do not fall in this category.) This point must be carefully watched when fitting attendance at an external training course into a programme of in-company training.

Fitting Together In-Company and External Training

Where the training programme involves a mixture of in-company and external training it is important that the in-company part is first put on a systematic basis and that the external part is then fitted to the in-company part.

External training should be approached as follows:

(a) The in-company training must be systematically organised.

(b) The external training is checked to see that it is appropriate to the trainees' needs and the company's requirements.

(c) If the external training is not precisely appropriate to either the trainees' or the company's requirements the course organisers should be told of the problem. Adjustments can often be made to meet requirements. Every external training establishment will welcome an approach of this sort.

(d) If the external training cannot be suitably adjusted the course which falls below requirements should be chosen. The in-company part of the programme must be expanded to meet the deficiency.

(e) If the external training cannot be obtained when it is wanted, careful adjustment of the in-company part must be made. It is important that the logical ordering of the programme is not upset. Problems of this sort are avoided if training requirements are planned carefully in advance.

(f) Finally, the in-company programme must be rechecked continually to ensure that trainees are given every opportunity to put into practice what they have learned from external sources.

TIMING THE PROGRAMME

Timing must be realistic and flexible.

Realistic because:

(a) the trainee needs sufficient time in which to learn;

(b) time costs money.

Flexible because:

(a) trainees vary in the speed at which they learn;

(b) instructors vary in the speed at which they promote the learning;

(c) conditions under which learning takes place vary from day to day (e.g. temperature, noise level, the mood of instructors or trainees).

<u>A Simple Procedure</u>

The following simple procedure will help to achieve timing which is both realistic and flexible:

1. The time needed by an average trainee is estimated for <u>each item or subject</u> of the programme. (First estimates and later adjustments can be made more accurately and sensibly if each item or subject of the programme is timed separately).

2. These estimated times are built into four-day units.

3. Each four-day unit is made the "target" for a five-day week. (Reaching a "target" gives both instructors and trainees a sense of achievement but the "targets" must be attainable by the slower trainee.)

4. The four-day units are then spread over the five-day week in the way which best suits the subject matter and the trainees. (This gives flexibility and allows for special attention to slower trainees. Make sure the quicker trainees are "stretched" by giving them extra work.)

PACE OF THE PROGRAMME

The level of ability of the trainees will to some extent determine the general pace at which skill and knowledge can be fed to them but there are other considerations:

(a) The length of time elapsed since the trainees were last in a formal training situation.   This may mean a slow start to acclimatise the trainees.

(b) The stages at which the rate of learning slows down.

There are points of time when the trainees are consolidating the material already learned.   These points of time are not easy to identify in advance but are most frequently found at the end of each part of the programme which is complete in itself.   This will mean varying the pace of the programme.

(c) The speed at which the trainee will be expected to perform his job at the place of work.   The pace of the programme should be intensified according to the speed of performance required.

It is often found that trainees learn more from a short programme at an intensive pace than they do from a longer programme covering the same material at a leisurely pace.   This is because the intensive programme is more challenging to the trainees, who respond by making greater effort.

THE LEVEL OF INSTRUCTION

A training programme which covers the right items or subjects may fail to achieve its objectives because it is pitched at the wrong level.   The level of instruction must be matched to the trainees' abilities.

When the material to be learned is at too high a level - The average trainee will be unable to learn.   Although he is not to blame the trainee will feel he has in some way failed.   This sense of failure could permeate the whole of his work.

The above-average trainee may be able to understand the subject matter.   He will not suffer a sense of failure, but he will find the job demands less of him than he was led to expect from the training programme.   He may either suffer a feeling of frustration or expand his responsibility beyond that expected by management.

When the material to be learned is at too low a level - Trainees often reject the whole of the programme even when some parts are at the right level if a lot of the material is at too low a level.

The question of "level" needs to be carefully assessed for trainees attending courses run outside the company.   Course organisers will welcome queries on this score.

THE NEED FOR "FEEDBACK"

To complete even a short training programme before checking whether the trainees have acquired the necessary level of knowledge or skill would create a position where any false learning or omissions could not be rectified within the time allocated to the programme.

At frequent intervals during the programme both the trainer and the trainee need to know how they are progressing.

The trainer needs to know whether:

(a) the items to be learned are being learned;

(b) there are gaps in his instruction;

(c) there are gaps in the programme;

(d) there are slower trainees who need special attention;

(e) there are quicker trainees who need extra work to keep them interested.

The trainee needs to know whether:

(a) he has correctly understood the information he has been given (knowledge);

(b) he can use the information on a job of work (skill).

Once the trainee has been tested he needs to know the result at the earliest possible time.

How to Provide for "Feedback"

Every instructor should provide for participation by the trainees in every session he gives but this will provide knowledge of progress only up to a point. It is also necessary to incorporate in the programme some sessions which are specifically designed to let both the trainee and the trainer know what is being achieved.   These may be formal tests or sessions which incorporate an element of test.

In the formal test the trainee is asked to talk or write about the information he has been given or to do something, e.g., a clerk to write a letter, an apprentice to make something, a manager to set up an appropriate organisation to meet a crisis situation.

The training sessions which provide most knowledge of progress are those which simulate the work situation, e.g., role play, syndicate and group exercises, business games, projects.

Whatever the form of the test it must be carefully devised with the following points in mind:

(a) the objective of the part of the programme being tested;

(b) the standard expected of the trainees;

(c) the type of trainee;

(d) the place at which the test is to be set;

(e) the ease with which the test can be marked or judged.

CHOICE OF TRAINING TECHNIQUE

The choice of training techniques is important to a successful training programme.   A programme which envisages all knowledge being put across in the form of "telling" and all practise of skill being done at the place of work will not be as successful as one which employs the different available training techniques to advantage.

The choice of training technique should be made with the following points in mind:

The end result to be achieved - For example, it is little use including in a training programme a first-class talk during which supervisors are told why their attitude should change, if at the end of it their knowledge is expanded but their attitude unchanged.   They may show more willingness to change if the discussion technique is used.   The trainees will then not feel they are being "preached at".

The person who is to give the particular session - It is often the case that several techniques may be suitable for a particular item of the programme but the person giving the session is better at one technique than another.

The type of trainee - To take two examples (a) practical men who have been doing a manual job for some years are unlikely to learn much from formal talks, (b) young persons may resent a talk given in a schoolroom atmosphere - they want to be regarded as adults.

    <u>The time of day</u> - For example, during the post-lunch period trainees are best kept physically active.

    <u>The technique used for other items of the programme</u> - Variety of technique helps to maintain the interest of the trainees.

    Whichever technique is selected, remember that the trainees will not learn unless they are interested. It will help maintain their interest if they are actively involved in the learning.

REDESIGNING THE TRAINING PROGRAMME

    In view of the wide variety of factors which have to be taken into account when designing the training programme, it would be surprising if the ideal programme is devised at the first attempt. It will invariably be necessary to make changes in the light of the results of the full evaluation which must follow the completion of every programme of training.

    As part of the process of evaluation it is necessary to keep progress records during the currency of the programme:

    (a) a record of the progress of each trainee;

    (b) a diary of the training officers'/instructors' impressions and suggestions for improvement.

TIPS FOR LESSON PREPARATION AND PRESENTATION[1]

Consider your overall objective

What is the objective of this particular lesson in relation to the total course?

What do you want the group to do better or to do differently, or what do you want them to know or understand as a result of your instruction? In other words, what do you want their "terminal behaviour" to be?

Try to keep the objective realistic, practical, useful, and always clearly defined.

Consider the group

How much do they already know about the subject?

What is their general attitude toward the subject likely to be?

What is their intellectual level? How fast will they be able to work? Is the group homogeneous from this point of view?

Does the group have any particular learning difficulties that must be taken into account?

What is the size of the group?

Consider the time available

How much time do you have to prepare?

What is the total time available for the lesson (including time for out-of-class reading and/or problem-solving)?

What time of the day or evening is the lesson to be given? Is this likely to affect the learning process in a predictable way? Can the lesson be planned to account for this?

Consider the resources available

Is the necessary equipment available for any special demonstrations?

Is there time to obtain it and set it up?

Is time available for the class to do preparatory reading?

Is a guest speaker, resource person, special film or other assistance required for the lesson? Have prior arrangements been made to have any of these available?

Plan and schedule the subject matter

Good instruction is dependent upon careful planning of the nature and amount of subject matter to be put across.

Most instructors have at their disposal only a limited time in which to give their lesson, therefore it is always advisable to 'grade' the subject matter carefully so as to ensure that the more essential ingredients of the lesson are put over and understood within the time allocated for instruction.

---

[1] See also the background reading - Session 5, "The Lecture Method".

The diagram below illustrates a suggested 'grading' of subject matter:

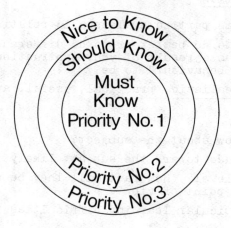

Priority No. 1 - MUST KNOW - Vital, basic information all of which must be put across at all costs; this includes problem-solving or practice exercises considered to be the basic minimum for learning. Includes fundamental facts, data, figures, symbols, etc., without which there can be no understanding whatsoever of the subject.

Priority No. 2 - SHOULD KNOW - Important information of which as much as possible should be put across, e.g. a breakdown or elaboration of the basic points in Priority No. 1.

Priority No. 3 - NICE TO KNOW - Incidental information which can be put across if time permits; background, historical or related information which is of general interest but not of intrinsic inportance to the understanding of the subject.

The instructor must plan how long it will take him to teach, and the group to absorb, the vital points of information, and decide how he will apportion the remaining time between Priorities No. 2 and 3. The amount of subject matter which can be put across and assimilated in a given period of time will depend upon:

- the skill of the instructor;

- the complexity of the subject;

- how much class activity (participation in exercises, discussion, questioning) is required, and of what kind;

- whether the group has any previous knowledge of the subject.

Thus a skilled instructor, given a simple subject and an experienced group, may be able comfortably to cover all three categories of information. On the other hand, an intricate subject and an inexperienced group may mean that he can only attempt satisfactorily to cover the MUST KNOW and SHOULD KNOW categories.

Develop the lesson material

Prepare suitable exercises, demonstrations, sample problems or illustrations (including visual aid displays) as appropriate, to reinforce the lesson. Review films or other supplementary material for suitability.

Prepare discussion questions and test questions if necessary.

Prepare handouts, plan chalkboard notes, etc.

Prepare a lesson plan

See that the order of presentation is logical from the group's point of view. Proceed from the known to the unknown, from the simple to the complex and from the particular to the general.

Note down in the plan where you will use prepared exercises or special demonstrations (including visual aids) or a discussion or question period.

Estimate the length of time to be used for each section of the lesson.

Classroom arrangements

Arrive in advance to check the physical arrangements in the classroom: layout of chairs and tables, positioning of visual aids or other equipment, chalk and eraser available, sufficient ventilation (open windows), etc.

Introduction

Start the lesson punctually.

Put the group at ease.

Announce the subject of the lesson briefly and concisely.

Relate the lesson to previous instruction and to the programme as a whole.

Try to get the interest of the group, and motivate them so that they want to learn.

Tell your class right at the beginning whether they need to take notes or not. If you have prepared a summary for distribution, tell them, but do not distribute it until the end of your talk. Much could be said about note-taking, but the essence of the matter is this: if they are feverishly trying to get down what you are saying, they cannot be listening at the same time. So you may be talking to nobody for about 50 per cent of the time. If your lesson contains a good deal of detail you certainly should prepare a handout - that is, of course, if you want them to remember what you said.

Body of the lesson

Use your lesson plan throughout.

Follow a logical sequence.

Use questions and answers to check understanding.

Keep track of the time; leave time for note-taking or other administrative matters.

Recapitulation

Review briefly the ground you have covered; memory is helped by repetition.

Use questions to reveal misunderstandings and clear them up.

Deal tactfully with incorrect answers.

Test

Make sure that questions, problems or exercises selected for testing purposes adequately cover the material which has been taught.

Make sure that questions are not ambiguous.

Go over the areas of weakness revealed by the test.

Make sure that students have a reasonable chance of answering the questions or completing the task in the time available.

Objective

To give participants an opportunity to:

- take part in an In-Basket Exercise in order to understand the method
- discuss their views on this experience
- evaluate the In-Basket Exercise as a training technique

Handout Material

I - The In-Basket, pp. 5-6

II - In-Basket Exercise - The Confidential File:
       Instructions to the Players, pp. 7-8, and
       Contents of the Confidential File, pp. 9-19

HANDOUT I, Session 1, Session Evaluation Form

Background Reading

Use of In-Basket Exercises, pp. 1-4

In-Basket Exercise: The Confidential File: Instructor's Notes, pp. 21-23

Recommended Reading

ILO, Man.Dev. Manual 28, In-Basket Exercises for Management Development

Special Equipment and Aids

If possible, an in-tray or in-basket should be provided for each participant

90 min.	**Session Guide 20**
	The contents of The Confidential File should be placed in each participant's in-basket before the session starts, covered with the Instructions to the Players or a blank sheet.
14:00	Briefly review the information in HANDOUT I, The In-Basket, so that participants understand the general idea of the In-Basket as a teaching method.
	Refer to the background reading, Use of In-Basket Exercises, for the detailed conduct of this session. Set the stage by outlining the position, Instructions to the Players, and HAND OUT this section. Allow time for participants to read it through and ask questions if necessary.
	Optional: In relation to Instruction 10, you may wish to have each participant write an outline of the report called for in the exercise, and/or write on each piece of paper in the In-Basket what he decides to do about the matter it contains.
14:15	Ask members to begin dealing with the contents of The Confidential File in their in-baskets.
	Remember that the element of frustration should be preserved. Some participants may want more information - it is not available.
15:00	Stop exercise. BREAK.
15:15	Discuss the decisions that were taken and review the finished work. Refer to Instructor's Notes for The Confidential File.
15:40	In summing up, emphasise that the In-Basket involves careful planning and organisation. The materials used should be pertinent to the particular job and level of trainees.
	Ask members to evaluate the session.
15:45	Collect evaluation forms and close the session.

USE OF IN-BASKET EXERCISES[1]

An In-Basket exercise consists basically of three parts:

A.   A set of instructions to the 'player'. This sets the background, tells him just what the circumstances are - such as his position in the business, who has died, why his superiors are out of reach, who the persons are whose requests, letters, etc. are found in his basket - an organisation structure, where this is necessary, and all other items necessary to set the stage and put him in the position as nearly as possible of a man arriving at work and sitting down for the day's work.

B.   The contents of the In-Basket. Each of these is on a separate sheet, some parts are handwritten, some are inter-office memos and others are letters or cables from outside the organisation.

C.   Notes for the guidance of the instructor or whoever is conducting the exercise.

The first two of these sections are designed for reproduction, so that each 'player' has his own full set of both. The third is not for distribution at all and is for the guidance of the man in charge.

There are many ways in which this type of activity can be used. We shall outline some of them, but the alert trainer will always be able to adapt these methods and develop his own.

The Group

As already stressed, the essence of this type of activity is that every man is on his own; but it can still be used with a group in this way. (There are, of course, variations.)

First explain to the group what an In-Basket exercise is. Then set the stage by outlining the position, "A" section above, and hand out this section. Allow time for it to be read for reinforcement and ask for questions.

Questions here - without the contents of the In-Basket - are designed to make sure that the participants are clear about their instructions. Additional information is not usually necessary, but if a player wants it, the instructor will have to make up his own mind what instructions to give. Someone may want to know whether the situation arises in winter or summer, how many employees the company has, whether the product is sold to retail consumers or industrial users. Now, if such matters are of real importance to the decision which the participants will be called on to make, they ought to be covered in the instructions - "A" section. If the answer is not there, it will rarely be important and the instructor should give an answer that seems relevant and realistic. In case such a situation should arise and in order to preserve the element of realism, the instructor should have the foresight to plan in advance for these questions and the answers he will give.

Having settled any such queries, hand out "B" section, the contents of the basket, one set to each person. Each man is now on his own. Some will want more information - it is not available. This is a really important feature of the whole exercise, because this is exactly what happens to us all in real life - we have to make decisions every day without having as much information as we would like to have. We just get as much information as we can and then do our best with it. It is essential, therefore, that this slight element of frustration be preserved. In fact, it is deliberately built into the exercises, so that they will be as realistic as possible.

---

[1] ILO: Extracts from In-Basket Exercises for Management Development, Man.Dev.Manual 28, Geneva, 1968.

Allow whatever time is considered reasonable for the exercise. Half an hour may be enough for some exercises or some groups. Flexibility is essential and the instructor must make his own judgments about this in the light of his students. The time allotted should, of course, be announced at the beginning or it can be built into the instructions by something like, "it is now 9 a.m. and you are required to present your report to the managing director at 9:45 a.m."

When time has expired, the whole thing is turned into a group discussion of the issues involved. Leading questions start it off, for example: "Well, what is the big issue here?" A good discussion leader will be able to keep the ball rolling and encourage each person to express his viewpoint, pitting one view against another and bringing out for discussion the main teaching points. These, of course, are suggested in "C" section of the exercise, but again, there is unlimited room for adaptation to the special needs of the group.

Another group approach is to start with Item 1 in the Basket (after individual action) and deal with it. The critical items will soon arise and participants will point out that Item 2 cannot be dealt with without taking Item 7 into consideration.

Having made decisions in the "on your own" session, the players have the opportunity to support their decisions with reasoned argument or to rebutt the ideas of others who think differently, or even to recognise that certain decisions were not well taken in their private exercise. In any case, the whole point of the exercise is not to wrap up the neat solution to the problem, but to give the participants an opportunity to try out their decisions and then to have the group discussion either show where they went astray or confirm their wisdom, or even a little of both.

As a Selection Technique

Where a number of persons are being considered for appointment or promotion, various group techniques are useful and many have been used. With the In-Basket exercise, the leader or instructor has the opportunity to observe how the players react under the circumstances of the exercise, what factors they take into consideration in arriving at decisions and how they justify their own ideas and meet those of others that may be contrary to their own. They will reveal aspects of character and attitude unconsciously which would be difficult to assess, or even to detect, in an ordinary interview. Where the members of the group are all considered possible contenders for the position or promotion, they can be compared in performance in a situation which has some reality in the exercise and a great deal of reality in the follow-up discussions. Of course, a great deal depends on the leader, both in promoting the discussion and in assessing the spontaneous performance.

Perhaps it is not necessary to add that this technique is not by itself a sufficient one in selection or deciding who to promote, but it does give a useful ancilliary guide.

To Decide Training Needs

Both in a firm and in a training institute, it is necessary to plan the training and development of executives in accordance with their needs. A well conducted In-Basket session will reveal the way players think, what elements in a situation they appreciate and how far they have developed diagnostic and decision-making skills. For example, it is common for important public relations features of an In-Basket situation to be completely overlooked; or some of the group will usually say that there is insufficient information for them to make a decision and others will insist that the responsibility required of them in the situation really belongs to a more senior person in the company.

The first of these requires that these persons are trained to appreciate the public relations aspects of decisions; the other two reveal that these persons avoid decision-making and require development in this executive area. An alert leader can learn a great deal about the players which will help him in planning or recommending their development programme.

In the same field is the use of the exercise as an opening gambit in a training course where the leader of the course does not know the participants. With an In-Basket exercise, he can lead the players to reveal themselves in a variety of ways which will help him to understand them, their needs, and how to develop the details of the course of training ahead.

EVALUATING THE PERFORMANCE

Returning to the use of the In-Basket exercise as a training device, which will be the concern of most readers of these notes, how does the instructor make a measurement of the success of his teaching? It is important to acknowledge that this is not a test of the trainee but a test of the effectiveness of the teaching. If the trainee shows an ability to understand the problems and shows some capacity in applying the skills which we set out to teach, this is a tribute to good teaching.

This overstates the position? Yes, perhaps it does, since one trainee may come to tuition rather more advanced or with more innate capacity for analysis and decision, but especially for developing countries where the trainees are likely to be sensitive, unwilling to lose face in a test, the stress on the testing of the method of teaching rather than the trainee is worth making.

In any case, what the instructor wants to know is whether he has got his points over successfully. How is he to evaluate the results of an In-Basket exercise?

First of all, there must be a classification of the different items in the exercise - that is, in the instructor's mind. In any In-Basket, there will be items of no particular importance - the red herrings and the atmosphere creators; then there will be a series of items of some importance which require action of some kind; and finally, the key papers on which vital decisions are needed.

The ability of the trainee to make this classification is critical. If he wants to deal personally with every minor detailed item, if he does not know how to delegate the unimportant or the less important - without giving offence to whoever originated the item - then he has not learned the first lesson of management.

This is the first point of evaluation then; does the trainee sort the key items from among the distracting ones and can he distinguish the items of prime importance?

Then, what does he do with the items of real importance? Most exercises call for some decision or some firm analysis or recommendation of action. At the same time, this often means that some other item which seems to clamour for attention has to be either delegated or ignored.

This is the second stage: having discarded the rubbish, how does the trainee deal with the rest? Does he rightly distinguish the items of primary importance from those of secondary importance?

Of course, if the discussion method (following individual study and decision), is followed, these questions are threshed out and different opinions encouraged. The instructor does not get the opportunity to make any more than a subjective assessment of each person's reactions because he is busy encouraging discussion and inter-play of ideas. However, he will usually be able to judge fairly accurately between those who are too concerned about the minor detail and those who come to the real aspects involved. Also, he will find those who have picked the No. 1 items will stand out from those who have not.

Finally, the question is: are the trainees developing skills, the skills for which the exercises are designed? It is not of primary importance that they are right; but are the skills emerging? If this is agreed, then it is not very important to make any more than subjective judgments.

Of course, if the In-Basket is being used as an examination technique or a testing technique for recruitment or determining training requirements, such rough and ready assessments are not good enough. In these cases, the instructor should classify every item in the Basket before he starts. On average, he will have three groups: the irrelevant, the important and the all-important.

As a first step after the trainee has completed his work (with his written comments) the instructor then divides the items according to his own pre-established groupings. If the trainee and the instructor agree, this is worth 25 points; where they do not agree, the instructor will have to determine how much deduction to make from the perfect score for this section, 25.

Next: did the trainee and instructor agree on the distinction between important and all-important? This is worth 50 points. Another 25, making 100 in all, is applied to evaluating the decision on what to do with the all-important items.

This scoring division gives the major weight to diagnosing the nature of the problem or the accuracy of the analysis. It assumes that this is the major emphasis in the structure of the exercise. If it is not, the instructor will need to decide where the weight lies and make up his scoring scale accordingly.

Another method is to consider each paper in the Basket quite separately and give the trainee's treatment of each paper an individual score between one and five (another alternative is three-point scoring, one, three or five, for each paper). The total score then becomes the addition of the scores for each paper.

It really depends on what the instructor wants the exercise to stress. With some groups, not advanced in the type of skills we are trying to teach, the most important first step may be to get a distinction between the "rubbish" and the rest. If so, then this distinction should be scored high; and so with other possible objectives the instructor has in mind.

If the instructor really wants to find out - say to develop a training programme for the trainee - something of the way the trainee thinks and what his ideas are on the subject of authority and decision and so forth, then scoring is important and should be thought out clearly so that it does score highly the desirable attitudes or skills which the instructor is investigating.

When the objective is to develop skills by giving the chance to experiment with realistic situations, scoring is unimportant. A good instructor will not need a score to show him he is successful and a score is of no importance at all to the trainee. It is getting the mental exercise that matters. If the sessions are well conducted by the instructor, it is implicit in the whole In-Basket idea that the skills will be developed by the exercise, and that is the objective.

REALISTIC PREPARATION

The contents of the Basket should look real. For instance, they should comprise different sizes, types and colours of paper as would be the case with such a mixed collection in true life events. If the paper would have been handwritten in real life, then it should be handwritten for the exercises. This would apply to office memos mostly or to mischief-making notes. It is not difficult to make stencils for roneo in handwritten form though it does take care and more time.

Office memos should look real, written or typed on paper headed "MEMO" or something else appropriate. This means care in printing this word on a stencil, but it can be done.

Where several items are handwritten, originating from more than one person, they should be written on the stencil by different persons.

Account forms and letterheads are more difficult unless the material is being prepared by offset or photographic process. This is usually too expensive for short runs unless the instructor has access to a modern photocopying machine. If he has, then it is worth borrowing some letterheads or even having them handset by a job printer. Account forms can sometimes be bought in a suitable form from ordinary stationery suppliers, though the colour will need to be watched if they are to be photocopied; they can be hand drawn for a stencil without much difficulty.

That red herring item, the intriguing love letter, is often written on coloured paper and sealed in a matching envelope. The sealed envelope can introduce not only realism, but an extra indecision - does the trainee open a sealed envelope addressed to another person or not? If he does not, what does he do with it - especially if the person to whom it is addressed is dead or away for six months.

A thumb print on printers' proofs requiring approval; some poor typing with mistakes and overstampings; corrections to a document made in ink; incorrect spelling or grammar from a worker who is employed because he is a skilled mechanic, not for his education - these are all facts and events in life and should be introduced to add reality to the whole appearance of the documents in the Basket.

THE IN-BASKET

Prepared at the United Nations
Institute for Training and Research (UNITAR)[1]

Definition

Developed originally as a possible measure of aptitude for the administrative components of the managerial role, the In-Basket is a simulation of a manager's workload on a typical day. The name is derived from the wire baskets that formerly were seen on almost every manager's desk, marked "in" and "out" for mail and memoranda.

Major Aims

As a diagnostic tool, the exercise provides information on how a participant handles a sequence of problems in a given situation, under some pressure, and thus some measure of his potential or his competency. As a training device, it can be used to help the trainee identify areas in planning, organising and administrative behaviour in which his skills need to be improved, as well as an opportunity to practice those skills in a situation in which he can obtain feedback on his performance.

Design and Methodology

The underlying idea of the In-Basket technique is that a person is required to assume the role of a fictitious executive or supervisor in a hypothetical situation. In the actual exercise, the participant is presented with numerous background materials so that he may become familiar with the organisational situation. They may include such items as financial statements, organisational charts, job descriptions, formal position papers and informal items such as descriptions of the personalities and performance of other characters in the test situation. Though they may vary in nature and content, they all share the common purpose of increasing the reality of the hypothetical situation for the participants by placing the tasks which they are to perform in context.

Once a player is familiar with the situation, the exercise itself is begun. Each player is presented with a group of letters, reports, notes and related items which have presumably accumulated in the In-Basket of the hypothetical manager. He is then asked to take any actions he deems appropriate with the In-Basket items within a limited time period.

Unlike some other types of exercise in which a participant merely tells what he would do, as an executive, the In-Basket player must actually do it. This means that he must actually write all his notes and memoranda, write out his conversations with others, and put down the contents of his telephone calls on paper. Thus, at the end of the exercise, there will be a written record of every action which each participant has taken.

An important dimension of the In-Basket experience is time pressure. The situation into which each participant is placed contains a time period during which all available work must be accomplished. At the end of that time period, for example, the participant may be scheduled as part of the exercise to attend a crucial meeting or conference at which at least some of the items in his In-Basket will be discussed. In order to be prepared for this conference, the participant is literally forced to scan many different items calling for different actions and deal with them by (1) setting priorities, and (2) delegating certain items to his subordinates for handling.

The In-Basket game also includes a procedure which allows players to explain their actions. The player's actions are either (1) scored in some manner, or (2) reviewed with him by an interviewer or instructor, or by a group of his fellow players, or both.

---

[1] From a draft manuscript by Sidney Mailick and Nancy A. Bord, "Experience in the US with New Techniques for Training Managers", UNITAR, December 1970.

Assessment of Effectiveness

The key to the In-Basket's effectiveness as a training device is the fact that it is rooted in real-life situations. If the selected situation is similar to one in which the participant actually has or expects he will function and if, in addition, it is constructed so as to call adequately for use of the participant's decision-making and problem-solving abilities, his behaviour in the game may be more natural than in some other types of training techniques.

One of the advantages of the In-Basket game is that it can be designed either to focus on the activities that are part of all executive positions, or to emphasise certain specific aspects of performance. For instance, if the objective is to develop or improve human relations skills, the In-Basket material can be weighed heavily with interpersonal conflicts, other responsibilities being held to a minimum. The In-Basket can also be adapted to the level of the position for which training is required. If first-line supervisors are participating, the problems can be constructed to emphasise such factors as providing staff services, supervising work, and technical aspects of production. If it is desired to train higher-level executives, the problems may be related to activities such as long-range planning, diversification, and decentralisation.

Like any other training technique, the In-Basket method has certain short-comings. It is handicapped by the fact that it is different to score or measure its effects. Further, since the In-Basket is a form of role-playing, it may become unrealistic, no matter how "realistic" the situational setting is made. This may stem from the fact that the In-Basket is essentially an individual and non-interactive device. Although each participant plays the "game", he plays it by himself, and with his own materials. Except for the post-game review period, there is little opportunity for interaction between participants. The trainee who participates in the In-Basket exercise is not constrained by other people's behaviour in a dynamic fashion. Decisions are made during the In-Basket exercise without the advantage of consultation. The In-Basket exercise thus provides little training for "team management" responsibilities.

The effectiveness of the technique, in summary, clearly depends upon the adequacy of the materials developed for the particular In-Basket exercise. They must demand a realistic and representative sample of managerial performance across a broad variety of relevant tasks. To avoid superficiality, as is the case in other simulations, it must be carefully planned and carefully guided by the training director. In contrast with the more complete simulation games, however, In-Basket should not be used as the sole training method in any given programme, but only in concert with other management training techniques.

IN-BASKET EXERCISE:

THE CONFIDENTIAL FILE[1]

INSTRUCTIONS TO THE PLAYERS

You are a member of a management consultant firm. The head of your firm has been called in on a consultant job which he has allocated to you after conducting the initial interview with the principal. He has given to you the attached confidential file with the following explanations:

1.   Your client is Mme. Phan Boon Tran, who is the widow of the proprietor of a chain of three retail stores, supported by a small metal manufacturing plant. Most of the products this plant manufactures are sold through the retail stores, but some products are manufactured there to meet government orders. These orders are normally obtained by tender. Your client's husband died four months ago and the widow has been trying to carry on the business with the assistance of her former husband's executives.

2.   These executives consist of a Managing Director, Mr. Alexander Boom, who has held this position with the company for almost four years; the Plant Manager Morgan and the managers of the three retail stores, Morales, Allen and Ang Soong. All of them have been with the organisation for some years.

3.   Your client speaks and understands English well and this is the language in which most of the business of the organisation is conducted. However, she does not read or write English and therefore has difficulty in understanding the books and documents on the company. In particular, she cannot understand the contents of the Confidential File which has been handed to you. She found it, locked, among her husband's papers after his death. She has tried to read it but without any success and she does not trust the Managing Director, Alexander Boom, so she has not discussed it with him.

4.   Since her husband's death, she has been living on money available from his estate and when she has asked Boom about the profits of the company, he says the organisation is losing money. She has asked him for accounts but he has put her off, saying that she will have to wait for the half-year results to be completed. In any case, she knows she will not be able to understand them.

5.   You do not know your client and you did not know her husband, but the head of your firm was well acquainted with them both for some years during the husband's lifetime. He is not able to add anything about the details of the organisation you are to investigate, as the late Mr. Tran was secretive and never talked about his business.

      It was rumoured that he had trouble with the taxation authorities over not revealing all his income. He had lived well and was reported to be wealthy, but whether as a result of his business or from successful gambling on his string of horses, no one ever knew.

6.   The head of your firm says he thinks it likely that the business was never properly incorporated but carried on without any structure other than the owner's personal control. Consequently, Boom's title is likely to be no more than a courtesy one, without legal significance.

7.   At this stage you are not to discuss anything with Boom or the store managers and your investigation is entirely confidential. What your client wants to know is: what are the significant contents of the confidential file and what do you recommend as a result of studying the file.

8.   Since your client knows nothing about this business, she cannot help you with any further information. But she has reached the point where she wants to have some sort of a showdown with Boom so that she can find out exactly where the business stands.

──────────

[1] Extracted from ILO: In-Basket Exercises for Management Development, Man.Dev. Manual 28, Geneva, 1968.

9.   As a final bombshell, the head of your company says that the whole question
      has suddenly become very urgent. The client has just telephoned him to say
      that Boom wants to see her urgently this very afternoon. She wants your
      company's representative to be present at the interview as her business
      adviser. Your boss adds that he wants your report in just one hour. He says
      he knows this is unreasonable, but that's how it is.

10.   Summing it up: Within one hour, with no other information than you have, you
      are to examine in detail the contents of the Confidential File and report on
      your findings, make recommendations on what should be done and (your boss adds)
      decide whether you should attend the meeting with Boom later in the day.

C O P Y

March 3rd, 1964.

Mr. Alexander Boom,

Dear Boom,

    We agreed today that you would be the Managing Director
of my enterprises and that you would be paid a salary of
£ 2000. a year, which I would reconsider each year according
to the profits we are making.

    In addition to this, you will have the free use of a car
belonging to the enterprises and all the costs of running it,
up to £ 700. each year can be charged to the firm's account.

    This is just a note on these things so that we are both
agreed on what we decided.

                        Phan Boon Tran.

Profit and Loss Account
(Consolidated)

	1964	1965		1964	1965
Stock B/F	247,312	229,716	Sales	690, 912	673,418
Purchases	542, 519	598,218	Stock C/F	229,716	211;419
Gross Profit	130,787	65,903			
	920,628	844,837		920,628	884,837
Salaries and Wages	27,619	28,217	Gross Profit	130,787	65,903
Stationery	950	922			
Rent	4,000	4,000			
Advertg.	2,060	1,997			
Repairs	190	220			
Bad Debts	226	184			
Net Profit	95,742	30,363			
	130,787	65,903		130,787	65,903

(handwritten: TAX -50000)

Notes to Instructor: This sheet should be rather crudely typed,
like the above. Do not imitate it exactly, but make a few errors
in lining up, some overstampings - but not bad enough to be really
obscure. The idea is to suggest that it has been typed by a poor
typist, maybe an amateur. This adds to the realism of the document.
Add the inked changes in ink as above.

Government Department Contacts

Public Works	Arossa Mobutu
Post and Telegraphs	Arnold Warne
Finance	Alwyn Mooros
Taxation	George Shan
Customs	Oris Tran
Harbours and Port	T.B. Shuon
Agriculture	Art Sawne
Education	Ellis George
Police	Aitken (Capt.)
Water and Irrigation	Amos Conn

Mr. Iran,

The staff of the factory is getting a bit restless because they think we are making a big profit.

Their wages are the same as they were two years ago but food costs are way up in that time.

What do you think we ought to do?

Alexander Boom

<u>1966</u>

<u>Profit and Loss Account</u>
<u>Consolidated</u>

Stock B/F	211,419	Sales	706,432
Purchases	690,316	Stock C/F	229,519
	935,951		935,951

Salaries and Wages	28,919	Gross Profit	34,216
Stationery	818		
Rent	4,000		
Advtg.	1,219		
Repairs	--		
Bad Debts	198	Net Loss	938
	35,154		35,154

<u>Note to Instructor</u> : Please refer to Sheet 2 ; same instructions
apply here.

DEPARTMENT OF TAXATION AND REVENUE

P.O. Box 5570
Bangaloops

5th March 1967.

Mr. Phan Boon Tran,
P.O. Box 33D,
<u>Bangaloops</u>

Dear Sir,

Further to the discussion in your office today, the Department will drop all investigation of your returns for tax purposes if you forward within seven days your cheque for £ 3,200 in full settlement of the Department's claims.

Kindly note that proceedings will be taken after seven days if this settlement is not made. Kindly note also that this letter refers only to your income up to the end of the year 1965.

Yours faithfully,

W. Q. Shan

W.Q. Shan
<u>Commissioner.</u>

"Cheque No 114 sent 6th March."

You ought to be telled that
your wife is not what you
think she is. She is carrying
on a affair with your managing
director. And this isn't the first
time she has been playing about
while you are busy with your
factory and byzness.

I won't tell you anymore or
who I am but I'm just
telling you so you know.

Argus, Springfield and Phoon

Solicitors and Business Agents

November 3rd 1966

Phan Boon Tran Esq.,

My dear Tran,

We have fully discussed with our client the proposal to buy your business.

Assuming that your accounts for 1965 and 1964 can be verified by our auditors; and that you will undertake not to start a similar business within ten miles of present sites, our clients are interested in discussing a firm price.

They consider that your valuation of £ 500,000 is too high, but this could be affected by the value of the stock. They suggest that a price of £ 200,000 plus actual value of stock as assessed by an independent valuer appointed by them but at your expense would be reasonable, always assuming the above provisos.

Will you let us know if this proposition is acceptable in principle. If it is, we will prepare an agreement to be signed by both parties.

sincerely yours,

Argus, Springfield and Phoon

Tran:

The government will give every encouragement to any
manufacturer, you or anybody else, who provides work and
goods. You cannot be protected from competitors starting up
unless you can get the government to declare you a pioneer
industry. This will give you tax exemptions, customs duties
to keep out imports and no-one will get any licences to
import goods that compete with you, or machinery to make them.

If you want this, you will have to start a new factory,
or produce a new range of goods. As the law stands, it is
only for new industries, so you will have to do something
more than just carry on as you have been doing. If you do
this, there's a good chance you can get the special status
above.

If you don't someone else might. Of course, this helps
you too but if you want to dominate the market you will have
to get in before your competitors and you might scare them
off. Once you are started and given the status, I think we
can see that new competitors don't have a chance to bring in
plant or machinery, so you would be a lot better off.

Why don't have a drink on Friday and talk it over?

Yours,

To   whom it is of concern:

This is my last will which I write while
of sound mind and full knowledge of what I am
doing.

I wish that all my goods and possessions,
whatever they are, should be given to my
daughter Ariadne Liew Tran and used for
her education and welfare — I do not wish
that my wife should receive anything
because I have well provided for her in
my life

Phan Boon Tran

First January 1966.

SUN WONG AND SIMPSON
CONSULTANTS

P.O. Box 173L
Bangaloops

__Confidential__   17th April 1966

Mr. Phan Boon Tran:

     You have asked us to look into the affairs of your
business quietly and to give you recommendations about its
future development.   You will find a great deal of detail in
the pages of our Report which follows, but this is a summary
as we see the position:

1.   Your factory produces goods for which there is an
     increasing need in this country and we think you ought
     to keep it going and consider expanding your output some-
     time within the next year. If you don't, the market will
     get bigger, you will be unable to supply all requirements
     and competitors will start.

2.   Your retail stores are located in the right places and
     you should consider starting another one at Rodcase, where
     there is a big workers'estate being started.

3.   The methods in your stores are out of date. They should
     be painted light colours inside and out, with plenty of
     colour. Shelving must be cleaned and painted and kept
     clean-looking. Your service counters should be covered
     with some light coloured plastic or something of that
     kind. If you brighten up everything it will help attract
     more customers and sell more goods. In the same way you
     should brighten your staff - give them bright coloured
     uniforms and make sure they keep them clean and tidy.

4.   Your accounts show that profits are declining. You should
     examine all expenses and see where you can cut them down.
     This is the best way to increase your profit.

5.   We think your managers are all OK, but you might try
     giving them a bonus on results so that they will try to
     work harder and make more sales.

     In the main Report all these items are discussed in full.
If you take our advice, we think your problems will soon disappear.

                              Yours faithfully,

                              Sun, Wong and Simpson
                              Consultants.

IN-BASKET EXERCISE:
THE CONFIDENTIAL FILE

INSTRUCTOR'S NOTES

General

The best impression will be given if the papers are different sizes and types and if the papers are handwritten where this is indicated. Other notes as to realistic presentation appear on individual papers.

Significance of the Papers

The papers consist of three groups:

- those that cover purely personal matters;
- the accounts of the business;
- other papers concerning the business which help
  to show its state of health.

The last group and the accounts are the most important for the state of the business. These are:

The Accounts (Sheets 2 and 5)

Any trainee ought to be able to note that profit has been falling. The important point, however, is that gross profit has been falling over the period of the accounts while at the same time, sales have been going up. Probably this would be picked up only by accountants or students of accountancy. Therefore, either the exercise should be confined to people with this interest, or the non-accountants should not be expected to see this point.

Suppose your group merely picks up the fall in net profit, the question you ask is: why is it falling? The obvious answer is that expenses are going up. Are they? Examination of the expenses after gross profit is determined (that is in the second part of each statement of account) will show that these costs are tending down, not up. Why then are profits falling? This leads to an examination of the gross profit. It is falling. Why? Sales are down? No, they are up. What about Stock carry-over each year? Not much change across the period. Purchases? Yes, they are going up. So what do we conclude?

Most likely that either the costs of individual items purchased have been creeping up - that is the firm has been paying rising prices for the same goods; or that sale prices have not been high enough. They may include too many items sacrificed at sales, allowed to become dirty or damaged so that they have to be sold at a discount. Somehow, volume has been sacrificed to profit. Turnover is up, gross profit on the turnover is down. Something is clearly wrong either with the buying policy or with the pricing policy, or both.

With an accounting group, a lively discussion can be provoked on this. With a non-accounting group, the accounts analysis gives the chance to talk about the folly of going for turnover only - a company can "go broke" even while its sales are buoyant.

The inked notes on accounts show Tran has been understating profit by a stock undervaluation or reserve. This is common enough and of no importance in revealing conditions in the business.

The Other Business Papers (Sheets 3, 4, 6, 8, 9, 11)

Sheet 3 - a list of government department contacts. This is a perfectly legitimate list. Every businessman needs this type of contact. Some trainees might want to suggest some corruption; not necessarily.

Sheet 4 - tells us little of importance, suggests that costs are not rising at the factory, but that there may be a bit of bother ahead. But how do we know Tran did not do something about the problem? Did he raise wages? What do the accounts reveal? On the other hand, the sheet suggests something about Boom, who signed it. He is the Managing Director. He ought at least to be making a recommendation, not asking for advice. This could lead to a discussion of the need for strong managers willing to tackle problems or at least recommend action which will solve them.

Sheet 6 - a red herring, of no importance. It does confirm that Tran had some difficulties with the taxation people, but it is settled and, in any case, tells us nothing about the present state of the firm.

Sheet 8 - is this a way out for the widow? Should she get in touch with this company and re-open discussions. We do not know what happened from this letter. Would the company be willing to offer the same price now? (See continued fall in profit to a loss position after the letter was written). Incidentally, are the ideas about independent valuation of stock and the suggested contract to keep out of similar business in the locality good ideas?

Sheet 9 - Here is another possibility - expand the manufacturing side. If the gross profit fall is due to higher cost per unit buying, it might be good business to manufacture your own in greater quantity and so control buying price. But there is another trap here. Gross profits include profits from the sale of goods manu- factured. It might be that they have been sold at too low a price and so have lifted turnover, but cut the profit. So the factory and the shops need separate investigation. Anyway, this is a proposition which is worth looking at as a solution to the firm's difficulties.

By the way, "Al" can be identified as the contact man at the Finance Dept. of the government so his advice should be reliable on that side.

Sheet 11 - The first item of the summary report supports the idea of expansion, and the second item writes off one possible cause of loss - bad locations.

Item 3 seems sound and sensible enough.

Item 4 is "up the creek" and should undermine confidence in this consulting firm. Expenses are down, not up - the cause of the losses lies somewhere else, as we have seen above. Then the consultants have just recommended increased costs - painting and so on. Finally, is cost-cutting the "best way to increase your profits"? This reveals a negative attitude. The best way to profit is more turnover at profitable levels. If this consultant's advice is followed and expenses are cut, this does not go to the root of the present problem because gross profit is down, and no cost cutting later will do much about that.

Item 5 suggests a bonus on results. What results? This is a question for discus- sion. Clearly, in the present result-of-business position, a bonus on increased sales might merely add to the loss - higher turnover in this company has been accompanied by falling profit. So we need a bonus on profit results. This is a good type of bonus for management at all times. A salesman may get a bonus on sales, since he is instructed on what his price is to be. A manager, though, must manage, not just sell.

On this sheet, the last question for discussion is: if the consultant's advice were followed, would the firm's difficulties be solved?

The Remaining Papers (Sheets 1, 7 and 10)

Sheet 1 - of no importance, it records an agreement which has no present effect on the situation. Boom may, of course, want his annual rise considered. Should he get it?

Sheet 7 - a red herring. Best destroyed.

Sheet 10 - This is something of a bombshell, but it ought not to divert attention from the main business in hand. The trainee has been asked to report on the apparent state of the business and what ought to be done about it. He should go ahead with this and carry out his instruction. It is not his affair whether the widow owns the business or not.

Of course, he cannot ignore it. Top treatment would be to report on it separately to his own boss, raising the question of whether he, the boss, should tell the widow about the "will" and advise her to get legal advice on whether it is valid and where she stands.

Final Observations

The best performance will be by those who quickly eliminate the unimportant items, dispose of the will by calling it to the attention of the boss, and then get down to analysing the firm's situation. Three possibilities are open: expand, try to sell or set the present business on its feet.

In any case, it will be necessary to get out separate accounts for the manufacturing side of the business and see what contribution it is making to the total position.

In view of the possible doubt about the widow's legal position, the boss might be advised to suggest she tell Boom she cannot give him time as requested for discussion and make an appointment for a couple of days later. This will give a breathing space for a more leisurely examination of and report on the accounts, etc...But, the trainee must not "trade" on this. He can recommend it, but he must still come up with his report and analysis, even if an interim one.

Objective

To explain how and when evaluation should be done, and what benefits can be derived from a systematic assessment of training and learning

To encourage participants to evaluate all training programmes they conduct

---

Handout Material

I   - Stages in Evolving an Evaluation Instrument (a diagram), p. 15

II - Course Review Form (to be handed in at Session 27), pp. 17-18

III - Individual Session Evaluation Sheet, p. 19

HANDOUT I, Session 1, Session Evaluation Form

Background Reading

Levels of Evaluation, p. 1

Evaluation of Training, pp. 3-8

Evaluating Management Training, pp. 9-14

Recommended Reading

Craig and Bittel, Training and Development Handbook, Chapter 5,
        "Evaluation of Training", by D. Kirkpatrick

Markwell and Roberts, Organisation of Management Development Programmes,
        Chapter 8, "Evaluation of Training"

Hesseling, Strategy of Evaluation Research in the Field of Supervisory and
        Management Training

Andrews, The Effectiveness of University Management Development Programmes.
        There is a summary and commentary on this book in an ILO general
        paper of the same title, reference Man.Dev./6 (1968)

Special Equipment and Aids

Prepare a display of the various types of evaluation forms and either
distribute them around the classroom or pin them on the bulletin board

45 min.	**Session Guide** 21
	During the week, you will have studied the session evaluation forms. Before this session, make a summary of the views expressed on these forms. (The Session Evaluation Form can be considered as a four-point scale; see background reading for suggestions on how to analyse the information).
16:00	Summarise the evaluation which participants have made of the different sessions in this course. Discuss the purpose and value of "evaluation at the reactions level". (See also the section on Immediate Outcomes in the background reading, Evaluating Management Training.)
	If time permits, compare different kinds of evaluation forms with the one used in this course: HANDOUT III (provided as a sample alternative), the seven-point scale in the background reading, some of the other types found in the recommended reading.
16:15	Give a 20-minute lecture on the other levels at which evaluation can take place. Refer to the background reading and Chapter 5 in Craig and Bittel.
	Intermediate summary. Emphasise that evaluation is a before, during and after process. Information obtained during or after a training programme should be seen, if possible, in the light of information gathered on the before-training situation. Peter Warr's article, Evaluating Management Training, discusses the need for early forms of evaluation.
16:35	Issue HANDOUT I, Stages in Evolving an Evaluation Instrument. Go over it; stress that:
	– attention must be given to each step if the evaluation of a training programme is to give an over-all picture;
	– objectives should be defined or specified as clearly as possible;
	– before-training evaluation is often necessary prior to specifying the objectives of a training programme; etc.
	Answer any questions members may have.
16:45	Distribute HANDOUT II, the Course Review Form, which is to be filled out by participants and handed in at Session 27. Mention that evaluation of the over-all course will be discussed at the concluding session.
	Close the session.

LEVELS OF EVALUATION

<u>Evaluation at the reactions level</u> provides:

- a short-term subjective assessment of the trainee's reactions to the course;
- an indication of those parts of the course which need immediate alterations;
- little in the way of value if it is the sole means of evaluating training.

<u>Evaluation at learning level</u> obtains information on the amount of learning that trainees acquire during the training programme - measures increased knowledge. Sometimes referred to as the level of <u>immediate</u> outcomes.

How: usually through examination or testing systems.

Benefits: enables trainer to establish base data; provides trainee with knowledge of results which helps him to identify his own area of need.

Drawbacks: measurement of increased knowledge alone is unsuitable - does not indicate manager's ability to use or apply it to his work.

<u>Evaluation at job behaviour level</u> discovers whether or not trainees have applied their learning in the form of changed behaviour on the job - measures effectiveness of training programmes in terms of on-the-job behaviour. Sometimes referred to as the level of <u>intermediate</u> outcomes.

How: many ways, depending on complexity of job - systematic appraisal on a before-and-after basis, trainer's observations through involvement in job situation.

Benefits: indicates whether or not training programme was effective; gets top and senior management involved.

Drawbacks: more difficult to evaluate than "reactions" and "learning" levels; time-consuming for the trainer.

<u>Evaluation at functioning level</u> measures the effects of the trainee's job behaviour on the productivity or efficiency of the trainee's department or on the morale of his subordinates. Sometimes referred to as the level of <u>long-term</u> or <u>ultimate</u> outcomes.

How: reduced turnover, reduced costs, reduction in grievances, increase in quality and quantity of production.

Benefits: evaluates training programme directly in terms of results desired.

Drawbacks: difficult to know how much of the improvement can be directly attributed to a specific training programme - depends partly on how specific the objectives of the training are.

EVALUATION OF TRAINING[1]

by A.C. Hamblin,
School of Management,
Bath University of Technology

Definition

Evaluation of training is used here in a broad sense, to mean any attempt to obtain information (feedback) on the effects of a training programme, and to assess the value of the training in the light of that information.

According to some experts on the evaluation of training, we should distinguish between validation (the assessment of whether the training has achieved its laid-down objectives) and evaluation (the measurement of the total effects of the training programme). In practice, however, this distinction is not always meaningful, since it may be impossible to obtain information on the total effects of training (which may be extremely complex). Therefore, any evaluation exercise involves selection between evaluation criteria and thus (by implication) the establishment of training objectives.

Why Evaluate?

Evaluation has two purposes. First, it can be used for assessing training effectiveness. Secondly, it can itself be used as a training aid.

The primary purpose of evaluation is to improve training by discovering which training processes are successful in achieving their objectives (to "sort out the good training from the bad"). Many trainers hope to obtain completely objective information on the results of training. In practice, this is usually impossible, since any evaluation exercise affects the nature of the situations studied. For example, if we ask trainees for information about their reactions to training, we change the nature of their reactions. If we set trainees an examination at the end of a course, we affect the nature of their learning. If we study a trainee's job behaviour after a course, we change his job behaviour. These changes are bound to occur so long as the trainee knows he is being evaluated.

This leads us to the second purpose of evaluation. Since evaluation affects learning, it can be put to use as a training aid (an aid to learning). Its effects are likely to be beneficial, since it is a primary principle of the psychology of learning that knowledge of results facilitates good learning. Evaluation can help trainees to learn more effectively.

Levels of Evaluation

The processes which occur as a result of a successful training programme can be divided into four levels. Evaluation can be carried out at any of these levels.

1. The Reactions level. Trainees react to the training (form opinions and attitudes about the trainer, the method of presentation, the usefulness and interest of the subject matter, their own enjoyment and involvement, etc.).

2. The Learning level. Trainees learn (acquire knowledge, skills and attitudes about the subject matter of the training, which they are capable of translating into behaviour within the training situation).

3. The Job Behaviour level. Trainees apply this learning in the form of changed behaviour back on the job.

4. The Functioning level (Efficiency and Costs). This changed job behaviour affects the functioning of the firm (or the behaviour of individuals other than the trainees). These changes can be measured by a variety of indices, many of which can be expressed in terms of costs.

---

[1] See A.C. Hamblin, "Evaluation of Training", in Industrial Training International, November 1970, pp. 33-36.

(Note: the "Learning", "Job Behaviour" and "Functioning" levels are
referred to by some experts as the "immediate", "intermediate" and
"ultimate" levels respectively.)

These four levels can be seen as a chain of cause and effect. The chain
can be broken at any of its links: a trainee may react correctly but fail to
learn; or he may learn, but fail to apply his learning on the job; or he may
change his job behaviour, but this may have no effect on the functioning of the
firms. Thus, ideally we should evaluate at every level. If we ignore the more
distant levels, we will only discover the more superficial changes. If we
ignore the immediate levels (reactions and learning), we are in danger of being
unable to explain any changes that we discover, because we have not followed
through every link in the chain. (For instance, we might discover the trainee's
job behaviour had deteriorated after the training; but unless we had evaluated
at the reactions and learning levels, we would not know why this had happened
and so would not be able to improve the training.)

In many cases, however, it may be impractical or undesirable to evaluate
at every level, e.g.:

- For simple forms of training with clearly defined objectives (e.g. training
  an operator to work a machine, where the skill components of the job have been
  precisely defined) it is possible to evaluate directly at the job behaviour
  and functioning levels.

- For very complex forms of training, with wide or ill-defined objectives
  (e.g. many forms of supervisory and management training) it may be impossible
  to evaluate at the more distant levels. For instance, we may be training
  supervisors to improve their communication with their subordinates (Job
  Behaviour level) but we may have no idea how to measure the effect of these
  changes on the functioning of the firm. Or we may know too little about the
  trainees' job content to be able to evaluate job behaviour, and we may therefore have to concentrate on the Reactions and Learning levels, and to set
  objectives at these levels only.

Objective Setting and Evaluation

The choice of evaluation criteria depends on the objectives of the training.
Therefore, post-training evaluation is intimately connected with the pre-
training investigation of training needs and the establishment of training
objectives.

Ideally, we should set the objectives of training at each of the four
levels. For instance, the objectives of a course for salesmen might be defined
in the following manner:

to establish a high level of involvement and interest (Reactions) in

order that trainees may effectively learn certain facts, certain skills

of salesmanship, and certain attitudes towards the salesman's job

(Learning) in order that they may use these facts and apply these

skills on the job (Job Behaviour) in order that the quantity of sales

may increase over a specified period (Functioning).

If these objectives were precisely defined and established, it would be possible
to evaluate at every level. The more precise the objectives, the more precisely
can training be evaluated. The level(s) at which training is evaluated should
be the level(s) at which the objectives of training are set.

When to Evaluate?

Evaluation data (at any of the four levels) can be obtained during training,
immediately after training, or at a specified time (or times) after the end of
training. In each case, it should if possible be compared with information on
the before-training situation.

Quantified or Unquantified?

Evaluation data can be either quantified (measured, systematic, numerical) or unquantified (descriptive, unsystematic, verbal). The two types of data have complementary advantages and disadvantages. Because of its narrowness and specificity, quantified data should never be taken at its face value, but should be interpreted in the light of unquantified data.

Techniques of Evaluation

There is a wide range of possible techniques at each level of evaluation; in fact, the range of evaluation methods is potentially as wide as the range of training methods. The selection of the correct technique (or combination of techniques) for a particular situation depends on the nature of the training objectives; the design of training and the training methods; the relationship between trainers, trainees and their superiors; the finance available; and other factors. Evaluation should be tailor-made to fit the needs of the situation.

However, all evaluation techniques (with the exception of some at the "functioning" level) are variations on the two themes of watching and asking (observation and questionnaire/interview). The advantages and limitations of these two types of technique are complementary, and they should be employed together whenever possible.

In the remainder of this article, a few techniques at each of the evaluation levels will be briefly described and discussed.

Level 1. Reactions

Information about trainees' reactions to training may be obtained during training, immediately after training, or some time later. During training the skilled and sensitive trainer will of course obtain a great deal of useful information about trainees' reactions simply by watching them and listening to their conversation. However, in some circumstances it may be desirable for him to supplement this unsystematic information by the use of rating scales for sessions. These are forms on which, at the end of each training session, trainees are asked to place a tick on a number of seven-point (or five-point) scales. For instance, a rating scale form might look like this:

I have found this session

| very well presented | 1 2 3 4 5 6 7 | very badly presented |
| very stimulating | 1 2 3 4 5 6 7 | totally unstimulating |

For me in my present job, the session has been

| extremely useful | 1 2 3 4 5 6 7 | totally useless |

The information on the forms can be quickly analysed in the form of histograms, and the results can, if desired, be fed back to the trainees and used as a basis for discussion.

Rating scales on immediate reactions are most useful for "steering" purposes, i.e. for deciding what to do next on an ongoing training programme. They should not be used if the training programme is so inflexible that changes cannot be made in the light of the information obtained. It is also risky to use them for deciding which sessions to include on repeats of the same programme; for this purpose it is better to obtain information on long-term rather than immediate reactions.

The traditional time for obtaining feedback on trainees' reactions is at the end of the training programme. But this is probably the least satisfactory time at which to obtain this information, since it has neither the advantages of immediacy nor those of objective distance.

Information on long-term reactions to training can be obtained from trainees by questionnaires or interviews some time after the end of a course. This approach can be most useful for restructuring training programmes, so long as it is not confused with an evaluation of learning or of job behaviour.

Level 2. Learning

The purpose of evaluation at this level is to obtain information on the amount of learning that trainees acquire during the training programme, irrespective of whether they go on to apply the learning on the job. Learning can be divided into knowledge, skills and attitudes, and the three will be discussed separately.

Knowledge learning can be evaluated by various forms of tests and examinations. The purest form of evaluation of knowledge learning is that used in programmed instruction, where knowledge is evaluated at every stage of the learning process. However, even if programmed learning is not being used, it is possible to construct tests consisting of multiple-choice questions (i.e. questions where the trainee must choose between the right answer and a number of wrong answers) which can be administered at the end of the training programme (and then repeated later, if desired, to measure the extent to which learning has been retained). In order to measure the amount of change caused by the training, the test must also be administered at the start of the training programme, except in cases when it can reasonably be assumed that the trainee knows nothing about the subject-matter before the training starts.

If the knowledge to be assessed is not simply factual knowledge but includes a large element of "intellectual understanding" it may be difficult to construct multiple-choice questions, and it may be necessary to use examinations of the academic type. Examinations, despite all their faults (which include unreliability, subjectivity of marking, and the intrusion of "examination technique" as a separate but irrelevant skill) are still the best method of evaluating some types of knowledge. Examinations do not have to be written; for many trainees oral examinations are better.

Skill learning can again be evaluated by tests, though in this case they must be practical tests in which the trainee is given the opportunity to demonstrate his skill. Here again the test must be performed at the beginning and at the end of training (and also, in the case of long training programmes, at one or more points during training) in order to measure the change effected by the training. Provided that the elements of the skill in question have been identified, it should be possible to assess the trainee's performance during demonstrations of skill. This is true even of social skills.

Attitude learning is an objective of most training programmes even when their primary objectives are in terms of knowledge or skills. To measure changes in attitudes, we can use elaborate attitude scales but their complexity, together with the narrowness of the range of attitudes measured, makes them inappropriate for most training programmes.

Semantic differential scales (SDs for short) provide a simpler and more effective approach. In this technique, trainees are given a sheet at the top of which the subject-matter of the training (for example, "Work Study") is stated, and below this are a number of seven-point or five-point scales stretching between pairs of adjectives with opposite meanings (for example, "complicated-simple", "inefficient-efficient", "friendly-hostile", and so on). Trainees are asked to rate the subject-matter of the training on each of these scales. They must do this at the beginning and at the end of the training programme, so that changes can be identified. The psychological theory of SDs is well advanced but in its simplest form the SD is an evaluation instrument which training officers can easily apply and adapt for their own purposes. It often reveals unexpected attitude changes, and provides invaluable information on what "really happened" during the training process.

Level 3. Job Behaviour

The purpose of evaluation at this level is to discover whether trainees have applied their learning in the form of changed behaviour on the job. A variety of evaluation techniques can be used, but perhaps the most important thing is that trainers should "get their feet wet": in other words, that they should actively involve themselves as far as possible in the job situation of their trainees, so that they obtain a large amount of unsystematic information about their job behaviour.

For manual jobs, where the knowledge and skill elements of the job have
been broken down, it is possible to evaluate job behaviour relatively completely
by means of systematic observation. For more complex jobs (e.g. managerial and
supervisory), it is not possible to obtain such complete information on job
behaviour, and it is necessary to choose between several approaches, or to
combine more than one approach. The following are among the techniques that can
be used:

Activity sampling - for discovering the percentage of time spent by the trainee
on different aspects of his job; and observer diaries, for obtaining a
continuous record of the trainee's pattern of activities. These techniques have
been widely used by the author and others on research projects, but their expense
makes them impracticable in many training situations.

Self-diaries - the trainee keeps a record of his own activities over a specified
period, often by ticking in the appropriate columns on a pre-designed form at
half-hourly or hourly intervals. They are both less expensive than observer
diaries, and also more acceptable to trainees, especially at managerial levels.

Observation of specific incidents - the trainer or evaluator observes the
trainee's performance during a specific incident related to the subject-matter
of the training. (For instance, in a course on interviewing techniques, the
trainer might sit in on a real-life interview and assess the trainee's
performance.) This is clearly similar to the tests of skill discussed above,
except that it takes place in a job setting instead of in a training setting.

Self-recording of specific incidents - devising tailor-made evaluation instruments through which the trainee can himself record details of the way in which
he performs certain incidents.

Appraisal by superiors - an obvious method of evaluating job behaviour after
training, but many conventional appraisal forms are ill-designed for this
purpose. It is necessary to tie the appraiser down by asking for concrete
descriptions of job behaviour (e.g. "Can you describe any specific incidents
in which he demonstrated this improvement in knowledge/skill/attitudes?")

Self-Appraisal - a variation of appraisal and can be used in conjunction with
other forms of appraisal.

All these methods can of course be used before training in order to identify
training needs and objectives, as well as after training in order to evaluate
its effects. In the case of training programmes which are spread out over a
long period, with the trainees returning to the job between training sessions,
they can also be used at various stages during the training process in order to
"steer" the training.

Level 4. Functioning

Evaluation at this level consists of any attempt to measure aspects of the
effects of trainee's job behaviour - whether on the productivity or efficiency
of the trainee's department, or on the morale of his subordinates as expressed
by absence rates, labour turnover rates, or the incidence of industrial disputes.
Any index of functioning which is related to the training objectives can be used;
and once the effect of the training on the functioning of the firm has been
isolated it is often a relatively small step to assess the cost benefits
resulting from the training.

The main difficulty is determining to what extent changes are the result of
the training rather than of other factors. If the objectives of training have
been very precisely defined (for instance, if supervisors are being trained in
quality control specifically with a view to reducing the percentage-reject rate
in their departments) it may be possible to evaluate at this level. In other
cases it will probably prove too difficult.

Control Groups

If one adopts a strictly scientific approach to the evaluation of training,
it is necessary to have a control group which does not undergo training, but is
carefully matched with the trainee group in respect of all other factors. One
can then compare changes in the trainee group with changes in the control group,

and so isolate the effects of the training. However, the practical difficulties of obtaining matched control groups in real-life industrial settings are usually insuperable. But it must be admitted that if there is no control group there is always an element of subjectivity (or perhaps we should call it 'intelligent guesswork') in assuming that any changes which are observed have resulted from the training, and not from the changes which have been going on at the same time. The more we can map out the complete chain of cause and effect between the training process and the ultimate changes, the more we can reduce the element of guesswork.

Is Evaluation Worthwhile?

Evaluation is simply the obtaining of selective information about the effects of training; the value of that information is determined by its usefulness for the people who receive it (e.g. trainers, trainees or their superiors). It must be remembered that evaluation exercises may themselves be costly and time-consuming, and may also have unforeseen side-effects. One should not evaluate by any method unless one foresees the use to which the evaluation data will be put, and judges that this usefulness makes the evaluation worthwhile.

REFERENCES

1. Hesseling, P.: Strategy of Evaluation Research (Assen, Van Gorcum, Netherlands, 1966).

2. Warr, P.B.: "Evaluating Management Training", in Journal of the Institute of Personnel Management, February 1969.

3. Hastings, Kenneth: "Managers Talking - A Means of Assessment", in Industrial Training International, July 1968.

4. Malt, Lillian G.: "Improving Performance - Role-Playing in Management and Supervisory Training", in Personnel Management, March 1965.

5. Fleishman, E.A., Harris, E.K., and Burtt, H.E.: Leadership Supervision in Industry (Columbus, Ohio State University, 1955).

6. Kerlinger, Fred N.: Foundations of Behavioural Research (London, Holt, Rinehart and Wilson, 1969).

7. Basey, Ray: "Training the King Man" in Industrial and Commercial Training, January 1970.

8. Thurley, K.E. and Hamblin, A.C.: The Supervisor and his Job (London, H.M. Stationery Office, 1963).

9. Bird, Michael: "Changes in Work Behaviour Following Supervisory Training", in Journal of Management Studies, October 1969.

10. Thompson, Michael (interviewed by John Wellens): "The Olsen Project", in Industrial Training International, October 1968.

EVALUATING MANAGEMENT TRAINING[1]

by Peter Warr

This is not as easy as evaluating operative training.
But a system can be devised for getting quick information,
with the prime aim of improving training.

There is general agreement that once a training programme is over we should, as a matter of routine, try to check its effectiveness. Unfortunately, this notion is largely mistaken - at least as far as management training is concerned. Merely to obtain information about the trainees' performance _after_ they have received training is to shut the door after the horse has bolted. It is much preferable to treat evaluation as a process that is carried on before, during _and_ after training. It then becomes more feasible actually to take practical steps towards evaluating training for managers. But many specialists, while appreciating the need for such evaluation, are uncertain how they should go about it.

For several years, a unit at the Psychology Department of Sheffield University has been working to develop evaluation schemes which are of practical value. Part of this research will be described here. Basic to our work is the belief that, because managers' jobs differ from those of operatives, principles about operative training will not always apply to management training.

It is usually fairly easy to draw up a job specification for an operative - especially if his task is repetitive, with a short cycle-time. From this specification, we can develop estimates of his training needs, and furthermore we can readily measure the success of efforts to alter his work behaviour (in terms of output, scrap, accidents, obvious mistakes and so on). For this reason it makes sense to advocate for operatives that we:

(a) ascertain their training needs by job specification and individual appraisal methods;

(b) evaluate the success of their training by observing performance on the job.

But when we turn to managers, it soon becomes clear that job specification in any degree of detail is a much more difficult proposition. Managerial work is so much more complex and variable that a complete job specification cannot be drawn without considerable delay - by which time it may already be partly out of date. This is not to say that short specifications are impossible; only that descriptions in sufficient detail for training use are often impractical. For the same reasons, it is also very difficult to obtain objective measures of a manager's performance on the job. It follows that the two recommendations made above for operatives might not necessarily apply in the context of management training.

Our research has suggested that this is in fact often the case. Manager's training needs are often better ascertained by more direct (and less comprehensive) methods. By concentrating on what a manager _cannot_ do, or confining ourselves to the key areas of his job, we can often formulate training policy relatively quickly. Such procedures need less time than is required for full investigations into all that a manager should do and into what he is already capable of doing. This simpler approach to assessing managers' training needs has been referred to as "training by exception"[2] by analogy with the "management by exception" philosophy.

A second implication of the difficulty of measuring a manager's behaviour is that training evaluation in terms of on-the-job performance appraisal is not at present usually practical. This does not mean that we should despair of being able

[1] This is reprinted with kind permission of the Institute of Personnel Management. See Peter Warr: "Evaluating Management Training", in the _Journal of the Institute of Personnel Management_ (Business Publications Limited, London, February 1969).

[2] Warr, P.B. and Bird, M.W.: _Identifying Supervisory Training Needs_ (London, HMSO, 1968) DEP Training Information Paper 2.

to evaluate manager's training programmes. Even though the measurement of their on-the-job performance is at present for most training officers an unrealistic proposition, there are still aspects of managerial training which are measurable. These can provide particularly valuable information to the training specialist who is concerned to do something about evaluation of management training.

Evaluation Defined

The evaluation framework which has developed from our research emphasises that the primary purpose of evaluation is to improve training. We must, of course, check how satisfactory a training programme has been. But unless we use this information to improve training arrangements, we are largely wasting our time.

With this in mind, a rather formal definition of training evaluation may be offered:

the systematic collection and assessment of information for deciding how best to utilise available training resources in order to achieve organisational goals.

The essential point is that training evaluation involves obtaining feed-back material which will help us to decide what training policies to adopt. Given that evaluation is a continuous process, the answer to the question, "when do we collect this information?", seems to be "right from the start".

Types of Training Evaluation: C-I-P-O

It is helpful to distinguish between four types of training evaluation. These are Context, Input, Process, and Outcome evaluation (C-I-P-O). They are of differing importance, depending upon whether we are talking about the training of managers or of operatives.

(a) Context evaluation. Obtaining and using information about the current operational context - that is, about individual difficulties, organisational deficiencies, and so on. In practice, this mainly implies the assessment of training needs as a basis for decision.

(b) Input evaluation. Determining and using facts and opinions about the available human and material training resources in order to choose between alternative training methods. (For example, in-company or external training? Which external course has a good reputation? Which costs least?)

(c) Process evaluation. Monitoring the training as it is in progress. This involves continuous examination of administrative arrangements and feedback from trainees.

(d) Outcome evaluation. Measuring the consequences of training. Three levels of outcome evaluation may be distinguished:

- Immediate outcomes. Changes in trainees' knowledge, skills and attitudes which can be identified immediately after the completion of training. Assessment involves some measures of how people have changed during a training programme.

- Intermediate outcomes. The changes in trainees' actual work behaviour which result from training. Assessment involves monitoring performance on the job.

- Long-term outcomes. The changes in the functioning of part or all of the organisation which have resulted from changes in work behaviour originating in training. Assessment is usually in terms of output or financial measures.

It may be a little surprising to find so many activities designated as "evaluation". But in order to evaluate management training, we need continuous feedback, so that evaluation is most definitely not something which is merely tacked on to the end of a programme. Indeed, the most delayed types of evaluation are those with least benefits.

Long-term and Intermediate Outcomes

Taking the levels of outcome evaluation in this C-I-P-O scheme one by one, let us first examine <u>long-term</u> outcomes. Is there any point in pinning our evaluation hopes on long-term <u>results</u> - measures of profitability, output, productivity, voluntary absenteeism, disputes and so on? These general organisational measures may in fact be available. But it appears from the published literature that no one has successfully demonstrated increases in, for example, productivity arising directly from one particular piece of management training.

Of course, we hope that such training <u>does</u> have beneficial results of this kind. But when so many organisational <u>factors</u> collectively contribute to productivity and related indices, we can hardly expect to be able to show that one relatively small event - a single management training programme - has by itself pushed up productivity levels.

These long-term outcomes are generalised changes in aspects of the organisation, rather than in the manager himself. They represent the goals which training should aim to help the organisation achieve. The work of the training specialist is only part of the organisation's total effort. Training, in isolation from actions initiated in other departments, is unlikely to make much impression on the organisation's over-all performance.

When we turn to the <u>intermediate</u> outcomes, as envisaged in the C-I-P-O scheme, we are interested in how the manager himself has changed his work behaviour as a result of training. It might be thought that this is the most appropriate type of evaluation measure. But, as said before, there are grave snags when it is <u>management</u> training which is involved. First, we cannot easily measure changes in <u>managerial</u> behaviour. And secondly, a person's behaviour is determined by so many factors that to single out only one of these (his recent training) for study may be taking an oversimplified view of the situation.

This point may be illustrated by a study conducted at Sheffield by Michael Bird. He investigated changes in work behaviour after a training course. Of those managers who had attended the course, most had altered their work routines in some way. But there were wide differences between people. The differences were in individual personality (some managers are more change-oriented than others) and in their bosses' interest in the development of their subordinates. Training was found to produce on-the-job changes to a particularly high degree when the trainee was change-oriented and when his boss was training-oriented. (With the opposite type of trainee and boss, changes following training were rare.) With these extra factors (and others as well) influencing behaviour at work, it is rather unfair to praise or blame managerial training simply on the basis of whether observable behaviour changes ensue.

These considerations provide theoretical reasons for suggesting that perhaps we should at present pay less attention to intermediate outcomes of management training. A more practical reason is that training specialists usually have insufficient time and facilities to evaluate management training this way. Our research would suggest that the <u>immediate</u> outcomes (as defined above) should be stressed more. This does not mean <u>that</u> we ignore behaviour at work. On the contrary, we can utilise research findings to improve this, so getting a better return on our training investments. Indeed, one urgent task is for training specialists to devote more attention to the involvement of superiors in their subordinates' training. We should aim to develop the kind of leadership and training climate which will increase the possibility of a favourable intermediate outcome of management training.

Immediate Outcomes

For the practising training officer who is unsure about what to do next by way of evaluation of management training an examination of the earlier stages of the C-I-P-O scheme might be recommended. Basically, this means stressing the systematic development of feedback loops up to and including the end of a training sequence. This is consistent with our definition above of training evaluation, which assumes that evaluation's primary purpose is to <u>improve</u> training, not simply to check on its value afterwards.

Why should we be concerned with these immediate outcomes, rather than with following up training's consequences into the workplace? Three major reasons may be advanced. First, we need quick, immediate information on which to base training decisions; information coming in after a delay of weeks or months may well be useless. (The kind of feedback information we have in mind here will provide measures of training efficiency and cost-effectiveness. For instance, the consequences of shortening a course by one day - more "efficient" training - can be assessed.)

Secondly, if a training programme is no good at the level of immediate outcomes, it is not likely to be much good in the longer term. And thirdly, some assessment of immediate outcomes of management training is already a practical proposition, both in terms of time and of resources required.

To evaluate training at the immediate outcome stage, we shall need some before-and-after measurements. The measurement might in fact be the same test administered twice. This development is absolutely vital, and deserves much more intensive practice by training officers. They are usually a little frightened of designing tests and questionnaires, and tend to neglect the opportunities they present. Another urgent task is therefore that training specialists should devote more attention to developing before-and-after and other measures in order to set up self-correcting training systems.

The idea of a "self-correcting training system" deserves some comment. If we are doing our evaluation work properly, we shall be obtaining a lot of information about our training which will help in remedying its faults. Adequate feedback loops ensure that a training programme "corrects itself". This is, of course, particularly applicable to off-the-job training courses which are repeated frequently for different groups of trainees. Such courses can readily become mummified, not changing from one generation to the next. The systematic intro-duction of feedback can effectively prevent this.

But what can we measure with these before-and-after tests? It is clear that a gain in knowledge can most easily be tested. Applying a standard questionnaire before and after training is an invaluable procedure. Its value does not only come from the information it yields to a trainer about how much his trainees have learned. Pre-tests and post-tests have all sorts of other beneficial consequences. For example, giving a pre-test at the beginning of a programme can actually lead to increased learning during that programme. And questionnaire construction is particularly useful in forcing a trainer (or his outside speakers!) to think carefully in advance about the objectives of the training programme.[1]

As well as knowledge, attitudes can be measured by means of fairly simple devices. And it is becoming more possible to study the changes in skills which follow management training programmes. The exact nature of the pre-tests and the post-tests will necessarily depend on the programmes in question. But the general principle guiding their design is clear. The test should embody whatever the trainer wants his trainees to be capable of at the end of training, but not to be capable of at the beginning. This, of course, reiterates the programmed instruction idea of "criterion behaviour or knowledge"; but it does also include the notion that poor performance before training is desirable - otherwise the training itself is unnecessary.

Context, Input and Process Evaluation

This brings us back to the first three categories in the C-I-P-O scheme outlined above. It is these, together with immediate outcomes, which training specialists can most fruitfully emphasise in their attempts to evaluate management training.

By process evaluation, we mean learning about the programme as it is going on. This is essential if we are to get feedback quickly enough to make use of it. The obvious procedure is to take the trainees into our trust. Their reactions are the important ones, and they often experience a training sequence very differently from the training staff. If we could systematically and reliably measure important trainee reactions to each part of a training programme, then we could rapidly learn where we were going wrong.

---

[1] Warr, P.B., Bird, M.W. and Rackham, N.H.: "Evaluating Management Training", Association of Teachers of Management Bulletin, 1968, 8, No. 2, 1-13.

One possibility is to make regular use of "session assessment forms" - simple rating scales which trainees complete _immediately after_ a session. The scales to be used will vary from situation to situation. But here is a set we have found useful:

Enjoyment of session

    Didn't enjoy it
    very much |___|___|___|___|___|___| Enjoyed it very much

Amount of new information picked up during session

    Taught me little
    I didn't know
    already |___|___|___|___|___|___| Taught me a lot

Relevance of session to own job

    Not very relevent |___|___|___|___|___|___| Very relevant to my job

Length of session

    Not enough time
    allocated to
    session |___|___|___|___|___|___| Too much time
                                                                             allocated to session

By calculating the average reaction on these four scales (scoring each scale from 1 to 6) we have acquired a lot of useful information for improving training courses. Together with the scales, trainees should be asked for more general comments. Members of management courses are typically very responsible and co-operative when they can see that training staff are seriously interested in improving their programmes, and this form of process evaluation has proved to be most valuable. But process evaluation is naturally not enough by itself, and should always be coupled with some form of outcome evaluation.

Another form of evaluation is _input evaluation_ - described above in terms of gaining information about what training resources are available both inside and outside the company. One widely known system of input evaluation is the De La Rue Index. In this, information is gleaned about alternative courses, their objectives and attainments. This kind of information, reliably obtained, is obviously a help. But as with other forms of assessment, input evaluation alone is not sufficient.

Finally, there is _context evaluation_. This is primarily a question of assessing training needs, and is coupled with the basic notion of "training by exception". Assessment of needs is an essential part of training evaluation. Our studies have from time to time identified training courses which bear little relationship to trainees' jobs and requirements. It is clear that in evaluating these courses we must judge them in relation to actual job needs.

In the C-I-P-O system outlined here, this judgment is made at several stages. It appears in intermediate outcome evaluation, where we examine changes in work behaviour; it appears in process evaluation, where we study trainees' assessments of the relevance of their training: and naturally it is also the core of context evaluation. Successive feedback loops of this kind go a long way to improving training - and improvement should be evaluation's major purpose.

Summary and Practical Conclusions

Evaluation is an ongoing process geared to the improvement of training. The stages of this ongoing process have been described as Context, Input, Process and (three types of) Output Evaluation. Each form of evaluation is important. But we should always try to incorporate more than one form into our programme.

As far as management training is concerned, emphasis should (for the present) shift from attempts to evaluate training in the work situation. Training staff currently have no techniques readily available for this form of evaluation. In any case, there is the possibility of greater practical rewards following from a concentration on _earlier_ forms of evaluation.

Two urgent tasks seem to face training staff at the present time.   These are:

(1) Training specialists should devote more attention to increasing the involvement of superiors in their subordinates' training.

(2) Training specialists should devote more attention to developing before-and-after and other measures in order to set up self-correcting training systems.

STAGES IN EVOLVING AN EVALUATION INSTRUMENT

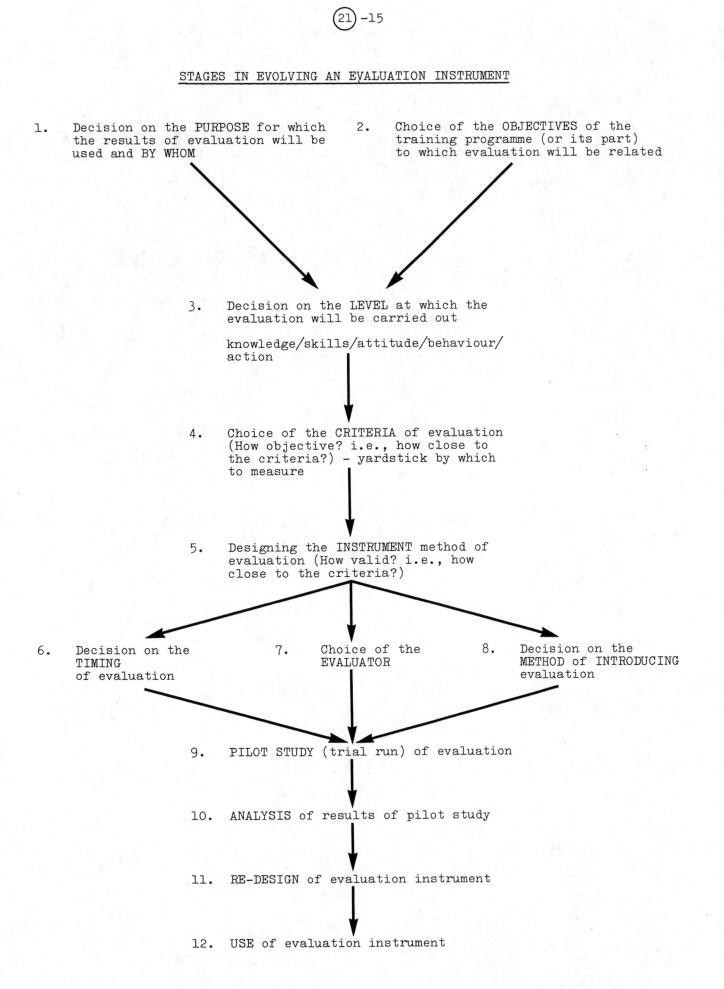

1. Decision on the PURPOSE for which the results of evaluation will be used and BY WHOM

2. Choice of the OBJECTIVES of the training programme (or its part) to which evaluation will be related

3. Decision on the LEVEL at which the evaluation will be carried out

   knowledge/skills/attitude/behaviour/action

4. Choice of the CRITERIA of evaluation (How objective? i.e., how close to the criteria?) - yardstick by which to measure

5. Designing the INSTRUMENT method of evaluation (How valid? i.e., how close to the criteria?)

6. Decision on the TIMING of evaluation

7. Choice of the EVALUATOR

8. Decision on the METHOD of INTRODUCING evaluation

9. PILOT STUDY (trial run) of evaluation

10. ANALYSIS of results of pilot study

11. RE-DESIGN of evaluation instrument

12. USE of evaluation instrument

COURSE REVIEW FORM:

COURSE CONTENT AND BALANCE

Please assume that the length of the course is fixed at 5 days. This means that if you wish to suggest other topics, some presently included must go, or be curtailed.

1. Name the 5 sessions you regard as MOST valuable (appraise the subject area – not the speaker or method of presentation).

NUMBER	TITLE

2. Name the 5 sessions you regard as LEAST valuable

NUMBER	TITLE

3. Suggest any topics, not presently included, which you would wish to have included in future courses:-

    _____

    _____

4. Suggest any topics in the present course for which you think more time should be allowed for a fuller treatment. (Here include sessions noted at (1) above, if appropriate).

    _____

    _____

5. Does the general arrangement and development of subject matter appear logical? YES/NO   If NO, suggest improvements:

    _____

    _____

    _____

6. Generally speaking, did you feel you had enough opportunity for discussion?
    YES/NO

    If NO, should this be by:

         (a) reducing the lecture element of sessions?   YES/NO

         (b) by issuing notes for prior reading?   YES/NO

    or ? (c)

7. On balance would you say that the Course objective was achieved?   YES/NO

8. Any further comments:

    _____

    _____

    _____

    _____

    _____

Handout III

INDIVIDUAL SESSION EVALUATION SHEET
(Sample)

Session No. and Title: _____

Session Leader: _____

Please evaluate the session as it appeared to you in relation to the nine points listed below. Place an X on the scale over the point between the two evaluations so that it indicates where your opinion lies. + indicates the optimum point on the scale.

1. OBJECTIVE EXPLAINED:

   Poorly |___|___|___|___|___| Clearly

2. OBJECTIVE ACHIEVED:

   No |___|___|___|___|___| Fully

3. SELECTION OF METHOD OF INSTRUCTION:

   Poor |___|___|___|___|___| Fully appropriate

4. CONTENT:
   Over-simplified, not enough foundation |___|___|___|___|___| Too sophisticated

5. PARTICIPANTS' ACTIVE INVOLVEMENT:
   Too little |___|___|___|___|___| Too much

6. LEADERSHIP PROVIDED BY TRAINER:

   Weak |___|___|___|___|___| Overdone

7. HANDOUTS AND VISUAL AIDS - QUALITY:

   Poor |___|___|___|___|___| Excessive

8. HANDOUTS AND VISUAL AIDS - QUANTITY:
   Too few |___|___|___|___|___| Too many

9. TIME ALLOTTED:
   Too little |___|___|___|___|___| Too much

Suggestions for improvement not covered by the above:

_____

_____

_____

Objective

To have participants apply what they have learned about the design of training programmes by:
- studying and preparing comments on a case history of a training programme
- designing a course programme in collaboration with other members

Handout Material

As for Session 19, especially HANDOUT I , A Systems Concept of Training
Instructions for Designing a Course Programme (prepared by the instructor)

Background Reading

As for Session 19

Recommended Reading

Special Equipment and Aids

Additional meeting rooms for the discussion groups
Chalkboard and flip chart in each room

Session Guide 22

Evening Study.

45 min. Each participant should read HANDOUT I from Session 19, A Systems Concept of Training, and prepare his comments and questions for Session 25.

60 min. Members divide into previously assigned groups to prepare the outline of a course programme which will be presented and discussed in Session 26.

You may wish to specify details of the assignment in a HANDOUT, explaining that each group should:

-   define their target audience;

-   state the objective of the course (related to organisational and participant needs);

-   outline the subjects to be covered, if possible, the time to be devoted to each and the sequence; specify the training methods to be used for each;

-   determine duration and organisation of the course.

The assignment can be made more precise by specifying the level of participants, the length or type of course (e.g., a residential one-week course for top managers), the subject or objective (e.g., an appreciation course in Management Information Systems). These choices should be related to the jobs and background of the participants in the course.

Groups should record their course outlines on a flip chart for easy presentation to the rest of the group in Session 26.

Objective

To show the value of practical exercises, projects, consultancy assignments and field visits as training methods by explaining their possible uses in various types of management training programmes

Handout Material

Background Reading

The Project Method in Management Education and Training, pp. 1-10

Field Studies in Management Education, pp. 11-13

Session 1, The Training and Consultancy Cycle in ILO Management
        Development Projects

Recommended Reading

Special Equipment and Aids

Chalkboard or flip chart

Show the "Alternatives for Scheduling Project Work", p. 5, either in freehand drawings on the chalkboard or flip chart, or on the flannel board

45 min.	**Session Guide** 23

8:30	As background, describe the reasons leading to an increasing use of practical assignments in management training programmes. Emphasise their importance in developing management skills and moulding attitudes. (Refer to Section I of the background reading, The Project Method, and see also Session 1, The Training and Consultancy Cycle in ILO Management Development Projects.)
8:40	Briefly review the various methods which belong to this category:

- practical exercises and demonstrations;

- application projects;

- consultancy assignments;

- visits to industry (field visits).

8:50	Conduct a discussion based on participants' and your own experiences with the use of these methods. Draw out such points as:

- how the practical assignment was integrated into the training programme (use the chalkboard to show the various ways of scheduling project assignments);

- selection of suitable practical assignments and visits;

- evaluation and follow-up of practical work;

- the trainer's role in the use of these methods;

- problems in planning and scheduling appropriate assignments;

- other drawbacks in using the methods.

9:10	In conclusion, re-emphasise the importance of "training by doing". Use of the project method and other practical in-plant activities can greatly facilitate the transfer of the results of management training to actual working life.
9:15	Close the session.

THE PROJECT METHOD IN MANAGEMENT EDUCATION AND TRAINING

by M. Kubr,
Management Development Branch
International Labour Office

I.   PURPOSE AND PRINCIPLES

The project method currently enjoys a great deal of attention from management teachers and trainers. A growing number of programmes and courses include work on practical application projects; in some cases the method has become the backbone of the entire course. Far from being a passing fad, its increasing use reflects some major developments in management training.

For many years one of the main problems in management education and training has been how to bring it closer to practical life and how to help the students to master the skills of practical application of general concepts, principles, methods and techniques of management to concrete situations. In an attempt to solve this problem a wide range of teaching and training methods has emerged; emphasis was put on developing methods which are likely to affect some of the skills a practising manager should possess. Thus the era of participative methods began, and was generally recognised as a step ahead in the methodology of management education and training.

Most institutes and centres confined themselves to restricting the use of classical ex cathedra methods and allocating more time in the classroom to participative methods, particularly the case study.

A number of management teachers and trainers, however, soon realised that participative methods in classroom instruction only improve certain features of the training process. These methods help to involve participants, arouse their interest in learning and sharpen their analytical capabilities; but they have little impact on some other important managerial skills. After all, even a highly sophisticated classroom simulation can embrace only a restricted number of the pressures, motives or obstacles which may underline a simple managerial problem. To communicate with other course participants who are temporarily released from their daily preoccupations and come to a course in order to learn is different from communicating with colleagues on the job. Furthermore in a training course there is no real responsibility for decisions made during simulation exercises. On the other hand, in practice, managers improve their skills by dealing with new and steadily more demanding situations, by overcoming obstacles in an environment which not only offers opportunities but at the same time forces them to seek their own solutions and to put these solutions into effect.

The realisation of this difference between learning in a training programme and learning in practice was reflected in the idea that training programmes could be complemented by a missing element which would bring them still closer to practice and adjust them better to the individual's training needs than methods such as case studies or business games were able to do. The project method is a result of this thinking. Thus project work is essentially in-plant work on practical management problems, carried out for the common good of the organisation and the trainee. It may also include special theoretical study, consultations and further training activities. The applied sciences and other disciplines have been using this approach for quite some time. In management education and training, however, the project method is a relatively recent element.[1]

---

[1] The project method in management education and training should not be confused with "project management" which is a system exercising managerial unity over all resources needed to achieve a specific goal.

The Management Development Programme of the ILO has been using this method in various ways since the early fifties and continues to use it in virtually all projects of technical co-operation in developing countries. A combination of classroom teaching and training with practical application in live situations has become the main methodological principle of the Programme.

R.W. Revans describes several training programmes in which the project method is an important element.[1] He has become the most active promoter of the method in management education and training. Under his guidance, Belgium's Inter-University Programme for Advanced Management was started in 1968 and project work is the core of the entire course.

For a number of years, various forms of the method have been used to complete the studies of economics and management at universities and in certain courses for managers in several Eastern European Socialist countries. In the Top Management Programme at the Institute of Management in Prague each participant works on an extensive and highly complex practical project. Project work is an essential element in many training programmes at the National Management Development Centre in Bucharest, established in 1967.

The Research Institute for Management Science in Delft has also included project work in its one year International Course on Management for Small-Scale Industries, intended mainly for trainees from developing countries.

In all these cases the type of project is chosen with regard to the objectives, content, duration and other features in the educational and training programmes. In particular, there is a difference between projects used in the training of functional managers and specialists and the training of general managers (see examples in Table 1, taken from various training programmes). Whereas the first group uses projects applying specific methods and techniques to structured, and as a rule well-defined problems belonging to one functional area of management, the latter deals with complex, multi-functional, and unstructured problems - a typical feature of general and top management practice.

Nevertheless, all project work has certain features in common:

. (a)   project work is guided by professional trainers;

(b)   projects cover non-routine work which is sufficiently demanding on the knowledge and skills of the trainee to offer a challenging training opportunity[2];

(c)   projects deal with practical issues important to the organisations in which they are carried out. "Artificial" projects which are not intended for any kind of application should be avoided, since they lack the desirable motivational strength and the necessary training impact.

An important advantage of the project method is its control and evaluation potential. A project produces evidence of what the trainee has learned in the preceding parts of a group training programme and studied individually. It demonstrates the trainee's ability to apply theory to live situations. That is why some educational and training programmes use application projects as part or all of the final examinations.

---

[1] See R.W. Revans, "Recent Experiences in Management Education" (paper for the UN Institute of Training and Research) Brussels, February 1970, or, by the same author, "Le Programme Interuniversitaire de Formation à la Direction", Synopsis, September/October 1969.

[2] Practical assignments, exercises and demonstrations helping the trainee to master routine methods and techniques are not considered as project method, although they are a useful part of many training programmes.

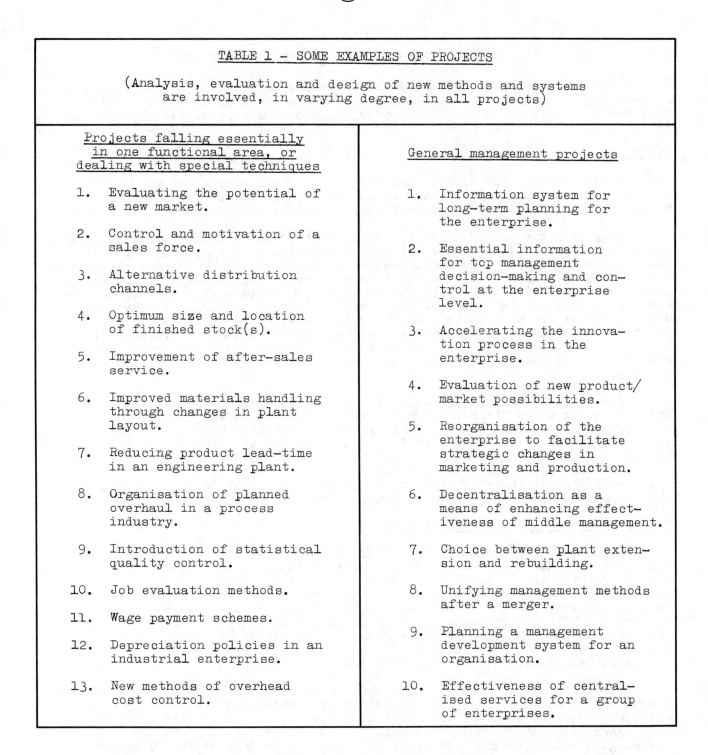

TABLE 1 - SOME EXAMPLES OF PROJECTS	
(Analysis, evaluation and design of new methods and systems are involved, in varying degree, in all projects)	
Projects falling essentially in one functional area, or dealing with special techniques	General management projects
1. Evaluating the potential of a new market.	1. Information system for long-term planning for the enterprise.
2. Control and motivation of a sales force.	2. Essential information for top management decision-making and control at the enterprise level.
3. Alternative distribution channels.	
4. Optimum size and location of finished stock(s).	3. Accelerating the innovation process in the enterprise.
5. Improvement of after-sales service.	4. Evaluation of new product/market possibilities.
6. Improved materials handling through changes in plant layout.	5. Reorganisation of the enterprise to facilitate strategic changes in marketing and production.
7. Reducing product lead-time in an engineering plant.	
8. Organisation of planned overhaul in a process industry.	6. Decentralisation as a means of enhancing effectiveness of middle management.
9. Introduction of statistical quality control.	7. Choice between plant extension and rebuilding.
10. Job evaluation methods.	8. Unifying management methods after a merger.
11. Wage payment schemes.	9. Planning a management development system for an organisation.
12. Depreciation policies in an industrial enterprise.	
13. New methods of overhead cost control.	10. Effectiveness of centralised services for a group of enterprises.

Nonetheless, the project method is not suited to every type of training programme. There is no real need to use it, for example, in short orientation programmes, nor would it be useful in programmes which broaden the managers' horizons and make them aware of new trends or possibilities in management, but do not aim at improving their skills.

Even in programmes where it plays an important if not key role, the project method is usually used in combination with other methods. There is a need to prepare participants for project work first (various other methods will be used for this purpose) and to complement project work by further training activities which cover topics that a project cannot embrace.

II. VARIOUS APPROACHES TO THE PROJECT METHOD

Although the project method is already being used in various ways, new types and combinations with other methods will undoubtedly be appearing in training programmes. Here we shall examine only a few of the more significant approaches to the method.

Individual or Group Approach

At the present time, individual projects prevail over group work. In addition to the fact that they are easier to organise, they provide a clear definition of the trainee's personal responsibility for the results of his work.

Group projects are assigned to small teams of participants in a training programme. They stress collective work on complex problems, sound division of tasks and co-ordination and communication within the team. In many cases, team work is the only appropriate way to tackle today's complex economic and managerial problems. There is, however, a danger that some members of the group will be interested only in their part of the total assignment and learn little about the other parts or the project as a whole. Less active team members may gladly rely on their more dynamic and productive colleagues and it will be difficult to compel them to contribute more to the team's work. To avoid this the group needs to select a good leader and develop a professional ethic which is accepted by all members.

In both individual and group projects the trainees use documents, reports and data prepared by the host organisation. In some cases this information may be prepared at the trainees' special request. Needless to say, seeking available information, using information produced and provided by other people or requesting new information is a normal feature of project work. However, the trainer must see to it that this supply of information does not exceed certain limits: it could well include the solutions which the trainees ought to find themselves and the project would thus miss its purpose.

The Trainee's Own or Other Enterprises

Most training programmes which include project work prefer it to be carried out in the trainee's own enterprise. This eliminates the difficulty of finding a host organisation. It is also easier to identify problems for project work and to obtain management's support for this form of training. This does not ensure, however, that management will automatically go along with the results of the work. Unless the trainee is himself in a high managerial position, the chances that top management will be really receptive to his suggestions will depend on such factors as management's interest in innovation and willingness to introduce change initiated by subordinates.

Some training programmes prefer the second approach. In the Belgian programme mentioned earlier a group of enterprises established a training consortium where each trainee works on an important project in an enterprise other than his own. According to Revans: "managers who undertake the study of the problems of others gain a new insight into their own (and) those interviewed by the action-oriented managers from another enterprise are more disposed to co-operate in the solution of the problems uncovered".[1]

For obvious reasons it is also necessary to seek host organisations for undergraduates in the final phase of their management studies. It is not unusual in such cases for the organisation to offer the student employment after graduation.

---

[1] R.W. Revans, op. cit., p. 7.

With or Without Implementation

Whether or not the training project should include implementation by the trainee is a crucial point. Experience affirms that wherever feasible, implementation should be included as part of the training process; on the other hand, there are practical considerations which sometimes make this impossible.

Relatively simple projects, particularly when carried out in the trainees' own enterprises, can usually be put into effect before the completion of the training programme. Complex projects intended to bring about a more substantial change in an organisation cannot be implemented in a short time and by the trainee alone, especially if the trainee has worked in an organisation other than his own. In the latter case, it is useful to determine the stage which the project should reach by the "cut-off" date of the training programme and to look for convenient ways of allowing the trainee to participate in the application of the project proposals after this date. Concrete arrangements will depend, amongst other things, on the trainee's actual position in management and his relationship with the organisation where the project was worked out.

III. THE METHOD'S PLACE IN TRAINING PROGRAMMES

Some general ways for combining classroom teaching with project work are indicated in Figure 1.

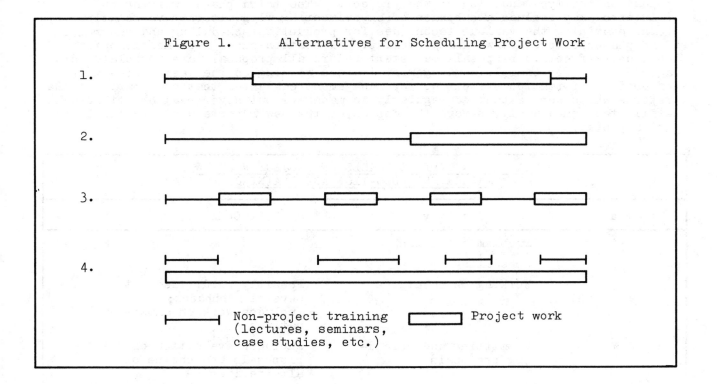

Figure 1. Alternatives for Scheduling Project Work

1.

2.

3.

4.

├─────┤ Non-project training (lectures, seminars, case studies, etc.)   ▭ Project work

Alternative 1 is a training programme which starts with a period of classroom study. During this period the participants are prepared for successive project work and the projects are selected and approved. This is followed by a period (usually substantially longer) of project work. Upon completion, the participants gather again for a brief discussion period on some or all of the projects. This exchange of experience gives everyone an opportunity to learn about a number of interesting practical applications. The ILO Management Development Programme mainly uses this alternative.[1]

Alternative 2 follows similar principles with the exception of the final period of group discussion on the projects. Projects are submitted (and possibly implemented) by the students. At the end of the programme an examining committee interviews each individual and evaluates his project. This alternative has replaced the final examination in many university programmes of management studies and also in some management training centres.

Alternative 3 involves a number of simple and short projects interspersed throughout the training programme. This arrangement is better suited to training in specific methods and techniques than to the training of general managers.

Alternative 4 represents a situation where formal classroom training is reduced to the minimum, and a complex project becomes the essence of the programme. Additional instruction such as consultations, lectures, group discussions, etc. is generated by the project and made available to the participants as the need arises. This approach is particularly suitable for internal training programmes for management succession in medium and large enterprises.

IV. PHASES OF THE METHOD

Projects generally pass through several major phases: a typical sequence is given in Table 2. A further division of these phases into subphases will depend on the type and size of the project. The third phase (working on solutions) may include a subphase of experimenting with alternative solutions (e.g. examining the various techniques for production scheduling and control). Some phases of project work may overlap: in certain cases implementation of obviously effective proposals may start before all proposals are formulated and agreed to. For example a management-trainee working on the design of a more effective information system for top management suggested that some parts of the reports which were submitted regularly to managers but never read or utilised be eliminated immediately, before the design of the new reports would be finalised and approved.

TABLE 2 - TYPICAL PHASES OF PROJECT WORK IN
MANAGEMENT EDUCATION AND TRAINING

Phase	Activity	Comment
1	Problem selection	
2	Scheduling	
3	Working on solutions	Possibly subdivided into several subphases; includes work on alternatives
4	Submitting and defending proposals	Includes evaluation of proposals and choice of alternatives
5	Implementation	
6	Evaluation of results	

[1] See ILO: "Improving Training in Modern Management Techniques" (paper for the UN Inter-Regional Seminar on the Use of Modern Management Techniques in the Public Administration of Developing Countries) Washington, D.C., 27 October-6 November 1970 (mimeographed).

Phase 1 - Problem Selection

Problem selection requires the collaboration of the trainer, trainee and host organisation. A consensus of opinion on the urgency of the problem and the practical usefulness of envisaged work must be reached if the project is to succeed. If one party lacks interest or motivation, the entire project may be jeopardised.

The trainer ought to eliminate problems which would require much more time than will be available or do not correspond to the profile of the students. He will equally refuse problems interesting to the host organisations but which do not offer a sufficient training opportunity to his students.

The trainee's participation in problem selection is a very important part of project work. Sometimes he is asked to consider problems put forward earlier by the trainer or by the organisation. But in many cases it is the trainee's responsibility to identify a problem, make the first brief analysis and convince both the trainer and the organisation that the project is worth while.

The host organisation should not be forced to agree to projects dealing with delicate issues which the management prefers to handle in a different way. The organisation must be prepared to offer certain information, the collaboration of its staff, and possibly other resources.

The attitude of receiving organisations to problem selection can be seen in the Belgian Inter-University Programme for Advanced Management. Revans reports that organisations give priority to non-structured and diffuse issues and willingly permit management trainees coming from other enterprises in the training consortium to tackle strategic issues affecting the future of the entire enterprise.[1]

Phase 2 - Scheduling

The over-all structuring and scheduling of the project is itself a very useful training exercise. Traditional scheduling methods may be used for simple and short projects (Gantt charts, project planning charts), and network planning (CPM, PERT) for the more complex.[2]

As a rule, the schedule of the time required to work on solutions (phase 3) will be rather detailed. In addition to the timetable it will be necessary to determine the resources which the trainee will need during this phase, i.e. necessary collaboration of the organisation's staff, cost of consultations with external specialists, cost of experimental work, study missions, document reproduction, etc.

Time scheduling and resource planning for implementation (phase 5) can, however, only be tentative at this stage. A detailed plan could hardly be submitted before determining the content and importance of the solutions the trainee will suggest in his report.

Phase 3 - Working on Solutions

During this phase, the trainee works out one or more solutions to the management problem which was selected for his project. At the beginning, the work is predominantly analytical. A sufficient amount of information must be collected and analysed to provide a solid base for successive work on solutions.

---

[1] R.W. Revans, op. cit.

[2] See D.I. Cleland, W.R. King: Systems Analysis and Project Management (McGraw-Hill, New York, 1968).

Needless to add that in a number of cases this may lead to a redefinition of the original problem. The findings ought to be synthesised by determining the main causes of difficulties and the main areas in which changes are needed.

This is followed by a period of studying solutions which were applied in similar situations by other organisations and determining the methods or techniques which are best suited to solving the given problem. Theoretical study complementing project work is thus highly action-oriented.

The trainee then proceeds to elaborate on his proposals. As mentioned, alternative solutions are frequently considered, e.g. in projects including investment proposals, dealing with geographical decentralisation of activities, suggesting redistribution of resources among areas of activities within the enterprise or in situations where alternative management techniques could be used.

If it is possible and the receiving organisation agrees, experiments with alternative solutions can be included in this phase. Alternative systems of scheduling, reporting, control, motivation, etc. can be tested in various organisational units within the organisation or, in other cases, in one unit successively.

Some frequently neglected principles must be underscored:

(a) the trainer ought to keep in touch with the trainee, know how work is advancing, and see to it that the trainee obtains the necessary professional advice including help from external specialists in the case of difficult projects;

(b) the receiving organisation should be continuously informed about the state of the project in order to avoid a situation where nobody in the organisation knows what the trainees actually do and whether their work will be of any use.

Project review meetings should be organised during this phase. Such meetings help to reassess the project plan, clear a number of issues and often revive collaboration between the parties concerned.

Phase 4 - Submitting and Defending Proposals

Management education and training programmes use various ways of submitting and defending project proposals. Generally a certain form of presentation for the project report is prescribed. It should include an economic evaluation of the project, especially the cost-benefit analysis relating to the various alternative solutions, and a more detailed time schedule and plan of resources needed for project implementation.

Proposals are examined and evaluated by the trainer and by the management of the receiving organisation. Frequently, external specialists are requested to give their professional opinions. This is followed, as a rule, by a meeting or seminar in which the project is reviewed. The student explains and defends his proposals. In some programmes this review meeting is actually the final examination, or part of it.

If the student is not requested to implement the project, phase 4 will complete his work. Proposals are then transmitted to the organisation concerned which will decide on further action. This phase, however, is no less significant if the trainees are requested to implement their projects. In any case, implementation needs to be preceded by a comprehensive review defining the project's suitability for application, choosing from alternatives, approving the time schedule and planned resources and ascertaining the trainee's competence to implement the project.

Phase 5 - Implementation

The implementation is difficult for everybody concerned: unforeseen obstacles will arise, and changed conditions may require modifications in proposals already worked out and accepted. In many cases the trainee must return to his regular job and will have to implement the project while dealing with many other practical problems. If he has to implement the project in another enterprise, he will face the problems that every outsider faces when trying to introduce changes.

As mentioned before, the learning value for the trainee in project implementation is indisputable. To secure this, the training institution must maintain contact with the trainee during this phase as well and provide further professional advice whenever it is needed, even if implementation was not considered to be part of the formal training programme.

The implementation phase will definitely show whether or not the project was based on a realistic appraisal of the organisation's needs and opportunities and carried out on an appropriate professional level. The number of consultancy reports and research projects which have remained in the drawers of the manager's desk is already large enough in many enterprises; the training projects should not add to this number.

Phase 6 - Evaluation of Results

In this phase we are concerned with two inter-related but different questions: the results of the project itself and the results of the training programme.

An evaluation of results obtained by the organisation demonstrates the practical usefulness of the total project. If the training project proves to be beneficial to the receiving organisation, management will support this method and become more interested in management training.

As a rule, if the organisation has received benefits from the project implementation, this is a sign that the training programme has helped the trainee to improve his competence. Nevertheless, a word of warning against oversimplified conclusions seems to be appropriate in this connection.

First, the trainee may work out and implement a highly effective project but he will learn very little if the project was not a challenge to him. It may also happen that the trainee does excellent work, but for various reasons (which he could not foresee or influence) a well-selected and elaborated project may not produce the desired results.

In order to assess the actual learning value of the project method, it is necessary to complement the analysis of the practical results of the given project with an analysis of further factors, especially long-term changes in the trainee's managerial skills and behavioural patterns.

Projects prepared by management trainees but implemented without their direct involvement need to be evaluated as well. It is useful to communicate to the former trainee the conclusions of this evaluation.

V. PERSPECTIVES

Although quite a few education and training programmes use variations of the method (it is sometimes given another name), it is notably less used than could be expected in view of its value. Some programmes, as mentioned earlier, do not actually need project work to attain their objectives. Many programmes, however, could make better use of one of the known types of the method, or develop their own alternative. It is fair to expect that this is going to happen in the not very distant future although it will mean that some training programmes will have to be restructured and numerous problems solved such as finding a sufficient number of organisations willing to co-operate in project work. It will make many training programmes more interesting, help to improve the control of their results, and provide better evidence about the usefulness of training than is now available.

Let us mention at least two from the many diverse possibilities for more extensive use of the project method:

- most management teachers, trainers, consultants or young managers from developing countries who go on fellowship programmes to industrialised countries do not actually do any project work during their fellowship. It could, however, substantially enhance the effectiveness of the fellowship programmes;

- practical application projects carried out by managers and functional specialists from public enterprises in governmental departments and by government officials in public enterprises could improve the mutual understanding between enterprises and administrations and improve the quality of management in the public sector.

Nevertheless, the project method should not be viewed as a panacea for management education and training. It is certainly useful, but like any other training method it is suited only to certain training programmes and objectives. Perhaps more than any other method, project work requires a solid preparation on the part of the students, a careful selection of problems to be dealt with, and working arrangements convenient to all parties concerned.

FIELD STUDIES IN MANAGEMENT EDUCATION

by R.T. Stiefel,
Centre d'Etudes Industrielles
Geneva

Introduction

Field studies normally appear among the set of teaching methods currently in use with management schools all over the world. And yet, looking at the situation more closely, it is in most cases a very unstructured activity and stands just for "going into the field".

In the following pages we want to present a more structured version of the method, which was introduced at the Centre d'Etudes Industrielles (CEI) a couple of years ago and enjoys an over-all acceptance among both teacher and student body. We will deal with the two versions of field studies; namely, the industry study trip and management systems study.

INDUSTRY STUDY TRIP

Criteria

We understand by the "Industry Study Trip" a teaching method that fulfils the following set of criteria:

- the visit of a well-chosen company;
- a well-prepared examination of the company's annual reports, the environment in which the company operates; a preparation of the expected problems should precede the trip;
- the participants must meet the policy-making level of the company;
- the participants have to report on their studies in the field;
- this report should not only record the situation in the company but should show the author's opinions about the problems and the way of tackling them practically.

Let us examine the various criteria in more detail.

1. The company must be an "interesting case". At the same time, the company must be assessed according to its openness and willingness to respond to questions. By "interesting case" we mean the company should have a striking strategy event in the recent corporate records. This can either be a take-over of a competitor, a development of a diversified product range or even simply an outstanding rate of growth, which makes it interesting to know more about it.

2. The participants want to know more about the company when meeting the management. Hence, they have to study the company's situation before they visit it. Assessing a company's situation means studying and analysing the latest annual reports, the competitive situation and the whole environmental sector in which it operates. Only then can the right questions be brought up, which may lead to a deeper understanding of the present situation.

At CEI a series of sessions on the environment sectors given by a guest lecturer - if necessary - premise the actual trip. At the same time, small study groups analyse different aspects of the company and present them in class so that enough background material on the company is available. For example, at one stage a Swiss aluminium company was selected which had the highest rate of growth among the competition. The participants were analysing the strength and weakness of the company beforehand by analysing the annual reports, the competitor balance sheets and annual reports, etc. Moreover, guest lecturers gave a series of sessions on the situation of the industry as well as on the environmental sectors of the companies. This preparation enabled the students to talk very competently with the managers they met.

3. It is absolutely necessary that the participants meet the top management people in the field. The most interesting issues normally have a strategic character. However, strategy is not formulated at middle management but at the top. If the participants only meet functional department managers, the

discussion necessarily focuses on administrative and operational matters and just deals with strategic issues to a minor extent due to the position of the managers in the company.

4.   At the end of an industry study trip, the participants come up with a report which reflects the visit in a strength and weakness balance after having had discussions with the responsible people.   This report is discussed in class and is also sent to the company.

Effectiveness

Looking at the industry study trip from a time dimension, we can distinguish certain phases of the trip as a teaching device:

- preparatory phase (gathering of information on the company, the competitive situation and environment);
- the actual visit to the company;
- preparation of a report on the company that has been visited;
- preparation and discussion of the reports.

It is, of course, an interesting question which phase contributes most to learning given a taxonomy of teaching objectives representing the different learn- ing domains.   It is hypothesized that the method on the whole has a comparative strength over other methods at the outset of the problem-solving cycle while the different phases might enhance knowledge, attitudes and skills unequally.

MANAGEMENT SYSTEMS STUDY

The second version of field study is a trip lasting several weeks to selected companies in different cultural, political and economical settings. The main features that distinguish the management systems study from the industry study trip are:

- the limited range of topics (mostly one theme);
- the number of companies, preferably operating in different environments;
- duration.

1.   The pre-selection of a topic known to both the students and the company people well in advance guarantees a certain depth in the discussion between them. If one does not confine the topic when visiting a company, the discussion will stay normally very much on the surface, due to the number of areas which are of general interest.   The chosen topics are generally very attractive.   The follow- ing list representing the topics chosen in the last years documents the areas of interest at the particular point of time:

- factors contributing to company growth;
- control of international operations;
- the effect of internationalisation, including foreign trade, on the organisation of the enterprise;
- technical innovation;
- motivation of man;
- training of managers and other personnel within the enterprise;
- practices and techniques in market research, sales promotion and distribution.

2.   The management systems study as a teaching method is especially powerful in international business education.   It is very intriguing to see, for example, how diversification strategies are pursued in different countries or how innova- tion is organisationally structured in different economic systems.   This method is particularly rewarding for a student who has to deal with international issues. It gives him a certain outlook and a feeling that there is not one panacea to tackle and handle business matters.   It prevents getting locked in with a certain type of thinking by being confronted with various approaches that are often equally successful.   It stimulates the readiness for becoming more creative and innovative, characteristics which are required in a business world that changes constantly.

3.   Use of this method must necessarily take longer.   Seeing two or three companies has only a minor impact.   In our opinion, it is a certain threshhold of exposure which leads to learning.   It is, however, a fairly expensive way of

learning.   Although there are no effectiveness studies on the method, it is well accepted in industry.   The Japanese participants of our courses are especially keen on using this method, a fact which is often referred to as the Japanese way of learning.

Timing of Field Studies

    Field studies are normally used in a longer management course.   Hence there is a legitimate question, how the timing should be arranged.

    It is our opinion that field studies should be placed towards the end of a course.   Especially when students have enjoyed a classroom exposure for a longer time, they face some difficulties in applying the new knowledge, skills and attitudes to a practical situation.   Field studies can be a "re-entry vehicle" in this respect by timing them at the end of a course, just before the students return to their companies.

Objective

To deal with a subject of special interest to the participants, but not covered by the Master Programme

---

Handout Material

Background Reading

Recommended Reading

Special Equipment and Aids

45 min. | **Session Guide 24**

To be prepared by the seminar leader. Some suggestions for the use of this session are:

- a training method not covered in the Master Programme, e.g., panel discussion, sensitivity training, management "plays", playlets, brainstorming;

- film show and discussion;

- special presentation by guest lecturer (or participant);

- application of teaching methods to particular subject areas - can be done in small interest groups.

Objective

To review the whole design process on the basis of an actual case history and to assess the validity of the principles covered in this case for other situations

Handout Material

As for Session 19, especially HANDOUT I , A Systems Concept of Training

Background Reading

As for Session 19

Recommended Reading

Special Equipment and Aids

Exhibits A, B and C from Session 19
Overhead projector and screen

45 min.	**Session Guide 25**
10:30	Ask one member of the course to introduce the discussion by presenting his views on the case history. He should point out items of general importance and give his critical comments on the procedure followed at RCA.
10:40	This should lead into a general discussion on the case, led by yourself or a participant previously designated. Since Session 19 has already dealt with the theoretical aspects of training design, the discussion should concentrate on the practical application of this theory as described in the case. Cover the following main phases, according to points brought out by participants:

Needs   - assessment by interview, and key findings
Assessment   - analysis of data, showing leadership styles
Process   - determination of training needs.

What are the views of participants as to the validity and practicability of this exercise? To what extent can the idea be used in their own training situations?

Objective   - Topic for debate: "The prime purpose of the
Setting   programme, then, would be to increase cognitive
Process   knowledge rather than to change behaviour or
                    attitude."

Design   - Participants may want to raise questions about
Process   individual sessions or point out features they
                    felt were most significant.

Evaluation   - The question of attitude change as revealed in
                    the final test and as reported by supervisors
                    may provoke some debate.

11:05	If it has not already come up in the discussion, ask participants to consider the extent to which they could use or adapt this approach in their own training.
	Sum up, emphasising that this case demonstrates the inter-relatedness of the various processes; that each stage in the design process benefits from close integration with the other stages.
11:15	Close the session.

Objective

To present, discuss and evaluate training programmes which participants have prepared in small groups

Handout Material

As for Session 19

Background Reading

As for Session 19

Recommended Reading

Special Equipment and Aids

Flip charts showing the outlines of course programmes

45 min.	**Session Guide 26**
11:30	Two course programmes should be selected from those prepared by the groups. Ask one of the members from each group to present the programme designed by his group.
	Presentation and discussion of the first programme.
11:50	Presentation and discussion of the second programme.
12:10	Summarise key points which were brought out in the discussions.
12:15	Close the session.

Objective

To stress the need for sound administration before, during and after a training programme

To advise on useful techniques, organisational arrangements, forms and check lists which can be used in course administration

Handout Material

I - The Organisation of Courses and Conferences, pp. 1-11

II - Organising Conferences, Study Groups and Courses - Check List, pp.13-16

Background Reading

Session 19, Handout III, Tips for Lesson Preparation and Presentation

Recommended Reading

Craig and Bittel, Training and Development Handbook, Chapter 29, "Planning and Scheduling" by James H. Morrison, and Chapter 31, "Training Records and Information Systems" by Jesse C. McKeon.

ILO, Man.Dev. Manual 35, Planning Training Courses by Network Analysis

Special Equipment and Aids

Possible film: How to Lead an Effective Sales Conference

45 min.	**Session Guide 27**
14:00	By now, the participants are familiar with the substance of the training process as well as its main phases. Give a talk on the administrative aspects of course design, implementation and evaluation. Emphasise the need for adequate preparation time and realistic scheduling; the need for well-prepared course materials and organised course records.
	Draw upon participants' experience with other training programmes. You will want to make extensive use of the chalkboard and/or flip chart when explaining techniques for scheduling training programmes.
	Cover the following points:
	- scheduling the preparation and implementation of training programmes;
	- administrative responsibility (including functions of the course director, administrative assistant, etc.);
	- organisational and administrative arrangements preceding the opening of the programme (use HANDOUT I);
	- course materials for the use of the training institution and for the participants;
	- course records.
	Issue the checklist in HANDOUT II, Organising Conferences, Study Groups and Courses.
14:40	Summarise the key points involved in course administration.
14:45	Ask members to hand in the Course Review Form.

THE ORGANISATION OF
COURSES AND CONFERENCES

by

Rex Strayton,
Associate Professor of
Personnel Administration,
International Centre for Advanced
Technical and Vocational Training, Turin

The notes which follow are fairly comprehensive and would assist
the reader to plan a major activity. The intention of preparing
them was to give too much information rather than too little and
leave the reader to select according to the occasion. The appen-
dices should be freely adapted to local conditions.

I am not going to waste any time trying to define what is a meeting or what
is a conference or what is the difference between a course and a seminar.

What I have to say really applies with equal force to all occasions where
we have:

    1.   an audience   3.   a place

    2.   a speaker   4.   an objective

                                    5.   an organiser

These, in my view, are the five common factors in all the various types of
activities which we will be required to organise and they are the main headings
of my talk.

On the one hand we know quite well that there is nothing complicated or
difficult in what we have to say on this subject. Indeed, you may not hear anything that you haven't heard before or that you wouldn't describe as "only common
sense".

On the other hand, we all know, from our own experience of attending meetings,
courses and conferences, that many of these factors are frequently neglected.
However enthusiastic the audience, however good the speakers, we may sometimes fail
to achieve our objectives precisely because we just can't spare the time to attend
to these details or because we write them off as being unimportant.

I shall have to go into some detail on the subject because I am trying to
cover a whole range of possible situations which you may have to face. It is not
claimed that every suggestion made is applicable to every situation. This handout
is an aide-memoire. You can select from it the items which you think are relevant
to the particular activity you happen to be planning.

Beware of over-organising and "fussing". This is almost as bad as the opposite!
What we should strive to achieve in the activities we organise is an atmosphere of
quiet efficiency.

1.   THE AUDIENCE AND WHAT IT EXPECTS

The courses, conferences, seminars, etc., with which we are concerned are not
organised in order to give speakers or organisers a chance to show off their talents.
They are organised for the benefit of the participants. Our first and most important
objective is to help the participants and we must keep this in mind at all times
when planning or organising this type of activity.

Of the five common factors which I have mentioned the most important, by far,
is THE AUDIENCE. They are the ones who pay the fees, give their time, who come to
learn, change their attitudes, or be persuaded. In their hands rests your reputation as an organiser and, by implication, the reputation of the organisation you
represent.

<u>Let us suppose that I am the audience and you are the organiser</u>. What do I expect from you?

A.   <u>Before the meeting - Good Publicity</u>

(i)   This does not mean expensive publicity. It means simple, attractive, well-presented. The outside cover should be attractive enough to invite people who see it lying around to pick it up and read it.

(ii)   Come to the point and tell me exactly what it is all about. Who is doing what? for what level of people? for people with what type of qualifications, previous experience, responsibilities? Give me the complete titles of the various sessions with sub-titles if necessary for clarification. Make sure that the titles of the sessions really do give a true indication of the content of the session. Don't change titles or dress them up in order to make them sound more impressive. There is nothing more annoying than to go to a course or conference expecting one thing and get something entirely different. Nothing will destroy your reputation and that of the institution you represent more quickly than this type of deception - for that is what it is. You may deceive me once but not twice! Nothing gets about more quickly than a bad reputation.

(iii)   Remember that my time is precious. When your pamphlet or brochure arrives on my desk my problem is to decide whether it's worth considering or not - whether it merits my time or not. If the pamphlet isn't simple, clear, attractive, it is highly probable that it will go straight from my in-tray to my waste-paper basket.

         Tell me something about the speakers in your pamphlet - what is their "authority" for speaking on this subject? This will help <u>you</u> to sell the programme and <u>me</u> to make a decision.

(iv)   How much notice should you give me? This may depend to some extent upon the custom of the country. But clearly, whatever the country, if your first notice reaches me two days or one day before the meeting you must not be surprised if I am not there.

         The length of notice which is appropriate for an activity tends to vary with the level of the activity, the distance the participants have to travel and the cost. For international conferences the date may be announced many months in advance. Many institutions which are engaged full-time in the organisation of training activities publish a programme for a complete calendar year and issue it at the beginning of the year. If your advance notice fixing the date is sent out more than three weeks before the actual date of the activity you may need to send me a reminder.

         If you are organising a series of activities over a period of several months there is something else you can do to help your members to remember. Some manufacturers of pocket-diaries insert in the diary a "reminder" sheet. It is a piece of paper the same width as a page of the diary and as long as the material you decide to put on it requires. The sheet is perforated horizontally into ten or twelve sections depending again on the material you decide to include, each horizontal section is a reminder of something specific, e.g., "my driving licence expires next week". The back of the sheet is adhesive and as soon as you buy the diary you separate the various reminders and stick them on the appropriate pages of your diary.

(v)   Make my acceptance easy. Incorporate a "tear-off" reply coupon in your pamphlet.

(vi)   Date, time, place, travelling instructions - make sure that all these are included and that they are correct. Add a small street map showing how to get to the meeting place if you cannot be sure that all participants are familiar with the location.

(vii)   If you have to organise a large number of courses, conferences, etc., you may like to consider the usefulness of a standard programme "cover". This can incorporate all the basic information which does not change in the short run - name of organisation, officials, telephone numbers, address plus a map inside the back page. In connection with each separate activity you now have only to prepare an "insert" and staple it inside the cover. It is a help to me if the document you send me is immediately recognisable as another programme from ".....". It is also better publicity for you.

B. At the meeting

(i)   Above all, to get the impression, right at the beginning, that you have been expecting me and have made certain arrangements for me. This is not a question of efficiency, it is a question of simple courtesy which a host always extends to his guests.

(ii)   Where to go. If the meeting room is in a large building such as a university for example, make sure that the hall porter knows how to direct people as they arrive. If there is no hall porter put a notice in a prominent place inside the main entrance.

(iii)   Hats, coats, lavatories. Make adequate arrangements and put up notices if necessary.

(iv)   Seating - get the most comfortable chairs that are available. You don't need pullman-type springing but it remains true that the mind's capacity to absorb is diminished if the body is very uncomfortable. Arrange the seats so that all participants can both see and hear. If the audience is large they will usually see better if you (a) stagger the chairs as they sometimes are in cinemas and (b) arrange the chairs in curved rows rather than straight rows.

(v)   Decide whether you ought to allow smoking or not. If you do allow it, provide ashtrays. If you decide not to allow it, put up readable notices in conspicuous places.

(vi)   Find out whether the speaker(s) are going to distribute summaries of their talks and tell the audience at the beginning so that they know whether to take notes or not.

(vii)   Prepare a list of the delegates and the organisations they represent and have copies of it available at the entrance to the lecture room so that the delegates can collect one as they come in.

(viii) Begin and end punctually.

(ix)   Make sure that the time allocated for questions and discussion does not disappear, no matter what has to be cut short or cut out.

(x)   If the activity you are organising consists of several sessions consider the usefulness of name cards for the tables or lapel badges for the participants. If you use lapel badges choose the sort that can be re-used and use the largest and thickest letters you can. Typing is not usually satisfactory. Make sure that you get the names of the delegates correctly spelled on name cards or lapel badges. People are often very sensitive about this.

2.   THE SPEAKER

There are two aspects of this: A. What the speaker expects from you

                                    B. What you expect from the speaker

A.   What the speaker expects from you

(i)   A good briefing - he needs to know, for example:

    (a)   What sort of audience will it be - what level of person - how many

    (b)   What is the general objective of the activity

    (c)   What do the audience already know, feel, think about the subject

    (d)   If there will be more than one speaker, what will the others be talking about

    (e)   Date, time, place, travelling instructions

    (f)   How much time is available

(ii)   <u>Equipment and printed material</u>

    (a)   Consider the usefulness of "Course and Conference Planning Sheet
        No. 2 - List of Speaker's Requirements" (see Appendix A)

    (b)   If you use this planning sheet (No. 2) and there are more than one
        session , summarise them all on Course and Conference Planning
        Sheet No. 3 (see Appendix B)

(iii)   <u>The duties of a host</u>

    (a)   Be at the place ahead of time to receive him when he arrives

    (b)   Introduce him adequately

    (c)   Thank him adequately at the end

    (d)   Enquire about expenses he may have incurred in connection with
        his talk and "see him off" the premises. Remember that many
        people do this type of work voluntarily.

(iv)   <u>Interruptions</u> - What do we do about late comers?

Remember that the first ten or fifteen minutes are among the most important
of the whole session. It is then that the speaker is trying to establish
contact with the audience and it is also during these few minutes that the
audience is "weighing up" the speaker. Give them both a chance. Once you
have fixed the starting time, decide how many minutes' grace you are going
to allow, then close the door and start. Don't let anybody enter then until
the first fifteen minutes are over. Then they can all enter at once and the
speaker can make his first intermediate summary - which is a good thing to
do anyway.

Have notices "Conference in progress" displayed at strategic points.

B.   <u>What you expect of the speaker</u>

(i)   If it is a formal lecture or a lesson persuade him to remain standing.
If it is an informal discussion it is not only permissible, it is
desirable for him to sit down.

(ii)   Try to dissuade him from reading prepared text.

(iii)   Try to persuade him to use appropriate audio-visual aids and offer help
and advice in advance.

(iv)   Try to dissuade him from falling into the common error of including in the
session more material than can reasonably be assimilated in the time available. Remember that the "saturation point" in a lecture tends to be reached
after 20 minutes, however good the speaker. Remember how quickly people
forget. Remember the iceberg - only about one-fifth of its total mass is
visible above the water. The same applies to the lecture. The other four-
fifths of the mass is there, under the water, invisible, but unquestionably
supporting all the rest which <u>is</u> visible.

(v)   Don't be afraid to tell your speakers exactly what you want them to do.
The role of the organiser in this respect is similar to that of the leader
of an orchestra. Not only must he control the participation of each instru-
mentalist but also ensure that each one of them harmonises with the performance of the others and that the melody is suited to the occasion.

All too often in the past speakers have simply been invited to "come and
talk about....." with no further briefing.

(vi)   The question of whether the speaker should smoke whilst lecturing is often
discussed and there are many points of view. In the opinion of the writer,
a speaker should not smoke whilst delivering a formal talk or lecture.
If he later sits down and conducts an informal discussion and everyone else
is smoking then naturally he may smoke too. The custom of the country
needs to be considered also in this connection.

3.   THE LECTURE ROOM

A.   Very often we have no choice. We have to take what is available and make the best of it. Get the best you can with the resources available. Visit the lecture room in advance. Familiarise yourself with its layout and its facilities:

windows	cloakrooms	furniture – type and
heating	lavatories	layout, power sockets,etc.

B.   Plan how you will use it:

(i)   In any handout on audio-visual aids there are detailed recommendations on how a room should be prepared for projection – the size, type and position of the screen, the position of the projector and loudspeakers, etc. Refresh your memory by looking at these notes.

(ii)   Consider the usefulness of arranging the chairs in curved rows rather than the traditional straight lines. "Stagger" them so that chairs in the second row are behind the spaces between the chairs in the first row and not directly behind the other. Consider the advantage of a centre aisle, especially if you are projecting.

(iii) Consider the usefulness of "open squares" formation or the "V" formation if the activity is a formal training course with 10 or 20 participants.

(iv)   Make sure that all of the basic necessities are available – lecterns, pointers, ashtrays, etc., You will already have prepared a detailed list of these necessities if you have completed your Course and Conference Planning Sheets Nos. 1, 2 and 3.

(v)   Don't crowd the platform with organisers and administrators. If there is to be any projection then the chairman will probably wish to leave the platform after introducing the speaker.

(vi)   Make sure that any organisers who may have to leave during the lecture if an emergency arises sit at the back near the door so that they can leave without creating a disturbance.

4.   THE OBJECTIVE AND THE ORGANISER

If you are the organiser, how should you approach your task?

A.   <u>Make an appreciation of the situation</u>. There are four steps:

(i)   <u>Objective</u>

What exactly am I trying to achieve? is it to inform, to persuade, to amuse, to explain, to advise, or exhort, to investigate, to teach a skill? or what?

(ii)   <u>Factors</u>

What are the factors which affect my objective?
Who else is planning or has already carried out activities in this field – what type of activity, and with what result?
What is the demand for this type of activity – from what type and level of people?
How many people are likely to be interested and how do I know this?
What are they likely to know, feel, think about this subject already?
How much will they be prepared to pay?
How much time will they be prepared to devote to this, and at what time of of the day?

(iii) <u>Alternatives</u>

What are the possible courses of action open to me, bearing in mind the general objective and the factors already listed above?

(iv)   <u>Plan</u>

Which of these alternatives will I adopt?

B.   The "selling" stage

     If you then have to "sell" the plan to other people such as top management
     for example, it may be helpful to present your proposal in the following
     form:

(i)   Objective

(ii)   Plan

(iii)   Advantages

(iv)   Cost

C.   Master planning and control sheet

     Once the plan is drawn up, prepare Course and Conference Planning Sheet No. 1 -
     Master Planning and Control Sheet (Appendix C). If you are dependent on other
     departments for co-operation in this activity you have to co-ordinate it very
     carefully. Give them adequate notice and be sure to thank them for their help.
     Use the Master Planning and Control Sheet for allocating responsibilities
     initially and for controlling the preparations.

D.   On the "day"

     If the activity you are planning is not just a single lecture but involves a
     number of sessions then you should remember that the first session and the
     last session are vitally important. You must try to begin with an impact
     and to end on a high note. Many training activities do not "conclude" they
     just "stop" - they fizzle out, or else they end with a "post-mortem". Try
     to avoid this. Try to arrange a final session which is forward-looking,
     which throws out a challenge to the participants which gives them some
     indication of where they go from here.

Course and Conference Planning Sheet No.2   APPENDIX A

List of Speaker's Requirements

Name of Speaker: _____

Activity: _____

Date: _____   Place: _____

From (time): _____   To: _____

Please tick the appropriate items and amplify where necessary

1. Chalkboard

2. Flip chart and stand

3. Chart stand

4. Flannel board

5. Projector for 35mm slides, colour/black and white

6. Projector for 35mm filmstrips, colour/black and white
    If it is a sound filmstrip and you want a record player or a tape
    recorder to be provided for you, fill in section 9 or 10 below

7. Projector for other sizes of slide - state size of slide: _____

8. Projector - 16mm film, colour/black and white
    sound/silent
    If it is sound, is it magnetic or optical sound?
    length of film _____ minutes
    can you produce the film 24 hours before the time of showing?
    operator required/not required

9. Record player - state speed of record - 33 - 45 - 78

10. Tape recorder
    state recording speed - 1-7/8 - 3-3/4 - 7-1/2 inches per second
    state size of spool - 3 - 5 - 7 inches
    Stereophonic/monophonic - with/without microphone

11. Episcope
    what type of material will you use with it?

12. Overhead projector

13. Printing or duplicating to be done - please specify: _____
    _____
    _____
    when will final draft be available? _____

14. If your session will not be given entirely in our conference room please
    specify: _____
    _____
    _____

15. Anything else - please specify: _____
    _____
    _____

APPENDIX B

Course and Conference Planning Sheet No. 3
Summary of Equipment Required

Item	Required for Session(s) Number
1. Chalkboard	
2. Flip chart stand	
3. Flannel board	
4. Slide projector - 35mm	
5. Filmstrip projector - 35mm	
6. Slide projector -	
7. Film projector - 16mm	
sound	
silent	
magnetic	
optical	
8. Record player	
9. Tape recorder	
10. Episcope	
11. Overhead Projector	
12.	
13.	
14.	
15.	
16.	

APPENDIX C

Course and Conference Planning Sheet No. 1
Master Planning and Control Sheet

Activity: _____

_____

Date(s): _____

Time(s): _____

Place: _____

Audience (type): _____

Audience (number): _____

Course Organiser: _____

Item	Who is responsible	Target Date	Done Date	Done Initials
1. Programme Preparation				
A. Preparation of draft				
B. Getting draft approved				
C.				
2. Speakers				
A. Selection				
B. Invitation				
C. Confirmation				
D. Sending out planning sheets No. 2				
E. Getting back planning sheets No. 2				
F.				
3. Programme printing				
4. Promotion				
A. Press				
B. Radio				
C. T.V.				
D.				
E.				
F.				

Item	Who is responsible	Target Date	Done Date	Initials
5. Enrolments				
A. Incoming queries				
B. Custody of enrolment forms				
C. Analysis of enrolment forms and selection of participants				
6. Programme Distribution				
A. Participants				
B. "External" speakers				
C.				
7. Joining Instructions				
A. Participants				
B.				
8. Fees				
A. Assessment				
B. Collection				
C.				
9. Teaching Equipment				
A. Planning Sheets No. 3 preparation				
B. Equipment reservation or procurement				
C. Ensuring it is in right place at right time				
D.				
10. Handouts				
A. Draft preparation				
B. Printing				
C. Custody and preparation for distribution				
D. Binders or folders procurement				
E. Ensuring they are in right place at right time				
F.				

Item	Who is responsible	Target Date	Done	
			Date	Initials
11. Food and Drinks				
A. Provision				
B. Cash collection				
C.				

Item	Who is responsible	Target Date	Done Date	Initials
12. Miscellaneous				
Pencils, rubbers, scratch-pads, name cards, lapel badges, flip chart paper, crayons, felt pens, ash-trays, procurement				

Item	Who is responsible	Target Date	Done Date	Initials
13. Lecture Room				
A. Selection				
B. Advance preparation including basic furniture				
Daily preparation including:				
Air conditioning				
Ventilation				
Blackout				
Lectern(s)				
Water on speaker's table				
Tidy up before and between sessions				
General over-all check-up				

14. Other Items - please specify:

ORGANISING CONFERENCES, STUDY GROUPS
AND COURSES: CHECK LIST[1]

Introduction

The Check Lists in this section are drawn to cover the organisation of a fairly large and important conference. For this reason, not all the items listed will be needed for small conferences, but it is better to work from comprehensive lists and ignore any unwanted features than to use shorter lists with the risk of missing some essential items.

The Check Lists are presented in the order in which they will be required, starting with the Preliminary Planning stage and working through to After the Conference. Many of the items occur more than once in the lists for the different stages; these are items which need checking more than once.

---

[1] This paper is drawn from Operating Manual No. 2 of the National Productivity Council, New Delhi, India.

Check List No. 1

PRELIMINARY PLANNING: 12 WEEKS AHEAD

___ Main subject of conference chosen

___ Purpose of conference defined

___ Topics for each session decided

___ Type of participants required decided

___ Method of selecting participants decided

___ Date tentatively selected and reserve dates

___ Speakers tentatively chosen, and reserve speakers

___ Chairman and inaugurator chosen, and reserves

___ Estimate of cost prepared

___ Venue selected

___ Duration and timing decided

___ Number of participants decided

___ Sponsors chosen

___ Invitation letter and/or brochure drafted

Check List No. 2

GENERAL ARRANGEMENTS: 8 WEEKS AHEAD

___ Agreement of sponsor to all 14 items of List No. 1

___ Agreement reached on who will work out details

___ Agreement reached on who will make arrangements

___ Agreement reached on who will send out invitations

___ Agreement reached on who will invite speakers, inaugurator

___ Amount of fees decided

___ Arrangement for collecting fees decided

___ Outline of general arrangements decided

Check List No. 3

GENERAL ARRANGEMENTS: 10 WEEKS AHEAD

___ Invitations to speakers, inaugurator, chairman, sent

___ Tentative arrangements for meeting hall made

GENERAL ARRANGEMENTS: 8 WEEKS AHEAD

___ Replies from speakers received, list finalised

___ Invitations to participants circulated

___ Speakers asked for details of any illustrations

___ Speakers asked to submit advance copies (if appropriate)

GENERAL ARRANGEMENTS: 6 WEEKS AHEAD

___ Gauge response

___ Firm arrangements for meeting hall made (see Check List No.4)

___ Invitations to special invitees sent

___ Background displays,exhibitions, decided

___ Films and projection equipment requisitioned

GENERAL ARRANGEMENTS: 4 WEEKS AHEAD

___ Initiate 'other arrangements' (see Check List No.5)

___ If response poor, initiate programme of personal contacts

GENERAL ARRANGEMENTS: 2 WEEKS AHEAD

___ Bibliography prepared

___ Final timings decided, final brochure, programme drafted

___ Speakers' charts and illustrations in preparation

Check List No. 4

CONFERENCE HALL ARRANGEMENTS

___ Seating arrangements, comfortable chairs, leg room
___ Platform, platform seats
___ Ash trays
___ Press bench
___ Lighting
___ Ventilation, fans
___ Projector stand, socket, voltage, AC/DC, blackout, screen
___ Ice water arrangements
___ Toilet facilities
___ Clock in meeting hall
___ Arrangements for meals and refreshments

Check List No. 5

OTHER ARRANGEMENTS

___ Press representation
___ Microphones/loudspeakers and standby battery
___ Conference badges
___ Advance summaries of speakers' talks
___ Any other handouts
___ Direction signs, motorists' signals
___ Blackboard and accessories
___ Any other platform display apparatus
___ Charts and illustrations needed by speakers
___ Arrangements for recording the speeches
___ Background displays, exhibitions, posters, photographs
___ Arrange secretarial desk
___ Notepaper, pencils
___ Transport arrangements
___ Accommodation arrangements
___ Arrangements for taking photographs
___ Any factory visits or associated activities
___ Arrange messages and greetings from notables

Check List No. 6

DURING WEEK PRECEDING THE CONFERENCE

___ Send reminders/invitations/final programme to participants
___ Send reminders to press
___ Arrange advertisements in the press
___ Send reminders to inaugurators/ chairman/speakers and special guests stating transport and accommodation arrangements
___ Check with manager of hall, all arrangements for conference room and refreshments
___ Check arrival of all literature
___ Check arrival of films and film equipment
___ Prepare any handouts/summaries/ leaflets
___ Check arrival of conference badges
___ Make arrangements for secretarial desk
___ Prepare cards with speakers' names
___ Check availability of blackboard and display apparatus
___ Check any background displays/ exhibitions/leaflet racks
___ Get a stock of inquiry forms
___ If response still poor, make personal contacts
___ Make transport arrangements
___ Check that microphone/loud- speaker arrangements are O.K.
___ Check and confirm accom- modation arrangements
___ Check any factory visits or associated activities
___ Make arrangements for vote of thanks
___ Prepare standby address in case a speaker fails to arrive
___ Prepare chairman's brief
___ Prepare Who's Who
___ Prepare list of addresses, tele- phone numbers, get timetables
___ Make arrangements for photographs
___ Get First-Aid Box
___ Make arrangements for checking and approving press releases

Check List No. 7	

THE DAY BEFORE THE CONFERENCE

___ Check that direction signs, motorists' signals have been arranged

___ Check seating for arrangement, comfort, leg room

___ Check platform arrangements

___ Check blackboard, chalk, duster, ruler

___ Check any other platform display apparatus

___ Check all charts/illustrations and methods of fixing

___ Check microphone equipment will be installed on time, complete with standby battery for power failure

___ Check press bench arrangements

___ Check toilet facilities

___ Check lighting, ventilation, fans, general noise level

___ Check film arrangements, films, films previewed, projector, projectionist, projector spares, screen, loudspeakers, blackout, voltage, socket and plug, converter if DC, all tested

___ Check sufficient ashtrays provided

___ Check arrangements for meals/refreshments

___ Check arrangements for water

___ Make arrangements for cleaning, emptying ashtrays, during break

___ Check arrangements for secretarial desk

___ Check list of addresses, telephone numbers, timetables

___ Check arrangements for collecting fees

___ Check First-Aid Box will be present

___ Check that standby arrangements have been made in case a speaker fails to turn up

___ Check conference badges are ready

___ Check that chairman's brief is ready

___ Check speakers' name cards are ready

___ Make arrangements for recording speeches, discussions

___ Check all posters, exhibition material, leaflet racks, literature displays

___ Check that notepaper and pencils are ready for participants

___ Check that pencil sharpening arrangements have been made

___ Check that all transport arrangements have been made

___ Check that all accommodation arrangements have been made

___ Check if daily money allowance ready

___ Check that press invitations issued

___ Check if vote of thanks arranged

___ Make arrangements for mutual introduction of speakers

___ Make arrangements for farewell tea, etc. for speakers

___ Make arrangements for welcoming inaugurator, special guests

___ Check that arrangements for taking photos have been made

Check List No. 8	

ON THE DAY: BEFORE CONFERENCE STARTS

___ Check direction signs, motorists' signals

___ Check seating for arrangement, comfort, leg room

___ Check platform arrangements

___ Check blackboard, chalk, duster, ruler

___ Check any other platform display apparatus

___ Check all charts/illustrations to be used by speakers, and method of fixing

___ Arrange attendant to expose charts

___ Test microphone/loudspeaker equipment

___ Arrange signalling system for volume control

___ Check standby battery is provided

___ Check press bench, enough chairs, pencils, cigarettes, ashtrays, Who's Who copies, advance speech copies

___ Check chairman's brief is at hand

___ Check lighting

___ Check ventilation, fans

___ Check for sufficient ashtrays

___ Check transport arrangements are working

___ Check water arrangements

___ Check films, films previewed, projector, projectionist, projector spares, screen, loudspeakers, blackout, lights control, spare reel, voltage, socket and plug, all tested

___ Check speakers' name cards on hand

___ Check posters, exhibition material

___ Check display of leaflets, booklets

___ Check conference badges are at hand

___ Check that literature for distribution to participants is at hand, advance copies, Who's Who, brochures, pencils and notepaper

___ Check secretarial desk, list of addresses, telephone numbers, inquiry forms, pencil sharpeners, stenotypists, timetables

___ Check daily allowance money ready, make arrangements for paying out

___ Check arrangements for clearing up during breaks

___ Initiate arrangements for introducing speakers to each other

___ Initiate arrangements for recording names of participants

___ Initiate arrangements for issue of conference badges

___ Initiate welcoming arrangements

Check List No. 9

ON THE DAY: AT THE BEGINNING
OF CONFERENCE

___ Check that the reception arrangements are working well
___ Check that the recording of
names is working well
___ Check that the issue of badges
is proceeding properly
___ Check that the issue of literature
is O.K.
___ Hand brief to chairman

___ If small conference, prepare name
and place schedule

Check List No. 10

ON THE DAY: DURING THE CONFERENCE

___ Check refreshment arrangements
___ Check clearing of ashtrays, etc.
during breaks
___ Check that all can hear and that
volume of sound is controlled
___ At small conference, hand name and
place schedule to chairman
___ Check arrangements for typing and
checking press reports
___ Exhibit telegrams, messages

___ Check functioning of ventilation

___ Check proposer of vote of thanks
has been briefed

Check List No. 11

AT THE END OF THE CONFERENCE

___ Check that transport arrangements
for participants are O.K.
___ Farewell tea for speakers and
main guests
___ Release of checked and approved
reports same day to press
___ Return to safekeeping of Centre's
literature and all equipment

Check List No. 12

AFTER THE CONFERENCE

___ Hold post-mortem. Make notes
___ Write letters of thanks to
speakers, chairman, etc.
___ Send short report to Headquarters
___ Edit speeches and points from
discussions, prepare summaries
___ Publish selections for edited
versions
___ Prepare list of participants
___ Send conference summaries to
participants, if appropriate
___ Clear all bills, determine
final cost
___ Prepare record file

___ Initiate follow-up action

Objective

To explain various types of follow-up activities

To emphasise that follow-up to training is an important element in the development of a manager, both in providing continuity of education and in facilitating the practical application of training

To inform participants of follow-up activities planned for this course

Handout Material

Background Reading

Follow-up of Management Training, pp. 1-5

Recommended Reading

ILO, Management and Productivity No. 35, "Management Education in the Second Development Decade", pp. 3-19

Special Equipment and Aids

Overhead projector, film screen

Exhibit A, "Overall Scheme of Follow-up" from the background reading, prepared on a transparency for the overhead projector

45 min.	**Session Guide 28**
15:00	Give a short introductory talk combined with discussion in which the participants will give their views and experiences on:
	– how management training tends to be followed up in practice;
	– what activities are included in follow-up;
	– who is responsible for follow-up;
	– what methods of follow-up have given the best results.
	Use Exhibit A, Over-all Scheme of Follow-up, as a visual aid.
15:35	Intermediate summary: Emphasise the points from the conclusion of the background reading, Follow-up of Management Training.
15:40	Discuss what kind of follow-up activities are envisaged (and what further activities are desired by the participants) for this particular course:
	– what kind of feedback can the participants expect to receive;
	– will they be supplied with further information on teaching and training methods and invited to further, more advanced or specialised training programmes;
	– what books and materials they might study.
15:45	Close the session.

FOLLOW-UP OF MANAGEMENT TRAINING

by M. Kubr,
Management Development Branch
International Labour Office

Concept of Follow-up

There is no precise and exhaustive definition of follow-up of management training. It is usually considered to be the various activities which are carried out after the completion of a training programme. The purpose of these activities is to examine and evaluate the practical usefulness of training, to help in the application of what has been learned, and to provide for a continuity of training and education. However, some people still restrict follow-up activities to the occasional contacts which a management centre maintains with former participants.

Although it is generally recognised that a formal (institutionalised) training course is only one step or event in the process of developing managers and properly utilising their skills, the value of follow-up is still frequently underestimated by both managers and course designers, and follow-up itself is often completely neglected. This is due to a number of reasons: follow-up demands co-ordination and a great deal of work on the part of the institutions and people involved; it requires solving delicate human problems in addition to professional ones; and it rarely shows any spectacular immediate results.

In order to indicate how these activities can be improved, this paper shall examine the principal areas of follow-up; emphasis will be put on methods of action and responsibility of organisations and persons. An over-all scheme of follow-up activities is given in Exhibit A.

Evaluation

As a rule, evaluation of training is subdivided into four phases or levels:[1]

(1) Reaction   (2) Learning   (3) Behaviour   (4) Results

The third and fourth phases are usually carried out after the completion of a training programme and may be considered as elements of follow-up. Indeed, evaluation at these two levels represents an important source of suggestions for further follow-up activities, especially for measures needed to remove obstacles impeding the application of what has been learned.

Quite frequently evaluating change in the behaviour of those who have passed through training programmes can be misleading since no notable behavioural change may be detected. A more extensive analysis frequently shows that the person concerned has tried to make at least some changes in his methods of work and behaviour. Unfortunately, numerous are the cases where the person gives up and re-adopts his previous behavioural patterns either because of the influence of established procedures, a lack of interest or even the difficulty in overcoming an aversion against innovation on the part of superiors and colleagues.

A valid criticism can be made that this type of "after training situation" is sufficiently known beforehand and that it would be much more effective, therefore, to consider these problems before a manager or staff specialist is sent to a course. More and more enterprises are responding to this problem through comprehensive management development planning, which co-ordinates training with plans for further growth and organisational improvements such as the introduction of a computer-based management information system or other measures intended to improve the quality of management.

---

[1] See Donald L. Kirkpatrick: "Evaluation of Training", in Robert L. Craig and Lester R. Bittel (eds.): Training and Development Handbook (New York, McGraw-Hill, 1967), pp. 650.

Experience shows that it is not very helpful to criticise higher managers for not supporting those who return from courses and who want to apply at least a modest part of what they have learned. It is much more useful to combine the training programmes for middle managers and staff specialists with shorter programmes for top managers and thus induce top management to adopt an attitude of enthusiasm towards modern management practices.

In the final stage the effectiveness of management training and of a manager's changed behaviour is tested through practical results. Improvements in the operation and performance of enterprises are, after all, the basic goal of management training. That is why evaluation should not be confined to behavioural change but should also be concerned with the results of practical applications as well.

There are, however, two major difficulties with evaluation at this level:

(a) Much of management training is aimed at improving the over-all level of managerial performance and affecting as many areas of activity as possible; it does not merely bring about isolated partial improvements, where the input and output is easily measurable.

(b) Furthermore, management training is only one of many factors which influence the performance of enterprises and other organisational units. Very often, training is intentionally combined with other factors. The "separation" of these factors for the purpose of evaluation is very difficult, if not impossible.

Consequently, it is rather exceptional to find an enterprise where improvements can be attributed exclusively to management training. Training programmes which teach special methods and techniques such as production scheduling, network planning, statistical quality control, stock control, etc., are easier to evaluate in terms of results than programmes concerned with broad management concepts and policies.

An evaluation of behavioural change and of the results of application is of tremendous value for further course planning, especially for improving curricula and selecting the right methods of teaching and training. Notwithstanding, it is only one part of follow-up.

Help in Practical Applications

The broad concept of follow-up of training activities includes help in practical application as its main part. During the application process, managers may need concrete, detailed advice on measures they intend to introduce or they may need certain services to be carried out for them by specialised departments or institutions. If this advice or service is not available, the manager may be unable to use in practice what he has learned.

Part of this help may be provided from outside, as an external service to management. Whereas some training institutions are still concerned with the running of a large number of courses only, there is a growing number of institutions which maintain contacts with their former course participants and try to be directly associated with projects and various other measures undertaken as a consequence of their training courses. This is particularly important in developing countries,[1] where managers do not have a network of local consultancy and service institutions at their disposal or are not able to pay a foreign firm for such services.

In some institutions it is the training staff who, in addition to their current teaching assignments, keep in touch with managers who need and are interested in further help. This advice and help may develop into regular consultancy assignments. The obvious advantage of consultancy work is that the trainers get direct feedback which helps them in their future teaching to create a better balance between theory and practice. A disadvantage of consultancy work may be that the training staff takes too much interest in consultancy itself and does not prepare the teaching assignments properly.

---

[1] See, for example, ILO: "Improving Training in Modern Management Techniques", working paper for the UN Inter-Regional Seminar on the Use of Modern Management Techniques in the Public Administration of Developing Countries, Washington, D.C. (Geneva, 1970) (mimeographed).

In other institutions teaching is organised separately from extension, consultancy, advisory and similar services and each part of the institution has its own professional staff. In this case, however, the rotation of staff between teaching and consultancy departments helps to utilise the experience of the consultants in teaching and gives the trainers an opportunity to do practical work.

However, the most important help in practical application has to be provided by superiors (chiefs) and colleagues within the enterprise. As we have seen in connection with the evaluation of behavioural change occurring after training, this help will depend on the professional competence of the managers and on their attitudes toward improvements suggested by their subordinates and colleagues.

Further Personal Development

Further personal development is an area of follow-up which is inseparable from the two previous ones. It should be viewed and handled in accordance with modern concepts of continuity of education and training during the manager's total career and as part of the over-all long-term development of the enterprise's managerial resources.

Here again, the main responsibility is to be assumed by the enterprise itself. As a rule, successful completion of a training course by a manager in post, a future manager or a staff specialist, provides a good base for other less formal and more individual types of further training and education. This may take a variety of forms depending on specific conditions; however, it is advisable to link further training with the practical application of what has been learned - and it should be done with clear objectives in mind.

Coaching on the job carried out with regard to the needs of the enterprise is a typical example. It may include various types of new work assignments, surveys, exercises, reading and projects executed individually or in groups. The chief should be personally responsible for the development of staff members designated for this form of further training and he should be available to give advice to the trainees.

Job rotation and similar methods belong to this area as well.

To complete the more individual and less formal methods of training on the job, management development systems should provide further courses; these may take one of the following orientations:

(1) more specialised courses (dealing with a selected subject area or method in greater detail and depth);

(2) more advanced courses (preparing the manager for promotion to a higher position);

(3) retraining courses (bringing managers up to date without preparing them for promotion);

(4) courses concentrating on management problems of a specific enterprise or plant.

Any of the above-mentioned types can be organised by the enterprise itself (if it can afford it) or by management development institutes as scheduled courses open to participants from various enterprises or as courses arranged upon request.

It has been pointed out that the various courses for further personal development of managers are essentially intended for managers who are on a mobile promotion stream, whereas the middle-aged managers' (not designated for promotion) further training needs are not properly met.[1] This criticism concerns many countries and should be very seriously considered by both enterprises and management development institutes.

Voluntary groups (circles) for self-education are sometimes set up by managers themselves. They meet more or less regularly to discuss various projects and topics. Professional trainers, consultants or extension officers may be asked to act as advisers to these groups.

---

[1] See A. Mant: The Experienced Manager - A Major Resource, London, British Institute of Management, 1969.

It should be mentioned, too, that some management associations and institutes give advice to individuals (as a rule members) on their further personal development, including advice on the choice of training programmes to be attended.

Liaison of Management Institutes with Former Course Participants

A number of management development institutes maintain regular contacts with their former course participants (alumni). These contacts have the following main purposes:

- to get feedback on the usefulness and effectiveness of training;

- to identify cases where the institute might assist in practical applications;

- to supply the alumni with recent and interesting information;

- to offer further training to them and other staff from their enterprises;

- to obtain help from the alumni in perfecting the teaching process.

It is useful to speak with former course participants about their jobs and what they think they have learned in a course. Sometimes associations of alumni are founded and conferences on topics of major interest are prepared by the institute's staff or by some of the alumni. Newsletters, documentation bulletins, reprints of important articles, etc., are sent to the alumni by some institutes. This, of course, only makes sense if the institute has a very good information service.

Management institutes, in their turn, can obtain valuable direct help from their former participants:

- case study materials can be drawn from their enterprises and prepared with their assistance;

- trainees may go to the alumni's enterprises to do practical work, exercises, consultancy work, etc.

- some alumni might become external collaborators and give lectures or lead case study discussions.

Conclusion

A broad concept of follow-up has been presented in the preceding. One might argue that some of the areas and activities mentioned above do not actually seem to be part of follow-up; this is relatively unimportant. The following points are vital in order to improve the process of follow-up:

- to understand that a specific training activity is only one event or phase in the total management education and development process;

- to agree that a specific training activity will make very little impact unless a number of other measures are taken and conditions for the practical application of modern management concepts and methods are improved;

- to see that the particular areas of follow-up cannot be separated from each other, but must be developed in their entirety.

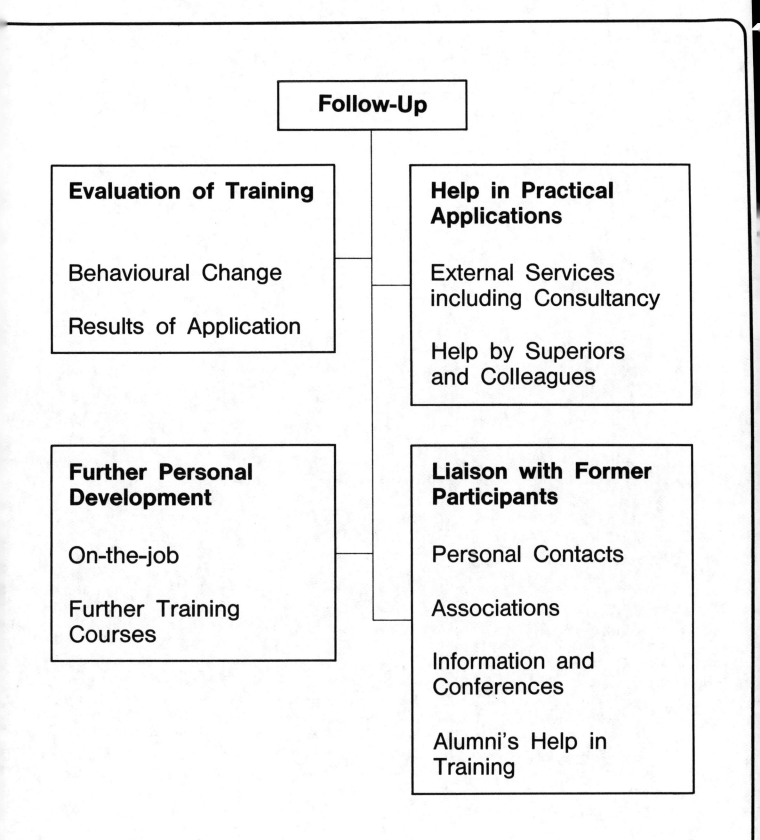

Follow-Up

Evaluation of Training

Behavioural Change

Results of Application

Help in Practical Applications

External Services including Consultancy

Help by Superiors and Colleagues

Further Personal Development

On-the-job

Further Training Courses

Liaison with Former Participants

Personal Contacts

Associations

Information and Conferences

Alumni's Help in Training

OVER—ALL SCHEME OF FOLLOW—UP

Objective

To summarise the main ideas on which the course was based

To give the seminar's organisers immediate feedback on the course

To inform participants on their progress during the course

Handout Material

Background Reading

Course Review Forms filled out by all participants

Recommended Reading

Special Equipment and Aids

45 min.	**Session Guide 29**

This session should be conducted in an informal and friendly manner. In addition to the course leader, other officials from the sponsoring organisation should be present.

Optional: Ask two members of the group to look at and summarise the Course Review Forms before the session.

16:00   If you have had the opportunity to look over the Course Review Forms (which should be studied in depth at a later date), or, if two members have prepared their summary, give a brief report on the prevailing views of participants about the course. Bring out any individual observations which are of particular interest.

16:15   Give your own evaluation of the course and of members' participation. Recall outstanding contributions, most valuable sessions for certain purposes, most apparent change or progress in the participants, etc.

Follow with an informal discussion. Refer again to the follow-up which participants can expect to obtain.

16:40   Thank anyone who merits appreciation for his contribution to the success of the course. If senior colleagues are present, ask them to close the seminar; if you are on your own, make the closing remarks.

16:45   Close the session.